D1163399

ADULT NONFICTION   c.1
Oversize
929.1 Sh31

Shea, Jonathan D
Following the paper trail :a multil
ingual translation guide

8000282217

WITHDRAWN

Following the Paper Trail:

A Multilingual Translation Guide

Following the Paper Trail:

A Multilingual Translation Guide

by

Jonathan D. Shea

&

William F. Hoffman

Avotaynu, Inc.

Copyright © 1994, Jonathan D. Shea and William F. Hoffman

All rights reserved. No part of this book may be reproduced or transmitted in any form or by any means, electronic or mechanical, including photocopy, recording, or information retrieval system, without prior permission from the publisher. Brief passages may be quoted with proper attribution.

Requests for permission to make copies of any part of this publication should be addressed to:

Avotaynu, inc.
P.O. Box 900
Teaneck, NJ 07666

Printed in the United States of America

99 98 97 96 95   2 3 4 5 6

ISBN 0-9626373-4-3

This book previously appeared in a softcover edition published by Language and Lineage Press, 1991, ISBN 0-9631579-0-6, Library of Congress Catalog Card Number 91-077564.

929.1
Sh31
c)

Dedication

To my immigrant ancestors:

Jan Kazimierz Bryzgiel,
a native of Wesołowo, Dąbrowa Białostocka, Poland

Zofia Józefa Kryszczyńska,
a native of Chrzanowo Cyprki, Łomża, Poland

John Alphonse Shea,
a native of Clonfanlough, Co. Offaly, Ireland,

Mary Ann Hosty,
a native of Ballandine, Co. Mayo, Ireland

— Jonathan D. Shea

and

To Waltraud Gutensohn Bartscht, Ph.D., Associate Professor, German
Department of Foreign Languages and Literatures, University of Dallas

— William F. Hoffman

FOND DU LAC PUBLIC LIBRARY

FOND DU LAC PUBLIC LIBRARY

Table of Contents

About the Authors

Jonathan D. Shea is a native of New Britain, Connecticut, and the grandson of Polish and Irish immigrants who settled in the Central Connecticut region near the turn of the century. He is the founder and current president of the Polish Genealogical Society of Connecticut, is a Director of the Polish Genealogical Society of America, and has authored numerous articles in the field of Polish genealogy for various genealogical and historical publications in the United States. He is also the author of several works, including *Russian Language Documents from Russian Poland: A Translation Manual for the Genealogist* and several indices to gravestone inscriptions from cemeteries in Poland and the Northeastern United States. He has additionally prepared indices to several church registers. Mr. Shea has also lectured extensively nationwide on the topic, including presentations at the Chicago Public Library and the National Archives in Washington, D.C.

Mr. Shea is a faculty member in the Department of Modern Languages at Central Connecticut State University. He is also the archivist at the Archives and Resource Center of the Polish Genealogical Society of Connecticut and serves as a consultant in the field of genealogical and heraldic sciences, specializing in Eastern Europe and Ireland, and is as well an interpreter and translator. He holds a B.S. degree from Georgetown University, Washington, D.C., as well as a Master's Degree in Slavic Languages and Literatures from the University of Massachusetts at Amherst and a Master's Degree in Library Science from Southern Connecticut State University in New Haven. Mr. Shea is currently a doctoral candidate in Russian.

William F. Hoffman was born in Paola, Kansas in 1951, and lived there and in Wichita, Kansas until 1963, when his family moved to the Fort Worth area. There he graduated from Monsignor Nolan High School in 1969 and attended the private University of Dallas, in Irving, Texas, on a full-tuition scholarship. He graduated from that institution in 1973 with a B.A. in foreign languages, specifically German, with Russian as a second language. He received an M.A. in foreign languages from the University of Texas at Arlington in 1976; during his studies there he worked as a graduate teaching assistant, giving courses in elementary and scientific and technical German. His academic honors include the Goethe Center Award (Dallas, 1973) and presidency of the Theta Pi chapter of the Delta Phil Alpha honor fraternity, 1975-1976. He works with English, German, Russian, Polish, and Latin, and the DOS computer programming language. He is a Director of the Polish Genealogical Society of America, and his published works include *Polish Surnames: Origins and Meanings* and the series *Obituaries and Death Notices Appearing in the Dziennik Chicagoski*, (with Thomas L. Hollowak). He edits *Rodziny*, the Journal of the Polish Genealogical Society of America, and typesets several publications, including *Plains Chess*. He is self-employed as a writer, translator, computer programmer, and specialty printer. He lives in New Milford, Connecticut, with his wife Jane and their daughter, Jennifer.

INTRODUCTION

Many individuals attempting to record the past histories of their families utilize American records not only to document family members who lived in the U. S. but also to discover a place of birth in the "old country." At this juncture, when the focus of research shifts across the ocean, researchers often encounter the need for concrete knowledge of a foreign language — a need numerous books and classes exist to satisfy. But the United States has been peopled by individuals from throughout the globe, and it follows that many of us are multi-ancestored Americans: our roots may trace back to several nations, so our research requires knowledge of several languages. The purpose of this work is to show researchers actual documents in not one but thirteen European languages, and to guide them through the process of unlocking the information held in those pieces of paper.

The languages chosen are divided by linguistic family: Germanic (German, Swedish), Romance (French, Italian, Latin, Portuguese, Romanian, Spanish), Slavic (Czech, Polish, Russian), and Other (Hungarian, Lithuanian). Multilingual documents have also been included so that two or three languages can be compared simultaneously (Ukrainian is featured in three such documents).

Each language section begins with a page showing the alphabet in print and cursive forms; a few notes are given on the alphabet's origin and unique features, along with some hints on pronunciation (meant only to give researchers a very rough notion of how words are sounded). Next come sample documents — whenever possible presented directly above or beside analysis of their components. Some hard-to-read documents have been retyped, conserving the same spacing as in the original, to facilitate comparison. In each section the sample documents are followed by a glossary of terms most likely to appear in such papers, and a sampling of personal names typical of that language.

The sample documents given here typify those the immigrant brought along to the New World as proof of identity or because they were required for international travel. Thus we have birth and baptismal certificates, passports, church administrative records, etc. We have chosen at random documents in various formats; some are long-form transcriptions from entries in registers, others are short-form versions of the same. All are representative of the material we may find in our attics among the possessions of our immigrant ancestors.

This volume, then, is an **introduction** to the translation of such documents. Not every word or portion of each document is translated; all the most important and frequently encountered material is. Further reading is strongly recommended so that the researcher can explore the intricacies and details of the language in question as well as gain additional knowledge on the types of records in each language and where they are housed in the country of origin. For this reason this work closes with a bibliography of handbooks and a list of ethnic genealogical societies.

Many of the documents presented here, and those you may have at home, are handwritten. The style of handwriting may range from elegant calligraphy to illegible scribbling. We have done our best to decipher what is written, and almost all handwritten entries are repeated in the analysis in a standardized script that should be easier to decipher.

When translating documents it is also important to conserve the proper rendition of the names given individuals at birth in their native language. While many of our ancestors chose (or were forced) to abandon their names in the U. S. (e. g., "Bronisława," "Calogero" and "Konstantinos" became "Bertha," "Charlie," and "Gus"), we need to know their original names to perform research in the country of origin. There were no "Sonnys" in Italy, "Walters" in Poland, or "Jessies" in Mexico.

We wish to thank a number of individuals and institutions who rendered valuable assistance in compiling this work: Anne Christine Beaulieu (French); Anabela Andrukonis (Portuguese); Dr. David A. Kideckel (Romanian); Dr. Nicholas Papp (Hungarian); Rosemary Guthrie of Alpena, Michigan and Ann C. Sherwin of Raleigh, North Carolina (German); John Murphy of Pittsburgh, Pennsylvania (German); Emma Swetzes of Manchester, Connecticut (Swedish); John A. Fischer of Sun City Center, Florida (French); Sherry Biskowski and Stanley Smelhaus (Czech); the Connecticut State Archives; the Archive and Resource Center of the Polish Genealogical Society of Connecticut. Several people in Lindsborg, Kansas were particularly generous in helping find usable Swedish documents: Marvin E. Johnson and the Archives Committee of Bethany Lutheran Church; Lenora Lynam, the Old Mill Museum; Richard L. Torgerson, Vice President and Academic Dean of Bethany College. A special thanks goes to Gary Mokotoff of Avotaynu, Inc. for his vital role in preparing this hardcover edition. Many thanks to them and to all who helped us produce what we believe will be a useful reference work.

Jonathan D. Shea
William F. Hoffman

The Germanic Languages

The Germanic languages are those belonging to the same family of languages as German (not languages coming from German, as some mistakenly assume the name means). All the Germanic languages — English, German, Swedish, Dutch, Norwegian, Icelandic, Danish, and a few others — have developed from a common ancestor which linguists call "Proto-Germanic" and which was spoken by Germanic tribes more than 2,000 years ago. This Proto-Germanic, in turn, was one of several major languages that had earlier developed from Primitive Indo-European, a language which existed perhaps 10,000 years ago and which was the source from which almost all the major tongues of Europe (and India) developed. Primitive Indo-European changed and split and evolved into "branch" languages, ancestral tongues roughly classified as Slavic, Germanic, Greco-Latin, and Indian (e. g., Sanskrit), all of which proceeded in turn to subdivide and evolve into the modern languages we know today. Thus Proto-Germanic evolved into modern Germanic languages much the same way Latin evolved into the Romance languages.

Linguists traditionally divide the Germanic languages into East, North, and West Germanic; some question the validity of these divisions, but they are adequate for our purposes. The East Germanic languages have mostly died out; West and East Gothic have some historical importance, but none of the East Germanic languages are of practical significance to genealogical researchers. The North and West Germanic languages, on the other hand, are very much alive and significant today.

North Germanic languages descended from the same source as Old Norse, the language of the Vikings (still spoken, almost unchanged, in Iceland) and a fascinating topic for study; modern North Germanic languages, besides Icelandic, are Faroese, Swedish, Danish, and Norwegian. These languages are of particular interest for genealogists because they characteristically describe family relationships with built-in precision; a Swedish uncle isn't just an uncle, he's a *morbror* (mother-brother) or a *farbror* (father-brother). Surnames in these languages are often simply patronymics: Thor Ericson is literally "Eric's son," and his daughter Klara is "Klara Thorsdottir" (allowing for variant spellings). Some linguists have argued that Russian's stress on patronymics and on separate terms for "mother-brother" and "father-brother" is inherited from Norse by way of the Viking founders of the earliest Russian settlements; but that contention is controversial and in any case is beyond the scope of our concerns.

The West Germanic languages are the ones "closer to home," so to speak: German, Dutch, Flemish, and the Angles', Saxons', and Jutes' dialects that ended up as English. Some Americans find these languages a little easier to work with because they can often include words or phrases close to English; others find it all the more frustrating that an occasional comprehensible word pops up in the midst of foreign babble. These languages really are closely related to English, however, and with a little study they yield their secrets.

In terms of difficulty for average English-speakers the Germanic languages stand about halfway between Romance and Slavic languages: Germanic languages are more highly inflected than Romance languages (i. e., they're more prone to change word endings according to grammatical usage), but far less so than the Slavic. Nouns and adjectives do take various endings, but recognizing the endings isn't as important for comprehension as in the Slavic languages. English verbs are formed and function much the same way German or Dutch verbs are. The North Germanic languages are a bit less familiar-seeming, but their basic structure and word-formation are still closely akin to that of English.

German, Dutch, and English use a separate word for the definite article, whereas the Scandinavian languages tend to use a suffix: German *das Haus,* English **the** house, Swedish *huset.* All the Germanic languages betray the Teutonic predilection for compound words (e. g., fireman, school-house), but German and Swedish tend to carry it farther than English, e. g., German *Geschwindigkeitsbegrenzung* (speed limit), Swedish *undervisningstimmar* (hours of instruction, course hours) and *medborgarkunskap* (civics, literally "citizenship-knowledge").

The verbs in Germanic languages tend to fall into two categories, called "strong" and "weak." The weak verbs — into which category the overwhelming majority of verbs fall — form their principal parts by tamely or weakly following a pattern; in English most weak verbs form the past tense by adding *-(e)d* (*love → loved*), in German the suffix is *-te* (*lieben → liebte*), in Swedish it's *-(d)de* or *-ade* (*älska → älskade*). The strong verbs are the exceptions in Germanic languages; they don't humbly follow the rules and add suffixes, instead they change internally, with vowels and consonants shifting according to fundamental linguistic rules. In English, *see, saw, seen* and *give, gave, given* are examples of strong verbs; in German the same verbs are strong, *sehen, sah, gesehen* and *geben, gab, gegeben;* in Swedish they're also strong, *se, såg, sett* and *ge, gav, givit.* Verbs in the various languages don't always correspond so obligingly, but the reason many do is because they share a common Proto-Germanic heritage.

In earlier days Germanic runes were used for ceremonial inscriptions (the word "rune" meant "secret writing"). But by the time Germanic tribes began to appreciate the value of writing in everyday life, Christianity had come to dominate Europe and Latin was the language of learning — so the Roman alphabet naturally came to be appropriated for writing all the Germanic languages, too. It proved necessary to invent or modify a few letters to fill in for sounds Germanic languages had and Latin didn't; but these unfamiliar letters need not terrify researchers.

The most confusing special character is the German *ß*, a combination of the German script forms for *s* and *z* (the letter's German name, *eszet,* simply joins the German names for *s* and *z*); for practical purposes the *ß* can simply be treated as a double *s: daß = dass* (or, in older writings, sometimes *dasz*). Swedish has the *å,* and Norwegian and Danish can intimidate one with *ø,* but there's nothing inherently incomprehensible about these letters. And genealogical researchers often find it unnecessary to worry about these letters; a cursory reading knowledge may require nothing more than the ability to recognize them.

It is, however, advisable to familiarize yourself with the pronunciation of any language with which you must work, because pronouncing a word may let the ear recognize a word that had looked utterly foreign to the eye. You will also often find yourself more often remembering a word's meaning if you can grasp the word as a sound rather than a mere unpronounceable jumble of letters. That is why pronunciation hints are given on the first page of each language section; the hints suffice only to develop a very rough approximation of the correct pronunciation, but that should be all a researcher needs. And of course, if you need more — if you want to develop a truly good accent and pronunciation — no book can do the job. Only extensive interaction with competent teachers and/or native speakers will enable you to develop the necessary skills.

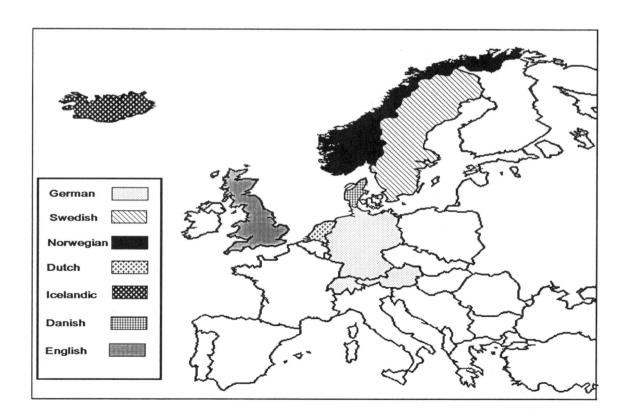

German	
Swedish	
Norwegian	
Dutch	
Icelandic	
Danish	
English	

Deutsch — The German Alphabet

Roman	Fraktur	Cursive
A, a	𝔄,a	*(cursive)*
B, b	𝔅,b	*(cursive)*
C, c	ℭ,c	*(cursive)*
D, d	𝔇,d	*(cursive)*
E, e	𝔈,e	*(cursive)*
F, f	𝔉,f	*(cursive)*
G, g	𝔊,g	*(cursive)*
H, h	ℌ,h	*(cursive)*
I, I	ℑ,i	*(cursive)*
J, j	ℑ,j	*(cursive)*
K, k	𝔎,k	*(cursive)*
L, l	𝔏,l	*(cursive)*
M, m	𝔐,m	*(cursive)*
N, n	𝔑,n	*(cursive)*
O, o	𝔒,o	*(cursive)*
P, p	𝔓,p	*(cursive)*
Q, q	𝔔,q	*(cursive)*
R, r	𝔕,r	*(cursive)*
S, s	𝔖,ſ,s	*(cursive)*
T, t	𝔗,t	*(cursive)*
U, u	𝔘,u	*(cursive)*
V, v	𝔙,v	*(cursive)*
W, w	𝔚,w	*(cursive)*
X, x	𝔛,x	*(cursive)*
Y, y	𝔜,y	*(cursive)*
Z, z	ℨ,z	*(cursive)*

Roman	Fraktur	Cursive
Ä, ä	𝔄,ä	*(cursive)*
Ö, ö	𝔒,ö	*(cursive)*
Ü, ü	𝔘,ü	*(cursive)*
ß	ß	*(cursive)*
ch	ch	*(cursive)*
sch	ſch	*(cursive)*
ck	ck	*(cursive)*
tz	tz	*(cursive)*

The rather intimidating typeface known in German as *Fraktur* was generally used in Germany until before World War II, but has since been replaced in common usage by the alphabet familiar to us. Even in the modern Roman-based alphabet there are a few modified letters used for special sounds in German, and these are listed on the right-hand side of the chart: *ä* (a-umlaut), *ö* (o-umlaut), *ü* (u-umlaut) and *ß* (eszet). The other letter combinations (*ch, sch, ck,* and *tz*) are shown because their printed or cursive forms can be hard to recognize; they are not regarded as separate characters and do not affect alphabetical order. Note also the alternate forms of lower-case *s* in *Fraktur* and cursive: ſ and / are the usual forms, s and ẞ are used at the end of words or at dividing spots in compound words. We've all seen similar usage in older English-language documents such as the Declaration of Independence, where the letters that look like uncrossed *f*'s are actually *s*'s.

German cursive script can be as intimidating as the printed *Fraktur*. Consider *(cursive)*, a familiar expression to most Americans; it looks like a series of angular scrawls (it's "Gesundheit," what you say when someone sneezes!). Any combination of *n (e)*, *c (c)*, *m (m)*, *n (n)*, *u (u)*, *v (v)*, and *w (w)* can be frustrating to decipher, especially if the penmanship is sloppy. The best approach is to identify the easier letters, such as *b*, *h*, *a*, and *v*; distinguish / *(s)* and/ or *f (h)* by their extending above and below the other letters; then start counting up-and-down strokes and trying to match them with problem letters. Hints: *u (u)* should always have that little curve over it, and *v (v)* and *w (w)* end with tailing curves that are usually discernable. Your odds improve if you have a limited list of candidate words to compare against; if you've inferred that the word might refer to parents, *(cursive)* can suddenly go from "M——r" to *Mutter,* "mother." So it's wise to refer constantly to the word-list at the end of this section.

The German Language

Until late in the 19th century there was no "Germany," just a hodge-podge of states, duchies, and monarchies in which varying dialects of German were spoken. The local dialect could vary enormously from one area to the next, and researching German records would be even more difficult than it is if not for historical developments personified by two men: Johannes Gutenberg and Martin Luther.

Gutenberg's significance is fairly obvious — the utilization of the printing press. Martin Luther may seem more controversial, especially to Catholics raised to think of him as the Devil incarnate, but to German linguists Luther is a towering figure. He grasped the value of making the Bible available to lay people in German — to counter the Catholic clerics who waved Latin Bibles and claimed the Good Book proved Luther wrong — so he translated the Bible into vivid, powerful German, which was spread far and wide with the help of the printing press. The impact of the Bible in the vernacular can hardly be exaggerated, and Luther's German became the basis for standard spoken German, *Hochdeutsch*.

Hochdeutsch means "High German," but it has nothing to do with social or moral elevation: it is German as spoken in the southern regions, where the elevation of the land is higher. (*Plattdeutsch*, "Low German," literally "Flat German") is the vernacular of the flatter northern parts of Germany.) The result of Luther's translation, spread by Gutenberg's printing-press, is the acceptance throughout Germany and Austria of a standard German that is understood by practically everyone and is used for official purposes. So when you try to study German documents, you often have printed forms to deal with, instead of scribbled hand-written ones, and you don't have to learn 58 different words for "father."

Of course nothing's allowed to be too easy, and German documents present their problems. But in the following pages lengthy analysis of sample documents will help with the grammar and vocabulary, and anyone who *The Empire Strikes Back* ever seen has and Yoda speak heard has can to the word-order eventually accustomed become!

German Pronunciation

The vowels in German are much like those of most European languages: *a* sounds like the *a* in "father," *e* like the *a* in "table," *i* like the *i* in "machine," *o* like the *oa* in "boat," and *u* like the *oo* in "boot." The short vowels are the same sounds, just not held as long; double vowels are pronounced as long vowels: in "Beethoven" the *ee* sounds just like a long German *e*. The vowels with umlaut, *ä, ö,* and *ü,* have had their sounds changed and shifted forward (which is what *Umlaut* means) from the back of the throat to the front: *ä* sounds like the *a* in "table" — in other words, the same sound as German *e* (in some regions it sounds more like the *a* in "cat"). The *ö* sounds like the vowel in "fir" without quite pronouncing the -r-. *Ü* sounds like the *ee* in "feet" pronounced with lips rounded to say "owe." The vowel *y,* found only in words of foreign origin, is pronounced just like the *ü.*

Of the diphthongs, *au* sounds like *ow* in "cow," *ai* and *ei* sound like the *i* in "mine," *eu* sounds like *oy* in "toy" (in some regions it is pronounced like the *i* in "mine"), *ie* sounds like the *ee* in "feet," and *ui* rhymes with "chop suey." *Ae, oe,* and *ue* are not true diphthongs; these are alternate ways of spelling *ä, ö,* and *ü,* a fact researchers must know to trace names. These alternate spellings may be used when one does not have access to a typewriter or other device with umlauts, so that *über* may be spelled *über* or *ueber* (but *über* is preferable if one has the capacity to reproduce it).

German consonants require considerable attention. The *c* by itself sounds like *ts* in "bats," but *ck* is pronounced like a simple *k;* initial *ch* sounds like a *k* (*Christus, Chor*), after the vowels *a, o,* or *u* it has the guttural pronunciation heard in the name "Bach," and in any other position it's a sound halfway between the *h* in "hue" and the *sh* in "ship." The *b, d,* and *g* are pronounced as in English except at the end of a word or a word-element in a compound word; then they devoice (i. e., are pronounced without sounding the vocal cords) to the sounds of *p, t,* and *k,* respectively; so *Guten Tag* (Good day) sounds like "goot-en tahk," and *Rad* (wheel) is pronounced the same as *Rat* (advice, counsel). The *g* is never pronounced like our *j,* but in a few French words it sounds like the *s* in "pleasure," e. g., *Genie;* also the suffix *-ig* is pronounced, not like *-ig* or *-ik,* but like German *ich.*

An *h* after a vowel is silent but indicates that the vowel is long; *sch* sounds like the *sh* in "ship," *tsch* sounds like *ch* in "church," and *dsch* is the closest German can come to our *j* sound in "jungle" (German *Dschungel*). Otherwise *h* is pronounced as in English. The *j* is always pronounced like our *y* in "yes." The combination *ng* is usually pronounced as in "ringer," not as in "linger." The *v* is pronounced like *f* (*vier* sounds much like our word "fear"), and *w* is always pronounced like our *v.* The *z* is pronounced like *ts* in "cats"; *q* is always followed by *-u-,* as in English, but the pair is pronounced like *kv.*

Before a vowel *s* sounds like our *z* in "zoo," but *sp* is pronounced like *shp* and *st* is pronounced like *sht*. When *s* occurs at the end of an element in a compound word — as in *Liebestraum,* for instance — the *s* and *t* are sounded separately, not as *sht*. Otherwise *s,* and *ss* or *ß,* is pronounced as in "sad."

The *r* is a difficult sound for Americans. It is properly pronounced in the back of the throat and it is rolled at the beginning of words. In some areas a trilled *r* made with the tip of the tongue, as in Spanish, is acceptable, and beginners should use that until they can have a chance to listen to Germans carefully and imitate the way they pronounce the *r*.

Document #1: A Family Record

This document (see opposite page) is a kind of generic family record. The darker, bolder script represents updates later added to the original. The document has several points of interest, both in terms of the script used and at least one point of grammar. The original is of poor quality and this reproduction has been electronically enhanced to make it easier to read., and it will be analyzed a section at a time. Here is the first section:

This same passage, given in a more standardized script, reads as follows:

Hausvater — "father of the house"
Geburts — "... of birth" (compound form)
Copulation — "marriage, wedding" (from the Latin word *copulatio,* a coupling or coming together; only later did *copulation* come to have a rather more specific meaning)
Tag Monat u. Jahr — "day, month, and year"
July — "July" (more often spelled *Juli* in modern times)
Marzellin Eyth — "Marzellin Eyth" (proper name)
Bürger — "citizen, burgher"
Musikant — "musician"
ausgewandert — "emigrated"
Oktbr. — abbreviation for *Oktober,* October

(1) (3)

[Ge]burts Tag [Mon]at u. Jahr	Hausvater	Copulation Tag Monat u. Jahr	Hausmutter	Geburts Tag Monat u. Jahr
July '91.	Marzellin Lisch Bürger u. Musikant ausgewandert 1863.	27 Oktbr 1813.	Mathia Kuglerin X † 23 Dec. 1849	10 Septbr 1790.
[Va]ter	Johann Lisch, Bader, vulgo der Schwarz	Jakob Kugler, X Magistratsgärtner	Vater
[Mu]tter	Agnes Rauterin X 14a	Weil. Mechtild X Kuglerin 65a	Mutter

(2) (4)

②

[Va]ter	Johan Eyth, des Peter, vulgo der Schwarz
[Mu]tter	Agnes Tautnerinn x14a

Vater Vater — "father"

Mutter Mutter — "mother"

Johan Eyth Johan Eyth — "Johan Eyth" (proper name)

des Peter des Peter — literally "of the Peter," in other words, "[son] of Peter"

vulgo vulgo — a Latin term meaning "in the common language," i. e., in German rather than in the educated language, Latin; this term often precedes a commonly-used nickname or by-name.

der Schwarz der Schwarz — "the Black." It is hard to tell whether the word is *Schwarz* (black) or *Schwanz* (tail), but "Peter the Dark" or "Peter the Black" seems more likely, although standard German would be *der Schwarze*. (*Schwarz* was a term sometimes applied to a blacksmith, especially in the context of surnames).

③

Hausmutter	Geburts Tag Monat u. Jahr
Matthia Kaplerinn 23 Dec. 1849	10 Septr 1790

Hausmutter Hausmutter — literally "mother of the house"

Geburts Tag, Monat, u. Jahr — see Section 1, above

Matthia Kaplerinn Matthia Kaplerinn — "Matthia Kaplerinn" (proper name)

Septr. — abbreviation for *September*

④ | *Jakob Kapeler, Magistratsperson* | *Vater* |

Jakob Kapeler, Magistratsperson	*Vater*
x	
Weib. Mechtild Kaplerinn	*Mutter*
x 65a	

Jakob Kapeler Jakob Kapeler — "Jakob Kapeler" (proper name)
Magistratsperson Magistratsperson — "town councilman"
Vater Vater — "father"
Weib Weib — "woman, wife" (the word *Frau* is more often used)
Mechtild Kaplerinn Mechtild Kaplerinn — "Mechtild Kaplerinn" (proper name)
Mutter Mutter — "mother"

TRANSLATION

Here is the information this document holds. The man of the house was Marzellin Eyth, a burgher and musician, born sometime in July 1791 (the date is cut off) to Johan Eyth, son of Peter, commonly known as *der Schwarz,* ("the Black," perhaps a blacksmith), and Agnes Sauter[inn]. A later notation mentions that Marzellin emigrated in 1863. On 27 October 1813 he married the lady of the house, Matthia Kapler[inn], born 10 September 1790 to Jakob Kapeler, a town councilman, and his wife Mechtild Kapler[inn]; a later notation says that Matthia died on 23 December 1849. (Presumably the bold letters and numbers are cross-references to other records.)

POINTS OF INTEREST

One fascinating grammatical point is clear from this record: that in German a man's wife or daughter could bear a form of his surname ending in *-in[n]*. The wife of Jakob Kapeler is Mechtild Kapler**inn**, and his daughter's maiden name was Kapler**inn**. The maiden name of Johan Eyth's wife was *Sauterinn*, which leads one to suspect her father's surname was *Sauter*. (Further documents of this family prove that this was in fact so.)

It is not uncommon for a female Slav's surname to be formed by adding a suffix (usually *-ova*) to the surname of her husband or father, but this record proves that German women sometimes did so, too. This is logical because in German almost any masculine noun can be applied to a female by adding *-in* (the extra *-n* is just an older or variant spelling of the same suffix). Thus a *Lehrer* is a teacher, a *Lehrerin* is a female teacher; and in this document a female *Kapeler* is a *Kaplerin(n)* (in German a medial *-e-* generally drops out when a suffix is added, so *Kaplerinn* is to be expected, rather than *Kapelerinn*).

This document is rather hard to decipher because the clerk formed the letters *-n, -e, -r,* and *-u* almost the same way, and it's almost a matter of faith that the word *Bürger* (Section 1) is *Bürger* rather than *Bünger* or *Bueger* or any one of a jillion other variations. Also interesting is the strange formation of *-h* (normally *f*) seen at the end of the name *Eyth,* and the *-p* in *Kapeler.* The latter looks more like a *-z,* and only after close comparison with several other documents for this family, and a good look at the *-p-* in *Magistratsperson,* does it become certain that the name was *Kapeler* and not *Kazeler* (the latter doesn't sound very German, whereas *Kapeler* does, but you can't always rely on that). Particularly maddening is that some letters are formed as they would be in Roman-based script: the *-p* in *Copulation,* the *S-* in *Septr* (*S,-* not *σ*), the *v-* (not Germanic *w*) in *vulgo.* It can't be mere coincidence that these words are all Latin; presumably the clerk used Roman script to write Latin words but Germanic script for German words.

Document #2: A Birth and Baptismal Certificate

The next document, reproduced on the opposite page, is in some ways more frustrating than the preceding one. One glance shows that much of it is printed, which should be good news — but the typeface is a fancified Gothic and is almost as difficult to read as standard *Fraktur*. Even more maddening is the handwriting: it's clear, well-formed, and the words in the top part of the document are quite legible. But then look at the handwriting under the columns!

The difference in writing style here is typical of many documents, and not just German ones. The more formal, official part at the top is written clearly and in Roman-style letters, as if here the clerk is on his best behavior; but once he starts filling out the columns he lapses into his usual — and, for us, difficult — scrawl. As if to have the last laugh on us, he returns to clear, familiar characters for the last lines and the signature.

This variation in handwriting was probably due to a conflict between training and force of habit. When writing words conveying the essential and primary facts, such as names and dates, clerks generally slowed down and formed their letters carefully, as they'd been taught to do; but when filling in familiar routine information, they would often fall back into their everyday, sloppy writing. In some documents the name of the person the document's about may be the only words decipherable amid the chicken scratches.

Here are the German words of the original document. Words originally appearing in type are given in normal Times Roman type; those originally appearing in cursive are given in italic.

Kronland: Schlesien
Bzrkshptmschft: *Freiwaldau*

Diözese: Breslau, österr. Anteil.
Pfarre: *Freiwaldau*
Nr. *183*

Geburts- und Taufschein

Aus dem hierpfarrlichen Geburts- und Taufbuche Tom. *XIX.* Pag. *148*
wird hiemit ämtlich bezeugt, dass im Jahre des Heiles:
Eintausend *acht* hundert *achtundneunzig (1898)*
am *vierundzwanzigsten April (24./4.)* in (der) *Freiwaldau,*
Dorf Haus Nr. *60* geboren und am *ersten Mai (1./5.)*
von dem hochwürdigen Herrn *Kaplane Franz Putze*
nach römisch-katholischem Ritus getauft worden ist:

Name des Täuflings	ehelich	unehelich	Vater Name, Religion, Stand, seine Eltern	Mutter Name, Religion ihre Eltern	Paten Name, Stand und Wohnort	Hebamme Name und Wohnort
Hoffmann Karl	✔		*Hoffmann, Karl, röm. kath. Weber in Dorf Frei-waldau, geb. am 7./8. 1868 in Vorst. Freiheit, Sohn des Webers Paul Hoffmann in Buchelsdorf und der Rosalia geb. Kauf von Dorf Freiwaldau*	*Frömel Rosalia geb. 13./12.1867 in Dorf Frei-waldau, Tochter des Oktavian Frömel, We-bers in Dorf Freiwaldau und der † Rosalia geb. Kreit v. Endersdorf*	*Gustav Schmidt, Tapezierer v. F. Anna Hoffmann, Tochter des Webers Paul Hoffmann in Buchelsdorf.*	*Marie Stöhr, Freiheit.*

Urkund dessen ist des Gefertigten eigenhändige Unterschrift und das beigedrückte Amtssiegel.
Katholisches Pfarramt *Freiwaldau,* am *30. März* 1908. — *I. V. Otto Birke, Kaplan.*

Kronland: Schlesien.   Diözese: Breslau, österr. Anteil.

Bzrkshptmschaft: *Freiwaldau*   Pfarre: *Freiwaldau*

                                                         Nr. *183*

Geburts- und Taufschein.

dem hierpfarrlichen Geburts- und Taufbuche Tom. *XIX* Pag. *148*
wird hiemit ämtlich bezeugt, dass im Jahre des Heiles:

Eintausend *acht* hundert *achtundneunzig*   (*1898*)

am *vierundzwanzigsten April (24./4.)* in der *Freiwaldau,*

Dorf   Haus Nr. *60* geboren und am *ersten Mai (1./5.)*

von dem hochwürdigen Herrn *Kaplane Franz Pütze*

nach römisch-katholischem Ritus getauft worden ist:

Name des Täuflings	ehelich	unehelich	Vater, Name, Religion, Stand, seine Eltern	Mutter, Name, Religion ihre Eltern	Paten Name, Stand und Wohnort	Hebamme Name und Wohnort
Hoffmann Karl	1		Hoffmann Karl röm. kath. Weber in Dorf Frei= waldau, geb. am 7./8. 1868 in Dorf Freiwald Sohn des Weber Karl Hoffmann in Lichtelsdorf und der Rosalia geb. Kirschner Dorf Freiwaldau.	Frömel Rosalia geb. 13./12.1867 in Dorf Frei= waldau, Tochter des Oklopiow Frömel, Weber geb. in Dorf Freiwaldau und der + Rosalia geb. Kirst u. Ludorsdorf	Gustav Schmidt, Lorzizimmer m. H. Anna Hoffmann Tochter des Weber Karl Hoffmann in Lichtelsdorf	Marie Stöhr, Freiwald.

Urkund dessen ist des Gefertigten eigenhändige Unterschrift und das beigedrückte Amtssiegel.

Katholisches Pfarramt *Freiwaldau,* am *30. März*   1908.

- 11 -

J. V.

Otto Birke,

Kaplan.

Here is a detailed analysis of the words appearing in this document, words that typically appear in most family history records and therefore need to be known.

Kronland: Schlesien — "Crownland: Silesia"; a *Kronland* was an administrative division used by the Austrians.

Diözese: Breslau, österr. Anteil — "Breslau diocese, Austrian section"

Bzrkshptmschft: Freiwaldau — no, *Bzrkshptmschft* is not a nightmarish monstrosity concocted by vowel-hating Teutons, but an abbreviation for *Bezirkshauptmannschaft*, literally "district captaincy" — another administrative subdivision for which there is no exact equivalent in English

Pfarre: Freiwaldau — "Freiwaldau parish"; a *Pfarre* can also be a vicarage or parsonage, but since Catholics are featured in this document "parish" seems the best translation.

Geburts- und Taufschein — this is an abbreviated way of saying *Geburtsschein und Taufschein*; this is a certificate *(Schein)* of birth *(Geburts-)* and of baptism *(Taufe)*. *Taufe* comes from the same root as our word "dip," and *taufen* means "to baptize."

Aus dem hierpfarrlichen Geburts- und Taufbuche — "from this parish's register *(Buch)* of births and baptisms"

Tom. XIX, Pag. 148 — Volume 19, page 148. These are Latin terms, *tomus* and *pagina,* and the Latin influence on European record-keeping may explain why in this section most of the letters are written in the Roman forms we're used to instead of the Germanic characters which predominate in the columns below.

wird hiemit ämtlich bezeugt, dass — "(it) is hereby officially certified that ..."

im Jahre des Heils — "in the year of our Lord" (literally, "in the year of salvation")

eintausend achthundert achtundneunzig — literally, "one thousand eight hundred eight and ninety"

am vierundzwanzigsten April — literally, "on the four-and-twentieth of April." This is the standard way of expressing dates in German: the preposition *am* (short for *an dem*) + the day number in ordinal form (usually ending in *-sten*) + the name of the month.

in (der) Freiwaldau — "in Freiwaldau." In some German expressions the definite article is needed — for instance, "in Switzerland" is *in der Schweiz* — so the *der* is printed in case it's needed; and when not needed, as here, it is simply crossed out or its omission otherwise indicated.

Dorf — village

Haus Nr. 60 — "house number 60"

geboren — "(was) born." In formal German different parts of compound verbs can end up all over the place. The basic structure of this clause is *dass...geboren...und...getauft worden ist: Hoffman, Karl* (that...born...and... baptized was: Hoffmann, Karl). To an English-speaker it may seem incredible that all this is said backwards and with various prepositional phrases thrown in here and there, but to a German-speaker the structure of the clause is familiar and not too hard to follow.

und am ersten Mai — "and on the first of May."

von dem hochwürdigen Herrn Kaplane Franz Putze — literally, "by the honorable Mr. Father Franz Putze." *Kaplan* comes from the same word as Polish *kapłan,* "priest," and English "chaplain." In passive clauses such as this ("Karl Hoffmann was baptized"), *von* translates as "by": he was baptized by *(von)* the Honorable Reverend Franz Putze.

nach römisch-katholischem Ritus — "according to [the] Roman Catholic rite"

getauft worden ist — "was baptized." In normal German this would be the end of the sentence, but in this document you first get the facts of the birth and baptism and only then the subject of the sentence, the name of the child being baptized.

Name des Täuflings — "Name of the one being baptized"

ehelich/unehelich — "legitimate/illegitimate." The appropriate column is checked, in this case showing that Karl Hoffmann was the legitimate *(ehelich)* son of a husband and his wife *(Ehefrau).*

Vater, Name, Religion — for once the obvious is correct: this means "father, name, religion."

Stand — here, "social standing" or "occupation" (in practical terms the two were almost the same thing). *Stand* is much like *stan* in Polish, *stato* in Italian, and *state* or *status* in English; depending on context, it can mean one's position (social or literal) or some aspect of the state in the political sense. Here *Stand* refers to the relative's position in society, but in many documents you will see the term *Standesbeamter,* "official of the state," which means specifically the registrar of births, marriages, and deaths.

seine Eltern — "his parents"

Mutter, Name, Religion, ihre Eltern — "mother, name, religion, her parents"

Paten — "godparents": *der Pate* is the godfather, *die Patin* is the godmother.

Wohnort — "residence, dwelling-place."

Hebamme — "midwife"

Hoffmann, Karl — the baptized child's name, Karl Hoffmann

Hoffmann, Karl, röm. kath. — "Karl Hoffmann [Senior], Roman Catholic"

Weber — "weaver," also a common German surname, but here definitely refers to Karl Hoffmann, Senior's occupation.

in Dorf Freiwaldau — "in [the] village of Freiwaldau"

geb. am 7.8.1868 in Vorst. Freiheit — "born 7 August 1868 in [the] suburb of Freiheit." The word *Vorstadt* means literally "in front of, before the city," and *Freiheit,* normally a noun meaning "freedom," must be the name of the suburb. See also the note on Marie Stöhr, below.

Sohn des Webers Paul Hoffmann — "son of the weaver Paul Hoffmann"

in Buchelsdorf — no tricks, it means "in Buchelsdorf"

und der Rosalia geb. Kauf — "and of Rosalia, née Kauf." German uses forms of *der* with personal names to make grammatical constructions like this clearer. Obviously when we're told Karl Hoffmann was the son of the weaver Paul Hoffmann there has to be another person he's the son of: his mother. In the expression *Sohn des Webers Paul Hoffmann...und der Rosalia* the genitive *des* (for a masculine noun) and *der* (for a feminine noun) make it clear that Rosalia is the mother even though a prepositional phrase *(in Buchelsdorf)* is stuck in there.

von Dorf Freiwaldau — "from [the] village of Freiwaldau." German sometimes uses *der* in places where we wouldn't use "the," as shown in the last note, and omits *der* in places where we do use "the."

Frömel Rosalia — simply the proper name, Rosalia Frömel

geb. 13./12./1867 — "born 13 December 1867." The abbreviation *geb.,* for *geboren,* means "born." It can be translated as "born," as it is here, but when used with a surname it means "née," as shown in the next note.

Tochter des Oktavian Frömel und der † Rosalia geb. Kreit v. Endersdorf — "daughter of Oktavian Frömel and of the late Rosalia née Kreit from Endersdorf." This is another case where *des* and *der* specify "of" in a phrase where we wouldn't use "the" at all. The little † or cross in front of Rosalia's name presumably indicates that she had died before this document was drawn up. In this context *geb.,* coming as it does before a surname, indicates a maiden name. Actually *geb. Kreit v. Endersdorf* could mean either "née Kreit, from Endersdorf," or "née Kreit von Endersdorf." There's no grammatical way to tell a difference. But *Kreit von Endersdorf* would be a name used only by nobility — weavers and tradesmen and peasants couldn't call themselves *"von"* anything, and there's no indication that anyone connected with this family was noble. It's difficult to imagine a noble woman in 1898 Silesia being allowed to marry a weaver, so it seems safe to translate this "Rosalia, née Kreit, from Endersdorf."

Gustav Schmidt, Tapezierer — "Gustav Schmidt, upholsterer." The word *Tapezier* or *Tapezierer* means "upholsterer" or "paperhanger." It's not clear which is more appropriate here.

v. F. — "from Freiwaldau"; *v.* is the standard abbreviation of *von,* and oviously *F.* would not be abbreviated unless the town referred to was obvious. "Freiwaldau" is the obvious choice.

Anna Hoffmann, Tochter des Webers Paul Hoffmann in Buchelsdorf — "Anna Hoffmann, daughter of the weaver Paul Hoffmann in Buchelsdorf."

Marie Stöhr, Freiheit. — The midwife *(Hebamme)* is Marie Stöhr, whose *Wohnort* (home, residence) is Freiheit. This is a bit tricky because "Freiheit" (freedom) seems an unlikely name for a town, and the expression *in Freiheit* can mean "at large," so in theory this could mean Marie (and Karl Hoffmann, Senior) came not from a village of Freiheit but from no fixed residence, i. e., were transients. But *Freiheit* has already been specified as the name of the *Vorstadt* or suburb where the father was born (see analysis of *geb. am 7.8.1868 in Vorst. Freiheit,* above), so that settles the issue.

Urkund dessen ist des Gefertigten eigenhändige Unterschrift und das beigedrückte Amtssiegel: "In witness whereof is the signature, in [my] own hand, of the prepared [document] and the seal of [my] office printed thereon." A painfully literal translation is "Witness of that is the prepared's own-handed underscript and the by-printed office-seal." It is not advisable to translate quite so literally, but it is easier to remember what *Unterschrift* means if you see the closeness to our words "under" and "script."

Katholisches Pfarramt Freiwaldau, am 30. März 1908. — If you have paid attention to this analysis you should have no trouble recognizing that this means "Catholic parish office of Freiwaldau, on 30 March 1908."

I. V. Otto Birke, Kaplan. — The *Otto Birke, Kaplan* part is easy — "Rev. Otto Birke." The abbreviation *i. V.* is a little harder. *I. V.* can stand for *in Vollmacht,* "in full power, with full authorization," or for *in Vertretung,* "representing, standing in for, signed for." The latter is probably appropriate here; Rev. Birke is not the official registrar, but is authorized to sign for him on documents such as this. This is another case where it's hard to be certain, so you go with the most probable explanation.

Here is a translation of Document 2, given in the same format as the original.

District: Silesia
Regional Captaincy: *Freiwaldau*

Diocese: Breslau, Austrian section
Parish: *Freiwaldau*
No. *183*

Birth and Baptismal Certificate

From this parish's birth and baptismal register, Vol. *XIX*. Page *148*
it is hereby officially certified that in the year of our Lord
One thousand *eight* hundred *ninety-eight (1898)*
on the *twenty-fourth of April (24./4.)* in *Freiwaldau,*
Village, House No. *60* was born and on the *first of Mai (1./5.)*
by the honorable *Reverend Franz Putze*
according to the Roman Catholic rite was baptized:

Name of the one baptized	legitimate	illegitimate	Father Name, Religion, Position, His Parents	Mother Name, Religion Her Parents	Godparents Name, Position and Residence	Midwife Name and Residence
Hoffmann Karl	✔		*Hoffmann, Karl, Rom. Cath. weaver in the village Freiwaldau, born on 7 August 1868 in the suburb Freiheit, son of the weaver Paul Hoffmann in Buchelsdorf and of Rosalia née Kauf from Freiwaldau village*	*Frömel Rosalia born 13 Dec 1867 in the village Freiwaldau, daughter of Oktavian Frömel, weaver in the village of Freiwaldau and of † Rosalia née Kreit from Endersdorf*	*Gustav Schmidt, upholsterer from F[reiwaldau]. Anna Hoffmann, daughter of the weaver Paul Hoffmann in Buchelsdorf.*	*Marie Stöhr, Freiheit.*

In witness whereof is my own signature of this prepared document and my office's seal printed hereon.

Freiwaldau Catholic parish office, on *30. March 1908. — Signed, Otto Birke, Priest.*

This document's format (except for the unusual typeface) and its vocabulary are thoroughly typical of many German-language birth, marriage, and death certificates. So it's worth close study.

Document #3: A German-Ukrainian Military Passport

This military passport is bilingual, with most entries in German but some terms also in Ukrainian. It was issued in Galicia in the Austro-Hungarian empire, and the bearer is a Pole!

Militär-Pass — "military passport"

Infanterist — "infantryman"

Johann Lech — "Johann Lech"

K. u. k. Infanterie-Regiment Prinz Friedrich August Herzog zu Sachsen Nr. 45 — "Imperial and Royal *(kaiserliches und königliches)* Prince Friedrich August, Duke of Saxony Infantry Regiment, No. 45"

10. Feld Compagnie — "10th Field Company"

Assentjahrgang 1896 — "Year of entry into the service: 1896"

Grundbuch-Blatt Nr. 383 — "Leaf No. 383 in the Land Register"

Ausrüstungs-Station: Sanok — "outfitting station: Sanok"

Charge: Infanterist — "Rank: infantryman"

Name: Johann Lech — "Name: Johann Lech"

Truppenkörper (Anstalt): (Infanterie-Regimt. No. 45) — "Body of troops (establishment): Infantry Regt. # 45"

Batterie- (Train-) Division — "battery (supply) division"

Unterabtheilung — "Subdivison: 10th Field Company"

Assentjahrgang [Рочникъ асєнтирунку] — "Year of entry into the service: 1896"

Los-Nr. [нумєръ лоса] — "Lot No. 1044"

Grundbuch-Blatt Nr. [нумєръ листа грунтовои книги] — "Land Register Leaf #383"

Dauernd beurlaubt [Трєкало оурлобованый]: *nach dem Dienstalter* — "Permanently discharged: by virtue of seniority"

Heimatsberechtigt (zuständig) in [Право домовности (приналєжности)] — "With right of domicile in:"

Ortsgemeinde [громада мѣстцєва]: *Wisłoczek* — "local community: Wisłoczek"

politischer Bezirk [повѣтъ политичный]: *Sanok* — "political district: Sanok"

Comitat [комитатъ] — "County"

Land [край]: *Galizien* — "Province: Galicia"

Zuständiger Ergänzungsbezirk Nr. [Приналєжный обводъ дополнитєльный] — "Jurisdictional Reinforcements District No. #45"

Stelle und Tag der Präsentierung — "Place and date of reporting"

Truppenkörper (Anstalt) des Präsentierten — "Body of troops [Establishment] of the one reporting: *Infant. Regmt. No. 45*"

Unterabtheiling des Präsentierten — "Subdivision of the one reporting: *10th Field Company*"

Assentjahrgang — "Year of entry into the service: *1897*"

Grundbuchblatt Nr. — "Leaf No. in the Property Registry: *383*"

Charge: Infanterist — "Rank: Infantryman"

Name: Johann Lech — "Name: Johann Lech"

Zuständiger Ergänzungsbezirk Nr. — "Jurisdictional Recruiting District No.: *45*"

Ist abzusenden (zu übergeben) — "Is to be detached (to be delivered)"

Militärärtzlicher Befund und Unterschrift — "Military medical examination results and signature." This space could have something like *gesund* (healthy) or *krank* (ill) written in.

Anmerkung — "Notes"

Geboren in [Родил ся] — "Was born in"

Ort [мѣстце]: *Wisłoczek* — "place: *Wisłoczek*"

politischer Bezirk [повѣтъ политичный] — "political district: *Sanok*"

Comitat [комитатъ] — "County"

Land [край]: *Galizien* — "Province: Galicia"

Jahr [рокъ] — "year: 1875"

Kunst, Gewerbe, sonstiger Lebensberuf — "Skill, craft, [or] other profession"

Hat besondere Merkmale [Мае особеннїи примѣты] — "Has distinguishing characteristics" (none noted)

Spricht [Говоритъ]: *ruthenisch* — "Speaks: Ukrainian" ("Ruthenian"). This line could also be filled in with *deutsch* deutsch, "German," *polnisch* polnisch, "Polish," or *russisch* russisch, "Russian."

Schreibt [Пише] — "Writes." Often this line will be blank, because most peasants had no opportunity to learn to read or write.

Körpergröße in Centimeter [Вeличина тѣла въ цeнтимeтрахъ] — "Height (literally, "body size") in centimeters: *163*"

Größenclasse der Fußbekleidung — "Shoe size (literally, "size-class of footwear")"

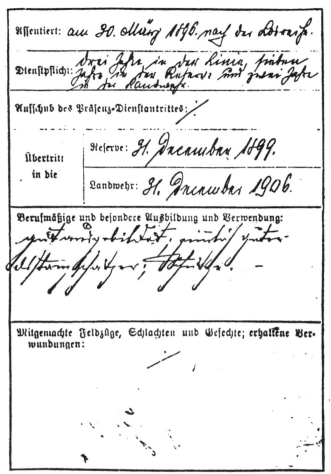

Page 5

Assentiert: am 30. März 1896 nach der Lobrnifh — "Entered the service: on 30 March 1896, in accordance with lot sequence"

Dienstpflicht: Drei Jahren in der Linin, sieben Jahren in der Reserve, und zwei Jahren in der Landwehr — "Term of service: three years on the line, seven years in the reserve, and two years in the *Landwehr*" (the *Landwehr* was something like a militia).

Aufschub des Präsenz-Dienstantrittes — "Deferral of reporting for commencement of duty."

Übertritt in die Reserve: 31. December 1899, [in die] Landwehr: 31. December 1906 — "Transfer into the Reserve: 31 December 1899; into the *Landwehr*: 31 December 1906."

Berufmäßige und besondere Ausbildung und Verwendung: gut ausgebildet, ziemlich guter Distanzschätzer; Schütze — "Professional and special education and skill: Well educated, fairly good judge of distance; marksman."

Mitgemachte Feldzüge, Schlachten, und Gefechte; erhaltene Verwundungen — "Campaigns, battles, and engagements participated in; wounds received."

Page 6

Besitzt Tapferkeits- (Erinnerungs-) Medaillen und sonstige Auszeichnungen: Jubiläums, Erinnerungs Medaillen — "Possesses medals for bravery (commemorative medals) and other decorations: Jubilee, Commemorative Medal"

Przemyśl, am 10. September 1899. K. u. K. Commando der Infanterie Regmts. Prinz Friedrich August Herzog zu Sachsen No. 45 — "Przemyśl, 10 September 1899. The Imperial and Royal Command of the Prince Friedrich August, Duke of Saxony Infantry Regiment, No. 45."

Ärztlich untersucht und gesund befunden. — "Examined medically and found to be healthy."

Sanok, am 10. September 1899. — "Sanok, 10 September, 1899."

Document #4: A Death Certificate

This death certificate (see opposite page — we added the line numbers) is instructive because its format is a common one, and because the darkness of the copy and the inconsistencies of the penmanship make it a representative example of the documents you'll encounter in real life. The first three documents were selected because they were comparatively easy to read once you began to get an eye for German script and for *Fraktur*. Here the *Fraktur* sections are the easy part; it's no exaggeration to say that if you don't know in advance what the handwritten parts should say, you'll never figure out what they do say.

The best way to proceed is to start by nailing down what can be determined for sure, then use that as a guide to clear up the unclear. Many find *Fraktur* difficult, but at least it is print and once you recognize a letter, you can feel confident it will be formed the same in line 25 as it was in line 2. So translating the *Fraktur* sections of the document should come first. Accordingly, here is Document #4 presented with the printed sections translated (to save space the written words are omitted); all the vocabulary terms used can be found in the word list beginning on page 26.

1) _____ on _____ 187_

2)   Before the below-signed registrar appeared today

3) by personality _____

4) _____ known

5) _____

6) residing in _____

7) and testified that _____

8) _____

9) _____ old _____ religion

10) residing in _____

11) born in _____

12) _____

13) _____ of (the)_____

14) _____

15) at _____

16) on the _____th of _____

17) of the year one thousand eight hundred seventy-__

18) _____ at _____ o'clock

19) has died_____

20) _____

21)   Read aloud, approved and _____

22) _____

23) _____

24)   **The Registrar**

25) _____

This translation is too literal and awkward, and the body of the text can be rephrased thus: "Today, before the registrar whose signature appears below, — appeared, personally known [to me], who lives at —, and he testified that —, — old, of the — religion, residing in —, born in —, — of —, died on the —th of —, 187_ — at — o'clock. Read aloud, approved, and —. The Registrar."

(1) _Müllrose_ am 14 Januar 187**6**

(2) Vor dem unterzeichneten Standesbeamten erschien heute

(3) der Persönlichkeit nach

(4) bekannt

(5) der Knecht Joseph Morawiak

(6) wohnhaft zu Müllrose Hof

(7) und zeigte an, daß Knecht Johann Stanislaus Wisniewski

(8) unverehelicht

(9) Zweiunddreißig Jahre alt katholischer Religion

(10) wohnhaft zu Müllrose Hof

(11) geboren zu Müllrose Hof 24 April 1843

(12)

(13) Sohn des Knecht Michael Wisniewski und

(14) seiner Ehefrau Margarethe geb. Kathausiak

(15) zu Müllrose Hof bei dem anzeigenden Gegenwart

(16) am dreizehn ten Januar

(17) des Jahres tausend acht hundert siebenzig und sechs

(18) Nachmittags um fünf ein halb Uhr

(19) verstorben sei

(20)

(21) Vorgelesen, genehmigt und wegen Schreibensunkunde

(22) von dem Anzeigenden mit seinem Handzeichen versehen

(23) XXX

(24) **Der Standesbeamte.**

(25) Janz

- 19

Before trying to read the handwriting in this document, a word about the origin of the document is in order; after all, documents aren't likely to just show up in your mailbox (believe me!), they come after searching a specific source in a specific place. This death certificate was obtained by an American researching her Polish ancestors; so although this certificate is in German, it's quite possible that some of the names will be Polish in origin. Many regions passed back and forth between Polish and German control over the centuries, so documents from them can be in or have names from either language, depending on when they date from. This can be a factor in understanding what the document says.

The first step in deciphering the written parts is to note any words or parts of words that are immediately recognizable. It may be simplest to assume that at this point to most readers nothing is immediately recognizable, and thus proceed with no assumptions.

The next step is to use the printed sections to gain clues as to what must logically follow them. In line 1, for instance, it's clear that am is followed by a date. The *14* isn't too hard to spot, the *1876* is obvious, so the inter-

① *Aullastra* ___ am *14 Januar* ___ 187*6*

vening word must be a month. There are only twelve possibilities to choose from, and a quick look at the word-list eliminates most of them: the word can hardly be *März, April, Mai, August, September, Oktober, November,* or *Dezember.* It's too long to be *Juni* or *Juli,* which leaves only *Januar* or *Februar.* The initial letter could be a *J* or *f,* but the 3rd letter can't be a *b,* so the word has to be *Januar.* So now we have some notion how this registrar wrote a capital *J* and the lower-case *a, n, r,* and *u,* and we know the date of the document is 14 January 1876.

With any luck this first discovery should prove applicable to some other section of the document, and a quick glance suggests that lines 16 and 17 deserve a closer look. The last word in line 16 looks a lot like the *Januar* in

⑯ am ___ *dreizehn* ___ ten ___ *Januar* ___

⑰ des Jahres tausend acht hundert siebenzig und ___ *sechs*

line 1. Line 17 clearly gives the year number, and odds are the year will be the same as that in the date of the document; this isn't always true, but it's what you should try first. By this logic the final word in line 17 could be the German word for "six," which the word-list shows is *sechs, sechs* — and so it proves to be. So what day is mentioned at the start of line 16? A good look at page 4 and the German alphabet suggests that the initial letter is *d, d,* and there appear to be about eight letters in the word; the word-list has only one numeral of eight letters beginning with d, *dreizehn* — dreizehn, "thirteen." The fifth letter does indeed appear to be a -z, and although the individual letters are too dark to be certain, *dreizehn* appears to fit. And it doesn't defy logic that a death occurring on 13 January 1876 would be reported to the registrar on 14 January 1876. (If we'd concluded that that first word was *dreißig* we'd have to explain how a death occurring on 30 January was reported on the 14th. Very suspicious!) So whoever died, died on 13 January 1876, and now we have samples of more letters, including *d, e, h, i,* and *z.*

The next line, line 18, appears to specify when on 13 January 1876 the death occurred; the final expression, *um — Uhr,* tells at what o'clock, and clearly there must be some indication of a. m. or p. m. The first word in line

⑱ *Nachmittags* ___ um *fünf ein halb* ___ Uhr

18 is hard to read, but if it's a choice between *vormittags* vormittags, a.m., or *nachmittags* nachmittags, p.m., the choice must be *nachmittags.* A close look reveals that that's what the word is, and this shows us how this clerk wrote -tt-, -a-, and -ach. Recognition of -h- and -a- suggests that the word right before *Uhr* is *halb,* "half," and just as English usually says "a half" or "one half," German usually says *ein halb* — so the word right before *halb* is not *nin (nin?)* but *ein, ein.* So the deceased died after noon at something-and-a-half o'clock. Again, there are only twelve possibilities to consider, and of the twelve *elf,* elf, "eleven," is the most likely. (Actually, it looks more like *Eilf,* but *eilf* is a variant spelling of *elf* which one occasionally sees, so that extra -i- need not concern us). So the deceased died at 11:30 p.m. on 13 January 1876.

Another line with which logic can help us is 9, which obviously tells how old the deceased was and of what religion. The religion is the first to tackle, because there are only a few possibilities. The most likely: *Katholisch*

9 ⟨*handwritten*⟩ alt ⟨*handwritten*⟩ Religion

katholisch "Catholic," ⟨*handwritten*⟩ *evangelisch*, "Evangelical, Lutheran," and ⟨*handwritten*⟩ *jüdisch* "Jewish." It's clear that *jüdisch* is out of the question here, but the second letter does look a bit like a -*v*-. Still, that first letter can't be an *e*-, it has to be a *k*-, and the second letter could be a sloppy -*a*-. All in all, ⟨*handwritten*⟩ *katholischer* is the best fit (the suffix -*er* is added for grammatical reasons, and in this case simply means "of") so "Catholic" it is.

As for the age, the first word starts with a *z*-, which suggests *zwei*, "two." The next word looks a lot like the first part of ⟨*handwritten*⟩ in line 16, and is in fact ⟨*handwritten*⟩ *drei*, "three." The last word clearly begins with *J*- (compare it with the first letter in *Januar,* lines 1 and 16), which suggests ⟨*handwritten*⟩ *Jahre,* "year." The word between *drei* and *Jahre* is hard to tell, but the first two letters look like *vi*- and the last three could be -*tel,* and the only word that fits is *Viertel,* "quarter." This makes sense, that the deceased was "two [and] three quarters years old."

By this point you should have started to get accustomed to this registrar's writing, and it's advisable to look over the document and see if any words or phrases have become recognizable, especially if they're repeated. There is an expression repeated several times, in lines 6, 10, 11, and the beginning of line 15; and the translation of the *Fraktur* tells us that in each case this expression refers to a place:

6 wohnhaft zu ⟨*handwritten*⟩   15 zu ⟨*handwritten*⟩

10 wohnhaft zu ⟨*handwritten*⟩

11 geboren zu ⟨*handwritten*⟩ 22 April 1873.

wohnhaft zu and geboren zu mean "residing in," "born in." So this must be the name of the town or village where the declarant lived and where the deceased was born and died. The first word is fairly clear: *Mierzewo.* The second word is harder, but comparison of the four times it's written suggests that it's either *Haf, Hof,* or *Huf. Haf* and *Huf* aren't words in German or Polish, but the word-list shows the German word *Hof,* which means "court, station." A *Hof* can be a courtyard or a noble's "court," e. g., a palace or manor house; it's the German equivalent of the Polish word *dwór,* which shows up in many Polish place names. That middle vowel looks more like a -*u*- than an -*o*-, but the final -*o* of *Mierzewo* in line 10 proves that the registrar sometimes got sloppy and formed his -*o*- that way. So all in all, *Mierzewo Hof* seems a reasonable guess at the name.

The second part of line 11 is also not too hard to read: "22 April 1873." Not only does this fill in one more part of the puzzle, it confirms the translation of line 9. If the deceased was born at Mierzewo Hof on 22 April 1873 and died at Mierzewo Hof on 13 January 1876, as lines 16-17 say, he would have been just about two and three-quarters years old.

What facts that should appear in a death certificate remain to be told? Obviously, the name of the person reporting the death and the name and relatives of the deceased. It's clear from the sense of the portions already translated that line 5 gives the name of the declarant, and lines 7-15 must give information on the deceased.

The first two words of line 5 are difficult, but knowing a person's name should appear on that line somewhere makes it easier to recognize the second two: *Joseph Marciniak.* (The surname could be *Morciniak* or *Moreśniak,*

5 ⟨*handwritten*⟩

but a little background in Polish suggests that those are very unlikely, whereas *Marciniak* is a common Polish surname. So without compelling evidence to the contrary, *Marciniak* it is.) As for the first two words, presumably they identify Joseph Marciniak in some way, probably by occupation. If so, the first word — three letters, beginning with *d*-, is very likely to be ⟨*handwritten*⟩ *der,* "the." The first letter of the second word has a little hook at the top, descending down and left and looping back around; the only capital letter formed that way is ⟨*handwritten*⟩, *K*-. The end of the word looks like like -*cht.* On this basis the word looks like *Knncht,* but German doesn't pack consonants together that way, so one of those -*n*'s must be -*n*- -*e*-. In the word-list *Knecht* is listed as a farmhand, stable-boy, or laborer (the same Germanic root gave English the word "knight"!). So the best guess is that the death report was made by the farmhand Joseph Marciniak, who lived in Mierzewo Hof.

Determining who made the report may be irrelevant except as an exercise in studying penmanship. But the person reporting was often an uncle or other close relative of the deceased, and thus the name may be worth noting as a possible member of the family under investigation.

At last we tackle the name that counts. Line 7 states that Joseph Marciniak testified (ʒeigte an, baß) that so-and-so died (verſtorben ſei, down in line 19). The three words that follow baß must be the name of the deceased. Of these the second and third words appear to be *Stanislaw Wisniewski* (notice, written not in Germanic but

(7) unb ʒeigte an, baß *Mielf. Jofn Stani: Lus Wisniewski*

(13) *Aefn ... veſ Basdeß Michael Wisniewski und*

(14) *ſeriin Efefefrau Margarethe ydn. Karbowiak*

Roman-style cursive, with -e- and -s- instead of -n- and -ſ-). The last part of the first word looks like -ſoſn -sohn, "—'s son." The same word appears line 13, right before what appears to be the name *Michael Wisniewski*. The first words in line 13 are definitely *Sohn des Sohn des*, "son of," so the mystery word is probably a description of Stanislaw Wisniewski's father, Michael, rather than an actual part of Stanislaw's name. The word appears to be *Wirth*, or in line 7 *Wirthsſohn*. A *Wirt* is an "innkeeper, host" (see word-list). Many German words now spelled with a -t- used to be written -th- (the -h- was silent, and eventually was dropped), so *Wirth* is an older variation of *Wirt*. If so, line 7 reads "and testified that innkeeper's son Stanislaw Wisniewski..."

Line 13, therefore, would read "*son of the innkeeper Michael Wisniewski...*" The last word is a little difficult to read, but if Stanislaw if the son *of* Michael, he had to be the son of Michael ***and*** someone else: *und und*, "and" makes sense and looks right. So line 14 must give the name of Stanislaw's mother, presumably Michael's wife. If so, the words *ſeiner Frau* or *ſeiner Ehefrau* (seiner Frau or seiner Ehefrau), "of his wife," should appear; and a close look at the first two words of line 14 confirms that they are there. Next should come the mother's first name, followed by *geboren geboren*, "née," and her maiden name. Knowing this, it is possible to read the next three words as *Margarethe, geb. Karbowiak*. (As with Marciniak's name in line 5, that surname is open to question, but comparison of the two surnames confirms that this reading is probably correct.)

This leaves only odds and ends to clean up. In line 1, the date is preceded by what is presumably the place where the document was written, apparently *Mielteckin* or *Mieltukin*. Close study of a map suggests that it is in fact *Mieltschin,* the German name of the town called Mielżyn" in Polish — and a few kilometers away the map shows a village "Mierzewo"!) In line 4 the prefix *be-* is added to ʀannt to form the word *bekannt*, which, with *der Persönlichkeit nach* in line 2, means "personally known, familiar." The rest of lines 3-4 provide room for the registrar to explain, if necessary, how the declarant identified himself.

Line 8's single word is hard to decipher, but the initial letter has over it the mark that usually accompanies a *u- u-*, and the middle of the word looks like *rſnirvt*. Under the circumstances *unverſnirvtſnt unverheirathet*, "unmarried," seems the best bet. (In modern spelling the

silent -h- has been dropped, so *unverheiratet* is the dictionary form.) It seems needless to state that someone who died at 2¾ was single, but the Germans' reputation for thoroughness is obviously well-deserved!

Line 15 has a rather tricky phrase following *zu Mierzewo Hof*: it looks like — *des* —ʒ—iɣ—*ə*— *Ɉnɣ*—*nvvurtſ*. Knowledge of German, or of the formal phrases typically found in German documents, suggests that this

(15) ʒu *Mierzewo Hof des Anzeigenden Gegenwarth*

phrase is *in des Anzeigenden Gegenwarth in des Anzeigenden Gegenwart[h]*, "in the presence of the one making the statement." *Gegenwart* (obsolete spelling *Gegenwarth*) is in the word-list and means "presence," and *der Anzeigende* means "the one who's making the statement" — this is the same word as the verb *zeigte an* in line 7.

Lines 21-23 are obviously some sort of legal formula, but the registrar scrawled his way through this *pro forma* statement so fast that it's very hard to read. But it stands to reason that the person making this statement

– 22 –

would be expected to sign it, and we see three X's in line 23; so it makes sense that lines 21-22 say something

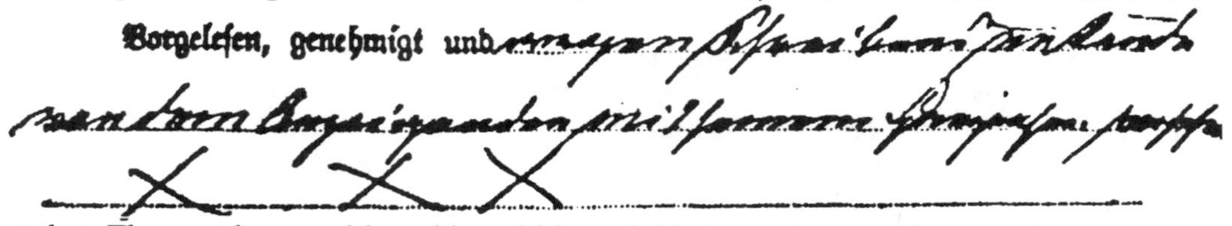
Vorgelesen, genehmigt und

about that. The next last word is so blurred it's probably beyond recognition, but the rest seems to be wegen Schreibensunkunde von dem Anzeigenden mit seinem ??? versehen: *wegen Schreibens-unkunde von dem Anzeigenden mit seinem ??? versehen,* "due to the illiteracy of the one making the statement, provided with his mark." The illegible word probably has something to do with Zeichen *Zeichen*, "sign, mark." Line 23 gives Joseph Marciniak's X, and lines 24-25 give the registrar's title and signature.

So here's the whole translation, with handwritten parts indicated by italics:

1) *Mieltschin (Mielżyn)* on *14 January* 187*6*
2) Before the below-signed registrar appeared today
3) by personality ________________________
4) ________________________ known
5) *the farmhand Joseph Marciniak* ____________
6) residing in *Mierzewo Hof* ____________
7) and testified that *innkeeper's son Stanislaw Wisniewski*
8) *unmarried* ________________________
9) *two, three quarter years* old *of [the] Catholic* religion
10) residing in *Mierzewo Hof* ____________
11) born in *Mierzewo Hof 22 April 1873* __________
12) ________________________
13) *son* of (the) *innkeeper Michael Wisniewski and* _____
14) *of his wife Margarethe née Karbowiak* __________
15) at *Mierzewo Hof, in the declarant's presence* _______
16) on the *thirteen*th of *January* ____________
17) of the year one thousand eight hundred seventy-*six*___
18) *after noon* at *eleven thirty* ____________ o'clock
19) has died________________________
20) ________________________
21) Read aloud, approved and *due to the illiteracy of*
22) *the declarant signed with his mark* __________
23) *XXX* ________________________
24) **The Registrar**
25) ________________________

Document #5: Contract for Passage on a Ship

The final document, reproduced on the opposite page, is a contract between Norddeutscher Lloyd (Lloyd's of North Germany) and a housewife named Basse Karaschik whereby Lloyd's would give her and her children passage from Bremen to New York. This is not a particularly difficult document to decipher — most of it is printed (granted, in *Fraktur*), with only a few words scribbled in — and it represents a kind of record researchers often succeed in finding or tracing. A line-by-line translation follows, but the reader may wish to try doing his/her own translation before looking at it. The words are all in the word-list beginning on page 26.

Vertrag über Beförderung nach einem außereuropäischen Hafen ohne Transportwechsel:
> Contract for passage to a port outside Europe without change of transport

Auswanderer-Verzeichnis No. M220/22 ... Norddeutscher Lloyd, Bremen ... Fahrkarte No.
> List (Register, Index) of Emigrants No. M220/22 ... Lloyd's of North Germany, Bremen ... Ticket No. — *[illegible]*

*Zwischen dem **Norddeutschen Lloyd** und dem unterzeichneten Reisenden (bei Familien als Familienvorstand) ist der nachstehende Beförderungsvertrag geschlossen worden:*
> Between the North German Lloyd and the traveler signed below (representing the family where families are involved) the following transportation contract has been agreed to:

*Die Beförderung, sowie Verpflegung für die Seereise wird übernommen von **Bremen** über **Bremerhaven (Nordenham)** am 7. Dec. 1912*
> Passage as well as meals for the trip by sea is undertaken from Bremen via Bremerhaven (Nordenham) on 7 December 1912 ...

im Auswandererdeck des deutschen Dampfschiffes Bülow
> ...on the emigrants' deck of the German steamship Bülow...

*des Norddeutschen Lloyd, auf dem Seeweg nach dem Hafen von **New York***
> ...of the North German Lloyd, on voyage to the harbor of New York...

*und von **New York** weiter nach ... Provinz (County) ... Staat ... mittelst Dampfschiff ... Eisenbahn (III Klasse)*
> ...and from New York on to ... Province (County) ... State ... via steamship ... railway (3rd class). [Since all this has been crossed through, passage was booked just to New York.]

2. Der Fahrpreis wurde für die nachstehend aufgeführten Personen wie folgt vereinbart:
> The fare was totaled for the persons hereinafter listed:

No. ... Zunamen... Vornamen... Alter (in Jahren)... Familienstand... Bisheriger Wohnort... Staat oder Provinz... Bezeichnung des Berufs... Stellung im Beruf... Fahrpreis für Seereise ab Bremen/ Weiterbeförderung ab New York
> #... Surnames... First names... Age (in years)... Marital Status... Previous Residence... State or Province... Description of Profession... Position in Profession... Fare for Voyage from Bremen (in Marks and Pfennigs)/ further Transport from New York

Karaschik, Basse, 49, v., Isaslaw, Rssl., Hsfrau, 170
> Basse Karaschik, [age] 49, married, [from] Isaslaw [a variant of the name of the village of Zaslavl in Byelorussia], Russia, housewife, 170 marks. [The two listed in lines 2 and 3 are apparently her children; the *Ang.* under "Stellung im Beruf" is probably short for *Angehörige*, "relatives, family," and their fares are half-price (85 marks instead of 170).]

Im Ganzen: 340
> Total: 340 marks, 0 pfennigs.

Außer diesem Betrage hat der Reisende für seine Beförderung, Gepäcktransport (abgesehen von etwaiger Ueberfracht), Beköstigung und Unterbringung bis zum außereuropäischen Hafen nichts mehr zu entrichten.
> Beyond this amount the traveler has nothing more to pay for his passage, luggage transport (aside from any charges for excess luggage), board and accommodation all the way to the port outside Europe.

3. Die Abfahrt [???] vom Hauptbahnhof/ vom Freihafen zu Bremen am ..., 191 ... um ... Uhr — Vorm. — Nachm.
> 3. Departure *[illegible]* from the main railway station/ from the free port at Bremen on ..., 191... at ... o'clock — a.m. — p.m.

Vertrag über Beförderung nach einem außereuropäischen Hafen ohne Transportwechsel.

Auswandererverzeichnis No. ___

Norddeutscher Lloyd, Bremen.

Fahrkarte No. ___

Zwischen dem **Norddeutschen Lloyd** und dem unterzeichneten Reisenden (bei Familien als Familienvorstand) ist der nachstehende Beförderungsvertrag geschlossen worden.

1. Die Beförderung, sowie Verpflegung für die Seereise wird übernommen von **Bremen** über Bremerhaven (Nordenham) am _____ mittelst Dampfschiff _____

und von **New York** weiter nach _____ des Norddeutschen Lloyd, auf dem Seewege nach dem Hafen von **New York** mittelst Dampfschiff — Eisenbahn (III. Klasse).

2. Der Fahrpreis wurde für die nachstehend aufgeführten Personen wie folgt vereinbart:

No.	Zunamen	Vornamen	Alter (in Jahren)	Familien-stand	Bisheriger Wohnort	Staat oder Provinz	Bezeichnung des Berufs	Stellung im Beruf	Fahrpreis für Seereise ab Bremen Mark / Pf.	Weiterbeförderung ab New York Mark / Pf.
1.										
2.										
1.	Najaschek	Josse (Rosi) (Chase)	49	v	Jsaslau					
2.		Chase	11	0						
3.			7							
4.										
5.										
6.										
7.										
8.										
9.										
10.										
								Im Ganzen:		

Außer diesem Betrage hat der Reisende für seine Beförderung, Gepäcktransport (abgesehen von etwaiger Uebertracht), Beköstigung und Unterbringung bis zum außereuropäischen Hafen nicht mehr zu entrichten.

3. Die Abfahrt
vom Hauptbahnhof
über den Freihafen } zu Bremen am _____ 191_ um _____ Uhr — Vorm. — Nachm.

German-English Word-List

This list of German words presents all words in three forms, first in standard Times Roman typeface, then in *Fraktur*, then in German cursive; this is meant to help those unfamiliar with the latter two recognize words as they might appear in documents. In addition to the general word-list — an alphabetized list of German words one is most likely to encounter in various documents — there are also two brief specialized lists, of months and of numerals; the words found in those lists also appear in the general list. A list of common German personal names follows.

Two points about German nouns must be stressed. First, German nouns form their plurals in a number of different ways, and trying to give all these plurals would complicate these lists a great deal; besides, any adequate dictionary gives the plurals, and it would be superfluous for these lists to try to cover ground adequately covered by dictionaries. Second, German words are very prone to forming compounds, e. g., *Dampf* "steam" + *Schiff* "ship" = *Dampfschiff* "steamship." No attempt has been made to list more than a few of the compound words a researcher is likely to encounter; any such attempt would mean trespassing on ground any good dictionary covers far more extensively and efficiently. These words can usually be solved by breaking them down into component parts, establishing what the components mean, and thus establishing what the compound should mean.

General

Abend Abend *Abend* — evening

abends abends *abends* — in the evening, at night

Abfahrt Abfahrt *Abfahrt* — departure, leaving

abgesehen von abgesehen von *abgesehen von* — with the exception of

abmelden abmelden *abmelden* — to report in on departure

absenden absenden *absenden* — to dispatch, send away

Abteilung Abteilung *Abteilung* — division

acht acht *acht* — eight

achtund- achtund- *achtund-*: — ...-eight (e. g., *achtunddreißig* = 38)

achthundert achthundert *achthundert* — eight hundred

achtzehn achtzehn *achtzehn* — eighteen

achtzig achtzig *achtzig* — eighty

alt alt *alt* — old

Altenteil → Ausgedinge

Alter Alter *Alter* — age

Amt Amt *Amt* — office (administrative position)

ämtlich ämtlich *ämtlich* — official

Amtssiegel Amtssiegel *Amtssiegel* — official seal

an an *an* — at, to, toward, by (also used with verbs, e. g., zeigte an is listed in the dictionary under anzeigen)

Angabe Angabe *Angabe* — statement, indication

Angehöriger Angehöriger *Angehöriger* — relative, family member

Angestellter Angestellter *Angestellter* — employee

anmelden anmelden *anmelden* — to report in on arrival

Anmerkung Anmerkung *Anmerkung* — notation, remark

Anstalt Anstalt *Anstalt* — establishment, institution

Anteil Anteil *Anteil* — section

anwesend anwesend *anwesend* — present

Anwesenheit Anwesenheit *Anwesenheit* — presence

Anzeigender Anzeigender *Anzeigender* — declarer, one making the statement

April April *April* — April

Arbeiter Arbeiter *Arbeiter* — employee, worker, laborer

Arzt Arzt *Arzt* — doctor

ärztlich ärztlich *ärztlich* — medical

assentiert assentiert *assentiert* — entered (or declared fit for) military service

Assentjahrgang Assentjahrgang *Assentjahrgang* — year of entry into military service

Aufenthalt Aufenthalt *Aufenthalt* — residence

aufgeführten Personen aufgeführten Personen *aufgeführten Personen* — persons cited

Aufschub Aufschub *Aufschub* — deferral, postponement

Augen Augen *Augen* — eyes

Augenfarbe Augenfarbe *Augenfarbe* — color of eyes

August August *August* — August

aus aus *aus* — out of, from

Ausbildung Ausbildung *Ausbildung* — education

ausgebildet ausgebildet *ausgebildet* — educated

Ausgedinge Ausgedinge *Ausgedinge* — = *Altenteil*, cottage or part of a farm reserved for the farmer after he hands his estate over to his son, so an *Ausdinger* is one who lives on that part, the *Ausgedinge* or *Altenteil*.

ausgegeben ausgegeben *ausgegeben* — issued

ausgewandert ausgewandert *[Kurrent]* — emigrated

Ausrüstung Ausrüstung *[Kurrent]* — equipment, outfitting

außer außer *[Kurrent]* — besides, except for

außereuropäisch außereuropäisch *[Kurrent]* — outside Europe

Auswanderer Auswanderer *[Kurrent]* — emigrant

auswandern auswandern *[Kurrent]* — emigrate

Ausweis Ausweis *[Kurrent]* — identification papers

Auszeichnung Auszeichnung *[Kurrent]* — decoration

Auszug Auszug *[Kurrent]* — extract

Bäcker Bäcker *[Kurrent]* — baker

Bahnhof Bahnhof *[Kurrent]* — railway station

Band Band *[Kurrent]* — volume

Barbier Barbier *[Kurrent]* — barber

Bart Bart *[Kurrent]* — beard

Bauer Bauer *[Kurrent]* — farmer, peasant

Bauernknecht Bauernknecht *[Kurrent]* — farmhand

Beamter Beamter *[Kurrent]* — official

Beförderung Beförderung *[Kurrent]* — transport

befunden befunden *[Kurrent]* — found (e. g., *gesund befunden,* found to be healthy)

Begräbnis Begräbnis *[Kurrent]* — burial

bei bei *[Kurrent]* — at, by, at the house of, in the case of

beigedrückt beigedrückt *[Kurrent]* — printed hereon

beiwohnen beiwohnen *[Kurrent]* — to attend; *beigewohnt* — attended

bekannt bekannt *[Kurrent]* — known

Beköstigung Beköstigung *[Kurrent]* — board

Belgien Belgien *[Kurrent]* — Belgium

belgisch belgisch *[Kurrent]* — Belgian (adj.)

Berg Berg *[Kurrent]* — mountain

Beruf Beruf *[Kurrent]* — occupation, profession

berufsmäßig berufsmäßig *[Kurrent]* — professional, occupational

Beschäftigung Beschäftigung *[Kurrent]* — occupation, employment

Beschneider Beschneider *[Kurrent]* — circumcisor

Beschneidung Beschneidung *[Kurrent]* — circumcision

besonder besonder *[Kurrent]* — special, particular

Bestätigung Bestätigung *[Kurrent]* — certificate

beurlaubt beurlaubt *[Kurrent]* — discharged, granted leave

Bezeichnung Bezeichnung *[Kurrent]* — description

bezeugt bezeugt *[Kurrent]* — testifies, testified

Bezirk Bezirk *[Kurrent]* — district

bisherig bisherig *[Kurrent]* — previous, up to now

Blatt Blatt *[Kurrent]* — leaf, sheet

blondhaarig blondhaarig *[Kurrent]* — blonde-haired

Böhmen Böhmen *[Kurrent]* — Bohemia

böhmisch böhmisch *[Kurrent]* — Bohemian (adj.)

Brauch Brauch *[Kurrent]* — custom, rite

Brauer Brauer *[Kurrent]* — brewer

Braut Braut *[Kurrent]* — bride

Bruder Bruder *[Kurrent]* — brother

Buch Buch *[Kurrent]* — book, register, record

Büchlein Büchlein *[Kurrent]* — booklet

Bulgarien Bulgarien *[Kurrent]* — Bulgaria

bulgarisch bulgarisch *[Kurrent]* — Bulgarian (adj.)

Bürger Bürger *[Kurrent]* — burgher, citizen

Bürgermeister Bürgermeister *[Kurrent]* — mayor

Charge Charge *[Kurrent]* — (military) rank

Chirurg Chirurg *[Kurrent]* — surgeon

Comitat Comitat *[Kurrent]* — county

Copulation Copulation *[Kurrent]* — marriage

Dampfschiff Dampfschiff *[Kurrent]* — steamship

Dänemark Dänemark *[Kurrent]* — Denmark

dänisch dänisch *[Kurrent]* — Danish (adj.)

das das *[Kurrent]* — *form of* der, q. v.

daß daß *[Kurrent]* — that (conjunction)

Datum Datum *[Kurrent]* — date

dauernd dauernd *[Kurrent]* — permanent(ly)

dem dem *[Kurrent]* → der

den den *[Kurrent]* → der

der der *[Kurrent]* — the, of the; who, which, that

des des *[Kurrent]* → der

dessen dessen *[Kurrent]* — form of *der* = "of which"

deutsch deutsch *[Kurrent]* — German

Deutschland Deutschland *[Kurrent]* — Germany

Dezember Dezember *[Kurrent]* (also sometimes spelled *December*) — December

die die *[Kurrent]* — form of *der* = "the"

Diener Diener *[Kurrent]* — servant

Dienst Dienst *[Kurrent]* — service

Dienstantritt Dienstantritt *[Kurrent]* — commencement of service

Dienstpflicht Dienstpflicht *[Kurrent]* — term of military service

Diözese Diözese *[Kurrent]* — diocese

Dorf Dorf *[Kurrent]* — village

drei drei *[Kurrent]* — three

dreihundert dreihundert _[Kurrent]_ — three hundred

dreißig dreißig _[Kurrent]_ — thirty

dreiund- dreiund- _[Kurrent]_ — ...-three (e. g., dreiunddreißig = 33)

dreizehn dreizehn _[Kurrent]_ — thirteen

Drittel Drittel _[Kurrent]_ — a third (1/3)

dritter dritter _[Kurrent]_ — third

Drucker Drucker _[Kurrent]_ — printer

durch durch _[Kurrent]_ — through, by

Ehe Ehe _[Kurrent]_ — marriage, matrimony

Ehefrau Ehefrau _[Kurrent]_ — wife

ehelich ehelich _[Kurrent]_ — legitimate, in wedlock

Ehemann Ehemann _[Kurrent]_ — husband

eigenhändig eigenhändig _[Kurrent]_ — by one's own hand

eilf eilf _[Kurrent]_ — variant spelling of _elf_, eleven

eins eins _[Kurrent]_ — one

einund- einund- _[Kurrent]_ — ...-one _(e. g., einunddreißig = 31)_

Eisenbahn Eisenbahn _[Kurrent]_ — railroad

elf elf _[Kurrent]_ — eleven

Eltern Eltern _[Kurrent]_ — parents

englisch englisch _[Kurrent]_ — English (adj.)

entrichten entrichten _[Kurrent]_ — pay

Erfolg Erfolg _[Kurrent]_ — success

Ergänzung Ergänzung _[Kurrent]_ — reinforcement, replacement, reserve

erhalten erhalten _[Kurrent]_ — to receive, received

Erlaubnis Erlaubnis _[Kurrent]_ — permission (_Erlaubnisschein_ — permit)

Ersatz Ersatz _[Kurrent]_ — replacement, reserve, training

erschien erschien _[Kurrent]_ — [he, she] appeared

erster erster _[Kurrent]_ — first

Estland Estland _[Kurrent]_ — Estonia

estländisch estländisch _[Kurrent]_ — Estonian

estnisch estnisch _[Kurrent]_ — Estonian (adj.)

etwaig etwaig _[Kurrent]_ — possible, eventual

evangelisch evangelisch _[Kurrent]_ — Lutheran, Evangelical

Fabrikant Fabrikant _[Kurrent]_ — manufacturer

Fabrikarbeiter Fabrikarbeiter _[Kurrent]_ — factory worker

Fahrkarte Fahrkarte _[Kurrent]_ — ticket

Fahrpreis Fahrpreis _[Kurrent]_ — fare

Familie Familie _[Kurrent]_ — family

Familienstand Familienstand _[Kurrent]_ — family or marital status

Familienvorstand Familienvorstand _[Kurrent]_ — family representative

Farbe Farbe _[Kurrent]_ — color

Färber Färber _[Kurrent]_ — dyer

Februar Februar _[Kurrent]_ — February

Feld Feld _[Kurrent]_ — field

Feldzug Feldzug _[Kurrent]_ — campaign

finnisch finnisch _[Kurrent]_ — Finnish (adj.)

Finnland Finnland _[Kurrent]_ — Finland

Firmelung Firmelung _[Kurrent]_ — confirmation

Fischer Fischer _[Kurrent]_ — fisherman

Fleischer Fleischer _[Kurrent]_ — butcher

Fluß Fluß _[Kurrent]_ — river

folgen folgen _[Kurrent]_ — to follow; _wie folgt_ = as follows

fortlaufende Zahl fortlaufende Zahl _[Kurrent]_ — consecutive number, number in a series

Fraktur Fraktur _[Kurrent]_ — Gothic typeface

Frankreich Frankreich _[Kurrent]_ — France

französisch französisch _[Kurrent]_ — French

Frau Frau _[Kurrent]_ — wife, woman, Mrs.

Fräulein Fräulein _[Kurrent]_ — girl, Miss

Freihafen Freihafen _[Kurrent]_ — free port

Friedhof Friedhof _[Kurrent]_ — cemetery

früh früh _[Kurrent]_ — early, in the morning

Fuhrmann Fuhrmann _[Kurrent]_ — carter

fünf fünf _[Kurrent]_ — five

fünfhundert fünfhundert _[Kurrent]_ — five hundred

fünfund- fünfund- _[Kurrent]_ — ...-five (e. g., _fünfunddreißig = 35_)

fünfzehn fünfzehn _[Kurrent]_ — fifteen

fünfzig fünfzig _[Kurrent]_ — fifty

Fußbekleidung Fußbekleidung _[Kurrent]_ — footwear

Gärtner Gärtner _[Kurrent]_ — gardener

Gastwirt Gastwirt _[Kurrent]_ — innkeeper

Gau Gau _[Kurrent]_ — district

ge-: _if a verb form starts with ge- and you can't find anything like it in the dictionary, try taking off the ge- (if there's a final -t, drop it and add -en) and looking for something like what's left; e. g., gesehen → sehen, gemacht → machen, geimpft → impfen and so on_

geb. geb. _[Kurrent]_ = abbreviation of _geboren_

geboren geboren _[Kurrent]_ — born, née

Geburt Geburt _[Kurrent]_ — birth

Geburtshelfer Geburtshelfer _[Kurrent]_ — midwife, birthing assistant

Geburtsort Geburtsort _[Kurrent]_ — birthplace

Geburtsschein Geburtsschein _[Kurrent]_ — birth certificate

Gefecht Gefecht _[Kurrent]_ — skirmish

das Gefertigte das Gefertigte _[Kurrent]_ — the document drawn up

Gegenwart Gegenwart _[Kurrent]_ — presence; _in seiner Gegenwart_ = "in his presence"

Geldverleiher Geldverleiher *[script]* — money-lender

Gemeinde Gemeinde *[script]* — community, congregation, parish

genehmigt genehmigt *[script]* — approved

genügt genügt *[script]* — satisfies, fulfills

Gepäck Gepäck *[script]* — baggage, luggage

Gerber Gerber *[script]* — tanner

Gericht Gericht *[script]* — court (of law) (also *Gerichtshof* means the same thing)

geschah geschah *[script]* — (it) happened

Geschlecht Geschlecht *[script]* — sex, gender

Geschlechtsname Geschlechtsname *[script]* — patronymic

geschlossen geschlossen *[script]* — closed, concluded (e. g., *ist geschlossen worden* = has been finalized, concluded)

Geselle Geselle *[script]* — journeyman

Gesetz Gesetz *[script]* — law

gesetzlich gesetzlich *[script]* — legal

Gesicht Gesicht *[script]* — face

gesund gesund *[script]* — healthy

getauft getauft *[script]* — baptized

getraut getraut *[script]* — wedded

Gewerbe Gewerbe *[script]* — skill, craft

Glaube Glaube *[script]* — religion, faith

Goldschmied Goldschmied *[script]* — goldsmith

Griechenland Griechenland *[script]* — Greece

griechisch griechisch *[script]* — Greek (adj.)

Größe Größe *[script]* — size, height

Großeltern Großeltern *[script]* — grandparents

Großmutter Großmutter *[script]* — grandmother

Großvater Großvater *[script]* — grandfather

Grundbesitzer Grundbesitzer *[script]* — landowner

Grundbuch Grundbuch *[script]* — land register

gültig gültig *[script]* — valid

Haar Haar *[script]* — hair

Haarfarbe Haarfarbe *[script]* — hair color

Hafen Hafen *[script]* — harbor, port

halb halb *[script]* — half (*ein halb* = one half, *elf ein halb Uhr* = 11:30)

Hälfte Hälfte *[script]* — half

Handelsmann Handelsmann *[script]* — dealer

Händler Händler *[script]* — dealer

Handwerker Handwerker *[script]* — artisan

Hauptbahnhof Hauptbahnhof *[script]* — main railroad station

Hauptmann Hauptmann *[script]* — captain (military)

Haus Haus *[script]* — house, home

Hausierer Hausierer *[script]* — peddler

Haustaufe Haustaufe *[script]* — baptism at home

Hausvater Hausvater *[script]* — man of the house, father

Hausmutter Hausmutter *[script]* — lady of the house, mother

Hebamme Hebamme *[script]* — midwife

Heil Heil *[script]* — salvation (e. g., *im Jahre des Heils* = in the year of our Lord)

Heim Heim *[script]* — home

Heimat Heimat *[script]* — home, homeland, native land

heimatsberechtigt heimatsberechtigt *[script]* — with right of domicile

Herr Herr *[script]* — master, lord, Mister

heute heute *[script]* — today

hier hier *[script]* — here

hierämtlich hierämtlich *[script]* — of the local office

hierpfarrlich hierpfarrlich *[script]* — of the local parish

Hirt Hirt *[script]* — shepherd

Hochdeutsch Hochdeutsch *[script]* — High German (standard spoken German)

hochwürdig hochwürdig *[script]* — honorable, reverend

Hochzeit Hochzeit *[script]* — wedding

Hof Hof *[script]* — court(yard), farm, manor house, station

Holland Holland *[script]* — Holland

holländisch holländisch *[script]* — Dutch (adj.)

hundert hundert *[script]* — hundred

ihr ihr *[script]* — her, their; (sometimes, but rarely = "you" or "your")

Impfbezirk Impfbezirk *[script]* — vaccination district

Impfliste Impfliste *[script]* — vaccination list

Impfschein Impfschein *[script]* — vaccination certificate

Impfung Impfung *[script]* — vaccination

in in *[script]* — in, to

Infanterist Infanterist *[script]* — infantryman

irisch irisch *[script]* — Irish (adj.)

Irland Irland *[script]* — Ireland

ist ist *[script]* — is (often used with other verbs, e. g., *ist getauft worden* = has been baptized)

Italien Italien *[script]* — Italy

italienisch italienisch *[script]* — Italian (adj.)

ja ja *ja* — yes

Jahr Jahr *Jahr* — year

Jahrhundert Jahrhundert *Jahrhundert* — century

Januar Januar *Januar* — January

jüdisch jüdisch *jüdisch* — Jewish

jung jung *jung* — young

Junge Junge *Junge* — boy

Juni Juni *Juni* — June

Juli Juli *Juli* — July

Kapitän Kapitän *Kapitän* — captain, e. g., ship's captain)

Kaplan Kaplan *Kaplan* — priest, chaplain

Kärrner Kärrner *Kärrner* — carter

katholisch katholisch *katholisch* — Catholic

Kaufmann Kaufmann *Kaufmann* — merchant

Kennzeichen Kennzeichen *Kennzeichen* — distinguishing marks

Kind Kind *Kind* — child (pl. *Kinder*)

Kirche Kirche *Kirche* — church

Kirchenbuch Kirchenbuch *Kirchenbuch* — church register

kirchlich kirchlich *kirchlich* — of, by, in the church

Klasse Klasse *Klasse* — class (e. g., *erste Klasse* = first class), classroom

Kleiderhändler Kleiderhändler *Kleiderhändler* — clothier

Knabe Knabe *Knabe* — boy

Knecht Knecht *Knecht* — farmhand, ploughman, servant, stable-boy

Konfirmation Konfirmation *Konfirmation* — confirmation

Körper Körper *Körper* — body

Kreis Kreis *Kreis* — district, region

Kronland Kronland *Kronland* — district, region, province, "crownland"

Kunst Kunst *Kunst* — art, skill

Kürschner Kürschner *Kürschner* — furrier

Land Land *Land* — land, region, province

Landvogt Landvogt *Landvogt* — bailiff

Landwehr Landwehr *Landwehr* — the *Landwehr*, militia, Territorial Reserve

Landwirt Landwirt *Landwirt* — farm-owner

laut laut *laut* — according to

Lebensberuf Lebensberuf *Lebensberuf* — profession

Lehrer Lehrer *Lehrer* — teacher

Lehrling Lehrling *Lehrling* — apprentice

Leistung Leistung *Leistung* — accomplishment

lettisch lettisch *lettisch* — Latvian (adj.)

Lettland Lettland *Lettland* — Latvia

Linie Linie *Linie* — line

Liste Liste *Liste* — list

Litauen Litauen *Litauen* — Lithuania

litauisch litauisch *litauisch* — Lithuanian (adj.)

Lohnarbeiter Lohnarbeiter *Lohnarbeiter* — hired hand

Los Los *Los* — lot

lutheranisch lutheranisch *lutheranisch* — Lutheran

Mädchen Mädchen *Mädchen* — girl

Mädchenname Mädchenname *Mädchenname* — maiden name

Magistratsperson Magistratsperson *Magistratsperson* — councilman

Mähren Mähren *Mähren* — Moravia

mährisch mährisch *mährisch* — Moravian (adj.)

Mai Mai *Mai* — May

Mal Mal *Mal* — time (e. g., *zum ersten Mal[e]* = the first time)

Maler Maler *Maler* — painter

Mann Mann *Mann* — man, husband

männlich männlich *männlich* — masculine, male

Mark Mark *Mark* — German mark (monetary unit)

März März *März* — March

Matrikenführung Matrikenführung *Matrikenführung* — registration of vital documents

Matrikenschein Matrikenschein *Matrikenschein* — vital document, birth certificate

Matrose Matrose *Matrose* — sailor

Medaille Medaille *Medaille* — medal

Meier Meier *Meier* — steward (of an estate)

Meister Meister *Meister* — master

Metzger Metzger *Metzger* — butcher

militärisch militärisch *militärisch* — military

Militärpaß Militärpaß *Militärpaß* — military passport

mit mit *mit* — with

mitgemacht mitgemacht *mitgemacht* — participated in

mittelst mittelst *mittelst* — by way of, via

Monat Monat *Monat* — month

Morgen Morgen *Morgen* — morning

morgen morgen *morgen* — tomorrow

Müller Müller *Müller* — miller

Mund Mund *Mund* — mouth

mündlich mündlich *mündlich* — oral(ly)

Musikant Musikant *Musikant* — musician

Mutter Mutter *Mutter* — mother

nach nach *nach* — to, according to, for, by, after

nachgefolgt nachgefolgt *nachgefolgt* — subsequent

nachmittags nachmittags *nachmittags* — in the afternoon, p.m.

nachstehend nachstehend *nachstehend* — following, subsequent

Nacht Nacht *Nacht* — night

nachts nachts *nachts* — at night

Name Name *Name* — name

Namensbeilegung Namensbeilegung *Namensbeilegung* — conferment of name

Nase Nase *Nase* — nose

nein nein *nein* — no

neun neun *neun* — nine

neunhundert neunhundert *neunhundert* — nine hundred

neunund- neunund- *neunund-* — ...-nine (e. g., *neununddreißig* = 39)

neunzehn neunzehn *neunzehn* — nineteen

neunzig neunzig *neunzig* — ninety

nicht nicht *nicht* — not

nicht mehr nicht mehr *nicht mehr* — no longer, no more

nichts nichts *nichts* — nothing

nichts mehr nichts mehr *nichts mehr* — nothing else

norddeutsch norddeutſch *norddeutsch* — North German

Norden Norden *Norden* — north

Norwegen Norwegen *Norwegen* — Norway

norwegisch norwegiſch *norwegisch* — Norwegian (adj.)

November November *November* — November

Nummer Nummer *Nummer* — number

ohne ohne *ohne* — without

Oktober Oktober *Oktober* — October

Onkel Onkel *Onkel* — uncle

Ort Ort *Ort* — place, site, spot

örtlich örtlich *örtlich* — local

Ortsgemeinde Ortsgemeinde *Ortsgemeinde* — local community

Osten Oſten *Osten* — east

Österreich Öſterreich *Österreich* — Austria

österreichisch öſterreichiſch *österreichisch* — Austrian

Pächter Pächter *Pächter* — farmer, tenant

Pag. Pag. *Pag.* — page (from Latin *pagus*)

Paß Paß *Paß* — passport

Pate Pate *Pate* — godfather

Paten Paten *Paten* — godparents

Patin Patin *Patin* — godmother

Pelzhändler Pelzhändler *Pelzhändler* — furrier

Person Perſon *Person* — person

Persönlichkeit Perſönlichkeit *Persönlichkeit* — personality (*der Persönlichkeit nach bekannt* = personally known)

Pf. = Pfennig

Pfarramt Pfarramt *Pfarramt* — parish office

Pfarre Pfarre *Pfarre* — parish

Pfarrer Pfarrer *Pfarrer* — parson, clergyman

Pfarrkirche Pfarrkirche *Pfarrkirche* — parish church

Pfennig Pfennig *Pfennig* — pennies

Pflicht Pflicht *Pflicht* — duty, requirement

Platz Platz *Platz* — place

Polen Polen *Polen* — Poland

polnisch polniſch *polnisch* — Polish (adj.)

Portugal Portugal *Portugal* — Portugal

portugiesisch portugieſiſch *portugiesisch* — Portuguese (adj.)

Präsentierung Präſentierung *Präsentierung* — presenting, reporting

Priester Prieſter *Priester* — priest

Probst Probſt *Probst* — pastor

Provinz Provinz *Provinz* — province

Rabbiner Rabbiner *Rabbiner* — rabbi

Register Regiſter *Register* — index

Reisender Reiſender *Reisender* — traveler

Religion Religion *Religion* — religion

Ritus Ritus *Ritus* — rite

römisch katholisch römiſch katholiſch *römisch katholisch* — Roman Catholic

Rumänien Rumänien *Rumänien* — Romania

rumänisch rumäniſch *rumänisch* — Romanian (adj.)

russischorthodox ruſſiſchorthodox *russischorthodox* — Russian Orthodox

Rußland Rußland *Rußland* — Russia

Sänger Sänger *Sänger* — singer

Schäfer Schäfer *Schäfer* — shepherd

Schauspieler Schauſpieler *Schauspieler* — actor

Schein Schein *Schein* — certificate, document, license

Schiff Schiff *Schiff* — ship

Schlacht Schlacht *Schlacht* — battle

Schlesien Schleſien *Schlesien* — Silesia

Schmied Schmied *Schmied* — smith

Schneider Schneider *Schneider* — tailor

Schnurrbart Schnurrbart *Schnurrbart* — moustache

schreiben ſchreiben *schreiben* — to write; *schreibt* [he, she] writes

Schreibensunkunde Schreibensunkunde *Schreibensunkunde* — illiteracy

Schreiber Schreiber *Schreiber* — clerk, scribe

Schriftzeichen Schriftzeichen *Schriftzeichen* — illiterate person's mark, made in place of a signature

Schuhmacher Schuhmacher *Schuhmacher* — shoemaker

Schultheiß Schultheiß *Schultheiß* — village mayor

Schulze Schulze *Schulze* — village mayor

Schuster Schuſter *Schuster* — shoemaker

Schütze Schütze *Schütze* — shot, marksman

schwarz ſchwarz *schwarz* — black

Schweden Schweden *Schwedisch* — Sweden

schwedisch schwedisch *schwedisch* — Swedish (adj.)

Schweiz Schweiz *Schweiz* — Switzerland

schweizerisch schweizerisch *schweizerisch* — Swiss (adj.)

Schwester Schwester *Schwester* — sister

sechs sechs *sechs* — six

sechshundert sechshundert *sechshundert* — six hundred

sechsund- sechsund- *sechsund-* — ...-six (e. g., *sechsunddreißig* = 36)

sechzehn sechzehn *sechzehn* — sixteen

sechzig sechzig *sechzig* — sixty

Seereise Seereise *Seereise* — sea voyage, sea journey

Seeweg Seeweg *Seeweg* — sea-route (*auf dem Seeweg* = by sea)

sei sei *sei* — (basically = is, was)

sein sein *sein* — to be

sein sein *sein* — his, hers, its (e. g., *in seiner Gegenwart* = in his presence)

Seite Seite *Seite* — page, side

September September *September* — September

sieben sieben *sieben* — seven

siebenhundert siebenhundert *siebenhundert* — seven hundred

siebenund- siebenund- *siebenund-* — ... -seven (e. g., *siebenunddreißig* = 37)

siebzehn siebzehn *siebzehn* — seventeen

siebzig siebzig *siebzig* — seventy (sometimes *siebenzig*)

slowakisch slowakisch *slowakisch* — Slovak (adj.)

Sohn Sohn *Sohn* — son

sonstig sonstig *sonstig* — other

spanisch spanisch *spanisch* — Spanish (adj.)

spät spät *spät* — late

Spekulant Spekulant *Spekulant* — speculator

Sprache Sprache *Sprache* — language

sprechen sprechen *sprechen* — to speak; *spricht* — [he, she] speaks

Staat Staat *Staat* — state

Stadt Stadt *Stadt* — city

Stand Stand *Stand* — position, class, occupation; the state

standesämtlich standesämtlich *standesämtlich* — by/of the Registry office

Standesbeamter Standesbeamter *Standesbeamter* — the Registrar of Vital Statistics

starb starb *starb* — died (from *sterben*)

Stelle Stelle *Stelle* — place

Stellung Stellung *Stellung* — position

sterben sterben *sterben* — to die

Stiefmutter Stiefmutter *Stiefmutter* — stepmother

Stiefvater Stiefvater *Stiefvater* — stepfather

Student Student *Student* — student

Stunde Stunde *Stunde* — hour

Süden Süden *Süden* — south

Tag Tag *Tag* — day

Tag(e)löhner Tagelöhner *Tagelöhner* — day-laborer

Tante Tante *Tante* — aunt

Tapezier[er] Tapezier[er] *Tapezier[er]* — upholsterer, paperhanger

Tapferkeit Tapferkeit *Tapferkeit* — bravery, gallantry

Taufbuch Taufbuch *Taufbuch* — baptismal registry

Taufe Taufe *Taufe* — baptism, christening

Täufling Täufling *Täufling* — the one being baptized

Taufname Taufname *Taufname* — given name

Taufpate Taufpate *Taufpate* — godfather, godparent

Taufschein Taufschein *Taufschein* — baptismal certificate

Taufzeuge Taufzeuge *Taufzeuge* — godparent

tausend tausend *tausend* — thousand

Tochter Tochter *Tochter* — daughter

Tod Tod *Tod* — death

todt → tot

Tom. Tom. *Tom.* — volume (from Latin *tomus*)

tot tot *tot* — dead (also spelled *todt*)

Totenschein Totenschein *Totenschein* — death certificate

totgeboren totgeboren *totgeboren* — stillborn

Transport Transport *Transport* — transportation

Transportwechsel Transportwechsel *Transportwechsel* — change of transport

Trauschein Trauschein *Trauschein* — marriage certificate

Truppenkörper Truppenkörper *Truppenkörper* — body of troops

tschechisch tschechisch *tschechisch* — Czech

Tschechoslowakei Tschechoslowakei *Tschechoslowakei* — Czechoslovakia

Tuchhändler Tuchhändler *Tuchhändler* — clothier

über über *über* — over, about, for

Überfracht Überfracht *Überfracht* — overweight, charge for excess luggage

übergeben übergeben *übergeben* — to deliver, surrender

übernommen übernommen *übernommen* — undertaken, taken on or over

Übertritt Übertritt *Übertritt* — transfer

Uhr Uhr *Uhr* — o'clock (e. g., *um sechs Uhr* = at six o'clock)

Uhrmacher Uhrmacher *Uhrmacher* — clock-maker

um um *um* — at

und und *und* — and

unehelich unehelich *unehelich* — illegitimate, out of wedlock

ungarisch ungarisch *ungarisch* — Hungarian (adj.)

Ungarn Ungarn *Ungarn* — Hungary

unter unter *unter* — under, below

Unterabt[h]eilung Unterabtheilung *Unterabtheilung* — subdivision

Unterbringung Unterbringung *Unterbringung* — accommodations

Unterschrift Unterschrift *Unterschrift* — signature

untersucht untersucht *untersucht* — examined

unterzeichnet unterzeichnet *unterzeichnet* — undersigned

unverheiratet unverheiratet *unverheiratet* — unmarried

Urkund Urkund *Urkund* — deed, voucher, document (e. g., *zu Urkund dessen* = in witness whereof)

Urlaub Urlaub *Urlaub* — leave, vacation

Vater Vater *Vater* — father

Veränderung Veränderung *Veränderung* — change

verheiratet verheiratet *verheiratet* — married

vermahlen sich mit vermahlen sich mit *vermahlen sich mit* — to marry

Verpflegung Verpflegung *Verpflegung* — meals, board

Versammlung Versammlung *Versammlung* — assembly

versehen versehen *versehen* — provided (*mit* = with)

verstorben verstorben *verstorben* — died

Vertrag Vertrag *Vertrag* — contract

Verwalter Verwalter *Verwalter* — bailiff (on an estate)

Verwendung Verwendung *Verwendung* — use, application, skill

Verwundung Verwundung *Verwundung* — wound, injury

Verzeichnis Verzeichnis *Verzeichnis* — list, register, index

Vetter Vetter *Vetter* — cousin

vier vier *vier* — four

vierhundert vierhundert *vierhundert* — four hundred

Viertel Viertel *Viertel* — a fourth, quarter

vierund- vierund- *vierund-* — ...-four

vierzehn vierzehn *vierzehn* — fourteen

vierzig vierzig *vierzig* — forty

Vogt Vogt *Vogt* — bailiff, provost

von von *von* — from, by, of

vor vor *vor* — before, in front of

vorgelesen vorgelesen *vorgelesen* — read aloud

vormittags vormittags *vormittags* — a.m., before noon

Vorname Vorname *Vorname* — first name

vulgo vulgo *vulgo* — in the vernacular

Waffe Waffe *Waffe* — weapon, arm

Waffenübung Waffenübung *Waffenübung* — military exercise

Wappen Wappen *Wappen* — coat of arms

Weber Weber *Weber* — weaver

wegen wegen *wegen* — because of, due to, on account of

Weib Weib *Weib* — woman, wife

weiblich weiblich *weiblich* — feminine, female

Weinhändler Weinhändler *Weinhändler* — wine merchant

weiter weiter *weiter* — further

werden werden *werden* — become, be

Westen Westen *Westen* — west

wie wie *wie* — as

wird wird *wird* — becomes, gets, is

Wirt Wirt *Wirt* — innkeeper, host

Wirtssohn Wirtssohn *Wirtssohn* — innkeeper's son

Witwe Witwe *Witwe* — widow

Witwer Witwer *Witwer* — widower

wo wo *wo* — where

wohnhaft zu wohnhaft zu *wohnhaft zu* — residing, living in/at

Wohnort Wohnort *Wohnort* — residence, dwelling

wurde wurde *wurde* — became, got, was (e. g., *wurde getauft* = was baptized)

Zahl Zahl *Zahl* — number, numeral, figure

zehn zehn *zehn* — ten

zeigte an, daß zeigte an, daß *zeigte an, daß* — stated that...

Zeit Zeit *Zeit* — time

Zeuge Zeuge *Zeuge* — witness

ziemlich ziemlich *ziemlich* — rather, fairly

zu zu *zu* — at, to

Zuname Zuname *Zuname* — surname

Zusatz Zusatz *Zusatz* — addition, addendum

zuständig zuständig *zuständig* — proper, authorized, competent, with jurisdiction

zwanzig zwanzig *zwanzig* — twenty

zwei zwei *zwei* — two

zweihundert zweihundert *zweihundert* — two hundred

zweiund- zweiund- *zweiund-* — ...-two

zwölf zwölf *zwölf* — twelve

zwischen zwischen *zwischen* — between

Months

Januar Januar *Januar* — January
Februar Februar *Februar* — February
März März *März* — March
April April *April* — April
Mai Mai *Mai* — May
Juni Juni *Juni* — June

Juli Juli *Juli* — July
August August *August* — August
September September *September* — September
Oktober Oktober *Oktober* — October
November November *November* — November
Dezember Dezember *Dezember* (sometimes spelled *December*) — December

Numbers

Virtually any of these words can appear with the suffix -[s]te, often ending with -n or -r. This suffix means the same as "-th" in English, e. g., *vier* = four, *vierter* = fourth, *vierzehn* = fourteen, *vierzehnter* = thirteenth, *vierzig* = thirty, *vierzigster* = thirtieth. Compound numbers such as twenty-five or thirty-eight are usually expressed as five-and-twenty, *fünfundzwanzig*, or eight-and-thirty, *achtunddreißig*, but in some documents this backwards order was reversed to make it easier to fill out the forms. These numerals also form their ordinal counterparts with the suffix -[s]te, e. g., on the twenty-fifth of June = *am fünfundzwanzigsten Juni*. This is also often written *am 25. Juni*, where the period shows it's an abbreviated ordinal.

acht acht *acht* — eight
achtund- achtund- *achtund-*: — ...-eight (e. g., *achtunddreißig* = 38)
achthundert achthundert *achthundert* — eight hundred
achtzehn achtzehn *achtzehn* — eighteen
achtzig achtzig *achtzig* — eighty
drei drei *drei* — three
dreihundert dreihundert *dreihundert* — three hundred
dreißig dreißig *dreißig* — thirty
dreiund- dreiund- *dreiund-* — ...-three (e. g., *dreiunddreißig* = 33)
dreizehn dreizehn *dreizehn* — thirteen
Drittel Drittel *Drittel* — a third (1/3)
dritter dritter *dritter* — third
eins eins *eins* — one
einund- einund- *einund-* — ...-one (e. g., *einunddreißig* = 31)
elf elf *elf* — eleven
erster erster *erster* — first
fünf fünf *fünf* — five
fünfhundert fünfhundert *fünfhundert* — five hundred
fünfter fünfter *fünfter* — fifth
fünfund- fünfund- *fünfund-* — ...-five (e. g., *fünfunddreißig* = 35)
fünfzehn fünfzehn *fünfzehn* — fifteen
fünfzig fünfzig *fünfzig* — fifty
halb halb *halb* — half (*ein halb* = one half)
Hälfte Hälfte *Hälfte* — half
hundert hundert *hundert* — hundred
neun neun *neun* — nine
neunhundert neunhundert *neunhundert* — nine hundred
neunund- neunund- *neunund-* — ...-nine (e. g., *neununddreißig* = 39)

neunzehn neunzehn *neunzehn* — nineteen
neunzig neunzig *neunzig* — ninety
sechs sechs *sechs* — six
sechshundert sechshundert *sechshundert* — six hundred
sechster sechster *sechster* — sixth
sechsund- sechsund- *sechsund-* — ...-six (e. g., *sechsunddreißig* = 36)
sechzehn sechzehn *sechzehn* — sixteen
sechzig sechzig *sechzig* — sixty
sieben sieben *sieben* — seven
siebenhundert siebenhundert *siebenhundert* — seven hundred
siebenund- siebenund- *siebenund-* — ... -seven (e. g., *siebenunddreißig* = 37)
siebzehn siebzehn *siebzehn* — seventeen
siebzig siebzig *siebzig* — seventy (sometimes *siebenzig*)
tausend tausend *tausend* — thousand
vier vier *vier* — four
vierhundert vierhundert *vierhundert* — four hundred
Viertel Viertel *Viertel* — a fourth, quarter
vierter vierter *vierter* — fourth
vierund- vierund- *vierund-* — ...-four (e. g., *vierunddreißig* = 34)
vierzehn vierzehn *vierzehn* — fourteen
vierzig vierzig *vierzig* — forty
zehn zehn *zehn* — ten
zwanzig zwanzig *zwanzig* — twenty
zwei zwei *zwei* — two
zweihundert zweihundert *zweihundert* — two hundred
zweiter zweiter *zweiter* — second
zweiund- zweiund- *zweiund-* — ...-two (e. g., *zweiunddreißig* = 32)
zwölf zwölf *zwölf* — twelve

Personal Names

Agnes Agnes *Agnes* — Agnes
Andreas Andreas *Andreas* — Andrew
Artur Artur *Artur* — Arthur
Bernhard Bernhard *Bernhard* — Bernard
Berta Berta *Berta* — Bertha
David David *David* — David
Eduard Eduard *Eduard* — Edward
Ernst Ernst *Ernst* — Ernest
Eugen Eugen *Eugen* — Eugene
Franz Franz *Franz* — Francis
Franziska Franziska *Franziska* — Frances
Friedrich Friedrich *Friedrich* — Frederick
Georg Georg *Georg* — George
Gunther Gunther *Gunther* — Gunther
Hans Hans *Hans* — John
Heinrich Heinrich *Heinrich* — Henry
Helene Helene *Helene* — Helen
Hermann Hermann *Hermann* — Herman
Irene Irene *Irene* — Irene
Jakob Jakob *Jakob* — Jacob, James
Johann Johann *Johann* — John
Johanna Johanna *Johanna* — Jean, Jane, Joan
Josef Josef *Josef* — Joseph

Karl Karl *Karl* — Charles
Kläre Kläre *Kläre* — Clare
Konrad Konrad *Konrad* — Conrad
Konstanze Konstanze *Konstanze* — Constance
Leonhard Leonhard *Leonhard* — Leonard
Leonore Leonore *Leonore* — Leonora
Ludwig Ludwig *Ludwig* — Louis
Luise Luise *Luise* — Louise
Margarete Margarete *Margarete* — Margaret
Marie Marie *Marie* — Marie
Matthias Matthias *Matthias* — Matthew
Michael Michael *Michael* — Michael
Peter Peter *Peter* — Peter
Richard Richard *Richard* — Richard
Rosa Rosa *Rosa* — Rose
Samuel Samuel *Samuel* — Samuel
Sara Sara *Sara* — Sarah
Saul Saul *Saul* — Saul
Stefan Stefan *Stefan* — Steven
Susanne Susanne *Susanne* — Susan
Viktor Viktor *Viktor* — Victor
Vinzenz Vinzenz *Vinzenz* — Vincent
Walter Walter *Walter* — Walter
Wilhelm Wilhelm *Wilhelm* — William

Printed	Cursive
A, a	$\mathcal{A}, a$
B, b	$\mathcal{B}, b$
C, c	$\mathcal{C}, c$
D, d	$\mathcal{D}, d$
E, e	$\mathcal{E}, e$
F, f	$\mathcal{F}, f$
G, g	$\mathcal{G}, g$
H, h	$\mathcal{H}, h$
I, I	$\mathcal{I}, i$
J, j	$\mathcal{J}, j$
K, k	$\mathcal{K}, k$
L, l	$\mathcal{L}, l$
M, m	$\mathcal{M}, m$
N, n	$\mathcal{N}, n$
O, o	$\mathcal{O}, o$
P, p	$\mathcal{P}, p$
Q, q	$\mathcal{Q}, q$
R, r	$\mathcal{R}, r$
S, s	$\mathcal{S}, s$
T, t	$\mathcal{T}, t$
U, u	$\mathcal{U}, u$
V, v	$\mathcal{V}, v$
W, w	$\mathcal{W}, w$
X, x	$\mathcal{X}, x$
Y, y	$\mathcal{Y}, y$

Printed	Cursive	Printed	Cursive
Z, z	$\mathcal{Z}, z$	Ä, ä	$\ddot{\mathcal{A}}, \ddot{a}$
Å, å	$\mathring{\mathcal{A}}, \mathring{a}$	Ö, ö	$\ddot{\mathcal{O}}, \ddot{o}$

Fortunately, the Swedish alphabet and the typefaces and handwriting styles used to print and write it do not present many serious problems for English-speakers (although documents from before 1790 were often written in German script — see German section, beginning on page 4). The only three unfamiliar letters are *Å å, Ä ä,* and *Ö ö,* which come after *z* in alphabetical order. The letters *c, k, w,* and *z* seldom appear except in words borrowed from other languages, but they are still listed in the alphabet and in dictionaries in the order familiar to speakers of English.

Vowels are long or short; the following examples are for long vowels, but the corresponding short vowels are the same sounds, just not held as long. The *a* is pronounced as in English "c<u>a</u>r." The *å* is pronounced like the *o* in "<u>or</u>." The *ä* is pronounced like *ai* in "<u>air</u>," but before an *-r* a short *ä* (or a short *e*) is pronounced like the *a* in "c<u>a</u>t." The long *e* is pronounced like *e* in English "th<u>ey</u>," except without any trace of a y-sound creeping in at the end. The long *i* is pronounced much like *ee* in "s<u>ee</u>" (also without the "y" at the end). The *o* is sometimes pronounced like *oo* in "m<u>oo</u>n," sometimes like *o* in "<u>or</u>." The *ö* is pronounced as in German, like *-ir* in English "s<u>ir</u>" but without actually saying the *r*. Long *u* is pronounced much like *u* in "Y<u>u</u>kon," but with the lips a bit more rounded. The *y* is pronounced like French *y* or German *ü*, saying "ee" but with lips rounded.

Most consonants are pronounced much as in English. A *j* sounds like *y* in "<u>y</u>acht," or in words of French origin like a French *j* (the same sound as the *s* in "plea<u>s</u>ure"). The *s* is always as in "<u>s</u>it," never as in "hi<u>s</u>," and *z* is pronounced the same way. The *r* is trilled slightly, as in Spanish or Italian, but the combinations *rd, rl, rn, rs,* and *rt* are pronounced with the *r* indistinct and almost eliminated; *rs* also sometimes sounds like the *sh* in "<u>sh</u>op." The combinations *dj, gj, hj,* and *lj* are pronounced like *y* in "<u>y</u>es." The *ng* is never as in "fi<u>ng</u>er," but always as in "si<u>ng</u>er." The combinations *kj* and *tj* are both pronounced like *ch* in "<u>ch</u>ild" (more precisely, as a palatalized *t* somewhat like the sound in "get <u>y</u>ou") The *ti* combination is pronounced like *sh* in the suffix *-tion,* and as *tsi* before *e* and *a* (this generally occurs only in words borrowed from other languages). *Sj, skj,* and *stj* are like *sh* in "<u>sh</u>oe."

Three special cases, usually pronounced as one would expect, change when followed by *e, i, y, ä,* or *ö.* (1) The *g,* generally pronounced as in English "go," sounds like the *y* in "<u>y</u>es", e. g., *ge* ("to give") is pronounced like "yay." (2) The *k,* usually like *k* in "<u>k</u>ite," becomes the *ch* sound described for *kj* and *tj,* so that Swedish *kind* (cheek) sounds much like the English word "chinned." (3) The *sk,* normally pronounced like *sk* in "<u>sk</u>y," sounds like *sh* in "<u>sh</u>oe," so that *skinn* (skin) is pronounced "shin." Before an *e* or an *i* in final unstressed syllables, however, all three take their normal pronunciations. The *g* also sounds like a *y* when it occurs in a final syllable after *l* or *r,* but before an *s* or *t* it tends to devoice to a *k*-sound.

All these hints on pronunciation may confuse readers more than help them, and for family research purposes one need only know enough to keep from being confused by the variant spellings and pronunciations that turn up in the records.

Swedish and the Other Scandinavian Languages

Of the Scandinavian languages — Swedish, Norwegian, Danish, Icelandic, and Faroese — the one most commonly encountered in the United States is Swedish; the 1991 *World Almanac,* citing the U. S. Immigration and Naturalization Service, gives total immigration, 1820-1989, as 1,245,000 from Sweden, 753,000 from Norway, and 370,000 from Denmark (from 1820-1868 Norway and Sweden were combined for counting purposes). So the numbers suggest that Swedish is the language to present in this book. But in fact, the Scandinavian languages are so similar that Swedes, Norwegians and Danes can often manage to converse with each other in their own languages; so it's reasonable to hope that analysis of Swedish documents may also prove useful to descendants of Norwegians and Danes.

Swedish, like German and English, is a Germanic language. A distinct Scandinavian branch of the Germanic family appears to have arisen by 550 A.D. at the latest; by 800-1000 A.D. this Common Scandinavian had split into Old East and Old West Scandinavian. The Old West developed further into Icelandic, Faroese, and one of the Norwegian branches, while Old East gave rise to the other Norwegian form and to Danish and Swedish. The main point is that these languages differentiated enough to deserve being called separate languages, but they still have a great deal in common. In fact, if one knows a little *Plattdeutsch,* the form of German spoken in Northern Germany, and compares it with any of the Scandinavian languages, many similarities become evident.

Norwegian has two different standard forms, *bokmål* ("book language," which used to be called *riksmål,* "national language") and *nynorsk,* ("New Norwegian," formerly called *landsmål,* "country language); but Swedish has one standard form, although of course dialectal differences can be found in different parts of Sweden. The Swedish vocabulary has been influenced by other languages, including Latin, French, English, and especially German. Low German loaned Swedish many words during the Middle Ages, and when the Reformation came to Sweden in the sixteenth century the language of Luther's Bible translation, High German, had a powerful effect on Swedish. Like German, Swedish tends toward compound words, e. g., *undervisningstimmar* (hours of instruction, course hours).

In one respect that should gladden the hearts of Americans, Swedish is more like English than German: the grammar is much simpler. Nouns and verbs both take fewer forms than in German, let alone Russian or Latin. The two most striking and troublesome grammatical features are the definite article and the verb's passive form with *-s.* In Swedish the definite article tends to attach to the end of its noun, e. g., *en dag* (a day), *dagen* (the day), *dagarna* (the days); *ett hus* (a house), *huset* (the house), *husen* (the houses); so it is wise to suspect its presence whenever a noun has one of the suffixes *-(e)n, -(e)t, -na,* or *-a. Den, det* and *de,* which normally function as the pronouns "it" and "they," can also precede a noun with the definite article when that noun is modified by an adjective: so *flickan,* "the girl," becomes *den vackra flickan,* "the pretty girl." As for the passive, *intyga* means "to certify," *intygas* means "it is certified." This particular word should be noted because it tends to show up often in documents.

A few variations in spelling, typical of Germanic languages, should be noted. The letters *ä* and *e* sound alike, and are sometimes used for each other; the same is true of *i* and *j*. A *k* may replace *c, ch, ck, g,* or *q*. Sometimes *s* is used for *c* or *z*. Other switches encouraged by similarity in sound are *v* for *w* or *f*, *t* for *d* or *th*, *sk* for *sch* or *stj*, and a single letter for a double, e. g., *s* for *ss* or *t* for *tt*. These and other variations became archaic as a standardized spelling for Swedish words came to be established, but variants still appear in documents of relatively recent origin, as will be seen several times in the sample documents.

Success in researching ancestors from Sweden requires having four pieces of information: 1) the ancestor's Swedish name, not an Americanized form 2) his/her date of birth, 3) the name of the parish (its name now), and 4) the name of the *län* and province. Some sources for further study are: "Genealogical Word List, Sweden," The Family History Library in Salt Lake City, Utah; the section on Sweden in Angus Baxter's *In Search of Your European Roots,* Genealogical Publishing Co., Inc., Baltimore 1988; and *Cradled in Sweden,* Carl-Erik Johansson. Angus Baxter considers Sweden the easiest country in Europe (or perhaps next after Switzerland) in which to trace ancestors.

Document #1: A "Moving" Certificate (Exit Permit)

Reproduced on pages 39-40 are the front and back sides of a *flyttningsbetyg,* a certificate *(betyg)* used to register a person or family's move *(flyttning)* from one place to another. The document is filled out by the local parish authority and is largely for ecclesiastical administrative purposes; but since Sweden does not have a civil registry, ministers of the Lutheran church have served as recorders of vital documents for both ecclesiastical and civil purposes. In this case the document was issued for a family emigrating from Sweden to the United States, but it also contains further information on children born in the United States. The vocabulary and format are quite instructive.

Utfl. N:o 25. Infl. N:o.__ Flyttningsbetyg (för äkta makar).

> *utfl., infl.* — These are abbreviations for *utflyttning,* "moving out," and *inflyttning,* "moving in." The certificate could be used for a family moving into or out of the parish by simply filling in a case number under the proper category. Here the family is moving out of the area, so this is the 25th certificate of *utflyttning. N:o* is an abbreviation meaning "number."
>
> *Flyttningsbetyg* — "Exit Permit." As one might deduce from the preceding note, *flyttning* means "moving," and a *betyg* can be a mark (as in a grade at school) or a certificate or permit.
>
> *för äkta makar* — "for a married couple." The standard modern meaning of *äkta* is "authentic," but an *äkta make* is a husband (*äktenskap* is marriage) and *makar* is plural of *make.* Either "married men" or "married couple" is a possible translation, and context favors the latter.

1. Målaren Johan David Liljedal och hans hustru Anna Maria Johansdotter
2. blefvo i äktenskap förenade genom vigsel den 24/3 1906.

> *målaren* — "the painter." The definite article *-en* is added to *målare,* "painter," but when a noun ends in a vowel the *-e-* of the suffix is omitted.
>
> *och hans hustru* — "and his wife"
>
> *Anna Maria Johansdotter* — Notice that the last name is a patronymic, literally meaning "Johan's daughter." Such patronymics are very common in Scandinavian countries, which is why one meets so many Johansons and Davidsons and Svensons and so forth; and *-dotter* is the female equivalent of *-son.*
>
> *blefvo i äktenskap förenade* — "were united in marriage." *Blefvo* is a past tense form of the verb *bli(va),* "to become, get," and this verb is often used with a past participle to express the passive voice. The participle *förenade* is from the verb *förena,* "to join, unite," so the whole verb here is *blefvo förenade,* "were joined." The preposition *i* means "in."
>
> *genom vigsel* — "by marriage ceremony"
>
> *den 24/3 1906* — "on 24 March 1906." Swedish dates are expressed with *den,* which one can think of as meaning "on the," followed by the day, month, and year.
>
> **Translation** — 1. The painter Johan David Liljedal and his wife Anna Maria Johansdotter 2. were joined in wedlock by a marriage ceremony on 24 March 1906.

MANNEN 3. är född den 15/3 1876 sjuttiosex/ HUSTRUN är född den 2/11 1884 åttiofyra
4. i Wånga församling i Östergötlands län,

> *MANNEN / HUSTRUN* — "The man / The wife." The *-nen* article added to *man* is an exception to the usual habit of adding simply *-en* to nouns ending in consonants; as for *hustrun,* it was noted above that nouns ending in vowels usually add just the *-n.* Note that from items 3 through 12 in this columnar format the same questions are entered for husband and wife; in this particular case the wife's entries agree with her husband's with the sole exception of the birthdate. So from item 4 on it is needless to give both and the second column is ignored.
>
> *är född* — "was born." The form *är* is the present tense of *vara,* "to be," and *född* is the past participle of *föda,* "to bear, give birth to."
>
> *1876 sjuttiosex* — It was standard procedure to give the year in numerals and then in writing; but since the first two digits seldom present any problem, the minister usually just writes out the last two digits, as here: *sjuttiosex* is "seventy-six."
>
> *i Wånga församling i Östergötlands län* — "in Wånga parish, in Östergötland district." The terms *län* and *församling* are vital for researching in Sweden. Östergötland is one *län* (district) of twenty-four in the country; in some cases a *län* is the same as a *ländskap* (province), in some cases there are more than one *län* in a *ländskap.* A *län* is divided into smaller units called *fögderi,* but for judicial administration they are divided into units called *härad.* A *län* is further subdivided into units called *församlingar,* parishes (once known as *socknar,* singular *socken*). [This information is taken from Angus Baxter's *In Search of Your European Roots.*]
>
> **Translation** — The man was born 15 March 1876 in Wånga parish in Östergötland district. The wife was born 2 November 1884 in Wånga parish in Östergötland district.

Utfl. N:o 25.

pr. 18 S. w.

Infl. N:o

Flyttningsbetyg

(för äkta makar).

1. Målaren Johan David Liljedal

och hans hustru Anna Maria Johansdotter

2. blefvo i äktenskap förenade genom vigsel den 24/3 1906.

MANNEN	HUSTRUN
3. är född den 15/3 1876 sjuttiosex	är född den 2/11 1884 attiofyra
4. i Wånga församling	i Wånga församling
i Östergötlands län,	i Östergötlands län,
5. är ——— vaccinerad	är ——— vaccinerad
6. är ——— döpt,	är ——— döpt,
7. har inom svenska kyrkan konfirmerats och äger godkänd kristendomskunskap,	har inom svenska kyrkan konfirmerats och äger godkänd kristendomskunskap,
8. har inom svenska kyrkan begått H. Nattvard,	har inom svenska kyrkan begått H. Nattvard,
9. är till Nattvardens begående oförhindrad	är till Nattvardens begående oförhindrad
10.	
11. åtnjuter ——— medborgerligt förtroende	åtnjuter ——— medborgerligt förtroende
12.	

15. Mannen är såsom värnpliktig inskr. N:o 20 48/1897.

16. Dessa makar flytta till N. Amerika församling i ——— län;

17. betygar S:ct Lars församling i Östergötlands län

18. den 29 Mars år 19 10.

C. V. Palmer

Kyrkoherde V. pastor Komminister.

Omstående makar åtföljas härifrån af nedanstående icke konfirmerade barn under 15 år:

Barnens namn m. m.	Födelsedag, månad, år (året jämväl med bokstäfver)	Födelseort	Döpt	Vaccinerad
1. *d. Mabel Wailet Maria*	23/5 1907 (*hundrasju*)	Kullerstad Östergs län	döpt ej	
2. *s. Olof Orving*	2/4 1909 (*hundranio*)	S:t Lars Östergs län	döpt v.	
3. *d. Mildred Ester Margareta*	24/2 1912 (*hundratolf*)	New Britain		
4. *d. Tella Florence Ingeborg*	18/1 1914 (*hundrafjorton*)	New Britain		

5. är vaccinerad, 6. är döpt, 7. har inom svenska kyrkan konfirmerats och äger godkänd kristendomskunskap, 8. har inom svenska kyrkan begått H. Nattvard, 9. är till Nattvardens begående oförhindrad, 11. åtnjuter medborgerligt förtroende

> *är vaccinerad* — "is vaccinated" (from the verb *vaccinera*).
>
> *är döpt* — "is baptized"
>
> *har inom svenska kyrkan konfirmerats* — "has been confirmed in the Swedish Church." The verb *har ... konfirmerats* shows the passive with -s, a distinctive feature of the Scandinavian languages. A verb is made passive by taking the corresponding active tense and adding -s (dropping final -r before adding -s). Thus *har konfirmerat* is "has confirmed," so *har konfirmerats* is "has been confirmed." This passive with -s is used somewhat less often than the other passive, *bli(va)* plus the past participle (see Document #6, *blef konfirmerad*).
>
> *äger godkänd kristendomskunskap* — "possesses satisfactory religious knowledge" (literally, "of Christianity"). The verb *äger* is the present tense of *äga*, "to own, possess."
>
> *har inom svenska kyrkan begått H. Nattvard* — "has taken Holy Communion in the Swedish Church." *Har ... begått* is the present perfect tense of *begå*, "to commit." *H. Nattvard* is sometimes seen as *H. H. Nattvard* (*Herrens Heliga Nattvard*, "the Lord's Holy Communion").
>
> *är till Nattvardens begående oförhindrad* — "is not barred from taking Communion." The verb *förhindra* means "to prevent," so *är förhindrad* means "is barred, is prevented." But here the participle has the negative prefix *o-*, so if one translated this painfully literally, it means "is to Communion's taking unprevented."
>
> *åtnjuter medborgerligt förtroende* — "enjoys civil trust."
>
> **Translation** — [The man/wife] 5. is vaccinated, 6. is baptized, 7. has been confirmed in the Swedish Church and possesses satisfactory religious knowledge, 8. has taken Holy Communion in the Swedish Church, 9. is not barred from taking Communion. 11. Enjoys civil trust.

15. Männen är såsom värnpliktig inskr. No. 20 48/1897. 16. Dessa makar flytta till N. Amerika. 17. betygar S:ct Lars församling i Östergötlands län. 18. den 29 Mars år 1910

Männen är såsom värnpliktig inskr. No. 20 48/97 — "The man is registered for conscription under No. 20
   48/1897." *Värnplikt* means "military service."
Dessa makar flytta till N. Amerika — "This married couple is moving to North America."
betygar S:ct Lars församling i Östergötlands län — "Certified: St. Lars parish, in the district of
   Östergötland."
år — "year"
Translation — 15. The man is registered for conscription #20 48/1897. 16. This couple is moving to North
America. 17. Certified: St. Lars parish, in the district of Östergötland, 18. 29 March 1910.

Omstående makar åtföljas härifrån af nedanstående icke konfirmerade barn under 15 år
   åtföljas — "are accompanied," another passive with *-s* (from *åtföljar*, "to accompany").
   härifrån — "herefrom," i. e., "from here."
   nedanstående — "listed below." *Stående* is a participle from the verb *stå*, "to stand," and it can be preceded by
      adverbs or prepositions; *nedan* means "below," so this means literally "standing below." *Omstående
      makar* is a similar construction, but *omstående* is easiest translated here as "this," i. e., the ones who are
      listed above, the ones under discussion.
   icke konfirmerade barn — "unconfirmed children." *Icke* or *inte* are adverbs meaning "not."
   Translation — This couple is accompanied from here by the unconfirmed children under 15 listed below.

Barnens namn, Födelsedag, månad, år (året jämväl med bokstäfver), Födelseort, Döpt, Vaccinerad
   barnens namn — "the child's name"
   födelsedag — "birthday"
   månad — "month"
   året jämväl med bokstäfver — "the year in letters as well," i. e., written out
   födelseort — "birthplace"
   döpt — "baptized"
   vaccinerad — "vaccinated"
   s. or *d.* — son/daughter
   Translation — The child's name, day, month, and year of birth (the year written out also), birthplace,
baptized, vaccinated: 1. daughter, Mabel Wailet (?) Maria, 23 May 1907 (hundred seven), Kullerstad,
Österg[ötland] district, baptized, ?; 2. son, Olaf Ärving, 2 April 1909 (hundred nine), St. Lars, Österg[ötland]
district, baptized, v[accinated]; 3. daughter, Mildred Ester Margareta, 24 February 1912 (hundred twelve), New
Britain [Connecticut]; 4. daughter Tella Florence Ingeborg, 18 January 1914 (hundred fourteen), New Britain
[Connecticut].

Document #2: A Report Card

A report card may seem insignificant at first glance, but a second glance shows that such records can convey a
great deal of information. It establishes a child's age and residence at a clearly defined time and place, and may
reveal quite a bit more. This card is reproduced on the next page.

Betyg från Stockholms Fortsättningsskolor
   fortsättningsskolor — "Secondary schools" may be the best translation, but this is a hard term because the
      Swedish education system is not organized like the American. Neither "high school" nor "trade school"
      seems quite appropriate; this student (a 15-year-old girl) is in a school *(skola)* with a two-year curriculum
      with an emphasis on business *(handel)* education, but she's graded in use of the *modersmålet* (mother
      tongue) and citizenship *(medborgarkunskap)* as well as knowledge of her field — a sort of hybrid high
      school and trade school. The term *fortsättningsskolor* literally means "continuation schools."

Kursbetyg från Fortsättningsskolan vid Kungsholms folkskola inom Stockholms skoldistrict, anordnad såsom
yrkesbestämd *fortsättningsskola i anslutning till handel samt omfattande två årskurser.*
   kursbetyg — "report card" is not literal but is the American equivalent.
   vid Kungsholms folkskola — "at Kungsholm *folkskola*." A *folkskola* is literally a "people's school."

BETYG FRÅN STOCKHOLMS FORTSÄTTNINGSSKOLOR

KURSBETYG

FRÅN

FORTSÄTTNINGSSKOLAN

vid _Kungsholms_ folkskola inom Stockholms skoldistrikt, anordnad såsom **yrkesbestämd** fortsättningsskola i anslutning till _handel_

samt omfattande två årskurser.

Clary Anna Matilda Mellström
(Fullständigt namn, tilltalsnamnet understruket.)

född den _12 augusti_ 1908, har under den första årskursen, som omfattat _190_ undervisningstimmar, deltagit i undervisningen _174_ timmar samt vid årskursens avslutande denna dag erhållit följande vitsord:

Arbetskunskap . . . . _Godkänd;_

Medborgarkunskap . . . _Godkänd;_
Modersmålet . . . . . _Icke utan beröm godkänd;_
Gymnastik . . . . .

Flit . . . . _Mycket god;_
Uppförande . . . . . _Mycket gott;_

Stockholm den _24_ maj 192 _3_.

H. Selling
Klassföreståndare.

Betygsgraderna äro:

för kunskaper och färdigheter:		för flit:	
Berömlig	(A)	Mycket god	(A)
Med utmärkt beröm godkänd	(a)	God	(B)
Med beröm godkänd	(AB)	Mindre god	(C)
Icke utan beröm godkänd	(Ba)	**för uppförande:**	
Godkänd	(B)	Mycket gott	(A)
Icke fullt godkänd	(BC)	Gott	(B)
Otillräcklig	(C)	Mindre gott	(C)
		Klandervärt	(D)

inom Stockholms skoldistrikt — "within Stockholm's school district"

anordnad såsom yrkesbestämd fortsättningsskola i anslutning till handel — Literally, "set up as a profession-defined continuation school in affiliation with commerce."

samt omfattande två årskurser — "and comprising two year-courses."

Translation — Report card from the secondary school at Kungsholm folk-school in the school district of Stockholm, established as a vocational secondary business school with a two-year curriculum.

Clary Anna Matilda Mellström (Fullständigt namn, tilltalsnamnet understruket) född den 12 augusti 1908, har under den första årskursen, som omfattat 190 undervisningstimmar, deltagit i undervisningen 174 timmar samt vid årskursen avslutande denna dag erhållit följande vitsord:

fullständigt namn, tilltalsnamnet understruket — "complete name, the name she goes by underlined." *Tilltalsnamnet* is literally *till* (to) + *tals* (speak, from the verb *tala*) + *namn* (name) + *-et* (the), so it's the "to-speak-name," the name one goes by.

har under den första årskursen — "has during the first year-course." Swedish is not as bad as German about splitting up its verb components, but it does often separate them; here *har* is the first part of a compound verb, and *deltagit,* in the next line, is the second. *Har* also teams up with *erhållit,* in the line after that, to produce the verb "has received."

som omfattat 190 undervisningstimmar — "which consists of 190 hours of instruction." *Som* is the standard relative pronoun, to be translated usually as "who, which, that." *Undervisningstimmar* is a compound noun, *undervisning* "instruction" + *timmar* "hours."

deltagit i undervisningen 174 timmar — "[has] participated in instruction 174 hours."

samt vid årskursen avslutande denna dag — "and with the year's course ending this day"

erhållit följande vitsord — "[has] received the following marks."

Translation — Clary Anna Matilda Mellström (full name, with the name she's called by underlined) during the first year's course, which consists of 190 hours of instruction, has taken part in 174 hours of instruction, and with the year's conclusion has received the following marks...

Arbetskunskap: Godkänd; Medborgarkunskap: Godkänd; Modersmålet: Icke utan beröm godkänd; Gymnastik — Flit: Mycket god; Uppförande: Mycket gott Stockholm den 24 maj 1923. H. Sjelling [?], Klassföreståndare.

arbetskunskap: godkänd — "knowledge of work: satisfactory"

medborgarkunskap — "citizenship [or civics]"

modersmålet: icke utan beröm godkänd — "mother tongue: not without praise, satisfactory"

gymnastik — "gymnastics"

flit: mycket god — "diligence: very good"

uppförande: mycket gott — "behavior: very good." The reason *flit* is described as *mycket **god*** but *uppförande* is *mycket **gott*** is because of grammatical gender: *uppförande* is a neuter noun and an adjective modifying it must take a neuter ending *(-tt)* while *flit* is common gender and its adjective appears in standard, unchanged form, *god.* Swedish has retained far fewer gender and adjectival endings than many other languages, but a few vestiges of inflection remain.

klassföreståndare — "schoolmaster," a compound noun from *klass* and *föreståndare,* "master, manager" (the feminine equivalent is *föreståndarinna*).

Translation — Subject knowledge: satisfactory. Citizenship: satisfactory. Swedish: satisfactory, not without praise. Gymnastics: —. Effort: very good. Behavior: very good. Stockholm, 24 May 1923. H. Sjelling [?], master.

Betygsgraderna äro — "The report's grades are:"

för kunskaper och färdigheter — "for skills (knowledge) and abilities"

berömlig — "commendable"; *godkänd* — "satisfactory"; *otillräcklig* — "inadequate"

med (utmärkt) beröm godkänd — "with (excellent) praise satisfactory"

icke fullt godkänd — "not fully satisfactory"

för flit — "for diligence"; *(mycket/mindre) god* — "(very/less) good"

för uppförande — "for behavior"; *(mycket/mindre) gott* — "(very/less) good"

klandervärt — "culpable, unacceptable"

Document #3: A Swedish Passport

(Innehåller 24 sidor.)

N:o 9147

Kungl. Maj:ts till Sverige Befallningshavande i Göteborgs och Bohus län anmodar alla vederbörande att låta innehavaren härav, svenske undersåten _Ernst Rudolf Karlsson_

född i _Halland_

boende i

2

vilken ....

....

....

....

avreser till _Amerikas Förenta Stater_

.... samt åter till Sverige

fritt och obehindrat passera samt lämna _honom_

skydd och bistånd i händelse av behov.

Detta respass är gällande till den _2 juni_ 19_20_

Göteborg den _3 juni_ 19_19_

(Innehåller 24 sidor.) — Contains 24 pages
Kungl. Maj:ts till Sverige befallningshavande i Göteborgs och Bohus län anmodar all vederbörande att låta innehavaren härav, svenske undersåten Ernst Rudolf Karlsson född i Halland boende i Halland

Kungl. Maj:ts till Sverige — "His Majesty the King of Sweden's"
befallningshavande — "Governor"
i Göteborgs och Bohus län — "in the district of Göteborg and Bohus"
innehavaren härav — "the bearer hereof"
svenska understäten — "the Swedish subject"
boende i Halland — "residing in Halland"
Translation — His Majesty the King of Sweden's Commander in Göteborg and Bohus district requests all concerned to let the bearer of this, the Swedish subject Ernst Rudolf Karlsson, born and residing in Halland...

vilken avreser till Amerikas Förenta Stater — "who is traveling to the United States of America"
samt åter till Sverige, fritt och obehindrat passera samt lämna honom skydd och bistånd i händelse av behov.
samt åter till Sverige — "and back to Sweden"
fritt och obehindrat passera — "to pass freely and without hindrance"
samt lämna honom skydd och bistånd — "and to grant him shelter and assistance"
i händelse av behov — "in case of need"
Translation — who is traveling to the United States of America and back to Sweden, to pass free and unhindered and to grant him shelter and assistance in case of need.
Detta respass är gällande till den 2 juni 1920 — This traveling pass is valid till June 2, 1920"
Göteborg den 3 juni 1919 — "Göteborg, 3 June 1919"

3

Passinnehavarens namnteckning:
(Unterschrift des Pass-Inhabers. Signature du Porteur.
Signature of the owner of Passport.)

Ernst Carlsson

Passinnehavarens signalement.

Född den ___ 21 sept. 1902

Längd: ___ 1·63

Hår: ___ blond

Ögon: ___ blå

Ansiktsform: ___ oval

Särskilda kännetecken: ___

Lösen ___ 2 kr. ___ öre

Översättnings-
avgift ___ 1

Stämpel ___ 2

Summa ___ 5

[Page 3]

[Photo of Ernst Carlsson]

Passinnehavarens namnteckning (Unterschrift des Pass-Inhabers. Signature du Porteur. Signature of the owner of the Passport.) — "Signature of the owner of the Passport" [in Swedish, German, French, and English].

Ernst Carlsson — "Ernst Carlsson" (this name was given as "Karlsson" on page 1 of the passport, but here it clearly seems to be written as "Carlsson"!).

[Page 5]

Passinnehavarens signalement — "Description of the owner of the passport"
Född den 21 sept. 1902 — "born 21 Sept. 1902"

Längd: 1.63 — "height: 1.63"
Hår: blond — "Hair: blond"
Ögon: blå — "Eyes: blue"
Ansiktsform: oval — "Face: oval"
Särskilda kännetecken: — "Distinguishing characteristics"

Lösen: 2 kr. ... öre — "Fee: 2 kronor [singular krona], 0 öre* [*krona* translates literally as "crown"]
Översättningsavgift: 1 — "Translation fee: 1 [krona]."
Stampel: 2 — "Stamp: 2 kronor"
Summa: 5 — "Total: 5 kronor"

Some other adjectives one might see used in the description of the bearer are: *skallig,* "bald"; *svart,* "black"; *brun,* "brown"; *grå,* "grey"; *rund,* "round" or *lång,* "long" (e. g., under *ansiktsform,* "shape of face").

Document #4: An Emigration Contract

On the opposite page is reproduced a contract between Carl Eriksson of Göteborg, an emigration agent, and Hilda Jonsson, emigrating to Hartford, Connecticut with her children Sigfrid and Elsa. The contract is in both Swedish and English and does not need comprehensive analysis, but a number of words and phrases seen in it are likely to appear in other contexts and may prove useful. Some of the expressions shown below are translated here rather more literally than in the English version of the contract so that the reader can more easily see how the Swedish words add up to their English translation.

utvandrare-kontrakt — "emigrant contract." *Utvandrare* is "emigrant," as opposed to *invandrare,* "immigrant."

Hvita Stjern Linien — "The White Star Line."

emellan/mellan — "between, among." The modern standard form of this word is *mellan.*

samt nedanstående utvandrare — "and emigrant listed below"

ålder — "age"

senaste vistelseort — "destination," literally "ultimate (last) staying-place"

jag förbinder mig härmed an — literally "I obligate myself herewith to"

från Göteborg till Hartford, Conn i Nordamerika —"from Göteborg to Hartford, Conn. in North America"

befordra — "to promote, move, forward"

nedan antecknade utvandrare — "[the] emigrant noted below" (*anteckna* means "to note, record")

härmed kvitterad afgift af Kr. 407.50 — "herewith paid fare of 407.50 *kronor*"

vid landning i Amerika — "upon landing in America"

resan — "the journey" (*resa* "journey," + *-n* "the")

med ångfartyg — "by steamship"

därifrån — "from there"

med järnväg — "by railroad"

å 3:de klass — "by third class"

senast inom 12 dagar — "at the latest within 12 days"

efter utvandrarens ankomst dit — "after the emigrant's arrival there"

med oceanångare — "by ocean steamer"

för ofvansagde afgift erhåller utvandraren — "for the abovesaid fare the emigrant shall receive." *Avgift* is the standard modern spelling of the word for "charge, fee"; *erhåller* is the present tense of the verb *erhålla,* "to receive."

för barn mellan 1 till 12 år — "for children between age 1 and 12"

landstigningsplatsen — "the landing place"

under uppehålen i England — "during the stay in England"

dock lämnas ingen ersättning — "but no compensation (*ersättning*) is [will be] allowed (*lämnas*)"

för effekterna — "for effects" (i. e., personal effects)

om skada eller förlust förorsakas — "if damage (*skada*) or loss (*förlust*) is caused (*förorsakas*)"

genom sjöolycka — "by accident at sea" (*sjö* is "sea," *olycka* is "accident")

till den främmande världsdelen — "to, at the foreign (*främmande*) country"

af vederbörande myndighet — "by involved authority" (*vederbörande* means "ones concerned" in the sense of "to whom it may concern")

på min bekostnad — "at my expense"

besörja utvandrarens återresa till Göteborg i Sverige — "to provide for the emigrant's return trip (*återresa*) to Göteborg in Sweden"

med underhåll — "with upkeep (or maintenance)"

Konungens Befallningshafvande — "Royal Governor"

på grund af detta kontrakt — "by the terms of this contract"

så fort omständigheterna medgifva — "as soon as the circumstances allow." *Medgifva* (modern spelling *medgiva*) is the present tense of the verb *medge* (from *med + ge*).

uppvisadt och godkändt — "exhibited and approved"

såsom upprättadt i öfverensstämmelse — "as found in accordance"

Mariied Berth.
Male Berth.
½ Female Berth.

Hvita Stjern Linien

N:r 591

UTVANDRARE-KONTRAKT
emellan

CARL ERIKSSON, Göteborg, befullmäktigad utvandrare-agent samt nedanstående utvandrare.

Jag CARL ERIKSSON, förbinder mig härmed att, på sätt här nedan närmare omförmäles, från

Göteborg till *Hartford Conn.* i Nordamerika befordra nedan

antecknade utvandrare mot en redan till fullo erlagd och härmed kvitterad afgift af allmän beskaffenhet.

hvari jämväl inräknats de vid landning i Amerika förekommande afgifter af allmän beskaffenhet.

Resan sker från Göteborg den

Utvandrarnes namn	Ålder	Senaste vistelseort
Mikla Jonsson	65	*Aurora*
Sophia	19	"
Ellen	7	"

Antages:

Göteborg den 19

Carl Eriksson

Uppvisadt och godkändt såsom upprättadt i öfverensstämmelse med Kungl. förordningen den 4 Juni 1884 och Kgl. Kung. den 28 Sept. 1905; intygas:

Göteborg i Poliskammaren den 19

Hvita Stjern Linien

I CARL ERIKSSON, hereby undertake, upon the following terms, to forward from Gothenburg

to *Hartford Conn.* in North-America, the emigrant

named below for the sum of *407.8* Kronor, which amount has been duly paid and

includes all ordinary charges upon landing in America.

—47—

Document #5: A Swedish-American Baptismal Certificate

On the opposite page is a reproduction of the first of three certificates issued by Swedish Lutheran churches in the United States involving the same individual. Swedish immigrants have tended to take their faith quite seriously, so these documents represented important points in a person's life — and as such were often carefully preserved and may well have survived. Establishing that a given person belonged to such-and-such a parish at a specific time can lead to the parish records, which typically have been preserved and may hold more data for the finding. And if, as in this case, the family still has one person's birth, confirmation, and marriage certificate, the documents may yield so many facts that one can trace almost his whole life's course.

These certificates often feature appropriate quotations from Scripture in Swedish. Lack of space makes it impossible to give translations of the lengthier passages, but anyone wishing to learn a little more about the language can profit from noting the citation of book, chapter, and verse and comparing the Swedish text with an English translation. Bible translations generally have played vital roles in the development of many European languages, and especially of the Germanic languages.

Dop-Attest. Härmed intygas att Oskar Leonard Johnson född i Marquette Ks den 28 Nov. 1889 döptes af mig i Marquette den 5 Mars 1890 i enlighet med Kristi befallning och den Evangelisk-Lutherska kyrkans bruk.

> *Dop-Attest* — "baptismal certificate"
>
> *härmed intygas att* — "It is hereby certified that..." This is a very popular beginning for many documents and may as well be memorized, for it will be seen again. *Härmed* can be remembered by thinking of it as "herewith" (anyone familiar with German will recognize this as similar to the German expression *hiermit*). *Intygas,* from the verb *intyga,* is the present-tense form *intygar* plus the passive suffix *-s* = *intygars,* and when the *-s* is added the preceding *-r-* is dropped: *intygas.* The word means literally "[It] is attested, is certified."
>
> *född i Marquette, Ks.* — "born in Marquette, Kansas"
>
> *döptes af mig* — "was baptized by me." *Döptes* is another example of the *-s* passive. Another formula one often sees in baptismal certificates states that a son *(son)* or daughter *(dotter)* "*blef af mig denna dag döpt i Guds, Fadrens och Sonens och den Helige Andes Namn, hvarvid barnet erhöll namnet: —.*" This translates as "was baptized by me this day in the Name of God the Father, the Son, and the Holy Spirit, whereupon the child received the name: (here the name is filled in)." Notice the other form of the passive, the proper tense of the verb *bli(va)* plus the past participle.
>
> *i enlighet med* — "in accordance with." The same thing can be expressed by the preposition *enligt.*
>
> *Kristi befallning* — "Christ's command." *Kristi* is from Latin *Christi,* the genitive of *Christus.* The pre-Luther influence of Latin and the Roman church often shows up in German and Swedish with such usages; the Lutheran church favored the vernacular, but some expressions from Latin were so familiar that they were retained even in official usage.
>
> *och den Evangelisk-Lutherska kyrkans bruk* — "and the Evangelical-Lutheran Church's custom."

Translation — Baptismal Certificate. It is hereby attested that Oskar Leonard Johnson, born in Marquette, Kansas the 28th of November, 1889, was baptized by me in Marquette on 5 March 1890 in accordance with Christ's command and the Evangelical-Lutheran Church's custom.

Föräldrar: Carl Wilhelm Johnson och hans hustru Helena Christina Johnson medlemmar af — förs. i —. Dopvittnen: Svan M. Peterson och Mrs. Johann Beata Svenson. E. M. Eriksson, pastor.

> *föräldrar* — "parents"
>
> *och hans hustru* — "and his wife"
>
> *medlemmar af — förs. i —:* "members of such-and-such parish in such-and-such a city." *Medlemmar* is the plural of *medlem,* "member."
>
> *dopvittnen* — "Witnesses of the baptism." Another word is *faddrar,* "godparents, witnesses."

Translation — Parents: Carl Wilhelm Johnson and his wife Helena Christina Johnson, members of — parish in —. Witnesses: Svan M. Peterson and Mrs. Johanna Beata Svenson. E. M. Eriksson, pastor.

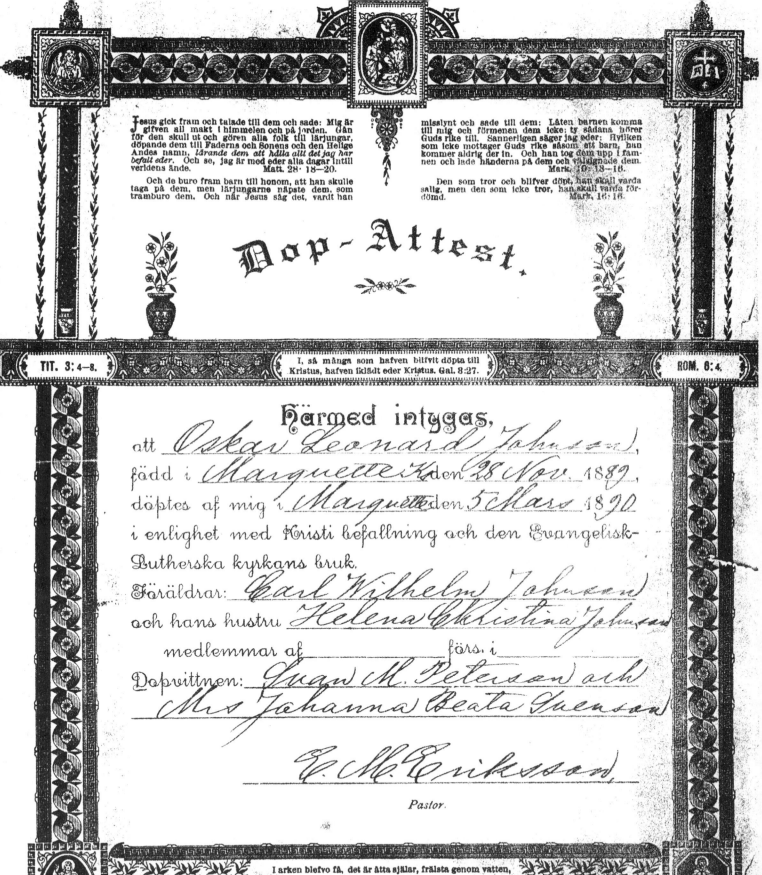

Jesus gick fram och talade till dem och sade: Mig är
gifven all makt i himmelen och på jorden. Gån
för den skull ut och gören alla folk till lärjungar,
döpande dem till Faderns och Sonens och den Helige
Andes namn, *lärande dem att hålla allt det jag har
befalt eder.* Och se, jag är med eder alla dagar intill
verldens ände.   Matt. 28: 18—20.

Och de buro fram barn till honom, att han skulle
taga på dem, men lärjungarne näpste dem, som
tramburo dem. Och när Jesus såg det, vardt han

misslynt och sade till dem: Låten barnen komma
till mig och förmenen dem icke; ty sådana hörer
Guds rike till. Sannerligen säger jag eder: Hvilken
som icke mottager Guds rike såsom ett barn, han
kommer aldrig der in. Och han tog dem upp i fam-
nen och lade händerna på dem och välsignade dem.
                              Mark. 10: 13—16.

Den som tror och blifver döpt, han skall varda
salig, men den som icke tror, han skall varda för-
dömd.
                              Mark. 16: 16.

Dop-Attest.

TIT. 3: 4—8.

I, så många som hafven blifvit döpta till
Kristus, hafven iklädt eder Kristus. Gal. 3:27.

ROM. 6: 4.

Härmed intygas,

att *Oskar Leonard Johnson*,

född i *Marquette K* den *28 Nov.* 1889,

döptes af mig i *Marquette* den *5 Mars* 1890

i enlighet med Kristi befallning och den Evangelisk-

Lutherska kyrkans bruk.

Föräldrar: *Carl Wilhelm Johnson*

och hans hustru *Helena Christina Johnson*

medlemmar af   förs. i

Dopvittnen: *Svan M. Petersan och*

Mrs Johanna Beata Svenson

E. M. Eriksson

Pastor.

I arken blefvo få, det är åtta själar, frälsta genom vatten,
hvilket ock nu i en motbild, dopet, frälsar eder — icke såsom
ett afläggande af köttets orenhet, utan såsom ett godt sam-
vetes förpligtelse till Gud — genom Jesu Kristi uppståndelse.
                              1 Petr. 3: 20, 21.

Document #6: A Confirmation Certificate

The next document is a *Konfirmations-attest,* a confirmation certificate. It is in the form of a single sentence, with appropriate facts filled in on a printed form. In this particular case the certificate does not add much to what was known about Oskar Leonard Johnson (except that his first name is now spelled in the more American form "Oscar" rather than the original "Oskar"), but it establishes he was still attending church in, and therefore presumably living near, McPherson in 1906. As might be expected, some Biblical influence is to be seen in the language of the text, as for instance the final sentence, *"vår Herre Jesu Kristi nåd och Guds kärlek och den Helige Andes delaktighet,"* a quotation from Paul's Second Epistle to the Ephesians, Chapter 13, verse 13. The quotation in the lower left is from 1 Cor. 3:11, *"Ty en annan grund kan ingen lägga, än den som är lagd, hvilken är Jesus Kristus"* (For other foundation no one can lay, but that which is laid, which is Christ Jesus).

Konfirmations-Attest. Härmed intygas *att Oscar Leonard Johnson efter behörig undervisning i Guds ord med ledning af Biblisk Historia och Luthers Lilla katekes samt Nja Testamentet blef i enlighet med den Evangelisk Lutherska kyrkans bruk* **konfirmerad**

> *härmed intygas att* — "It is hereby certified that..." (see note to Document #5)
> *efter behörig undervisning* — "after due instruction"
> *med ledning af Biblisk Historia* — "with guidance *(ledning)* of Bible history"
> *och Luthers Lilla katekes* — "and Luther's little catechism"
> *samt Nya Testamentet* — "and the New Testament"
> *blef... konfirmerad* — "was confirmed"
> *i enlighet med den Evangelisk Lutherska kyrkans bruk* — "in accordance with the Evangelical Lutheran church's custom"

Translation — Confirmation Certificate. It is hereby attested that Oscar Leonard Johnson, after due instruction in God's word with the guidance of Biblical History and Luther's little catechism and the New Testament, was confirmed in accordance with the Evangelical Lutheran Church's custom...

i den Sv. Ev. Luth. McPherson församlingen i McPherson, Ks den 13:de Maj 1906 och att han är medlem af den Sv. Ev. Luth. församlingen i McPherson, Ks.

> *i den Sv. Ev. Luth. McPherson församlingen i McPherson Ks* — "in the McPherson Swedish Evangelical Lutheran parish in McPherson, Kansas"
> *och att han är medlem af den Sv. Ev. Luth. församlingen i McPherson* — "and that he is a member of the," etc. The word *medlem,* "member," has been seen in its plural form, *medlemmar,* in Document #5.

Translation — ...in the McPherson Swedish Evangelical Lutheran parish in McPherson, Kansas, the 13th of May, 1906, and that he is a member of the McPherson Swedish Evangelical Lutheran parish in McPherson...

samt eger tillträde till Herrens heliga nattvard, och lemnas honom detta intyg med innerlig tillönskan af vår Herre Jesu Kristi nåd och Guds kärlek och den Helige Andes delaktighet. J. W. Engwall, Pastor.

> *samt eger tillträde till Herrens heliga nattvard* — "and has access to the Lord's Holy Communion." *Eger* is spelled *äger* in modern standard Swedish (compare item 7 in Document #1).
> *och lemnas honom detta intyg* — "and this certificate is issued to him." *Lemnas,* or in standard modern spelling *lämnas,* is the passive (with *-s*) of *lämna,* "to let." *Honom* is the object form of the pronoun *han* — like English "he/him," Swedish has only two forms of this pronoun, *han* and *honom,* while "she/her" is *hon/henne.*
> *med innerlig tillönskan af* — "with fervent wishes for"
> *vår Herre Jesu Kristi nåd* — "our Lord Jesus Christ's grace"
> *och Guds kärlek* — "and God's charity"
> *den Helige Andes delaktighet* — "the Holy Spirit's fellowship"

Translation — ...and [he] is admitted to the Lord's Holy Communion, and this certificate is issued to him with fervent wishes for the grace of our Lord Jesus Christ and the charity of God and the fellowship of the Holy Spirit. J. W. Engwall, pastor.

KONFIRMATIONS-ATTEST.

Härmed intygas,

att Oscar Leonard Johnson efter behörig undervisning i Guds ord med ledning af Biblisk Historia och Luthers Lilla katekes samt Nya Testamentet blef i enlighet med den Evangelisk-Lutherska kyrkans bruk

konfirmerad

i den Sv. Ev. Luth. McPherson församlingen i McPherson K. den 13:de Maj 1906 och att han är medlem af den Sv. Ev. Luth. församlingen i McPherson K., samt äger tillträde till Herrens heliga nattvard, och lemnas honom detta intyg med innerlig tillönskan af vår Herre Jesu Kristi nåd och Guds kärlek och den Helige Andes delaktighet.

J. W. Engwall
Pastor

En annan grund kan ingen lägga än den som är lagd, hvilken är Jesus Kristus.

Document #7: A Marriage Certificate

The last of Oscar Johnson's three documents is his marriage certificate.

Härmed Intygas

att _Oscar L. Johnson_   _Nannie C. Patrick_
från _McPherson_   och från _Lindsborg_
Staten _Kansas_   Staten _Kansas_

blefvo af mig förenade i

Det Heliga Äktenskapet

i enlighet med

Guds Ord och Staten _Kansas_ Lagar

i _Lindsborg, Kansas_ den _25 Februari_

år _Nitton Hundra Tjugu_

Alf. Bergin
(pastor)

Vittnen: _Ellen Blomquist_
Arthur Patrick

Hvad således Gud har sammanfogat må människan icke åtskilja.

Härmed intygas att _Oscar L. Johnson från McPherson Staten Kansas och Nannie C. Patrick från Lindsborg Staten Kansas blefvo af mig förenade i_ **Det Heliga Äktenskapet** _i enlighet med Guds Ord och_

Staten Kansas Lagar i Lindsborg Kansas den 25 Februari år Nitton Hundratjugo. Alf. Bergin [?] pastor. Vittnen: Ellen Blomquist, Arthur Patrick

   härmed intygas att — "It is hereby certified..." See note to document #5.
   från Staten — "from the state"
   blefvo af mig förenade — "were by me joined."
   i det heliga Äktenskapet — "in the Holy Matrimony." Swedish adds the definite article, English does not. When a Swedish noun with the definite article is preceded by a qualifying adjective, the adjective is preceded by *det* (neuter), *den* (nonneuter), or *de* (plural); thus *det heliga Äktenskapet*.
   i enlighet med — "in accordance with"
   Gods Ord — "God's Word"
   Lagar — "laws" (singular *lag*)
   år nitton hundratjugo — "the year nineteen hundred twenty"
   vittnen — "witnesses"
   Translation — It is hereby attested that Oscar L. Johnson from McPherson, the State of Kansas, and Nannie C. Patrick, from Lindsborg, the State of Kansas, were by me united in holy wedlock in accordance with God's Word and the Laws of the State of Kansas in Lindsborg, Kansas, on the 25th of February, the year 1920. Alf. Bergin, Pastor. Witnesses: Ellen Blomquist, Arthur Patrick.

In summary, Documents #5, 6, and 7 yield the information that Oscar Leonard Johnson was born in Marquette, Kansas on November 28, 1889, to Carl Wilhelm Johnson and his wife Helena Christina Johnson; was baptized by Pastor E. M. Eriksson in Marquette on March 5, 1890, with Svan M. Peterson and Mrs. Johann Beata Svenson as witnesses; was confirmed at the Swedish Lutheran church in McPherson on May 13, 1906 by Pastor J. A. Engwall; and married Nannie C. Patrick of Lindsborg, Kansas in Lindsborg on February 25, 1920 by Pastor Alf. Bergin, with Ellen Blomquist and Arthur Patrick as witnesses. This much data should provide his descendants with enough material to look successfully for census records, tax records, land transfers, Social Security records, military service records, obituaries in the local paper, etc. Not bad for three pieces of paper covered with pretty pictures and scripture quotations!

*   *   *   *   *

Selected Vocabulary Terms

A list of Swedish vocabulary has much in common with English vocabulary. For one thing, pronouncing Swedish correctly is not always as easy as it looks; like English, a number of sounds can be pronounced several different ways — and this makes the words harder to learn and remember correctly. But most of the other similarities with English simplify a reader's task; both Swedish and English have lost much of the grammatical inflection that makes Russian or Latin difficult for Americans. For a given noun, one need not learn sixteen or even six different forms; most have a singular form, a slightly different plural — usually easy to recognize — and perhaps the slight complication of a suffix comprising the definite article. Thus in the phrase *Amerikas Förenta Staterna* it is no great challenge to discern that the second word is *stat*, "state," plus the common plural ending *-er*, with the *-na* definite article tacked onto the end; so *Staterna* is "the states," and *Amerikas Förenta Staterna* is specifically "the United States of America."

In this list nouns are given in their singular form; no plural form is given if the noun adds the normal plural suffixes *-ar*, *-er*, *-or*, *-n*, or no suffix at all. If there is something a little unusual about the plural, that form is given, e. g., the plural of *son* is *söner*, and that form is given so readers can see and note the vowel change *-o-* → *-ö-*. Since a noun's gender dictates whether the definite article is *-(e)n* or *-(e)t*, neuter nouns are noted as "(neut. noun)" and all others are simply noted as "(noun)." No special note is made of the possessive because once readers see the form *skola*, "school," for instance, they should have no trouble recognizing that *skolan* is "the school," *skolans* is "the school's," *skolorna* is "the schools," and *skolornas* is "the schools'." The pattern is so regular and easy to learn that calling too much attention to it would probably complicate it more than if readers are simply allowed to pick it up as they go.

Most pronouns are enough like English to be easy: thus *han* is "he," *hans* is "his," and *honom* is "him". One needs to note the triple pattern that shows up with many pronouns and adjectives: *den, det, de* means *den* is the non-neuter singular, *det* is the neuter singular, and *de* is plural. A similar pattern appears with *min*, "my" *(min, mitt, mina)*, *sin*, "his, her, its," *(sin, sitt, sina)* and so on.

Adjectives are listed in the standard, nominative non-neuter form; thus *röd* is the standard form of the word for "red," but when it modifies a neuter noun it takes the form *rött, blå* ("blue") becomes *blått*, and so on. It may be helpful to note that "the boy" is *pojken*, but when an adjective is added a prepositive article is added, thus: "the big boy" is *den stora pojken*. "A house" is *ett hus*, "the house" is *huset*, "a big house" is *ett stort hus*, "the big house" is *det stora huset*, "his big house" is *hans stora hus*, and so on. Memorizing the endings is far less important than simply recognizing the patterns when they occur; *det* can also mean "it" and one could become pretty perplexed trying to translate *det stora huset* as "it big the house"!

Swedish verbs and English verbs follow the same basic pattern. There are a few dozen so-called "strong" verbs, such as *ge, gav, givit* ("give, gave, given") whose principal parts change internally, and almost all the rest are "weak" verbs that form their parts by a simple, regular pattern: *tala, talade, talat* ("talk, talked, talked"). Researchers do not usually need to devote a great deal of time to studying verbs, because documents typically use a limited number of verbs in a limited number of forms. If you know *är* ("is"), *har* ("has"), *var* ("was"), and *ble(f)vo* ("became, was") and can recognize participles of other verbs (usually ending in *-ande/-ende* and *-(a)d/- (a)t/- en/-et*) you can puzzle out most verb forms that appear in documents. So this list does not devote a great deal of space to verb forms, but simply lists the infinitive (and occasionally a participle) of the most frequently seen verbs.

The "supine" is noted for some verbs and should be explained briefly. The past participle, in English the third principal part of a verb (eat, ate, <u>eaten</u>; say, said, <u>said</u>), is in Swedish used only as an adjective or adverb or with a form of *vara* or *bli(va)*. The present perfect and past perfect tenses in English are formed with the present or past of "have" and that third principle part: have <u>eaten</u>, had <u>said</u>, etc. In Swedish the present or past of *ha*, "to have," is used and it is paired with the third principle part, but that is not the participle; it is a special form called the "supine," which resembles the participle but usually ends in *-at, -t, -it,* or *-tt*. For example, in Document #6 the passive "he was confirmed" is rendered with *blef konfirmerad*, a form of *bli(va)* plus the past participle; but in Document #1 the same thing is said *har ... konfirmerats*, where a passive *-s* is tacked onto the present perfect *har konfirmerat*, "has confirmed" — *konfirmerad* is the past participle, *konfirmerat* is the supine. Observant readers trying to form a concept of how Swedish works may note and be puzzled by the difference; this explanation is meant for their benefit.

The words below are listed in Swedish alphabetical order, which differs from English only in that *å*, *ä*, and *ö* always follow *z* in the listing; so *så* comes after *systerson* and not at the start of the *s* listings.

1:a — (abbr. *första*) first

2:a — (abbr. *andra*) second

3:e, 4:e etc. — (abbr.) third, fourth, etc.

adel — (noun) nobility

adoptera — (v.) to adopt; *adopterad* — adopted

af → *av*

af mig — "by me"

afgift → *avgift*

all, allt, alla — (adj.) all

alltid — (adv.) always

allting — (pron.) everything

Amerika — (noun) America

ande — (noun) spirit, ghost

andra — (adj.) second

ange — (v.) to state, report; *angiven* — (part.) stated

ankomst — (noun) arrival

anledning — (noun) occasion, case

anmärkning — (noun) remark, observation

annan — (adj.) other, different; *en annan* — another

anordnad — (part.) arranged, set up, established

ansikte — (neut. noun) face

ansiktsform — (noun) facial shape

anslutning — (noun) connection, affiliation

anteckna — (v.) to note, record; *antecknade* — (part.) noted

april — (noun) April

arbetare — (noun) worker, laborer

arbetskunskap — (noun) knowledge of one's work or field

arton — (num.) eighteen

artonde — (adj.) eighteenth

arv — (neut. noun) inheritance

att — (conj.) that

attest — (noun) certificate

augusti — (noun) August

av — (prep., sometimes spelled *af*) of, by, for, from

avgift — (noun) fee, charge, fare

avgång — (noun) departure

avlida — (v.) to pass away, die

avresa — (v.) to depart from; (noun) departure

avslutande — (part.) ending, finishing

avslutning — (noun) end

bagare — (noun) baker

bar — (past tense) → *bära*

bara — (adv.) only

barn — (neut. noun) child

barnbarn — (neut. noun) grandchild

barnlös — (adj.) childless

barnmorska — (noun) midwife

befallning — (noun) command, order

befallningsha[f]vande — (n.) Governor, commander

befolkning — (noun) population

befordra — to promote, move, forward

begravning — (noun) burial, funeral

begravningsplats — (noun) graveyard

begå — (v.) to commit, do, take

begående — (part.) → *begå*

begått — (supine) → *begå*

behov — (noun) need

behörig — (adj.) due, proper

berg — (neut. noun) mountain

bergsman — (noun, plur. *-män*) miner

beröm — (noun) praise

berömlig — (adj.) laudable

beskrivning — (noun) description

besörja — (v.) to see to, take care of, provide

betyg — (neut. noun) certificate

betyga — (v.) to report

betygsgrader — (plur. noun) grades

bevis — (neut. noun) proof, token, certificate

biblisk — (adj.) Biblical

bistånd — (neut. noun) assistance

blef → *bli(va)*

blefvo → *bli(va)*

bli(va) — (v., past tense *blev*, *ble[f]vo*) become, get, be

blond — (adj.) blond, fair

blå — (adj.) blue

blått → *blå*

bo — (v.) to live, reside; *boende* — (part.) residing, living

bok — (noun, plur. *böcker*) book

bokhållare — (noun) bookkeeper

bokstav — (noun, plur. *bokstä[f]ver*) letter (a, b, etc.)

bonde — (noun, plur. *bönder*) peasant

borg — (noun) castle

borgare — (noun) citizen, burgher

borgmästare — (noun) mayor

bostad — (noun, plur. *bostäder*) house, residence

bouppteckning — (noun) probate

broder → *bror*

bror — (noun, *bröder*) brother

brorsdotter — (noun, plur. *-döttrar*) niece

brorson — (noun, plur. *-söner*) nephew

brud — (noun) bride

brudgum — (noun, plur. *-gummar*) bridegroom

bruk — (neut. noun) custom

brukare — (noun) tenant farmer

brun — brown

bryggare — (noun) brewer

bröllop — (neut. n.) wedding

by — village

byggmästare — (noun) builder

bära — (v.) to bear, carry

därifrån — from there

dag — (noun) day

dagkarl — (noun) day-laborer

dam — (noun) lady

dansk — (adj.) Danish

datum — (neut. noun) date

de → *den*

december — (noun) December

del — (noun) part, share

delaktighet — (noun) fellowship, participation

delta — (v., present *deltar*, past *deltog*, supine *deltagit*) to take part, participate

dem — (pron.) them

den, det, de — (art.) the; (pron.) it, that; *den där* — (pron.) that; *den här* — this

denna/denne, detta, dessa — (demonstrative pron. and adj.) this

deras — (pron.) their

dess — (pron.) his, her, its

dessa → *denna*

det → *den*

detta → *denna*

din, ditt, dina — (poss.) your

dit — (adv.) there

dock — (conj.) but, yet

dom — (noun) judgment, verdict

domare — (noun) judge

dombok — (noun, plur. *-böcker*) court record

domsaga — (noun) judicial district

domstol — (noun) court

dop — (neut. noun) baptism, christening; *dop-* — (prefix) baptismal

dop-attest — (noun) baptismal certificate

dopnamn — (neut. noun) given name

dopvittne — (neut. noun) witness of the baptism

dotter — (noun, plur. *döttrar*) daughter

dotterdotter — (noun, plur. *-döttrar*) granddaughter

dotterson — (noun, plur. *dottersöner*) grandson

där — (adv.) there (see also *den, det*)

därifrån — (adv.) from there, thence

dö — (v., past *dog*, supine *dött*) to die

död — (adj.) dead; (noun) death

dödsorsak — (noun) cause of death

döpa — (v.) to baptize, to christen

döpelse — (noun) christening

döpt — (part.) baptized

döv — (adj.) deaf

eder — (pron.) you

effekt — (noun) baggage, personal effects

efter — (prep.) after; *lämnat efter sig* — was survived by

eftermiddag — (noun) afternoon

efternamn — (neut. noun) surname

egendom — (noun) property

eger (present tense v.) → *äga*

elfte — (adj.) eleventh

eller — (conj.) or

elva — (num.) eleven

emellan — (prep.) among, between

emigrationshandling — (noun) emigration record

en — (art. and num., neut. *ett*) a; one; *en* (or *ett*) *hundra* — one hundred

-en, -et — (suffix) the

engelsk — (adj.) English

enlighet — *i enlighet med* in accordance with

enligt — (prep.) according to

er — (pron.) you; your; yourselves

erhålla — (v. pres. *erhåller*, past *erhåll*, supine *erhållit*) to obtain, get

ersättning — (noun) compensation

ett → *en*

evangelisk-luthersk — (adj.) Evangelical Lutheran

fadder — (noun, plur. *faddrar*) godparent, witness

familj — (noun) family

fa(de)r — (noun, plur. *fäder*) — father; *fadrens* — "the father's"

farbror — (noun, plur. *farbröder*) uncle

farfar — (noun, plur. *farfädder*) grandfather

farföräldrar — (plur. noun) grandparents

farmor — (noun, plur. *farmödrar*) grandmother

fartyg — (neut. noun) ship

faster — (noun, plur. *fastrar*) aunt

februari — (noun) February

fem — (num.) five

femte — (adj.) fifth

femtio — (num.) fifty

femtionde — (adj.) fiftieth

femton — (num.) fifteen

femtonde — (adj.) fifteenth

finsk — (adj.) Finnish

fiskare — (noun) fisherman

fjol — (noun) last year

fjorton — (num.) fourteen

fjortonde — (adj.) fourteenth

fjärde — (adj.) fourth

flicka — (noun) girl

flicknamn — (neut. noun) maiden name

flit — (noun) diligence

flod — (noun) river

flytta — (v.) to move

flyttning — (noun) move, moving

flyttningsbetyg — (neut. noun) exit permit, moving certificate

folkskola — (noun) "people's school"

folkvisa — (noun) folk song

fortsättningsskola — (noun) "continuation school," secondary school

Frankrike — (noun) France

fransk — (adj.) French

fredag — (noun) Friday

friherre — (noun) baron

fritt — (adv.) freely

fru — (noun) Mrs.

från — (prep.) from

främmande — (adj.) foreign, strange, alien

fullständig — (adj.) complete, total

fyra — (num.) four

fyrtio — (num.) forty

fyrtionde — (adj.) fortieth

färdighet — (noun) skill, ability

färg — (noun) color

fästman — (noun, plur. *-män*) fiancé

fästmö — (noun) fiancée

föda — (v.) to bear, give birth to; *född* — (part.) born

födelse — (noun) birth

födelsebok — (noun, plur. *-böcker*) birth record

födelsedag — (noun) birthday

födelseort — (noun) birthplace

fögderi — (noun) subdivision of a *län*, "county"

följande — (adj.) next, following

för — (prep.) for; (conj.) for

förbinda sig — (v.) contract, obligate oneself

förena — (v.) to unite, join; *förenade* — (part.) joined, united

Förenta Staterna — (adj. and noun, plural) the United States

föreståndare — (noun) manager, headmaster (feminine: *föreståndarinna*)

förhindra — (v.) to hinder, prevent

förlust — (noun) loss

förmiddag — (noun) morning

förnamn — (neut. noun) first name

förorsaka — (v.) to cause

förra — (adj.) previous, prior

församling — (noun) parish

församlingsbok — (noun, plur. *-böcker*) parish records

första — (adj.) first

förtroende — (neut. noun) confidence, trust

föräldrar — (plur. noun) parents

gammal — (adj.) old

garvare — (noun) tanner

genom — (prep.) through, by

gesäll — (noun) journeyman

gift — (adj.) married; (neut. noun) poison

gifta sig — (v.) to marry *(med)*

giltig — (adj.) valid

god — (adj.) good

godkänna — (v.) to approve of; *godkänd* — satisfactory

gott → *god*

greve — (noun) count, earl

grevskap — (neut. noun) county

grund — (noun) cause, ground; *på grund av* — on account of

gruva — (noun) mine

gruvarbetare — (noun) miner

grå — grey

gräns — (noun) border, limit, boundary

Gud — (noun) God

gudfa(de)r — (noun, plur. *gudfäder*) godfather

gudmo(de)r — (noun, plur. *gudmödrar*) godmother

gymnastik — (noun) gymnastics

gå — (v., past *gick*, supine *gått*) to go

gård — (noun) farm, yard

gällande — (adj.) valid

ha — (v., pres. *har*, past *hade*, supine *haft*) to have

han — (pron.) he

hand — (noun, plur. *händer*) hand

handel — (noun) business, commerce

handelsman — (noun, plur. *handelsmän*) tradesman

-handlare — (suffix, 2nd part of compound noun) dealer

hans — (pron.) his

har → *ha*

hava → *ha*

havande — (adj.) pregnant

helig — (adj.) holy; *den Heliga Ande* — the Holy Spirit

hembiträde — (neut. noun) housemaid

hem — (neut. noun) home

hemmafru — (noun) housewife

henne — (pron.) her

hennes — (pron.) her

herre — (noun) Mister, Lord

herrfrisör — (noun) barber

herrgård — (noun) manorhouse

hertig — (noun) duke

hinderlös — (adj.) unhindered, free

historia — (noun) history

hjälp — (noun) help, aid

hjärta — (neut. noun) heart

hon — (pron.) she

honom — (pron.) him

hos — (prep.) at

hundra — (num.) hundred

hundrade — (adj.) hundredth

hus — (neut. noun) house

husförhörslängd — (noun) house examination rolls

hustru — (noun) wife

hvarvid — (adv.) whereupon

hår — (neut. noun) hair

hälft — (noun) half

händelse — (noun) event, occurrence

här — (adv.) here; → *den, det*

härad — (noun) civil district

härav — (adv.) hereof

härifrån — (adv.) herefrom

härmed — (adv.) herewith, hereby

i — (prep.) in, at, for, to; *i enlighet med* — in accordance with; *i dag* — today; *i fjol* — last year; *i går* — yesterday; *i morgon* — tomorrow

icke — (adv.) not; *icke fullt* — not fully

inflyttning — (noun) moving in

ingen — (pron.) no, none, not any, no one

innehavare — (noun) bearer, owner

innehålla — (v.) to contain

inom — (prep.) within

intyg — (neut. noun) certificate

intyga — (v.) to certify, attest

invandrare — (noun) immigrant

ja — (adv.) yes (opposite of *nej*)

jag — (pron.) I

januari — (noun) January

jord — (noun) earth

jordebok — (noun, plur. *jordeböcker*) property record

jude — (noun) Jew

judisk — (adj.) Jewish

juli — (noun) July

juni — (noun) June

jägare — (noun) hunter

järnväg — (noun) railroad

kalla — (v.) to call; *kallad* — (part.) called

karl — (noun) man, male, fellow

katekes — (noun) catechism

katolsk — (adj.) Catholic

kind — (noun) cheek

klandervärt — (adj.) culpable

klassföreståndare — (noun) class master

konfirmations-attest — (noun) confirmation certificate

konfirmera — (v.) to confirm; *konfirmerad* — (part.) confirmed

kontor — (neut. noun) office

kontorist — (noun) clerk

kontrakt — (neut. noun) contract

Konungens Befallningshafvande — "Royal Governor"

kr. → *krona*

krig — (neut. noun) war

krigsfånge — (noun) prisoner of war

kristendomskunskap — (noun) religion, knowledge of Christianity

Kristus — (noun, possessive *Kristi*) Christ

krona — (noun, plur. *kronor*) crown (money)

krukmakare — (noun) potter

kung — (noun) king

kungarike — (neut. noun) kingdom

kunglig — (adj., abbr. *kungl.*) royal

kunskap — (noun) knowledge

kursbetyg — (neut. noun) report card

kusin — (noun) cousin

kvinna — (noun) woman

kvinnkön — (neut. noun) female

kvinnlig — (adj.) feminine

kvittera — (v.) to receipt; *kvitterad* — (part.) paid

kväll — (noun) evening

kyrka — (noun) church

kyrkogård — (noun) cemetery

kännetecken — (neut. noun) characteristic

kärlek — (noun) love

kön — (neut. noun) sex

köpman — (noun, plur. -*män*) merchant

körsnär — (noun) furrier

lag (plur. *lagar*) — law

laglig — (adj.) legal

land — (neut. noun, plur. *länder*) land, country

landning — (noun) landing

landstigningsplats — (noun) landing place

ledning — (noun) guidance

lemnas → *lämnas*

leva — (v.) to live

levande — (part.) alive

lik — (neut. noun) corpse; (adj.) like

lilla — (adj.) little

liten — (adj.) little

liv — (neut. noun) life

lutersk — (adj.) Lutheran

lysning — (noun) banns

låg — (adj.) low

lång — long

låta — (v.) to let

läkare — (noun) doctor

lämna — (v.) to leave; *lämnas* — is let, issued

län — (neut. noun) province, county

ländskap — (noun) province, district

längd — (noun) length; roll, record

lärare — (noun) teacher

lärling — (noun) apprentice

lördag — (noun) Saturday

maj — (noun) May

Maj:ts — abbreviation of *Majestäts,* Majesty's

maka — (noun) wife

make — (noun, plur. *makar*) — husband

man — (noun, plur. *män*) man

manlig — (adj.) male

mantalslängd — (noun, plur. -*längder*) census

mars — (noun) March

med — (prep.) with; *med ledning af* — with the direction/guidance of

medborgare — (noun, plur. same) citizen

medborgarkunskap — (noun) civics, citizenship

medborgerlig — (adj.) civil

medge — (v., pres. *medgiva*) to admit, grant

medgi[f]va → *medge*

medlem — (noun, plur. *medlemmar*) member

mellan — (prep.) between

middag — (noun) noon, midday

mig — (pron.) me

militär — (adj.) military

min, mitt, mina — (poss.) my, mine

mindre — (adj.) smaller, lesser

mjölnare — (noun) miller

modersmål — (neut. noun) mother tongue, native language

mo(de)r — (noun, plur. *mödrar*) mother

morbror — (noun, plur. *morbröder*) uncle

morfar — (noun, plur. *morfädder*) grandfather

morföräldrar — (plur. noun) grandparents

morgon — (noun, plur. *morgnar*) morning

mormor — (noun, plur. *mormödrar*) grandmother

moster — (noun, plur. *mostrar*) aunt

mun — (noun, plur. *munnar*) mouth

murare — (noun) bricklayer

mycket — (adv.) very

myndighet — (noun) authority

målare — (noun) painter

månad — (noun) month

måndag — (noun) Monday

namn — (neut. noun) name

namnteckning — (noun) signature

natt — (noun, plur. *nätter*) night

Nattvard — (noun) Communion

nedan — (adv.) below

nedanstående — (adj.) listed below

nej — (adv.) no (opposite of *ja*, "yes")

ni — (pron.) you

nio — (num.) nine

nionde — (adj.) ninth

nittio — (num.) ninety

nittionde — (adj.) ninetieth

nitton — (num.) nineteen; *nitton hundratjugo* — 1920

nittonde — (adj.) nineteenth

nord — (noun) north

Nord-Amerika — (noun) North America

Norge — (noun) Norway

november — (noun) November

ny(a) — (adj.) new

nyfödd — (adj.) newborn

nytt → ny

nåd — (noun) grace, mercy

någon — (pron.) someone, anyone

något — (pron.) something

när — (adv.) where; (conj.) when

o- — (prefix) un-, non- (e. g., *odöpt* unbaptized)

obehindrat — (adv.) unhindered, not prevented

oceanångare — (noun) ocean steamer

och — (conj.) and

oförhindrad — (adj.) unhindered

ofvansagde → ovansagde

oktober — (noun) October

olycka — (noun) accident, misfortune

om — (conj.) if; (prep.) around, about

omfatta — (v.) to comprise, include; *omfattande* — (part.) including; *omfattat* — (supine) included

omstående — (part.) the ones under discussion

omständighet — (noun) circumstance

onsdag — (noun) Wednesday

ord — (neut. noun) word

ordbok — (noun, plur. *-böcker*) dictionary

orsak — (noun) cause

ort — (noun) place

oss — (pron.) us

otillräcklig — (adj.) insufficient, inadequate

oval — (adj.) oval

ovan — (adv.) above

ovansagde — (adj.) named above

oäkta — (adj.) illegitimate

pass — (neut. noun) passport

passera — (v.) to pass

passinnehavare — (noun) passport bearer

personalakt — (noun) personal record

pingst — (noun) Pentecost, Whitsunday

plats — (noun) place, spot

pojke — (noun) boy

prost — (noun) dean

präst — (noun) clergyman

på — (prep.) on, about, at, upon

påsk — (noun) Easter

register — (neut. noun) index

resa — (noun) journey, trip, travel

respass — (neut. noun) traveling pass, passport

rike — (neut. noun) country, state, realm

riktig — (adj.) right, correct

rit — (noun) rite

rund — round

rysk — (adj.) Russian

Ryssland — (noun) Russia

ryttare — (noun) cavalryman, rider

råd — (neut. noun) advice

rådgivare — (noun) counselor

rådman — (noun, plur. *-män*) councilman, magistrate

rätt — (noun) justice; (adj.) right, appropriate

röd — (adj.) red

S:ct — abbr. meaning "Saint"

samma — (adj.) same

samt — (conj.) and, along with

sen — (adj.) late; *senast inom 12 dagar* — at the latest within 12 days

september — (noun) September

sex — (num.) six

sextio — (num.) sixty

sextionde — (adj.) sixtieth

sexton — (num.) sixteen

sextonde — (adj.) sixteenth

sida (noun, plur. *sidor*) side, page

sig — (pron.) [him-, her-, it]self; themselves

signalement — (neut. noun) description

sin, sitt, sina — (poss.) his, her, its, their

sju — (num.) seven

sjuk — (adj.) sick

sjunde — (adj.) seventh

sjuttio — (num.) seventy; *sjuttiosex* — seventy-six

sjuttionde — (adj.) seventieth

sjutton — (num.) seventeen

sjuttonde — (adj.) seventeenth

själv — (pron.) self, selves

självmord — (neut. noun) suicide

sjätte — (adj.) sixth

sjö — lake; *sjöolycka* — accident at sea

sjöman — (noun, plur. *sjömän*) sailor

skada — (noun) injury, damage

skallig — (adj.) bald

skatt — (noun) tax

skepp — (neut. noun) boat

skilsmässa — (noun) divorce

skogvaktare — (noun) forester, woodsman

skola — (noun) school

skollärare — (noun) schoolmaster, teacher

skomakare — (noun) shoemaker

skråhandling — (noun) trade guild

skräddare — (noun) tailor

skydd — (neut. noun) protection, shelter

slaktare — (noun) butcher

slut — (neut. noun) end

släkt — (noun) family

släktforskning — (noun) genealogy

smed — (noun) smith

små — (adj., used in plural) small, little

snickare — (noun) carpenter

socken (noun, plur. *socknar*) parish

soldat — (noun) soldier

som — (rel. pron.) who, which, that; (conj.) as

sommar — (noun) summer

son — (noun, plur. *söner*) son

sondotter — (noun, plur. *sondöttrar*) granddaughter

sonhustru — (noun) daughter-in-law

sonson — (noun, plur. *sonsöner*) grandson

språk — (neut. noun) language

stad — (noun, plur. *städer*) city

stampel — (noun) stamp, seal

stat — (noun) state; *Staterna* — the States

stjärna — (noun) star

stor — (adj.) big, large, great

Storbritannien — (noun) Great Britain

styv- — prefix like "step-" in English, e. g., *styvbarn* — stepchild, *styvfar* — stepfather, etc.

stånd — (neut. noun) stand, status, position

summa — (noun) total

svar — (neut. noun) answer, reply

svart — (adj.) black

svensk — (adj.) Swedish

Sverige — (noun) Sweden

svåger — (noun) brother-in-law

svägerska — (noun) sister-in-law

svär- — prefix meaning "in-law, e. g., *svärdotter* — daughter-in-law, *svärfar* — father-in-law, etc.

syd- — (prefix) South

syster — (noun, plur. *systrar*) sister

systerdotter — (noun, plur. -*döttrar*) niece

systerson — (noun, plur. -*söner*) nephew

så — (conj.) so, so that; (adv.) how, so, such; *så fort* — immediately

såsom — (conj.) as, like

särskild — (adj.) special, particular

söder — (noun) south

söndag — (noun) Sunday

tant — (noun) aunt

testamente — (neut. noun) will

tid — (noun) time

till — (prep.) to, for, until, till

tillräcklig — (adj.) sufficient, adequate

tillsammans — (adv.) together

tillstånd(sbevis) — (neut. noun) permit

tilltalsnamn — (neut. noun) name one goes by

tillträde — (neut. noun) admission, entrance, access

tillåtelse — (noun) permission

tillönskan — (noun) wish, desire

timme — (noun, plur. *timmar*) hour

tio — (num.) ten

tionde — (adj.) tenth

tisdag — (noun) Tuesday

Tjeckoslovakien — (noun) Czechoslovakia

tjugo — (num.) twenty; *tjugoen* or *tjugoett* — twenty-one; *tjudoandra* — twenty-second; *tjugotredje* — twenty-third, etc.

tjugonde — (adj.) twentieth

tjänsteman — (noun, plur. -*män*) official

tolfte — (adj.) twelfth

tolv — (num.) twelve

torsdag — (noun) Thursday

tre — (num.) three

tredje — (adj.) third

trettio — (num.) thirty

trettionde — (adj.) thirtieth

tretton — (num.) thirteen

trettonde — (adj.) thirteenth

tusen — (num.) thousand

tusende — (adj.) thousandth

tvillingar — (plur. noun) twins

två — (num.) two

tysk — (adj.) German

Tyskland — (noun) Germany

under — (prep.) under, during

underhåll — (neut. noun) upkeep, maintenance

undersåte — (noun) subject

underskrift — (noun) signature

understruket — (part.) underlined

undertecknad — (part. used as noun) the undersigned

undervisning — (noun) instruction

Ungern — (noun) Hungary

uppehåll — (neut. noun) pause; *under uppehållen* — during the stay

uppförande — (neut. noun) behavior, conduct

uppgavs — (v., from *uppge*) was stated, declared

upprättadt — (part.) found, established

uppvisadt — (part.) exhibited, shown

utan — (prep.) without

utflyttning — (noun) moving out, away

utländsk — (adj.) foreign

utmärkt — (adj.) excellent

utvandrare — (noun) emigrant

vaccinera — (v.) to vaccinate; *vaccinerad* — (part.) vaccinated

vad — (pron.) what

vagnmakare — (noun) cartwright

vapen — (neut. noun) weapon; coat of arms

var — (conj.) where; (adv.) where; (pron.) each; (v.) → *vara*

vara — (v., pres. *är,* past *var,* supine *varit*) to be

vecka — (noun) week

vederbörande — (adj.) the ones concerned, involved, competent

vem — (pron.) who

vi — (pron.) we

vid — (prep.) on, by; (adj.) wide

vigsel — (noun) marriage

vilken, vilket, vilka — (pron.) who, which, that

vinter — (noun, plur. *vintrar*) winter

vistelseort — (noun) place of residing, of staying

vit — (adj.) white

vittne — (neut. noun, plur. *vittnen*) witnesses

vår — (noun) spring; (poss. pron. or adj.) our

vänster — (adj.) left

värdshusvärd — (noun) innkeeper

världsdel — (noun) continent

värnplikt — (noun) military service

värnpliktig — (noun) conscript

väster — (noun) west

vävare — (noun) weaver

yrke — (neut. noun) profession, occupation

yrkesbestämd — (adj.) professional, occupational

å — (noun) river; (prep.) at, on: *å 3:de klass* — by 3rd class

ålder — (noun, plur. *åldrar*) age

ångfartyg — (neut. noun) steamship

år — (neut. noun) year

århundrade — (neut. noun) century

årskurser — (noun) year's worth of courses

åt — (prep.) to, towards

åter — (adv.) again, back

återresa — (noun) return trip, trip back

åtfölja — (v.) to accompany; *åtföljas* — is accompanied

åtnjuta — (v.) enjoy

åtta — (num.) eight

åttio — (num.) eighty; *åttiofyra* — eighty-four

åttionde — (adj.) eightieth

åttonde — (adj.) eighth

äga — (v.) to own, possess; *äger* — has

äkta — (adj.) legitimate, authentic; *äkta make* — husband

äktenskap — (neut. noun) marriage

äldre — (adj.) older, elder

äldste — (adj.) oldest

änka — (noun) widow

änkling — (noun) widower

är (present tense verb) → *vara*

ö — (noun) island

öga — (neut. noun, plur. *ögon*) eye

ögonvittne — (neut. noun) eyewitness

öra — (neut. noun, plur. *öron*) ear

öster — (noun) east

översättning — (noun) translation

Selected First Names

This is hardly a comprehensive listing of Swedish personal names. Most Swedish names, however, are familiar enough to Americans, or look enough like their English counterparts, to cause little trouble. The names given below are a few that look just enough unlike their English counterparts to be a source of confusion. Several distinctively Swedish or Scandinavian names — "Björn" and "Sven," for example — are also given, just so readers can be familiar with them and not waste hours peering through dictionaries trying to find out what an "Ingmar" is.

Researchers should keep three points in mind. The first is that an **equivalent** name is not the **same** name; that is, "Per Eriksson" might be called "Peter Eriksson" by speakers of English (and if he moved to the United States he probably would come to be called "Peter," which is why we offer this list), but one should not forget that his name was "Per," not "Peter." The second point is that many Swedish surnames began as patronymics, so this list is the source of many surnames as well: Andersson, Henrikson, Johanson, and so on. The third is that Swedish spelling has shown variation over the centuries and archaic spellings of names have a particular tendency to survive, so one should expect to see variations, e. g., *Gustaf* as well as *Gustav*, *Pär* as well as *Per*, and so forth.

Anders — Andrew

August — Augustus

Bernhard — Bernard

Björn — Björn

Dorotea — Dorothy

Edit — Edith

Edvard — Edward

Elisabet — Elizabeth

Frans — Francis

Fredrik — Frederick

Greta — Margaret

Gustav — Gustave

Harald — Harold

Henrik — Henry

Hjalmar — Hjalmar

Horatius — Horace

Ingmar — Ingmar

Ingvar — Ingvar

Isak — Isaac

Johan — John

Karin — Catherine

Karl — Charles

Katarina — Catherine

Kristofer — Christopher

Lars — Lars

Lena — Helen

Ludvig — Louis

Markus — Mark

Märta — Martha

Matteus — Matthew

Mikael — Michael

Olaf — Olaf

Per — Peter

Petrus — Peter

Petter — Peter

Rickard — Richard

Rolf — Ralph

Sigfrid — Siegfried

Sven — Sven

Tor — Thor

Vilhelm — William

The Romance Languages

The Romance languages are derived from Latin and are spoken not only in their European places of origin and development but also on distant continents where colonies were established by Romance-speaking European nations — notably Spain, Portugal, and France — starting in the 1500's.

Influenced by factors such as native languages, geographical isolation, and borrowings from non-Latin-based adstrate languages (e. g., the Slavic influence in Romanian), these languages nonetheless have a rather high rate of cognancy, that is, words with similar forms and lexical meanings. Similarities in grammatical structure, morphology, word order, and other features foster additional intercomprehensibility.

Spanish is by far the most widely spoken of the languages, as can be seen from this brief summary of which languages are spoken where:

Spanish — spoken in Spain, Latin America, present and former Spanish possessions in Africa and in large immigrant communities in North America. Also worthy of note is Catalán, spoken on Spain's eastern coast, and Gallego, spoken in northwest Spain, north of Portugal.

Portuguese — spoken in Portugal, Brazil, and in former and present Portuguese colonies in Africa and Asia

Italian — spoken in Italy, parts of Switzerland, and large immigrant colonies in North and South America, notably the United States, Canada, and Argentina

French — spoken in France, Canada, numerous former and present French possessions worldwide

Romanian — spoken in Romania and parts of the former U.S.S.R., as well as in immigrant colonies in the Americas and Australia

Romansch and other varieties — used by small groups of speakers in Northern Italy, Switzerland, and Yugoslavia

---

Many family history researchers are sharply cognizant of dialectal and regional forms of the standard language — for example, Sicilian versions of Italian versus the type of Italian spoken near Bologna. The variants in these types of spoken (and sometimes written) languages will not play a significant role in translating vital records such as those under examination here as these are official government documents where the standard language is used, a language which generally comes under the scrutiny of various normative mechanisms. When attempting to read old letters, however, the knowledge of the dialects may become a necessity.

The same holds true for non-European varieties of a widely diffused language such as French. Documentary language will be similar in Montréal, Senegal, Haiti, or Tunisia, although the spoken variety will indicate a broad spectrum of variation.

It may be surprising to see several pages of this section devoted to Latin, but even a brief review of the Romance languages in the context of family history research would be incomplete without some attention to the language of the Roman Empire and the Roman Catholic Church. Its role as the source of the Romance languages may interest only linguists, but even the most practically-minded genealogist will find a nodding acquaintance with Latin of considerable merit. If one succeeds in tracing European family lineage back more than a few generations, the probability of encountering documents in Latin rises dramatically; it was, after all, Europe's language of learning and scholarship — including record-keeping — for centuries, and the use of the vernacular for such purposes is historically a relatively recent development. Anyone whose research leads back into the territory of the Austro-Hungarian Empire much more than a hundred years, for instance, will find documents in two or more languages, one of which is Latin; a Polish-American tracing an ancestor from an area and time where Ukrainian was the vernacular and German the official language might be very grateful for the sight of the comparatively familiar Latin words that appear in the sample documents. Latin's use as the *lingua franca* of European civilization still has benefits for researchers today.

As for the tongues based on Latin, many have eliminated the complicated inflections of that language. Some prominent grammatical features of the Romance languages of which the family history researcher should be aware include:

1. Pluralization — *-s/-es,* as in English, is widely used as a pluralizing suffix in Spanish, French, and Portuguese, while Italian prefers vocalic alternations, e. g., *-o → -i.*

2. Gender — while the Romance languages have grammatical gender, as opposed to the natural gender of English (the Spanish word for "table" is feminine in gender), certain categories of words referring to people will yield important clues to the family history researcher. For example, certain Spanish and Italian nouns and participles have both masculine and feminine variants. When confronted with a highly illegible document, the gender marker may be one of the means of identifying the gender of the certificate's bearer, i. e., Italian *nato* (masculine) vs. *nata,* "born," Spanish *niño* (masculine) vs. *niña,* "boy/girl," French *né* (masculine) vs. *née* (feminine), "born." Articles, both definite and indefinite, are also marked for gender, and this fact may also be of assistance in translation.

The map below is certainly far too general to be of any use to a serious student of European languages or history, but it may help beginners visualize the countries in which the Romance languages originated and with which they are most closely identified. It is important to note that French, for instance, is widely spoken not only in France but also in Belgium and in Switzerland; Italian, too, is commonly spoken in Switzerland, as is German (as is indicated on the map on page 3). A map of the Americas could well have been added, but surely most researchers know that French is widely spoken in Canada and parts of this country, as well as in many Caribbean countries, and that Spanish dominates Central and South America (with the enormous exception of Brazil, where Portuguese is spoken!), so it seems superfluous to repeat the facts visually.

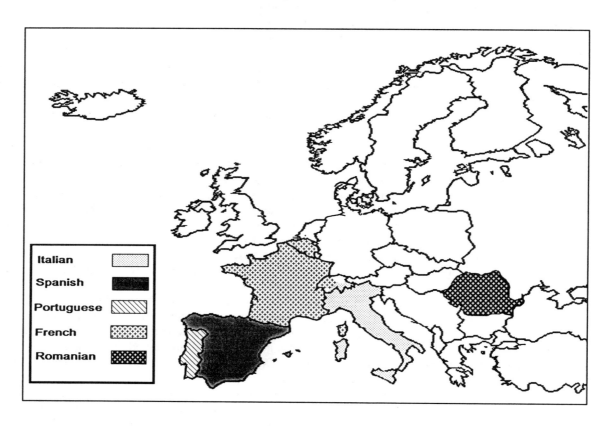

Italian

Spanish

Portuguese

French

Romanian

Français The French Alphabet

Printed	Cursive
A, a	*A, a*
B, b	*B, b*
C, c	*C, c*
D, d	*D, d*
E, e	*E, e*
F, f	*F, f*
G, g	*G, g*
H, h	*H, h*
I, I	*I, i*
J, j	*J, j*
K, k	*K, k*
L, l	*L, l*
M, m	*M, m*
N, n	*N, n*
O, o	*O, o*
P, p	*P, p*
Q, q	*Q, q*
R, r	*R, r*
S, s	*S, s*
T, t	*T, t*
U, u	*U, u*
V, v	*V, v*
W, w	*W, w*
X, x	*X, x*
Y, y	*Y, y*
Z, z	*Z, z*

Printed	Cursive	Printed	Cursive
À, à	*À, à*	Ê, ê	*Ê, ê*
Â, â	*Â, â*	É, é	*É, é*
Ç, ç	*Ç, ç*	Ô, ô	*Ô, ô*
È, è	*È, è*	Û, û	*Û, û*

The French alphabet is the same as the English (*k* and *w* tend to appear in words of foreign origin), but a few special diacritical marks distinguish certain sounds: thus ç is always a soft "s" sound, but *c* can be hard as in "card" or soft as in "certain." Vowels are sometimes seen with what looks like a German umlaut, e. g., *ë*, but this diacritical mark, called a "dieresis," means only that that vowel is sounded separately, not merged with preceding ones. The letters shown here on the right side of the chart are not considered separate characters and do not affect alphabetical order; they are listed only so that readers can become familiar with them.

French is notoriously difficult for Americans to learn to pronounce well; one must listen attentively to native speakers and imitate them again and again. Still, a few very general and very imprecise clues to French pronunciation may help the reader sound out words adequately, a process vital to figuring out and remembering words' meanings.

French vowels, in particular, deserve a great deal of attention. In general the *a* is like that in "father," and the *e* like the vowel in "let." The *i* or *y* is normally like the *i* in "machine," but *-in*, *-im*, *-ym* or *-yn* are somewhat like the nasal sound of English "hang" (well-known examples are the name of the sculptor Rodin and the term *vin ordinaire*). The *o* is basically the long "o" sound in "hotel," and the *u* is like the vowel in "feet" pronounced through rounded lips (like a German *ü*). All these vowels undergo extensive modifications, some of which are indicated by diacritical marks, e. g., *é*, *è*, *ô*, *ò*, etc.; they have nasal versions which are quite different from their normal values, and yet other sounds when joined into combinations such as *ai, au, ei, eu, oe, oeu, oi, ue*, and so on. Most of the distinctions between these sounds cannot be adequately described in print and must be heard to be imitated successfully.

Consonants are a bit less intimidating; most are pronounced somewhat as in English, but almost all French sounds are produced with greater muscular tension and less aspiration than their English counterparts. The *c* is usually hard as in "car," but *ce, ci, cy* and ç are soft as in "certain"; *ch* can be an "sh" sound, as in "champagne," or a "k" sound, as in "orchestra." The *g* is usually hard as in "go," but *ge, gi, gy* or *j* have the sound of "s" in "pleasure," and *gn* sounds like the "ny" in "canyon." The *h* is never sounded, *l* is generally very soft and liquid, and *ll* sounds like the *y* in "yield." The *th* sounds like *t*, but French *d* and *t* are pronounced with the tongue up against the teeth. The *r* is a uvular sound difficult for many Americans to learn, but a trilled *r* like that in Spanish is standard in Canada and scome parts of rural and southern France, and is always preferable to pronouncing *r* the way we do in English... As anyone knows who's ever tried to pronounce "qu'est-ce que c'est?" the way it looks, half the secret of good French pronunciation is knowing what not to pronounce!

CONFÉDÉRATION SUISSE.

CANTON DE

BERNE.

ARRONDISSEMENT D'ÉTAT CIVIL d' *Courroux*

EXTRAIT DU REGISTRE DES NAISSANCES.

(EXTRAIT DE NAISSANCE.)

VOL. *A. III.* FOL. *8.*

Le *Vingt six Mai* mil neuf cent *dix*
1910 à *huit* heure *4* minutes du *matin*
est né e à *Courroux, canton pl. Flena*
Douze Louise
fil *s* légitime
de *Félicien Joseph Dorga*, Profession : *Menuisier*
de *Breuleux Berne* domicilié à *Courroux*
et de *Rosalie Élisabeth née Schach*
de *Besançon, par option*

Pour extrait conforme,

Courroux le *23 février* 19*10*

L'OFFICIER DE L'ÉTAT CIVIL:

−64−

Document #1: Civil Birth Certificate

On the opposite page is reproduced a French-language civil birth certificate (in this case from Switzerland). Here is an analysis of its contents.

Confederation Suisse. Canton de Berne. Arrondissement d'état civil *de Courroux*
> *arrondissement* — "district"
> *état civil* — "vital statistics, civil registration"
> *canton* — "canton." The names of civil territorial divisions vary in French-speaking nations. In Switzerland *canton* is used, in France *département*, and in Canada *province*.
> ***Translation*** — Confederation of Switzerland. Canton of Berne. Civil registration district of Courroux.

Extrait du Registre des Naissances (Extrait de Naissance). Vol. *A.III, Fol. 8*
> *extrait* — "extract, certificate"
> *du* — "from the" (*de* + *le*)
> *naissance* — "birth"
> *vol.* — "volume" (abbreviation of *volume*)
> *fol.* — "folio, page" (abbreviation of *folio*)
> ***Translation*** — Extract from the Register of Births (Birth Certificate), Volume A.III, folio 8.

Le vingt six Mai mil neuf cent six 1906 à huit heures — minutes du matin
> *vingt six* — "twenty-six"
> *mil neuf cent six* — "one thousand nine hundred six" (1906)
> *à huit heures -- minutes* — "at eight o'clock" (-- minutes)
> *du matin* — "of the morning"
> ***Translation*** — On the twenty-sixth of May 1906 at eight o'clock, — minutes in the morning...

est né e à Courroux, canton du Berne
> *est née* — "was born" (*née* is feminine, *né* masculine)
> ***Translation*** — ...was born in Courroux, canton of Berne...

Donzé Louise fille légitime de Felicien Joseph Donzé Profession: Menuisier des Breuleux, Berne domicilié à Courroux
> *fille* — "daughter"   *fils* — "son"
> *menuisier* — "carpenter"
> *des Breuleux, Berne* — "from Breuleux, Berne"
> *domicilié à Courroux* — "residing in Courroux"
> ***Translation*** — Louise Donzé, legitimate daughter of Felicien Joseph Donzé, profession carpenter, from Breuleux, Berne, residing in Courroux...

et de Rosalie Elisabeth née Schach de Besançon, par option
> *née* — literally "born," but in this context indicates maiden name
> ***Translation*** — and of Rosalie Elisabeth, maiden name Schach, of Besançon.

Pour extrait conforme, Courroux le 23 février 1907. L'officier de l'état civil:
> *pour extrait conforme* — "this certificate is in conformance" [with the original]
> *l'officier de l'état civil* — "Registrar of Vital Statistics"
> ***Translation*** — This certificate [or extract] is in conformance with the original. [Dated] Courroux, 23 February 1907. [Signed] Registrar of Vital Statistics.

Document #2: Baptismal Certificate

On page 66 is a hand-written extract or certificate from the baptismal records of a Canadian parish.

Extrait du registre des baptêmes, mariages et sépultures de la paroisse de Saint-Damien de Brandon pour l'année mil neuf cent six.

Le neuf septembre mil neuf cent six nous, prêtre soussigné avons baptisé Joseph Antonio François Xavier, né la veille, fils légitime de Frédéric Cédras, cultivateur qui a déclaré ne savoir signer et de Marie Robert de cette paroisse. Le parrain a été Joachim Robert, cultivateur du lieu et la marraine Philomène Robert qui ont signé avec nous. Lecture faite.

J. Robert
P. Robert
Jos. Brien Ptre

Copie conforme à l'original.

J. Jodoin, Curé.

Saint-Damien de Brandon le vingt-trois Mai mil neuf cent vingt-deux.

Extrait du registre des baptêmes, mariages et sépultures de la paroisse de Saint-Damien de Brandon pour l'année mil neuf cent six.

extrait — "extract, certificate"
baptême — "baptism"
mariage — "marriage"
sépulture — "burial"
paroisse — "parish"
année — "year"

Translation — Extract from the register of baptisms, marriages and burials of the parish of Saint-Damien in Brandon for the year 1906.

Le neuf septembre mil neuf cent six

neuf — "nine"
septembre — "September"
mil neuf cent six — "one thousand nine hundred six" (1906)

Translation — On 9 September 1906...

nous, prêtre sousigné avons baptisé Joseph Antonio François Xavier

    nous — "we"

    prêtre — "parish priest"

    soussigné — "undersigned"

    avons baptisé — "have baptized" (from *baptiser*)

    Translation — we, the undersigned parish priest, have baptized Joseph Antonio François Xavier...

né la veille, fils légitime de Frédéric Cédras, cultivateur qui a déclaré ne savoir signer

    né — "born" (*née* when referring to a female)

    la veille — "the day before" (other possibilities are *ce jour*, "today," and *l'avant veille*, "the day before yesterday")

    fils légitime de — "legitimate son of" ("daughter" would be *fille*, cmp. Document #1)

    cultivateur — "farmer"

    qui — "who"

    a déclaré — "has declared"

    savoir — "to know, to know how"

    signer — "to sign"

    Translation — born the day before legitimate son of Frédéric Cédras, a farmer, who has declared he does not know how to sign [i. e., write]...

et de Marie Robert de cette paroisse

    cette — "this"

    paroisse — "parish"

    Translation — and of Marie Robert, of this parish.

Le parrain a été Joachim Robert cultivateur du lieu

    le parrain — "the godfather"

    a été — "was" (from *être*, "to be")

    du lieu — "from here"

    Translator — The godfather was Joachim Robert, a local farmer.

et la marraine Philomène Robert qui ont signé avec nous

    la marraine — "the godmother"

    qui ont signé — "who have signed" (**have** signed, i. e., both Joachim and Philomène Robert signed)

    avec nous — "with us"

    Translation — and the godmother [was] Philomène Robert, who have signed along with us.

Lecture faite. J. Robert P. Robert Jos. Brien Ptre. Copie conforme à l'original. J. Jodoin, curé

    lecture — "reading"

    faite — "done" (from *faire*, "to do, to make")

    Ptre. — abbreviation of *prêtre*, "priest")

    curé — "parson, parish priest, vicar"

    conforme à l'original — "The copy conforms to the original"

    Translation — A reading was done... *[The signatures of J. Robert, P. Robert, and Father Jos. Brien follow]*. This copy conforms to the original. [Signed] J. Jodoin, *curé*.

Saint-Damien de Brandon le vingt-trois mai mil neuf cent vingt-deux.

    le vingt-trois mai — "the 23rd of May"

    mil neuf cent vingt-deux — "one thousand nine hundred twenty-two"

    Translation — [Dated] Saint Damien in Brandon, 23 May 1922.

Document #3: French Passport

Republique Française — Passeport a l'Etranger — Carnet contenant 16 pages
>   republique française — "Republic of France"
>   Passeport a l'Etranger — "Passport for foreign travel" (étranger — foreign, strange, foreigner; a l'étranger — abroad)
>   carnet — "book, booklet"
>   contenant — "containing, consisting of" (from contenir)
>   **Translation** — Republic of France — Passport for Foreign Travel — Book containing 16 pages.

Département de la Seine — N° du Registre: 25802
>   département — an administrative subdivision in France (cmp. note on canton in analysis of Document #1)
>   **Translation** — Departement of La Seine, Registry #28502

Le présent PASSEPORT valable pour UN AN à partir du 11 août 1915 a été délivré à Mr Kirpitchnik Etienne Nationalité Russe
>   présent — "present, this"
>   valable — "valid"
>   pour un an — "for one year"
>   à partir de — "to commence with, beginning with"
>   août — "August"
>   a été délivré à — "has been issued to" (from délivrer, "to deliver, issue")
>   nationalité — "nationality"
>   Russe — "Russian"
>   **Translation** — The present passport, valid for one year beginning August 11, 1915, is issued to Mr. Etienne Kirpitchnik, nationality Russian.

Profession: *Monteur en bronze*

né à *Paris*

domicilié à *Paris 150 faubg. St. Antoine*

département d—

qui, en compagnie de —

se rend à ux *Etats-Unis*

> *monteur en bronze* — "jeweler" (specifically, one who sets jewels in bronze)
>
> *né à Paris* — "born in Paris"
>
> *domicilié à Paris* — "residing in Paris"
>
> *faubg. St. Antoine* — "suburb of St. Antoine" (*faubg.* is an abbreviation of *faubourg,* "suburb, outskirts")
>
> *qui, en compagnie de* — "who, in the company of..."
>
> *se rend* — "is going" (from *se rendre*)
>
> *aux Etats-Unis* — "to the United States"
>
> **Translation** — Profession, setter in bronze, born in Paris, residing in Paris, 150, suburb St. Antoine, département of —, who, in the company of —, is going to the United States.

Fait à *Paris* le *Onze Août Mil neuf cent quinze.* Signature du porteur: *Etienne Kurpitchnik*

> *fait* — "done"
>
> *le Onze Août* — "the eleventh of August"
>
> *Mil neuf cent quinze* — "[one] thousand nine hundred fifteen" (1915)
>
> *porteur* — bearer
>
> *Translation* — Done in Paris, 11th August 1915. Signature of bearer: Etienne Kurpitchnik.

For more samples of French-language passports, see Hungarian Document #2, Polish Document #6, and Czech Document #3.

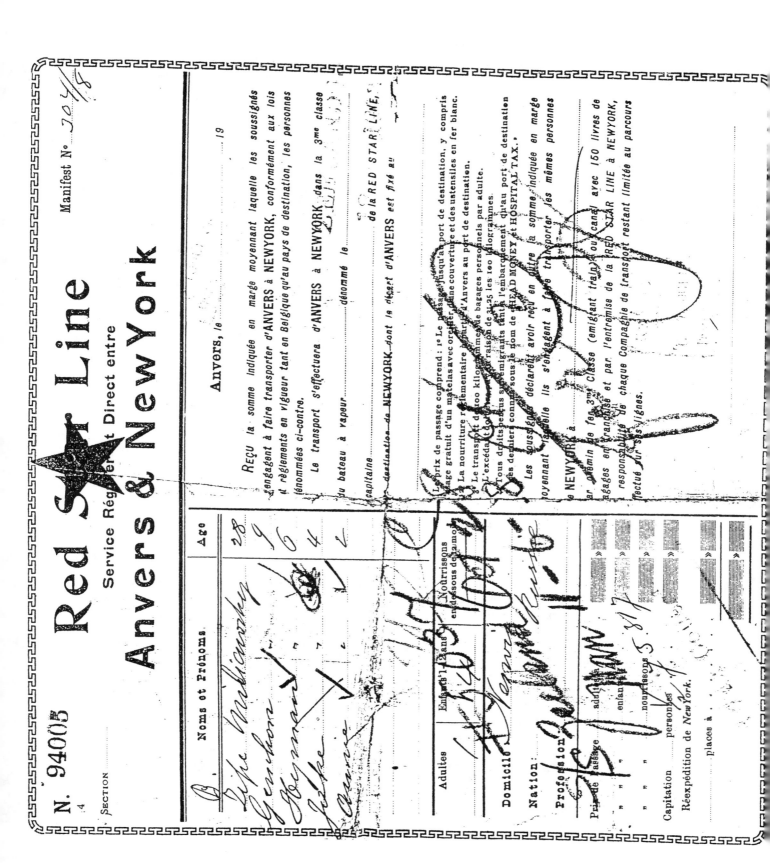

Document #4: Steamship Ticket

On the opposite page is a reproduction of a battered but legible steamship ticket issued in Anvers, Belgium. Most of the information on the left side of the ticket, relating to the passengers, consists of words so like their English counterparts that little translation is needed. *Noms et Prénoms* obviously means "Names and First Names"; *Adultes, Enfants 1-12 ans,* and *Nourrissons en dessous de 12 mois* clearly mean "Adults, Children age 1-12 years, and nursing children under 12 months." *Domicile, Nation,* and *Profession* are obvious, and *Prix de Passage* is clearly "price of passage," i. e., fare.

The printed information on the right two-thirds of the ticket is more or less legalese, but the terminology is precisely the sort one might expect to encounter while researching an immigrant's paper trail. So a brief analysis and translation may be helpful. (The various bits of information written and scribbled on the ticket are ignored as self-explanatory or insignificant). This document helps us understand the conditions of the voyage and the accommodations our ancestors had.

Reçu la somme indiquée en marge moyennant laquelle les soussignés s'engagent à faire transporter d'ANVERS à NEWYORK, conformément aux lois et règlements en vigueur tant en Belgique qu'au pays de destination, les personnes dénommées ci-contre.

    reçu la somme — "received: the sum"
    indiquée en marge — "indicated in the margin [or space]"
    moyennant laquelle — "by means of which"
    les soussignés — "the undersigned" (plural)
    s'engagent à faire transporter — "undertake to make transport, promise to provide transportation" [for] (from *s'engager,* "to undertake, promise, engage")
    conformément aux lois et règlements en vigueur — "in accordance with the laws and regulations in effect"
    tant en Belgique qu'au pays de destination — "both in Belgium and in the country of destination"
    les personnes dénommées ci-contre — "the persons named opposite"
    Translation — The sum indicated in the space having been received, the undersigned promise to provide transportation from Anvers to New York, in accordance with the laws and regulations in force in Belgium and in the country of destination, for the persons named opposite *[i. e., on the left side of the ticket].*

Le transport s'effectuera d'ANVERS à NEWYORK dans la 3me classe du bateau à vapeur — dénommé le [ZEELAND] capitaine — de la RED STAR LINE, à destination de NEWYORK dont le départ d'ANVERS est fixé au —.

    s'effectuera — "will be performed, carried out" (from *s'effectuer*)
    dans la 3me classe — "by third class"
    bateau à vapeur — "steamship"
    à destination de New York — "bound for New York"
    dont le départ d'Anvers est fixé au -- — "of which the departure from Anvers is set for"
    Translation — Passage will be effected from Anvers to New York by third class on the steamship Zealand, [with] captain —, of the Red Star Line, for the destination of New York, for which the departure from Anvers is set for ... *[the date either was not filled in or has faded to illegibility].*

Le prix de passage comprend: 1° Le passage jusqu'au port de destination, y compris passage gratuit d'un matelas avec oreiller, d'une couverture et des ustensiles en fer blanc.

    prix de passage — "price of passage, fare"
    comprend — "includes, comprehends" (from *comprendre*)
    jusqu'au port de destination — "[as far as] to the port of destination"
    y compris — "including"
    usage gratuit — "free (gratuitous) usage"
    d'un matelas avec oreiller — "of a mattress with pillow"
    couverture — "blanket, coverlet"
    ustensiles en fer blanc — "tin utensils"
    Translation — The fare includes: 1. Passage to the port of destination, including free usage of a mattress with pillow, a blanket, and tin utensils.

2° La nourriture réglementaire à partir d'Anvers au port de destination.

    la nourriture réglementaire — "regular nourishment"

    Translation — 2. regular meals beginning in Anvers up to the port of destination.

3° Le transport de 100 kilogrammes de bagages personnels par adulte. L'excédant dont être payé à raison de 31.25 les 100 kilogrammes.

    l'excedant — "the surplus, excess"

    être payé — "to be paid for"

    à raison de — "at the rate of"

    Translation — 3. transportation of 100 kg of personal luggage per adult. The excess of which to be paid for at the rate of 31.25 per 100 kg.

4° Tous droits perçus sur emigrants tant a l'embarquement qu'au port de destination ces derniers connus sous le nom de «HEAD MONEY et HOSPITAL TAX. »

    tous — "all" (from *tout*)

    droits — "fees" (in other contexts it usually means "rights")

    perçus — "collected" (from *percevoir*)

    sur emigrants — "from emigrants"

    tant a l'embarquement qu'au port de destination — "at embarkation and the destination port"

    ces derniers — "the latter"

    connus sous le nom de — "recognized" (from *connaître*) under the name of

    Translation — 4. all fees collected from emigrants at embarkation and at the destination port, the latter covered under the name of "head money" and "hospital tax."

Les soussignés déclarent avoir reçu en outre la somme indiquée en marge moyennant laquelle ils s'engagent à faire transporter les mêmes personnes de NEWYORK à —

    les soussignés — "the undersigned [ones]"

    déclarent avoir reçu — literally, "declare to have received"

    en outre — "besides, in addition, moreover"

    les mêmes personnes — "the same persons, said persons"

    Translation — The undersigned declare that they have received in addition the sum indicated in the space by means of which they promise to transport said persons from New York to — *[this is left blank, so no additional money was paid for transportation to some further point in America].*

par chemin de fer 3me classe (emigrant train) ou canal avec 150 livres de bagages en franchise et par l'entremise de la RED STAR LINE à NEWYORK, la responsabilité de chaque Compagnie de transport restant limitée au parcours effectué sur ses lignes.

    par chemin de fer — "by railway"

    ou canal — "or canal"

    livres — "pounds"

    en franchise et par l'entremise — "duty-free and through"

    la responsabilité de chaque Compagnie de transport — "the responsibility of each transportation company"

    restant limitée — "remaining limited"

    au parcours effectué sur ses lignes — "to the route covered by their lines"

    Translation — by 3rd-class railway (emigrant train) or canal with 150 pounds of baggage duty-free and through the Red Star Line in New York, the responsibility of each transport company remaining limited to the route covered by their lines.

Document #5: Death Certificate

The document on page 73 (used by kind permission of John A. Fischer of Sun City Center, Florida) is not the easiest to read, but for that very reason is worth a look. The point is that even when the handwriting is atrocious or the quality of the copy discouraging, one can hope to decipher it by looking for those expressions that must be

Du Vendredi neuvième jour
du mois de novembre l'an mil
huit cent trente deux, à cinq heures
du soir. _____

Acte de Décès de Frédéric
__Hoffman__, Maçon décédé aujourd'hui
à six heures du soir, âgé d'environ
quarante trois ans, né à Riedelberg,
Département de la Moselle & demeurant
au Havre, rue Beauxville, fils de
feu Daniel Hoffman & de feu
Marie Eve __Spiéttl__ Epoux de
Anne Barb. __Black__, marié
en la Paroisse de Rulsbronn,
Département de la Moselle le trois
Février mil huit cent huit. ainsi
Déclaré. _____

Sur la Déclaration à nous faite
par Pierre Louis de Fonckherre, Husi..
âgé de trente cinq ans, & Pierre Jordan
âgé de cinquante ans, tous deux amis
du Défunt & demeurant au Havre.

Lesquels ont signé avec nous après
lecture faite...

[signatures]

there and using them, by comparison, to figure out the rest. (In this instance the task is a bit easier because Jeannine Guez, the Secrétaire Adjointe of the Centre Havrais de Recherche Historique, Les Amis du Vieux Havre, provided a transcription to Mr. Fischer along with the copy of the certificate — a service one can always request when paying for a copy of a given document, although of course there's no guarantee that request will be granted).

*Du vendredi neuvième jour
du mois novembre l'an mil
huit cent trente deux à cinq heures
du soir*

> *vendredi* — "Friday"
> *neuvième jour* — "ninth day"
> *mois* — "month"
> *l'an mil huit cent trente deux* — "the year one thousand eight hundred thirty two (1832)"
> *à cinq heures du soir* — "at five o'clock in the evening"
> **Translation** — On Friday, the 9th day of November, 1832 at 5 o'clock p.m....

*Acte de décès de Frédéric
Hoffman maçon décédé ce jourd'hui
à dix heures du soir, agé d'environ
quarante sept ans, né à Riedilberg
département de la Moselle et demeurant
au Havre rue de Percanville*

> *act de décès* — "death certificate"
> *maçon* — "mason"
> *décédé* — "deceased, died"
> *ce jourd'hui* — "today"
> *à dix heures du soir* — "at ten o'clock in the evening"
> *âgé d'environ quarante sept ans* — "approximately forty-seven years old"
> *né à Riedilburg* — "born in Riedilberg"
> *département de la Moselle* — "province of Moselle"
> *demeurant* — "residing, living"
> *rue de Percanville* — [address] "Rue [street] de Percanville"
> **Translation** — Death certificate of Frédéric Hoffman, mason, deceased today at ten p.m., age approximately 47, born in Riedilberg, Moselle province, and residing in Le Havre on the Rue de Percanville...

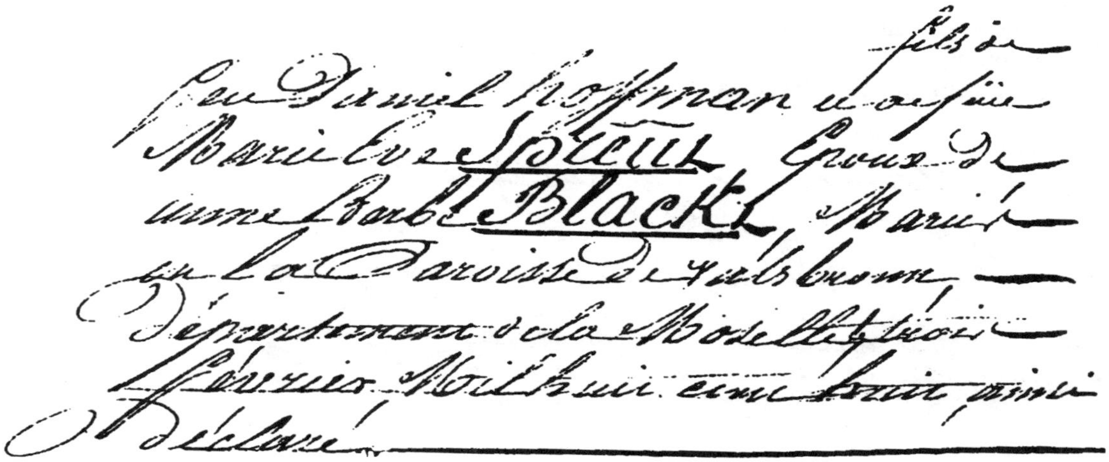

[handwritten facsimile]

fils de

et fils de
feu Daniel Hoffman et de feuë
Marie Eve Spreut, Epoux de
mme Barbe Black, Mariés
en la paroisse de Valsbronne,
département de la Moselle le trois
février mil huit cent huit ainsi
déclaré————————

> fils — "son"
>
> feu — "deceased, late" (this is the masculine form, *feuë* is feminine)
>
> epoux — "husband"
>
> mme. — abbreviation for *Madame*
>
> marié — (adj., participle of *marier,* "to wed") "married"
>
> paroisse — "parish"
>
> le trois février mil huit cent huit — "the third of February, one thousand eight hundred eight" (1808)
>
> ainsi déclaré — "declared thus"

Translation — and son of the late Daniel Hoffman and of the late Marie Eve Spreut, husband of Madame Barbe Black, married in the parish of Valsbronne, Moselle province, on 3 February 1808, made a statement to this effect...

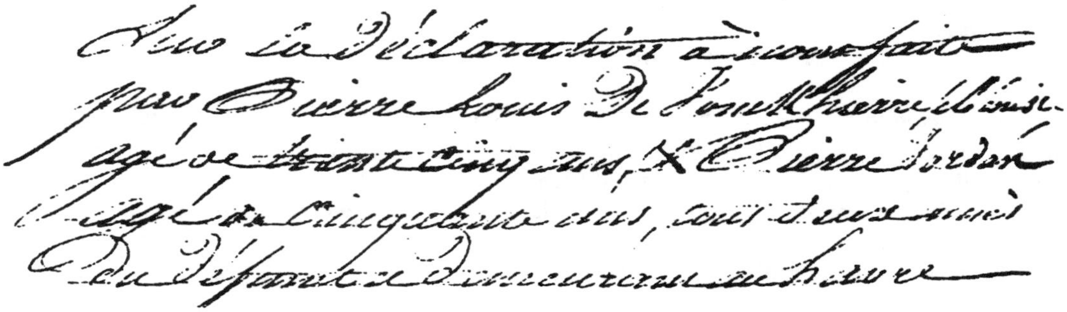

[handwritten facsimile]

Sur la déclaration à nous faite
par Pierre Louis de Jonckhierre, ébéniste
agé de trente cinq ans, et Pierre Jordan
agé de cinquante ans, tous deux amis
du défunt et demeurant au Havre.

> sur la déclaration — "according to the statement"
>
> à nous faite par — "made to us by"
>
> ébéniste — "cabinet-maker"
>
> âgé de trente cinq ans — "36 years old"
>
> âgé de cinquante — "30 years old"
>
> tous deux amis du défunt — "both friends of the deceased"

demeurant au Havre — "residing in Le Havre"

Translation — According to the statement made to us by Pierre Louis de Jonckhierre, cabinet-maker, age 36, and Pierre Jordan, age 30, both friends of the deceased and residing in Le Havre.

Lesquels soussigné aprés lecture faite
le présent acte fait double en leur présence et
constaté suivant la loi par nous Jacques
Joseph Grégoire Lahoussaye adjoint de Mr Le Maire
de la ville du Havre, de son adjoint remplissant
les fonctions d'officier public de l'etat civil

    Lesquels — "who" (plural)

    aprés lecture faite — "after it was read"

    fait double in leur présence — "copied in their presence"

    constaté — "reported, stated" (from *constater*)

    suivant la loi — "according to the law, in accord with the law"

    par nous — "by us"

    adjoint de Mr Le Maire de la ville du Havre — "deputy of the mayor of the city of Le Havre"

    de son adjoint — "of his assistant"

    remplissant — "fulfilling, carrying out"

Translation — Who after it was read signed the present document, copied in their presence and drawn up in accordance with the law by us, Jacques Joseph Grégoire Lahoussaye, assistant to the mayor the city of Le Havre, his deputy carrying out the functions of public officer of the Civil Registry. *[The last few words are very hard to make out, but since this a legalistic formula often found at the end of documents such as this, it is reasonable to assume that they say this or words very much to this effect.]*

Selected Vocabulary Terms

Nouns are generally given in the singular, but most French names form their plurals as do English nouns, by adding *-s,* so plural forms should cause little trouble. Adjectives and participles are given in their masculine form, but the feminine is usually made by adding *-e,* so it's not difficult to recognize that *née* is just the feminine form of *né,* "born," or *faite* is the feminine of *fait,* "done, completed"; the plural of adjectives and participles almost always is formed by adding *-s,* so *mariés* is not hard to recognized as a plural form of *marié,* "married." Verb forms are accompanied by their corresponding infinitive, the standard form under which they'd be found in the dictionary.

a — [he, she, it] has (from the verb *avoir*), also used with participles to form perfect tenses, e. g., *a déclaré* = [he, she, it] has declared, stated; *a été delivré* — has been issued

à — (preposition) at, to

à partir de — to commence with, beginning with

acte — (masc. noun) record, certificate

adjoint — (masc. noun) deputy, assistant

adulte — (masc. noun) adult; *per adulte* — per adult

âge — (masc. noun) age; *âgé* — old, of age

ainsi — thus, to that effect

ami — (masc. noun) friend

an — (masc. noun) year

année — (fem. noun) year

août — (masc. noun) August

après — (prep.) after

arrondissement — (masc. noun) district, ward

au — (= *à* + *le*) at the, to the

aux — (= *à* + *les*) at the, to the

avec — (prep.) with

avoir — to have; *avons* — "we have"; *avons baptisé* — "we have baptized"

avril — (masc. noun) April

baptême — (masc. noun) baptism

bateau — (masc. noun) boat; *bateau à vapeur* — steamship

canton — (masc. noun) canton (Swiss administrative unit)

capitaine — (masc. noun) captain

carnet — (masc. noun) book, booklet

ce — this, that (feminine form *cette*, plural *ces*)

cent — hundred

ces — this, that (plural form of *ce*)

cette — this, that (feminine form of *ce*)

chaque — each, every

chemin — (masc. noun) path, road, way; *chemin de fer* — railroad

ci-contre — opposite

cinq — five; *le cinq avril* — the 5th of April; *à cinq heures* — at 5 o'clock

cinquante — fifty

cinquième — fifth

civil — (adj.) civil, civic; *l'état civil* — registrar of vital statistics, civil status; (noun) layman, civilian

classe — (fem. noun) class; *dans la 3me classe* — by 3rd class

compagnie — (fem. noun) company

comprend (from *comprendre*) — includes

compris — (from *comprendre*) included

confédération — (fem. noun) confederation

conforme (from *conformer*) — agrees, conforms; *conforme à l'original* — conforms to the original

conformément — in accordance (with: *à*)

connu — (from *connaître*) recognized

constat — (from *constater*) drawn up, reported, established

contenant — (from *contenir*) containing

copie — (fem. noun) copy

couverture — (fem. noun) blanket, coverlet

cultivateur — (masc. noun) farmer

curé — (masc. noun) parson, parish priest, rector

dans — (prep.) in, within

de — of, from (*d'* before a vowel or a silent h, *du = de le*, *des = de les*)

décédé — (from *décéder*) deceased

décembre — (masc. noun) December

décès — (masc. noun) decease; *act de décès* — death certificate

déclaration — (fem. noun) statement, declaration

déclaré — (from *déclarer*) declared; *déclarent* — (from *déclarer*) they declare, state

défunt — (adj.) deceased

demeurant — (from *demeurer*) residing

dénommé — (from *dénommer*) named

départ — (masc. noun) departure

département — (masc. noun) département, province

dernier — (adj.) last, latest, final

des — of the (*de + les*)

deux — two; second; *deux cents* — two hundred

dimanche — (masc. noun) Sunday

dix — ten, tenth; *à dix heures du soir* — at ten o'clock in the evening; *dix-huit* — eighteen; *dix-neuf* — nineteen; *dix-sept* — seventeen

domicilié — residing

dont — of which, whom; whose; by whom

double — (masc. noun) double, copy; (adj.) double; *fait double* — copied

douze — twelve

droit — (masc. noun) fee, right

droite — (fem. noun) right (hand)

du — of the (*de + le*)

ébéniste — (masc. noun) cabinet-maker

effectué — (from *effectuer*) achieved, carried out, covered

embarquement — (masc. noun) embarkation

en — (prep.) in, among, at

entremise — (fem. noun) mediation, intervention; *par l'entremise* — through

environ — (masc. noun) vicinity, neighborhood; (adverb) about, nearly; *d'environ* — about

épouse — (fem. noun) wife

époux — (masc. noun) husband

est — (verb, from *être*) is; (masc. noun) east; (adj.) eastern

état — (masc. noun) state, profession; *Etats-Unis* — United States; *l'état civil* — registry of vital statistics, civil status

été — (from *être*) been; *a été* — has been, was

étranger — (adj.) foreign, strange; (masc. noun) foreigner; *a l'étranger* — abroad

être — to be

excédant — (adj.) excess, surplus

excédent — (masc. noun) excess, surplus

extrait — (masc. noun) extract, excerpt; certificate

faire — to do, make (used with a great many prepositions, nouns, and other verbs in idiomatic expressions, e. g., *faire transporter* — to have transported, to provide transportation for)

fait — (from *faire*) done, completed, finished; (noun) fact, deed

faubg. — (abbreviation of *faubourg*, masc. noun) suburb, outskirts

femme — (fem. noun) woman, wife

fer — (masc. noun) iron; *fer blanc* — tin

feu — late, deceased (feminine form *feuë*)

février — (masc. noun) February

fille — (fem. noun) daughter

fils — (masc. noun) son

fixé — (from *fixer*) set, established; *est fixé au ...* — is set for the ...th

fol. — (abbreviation of *folio*) folio

fonction — (fem. noun) function, duty

français — (adj.) French

franchise — (fem. noun) exemption, freedom; *en franchise* — duty-free

gratuit — free, for free

heure — (fem. noun) hour, o'clock; *à 8 heures du matin* — at 8:00 a.m.

huit — eight, eighth; *huit cent* — eight hundred

il — (pronoun) he

ils — (pronoun) they

indiquée — (from *indiquer*) indicated, pointed out

janvier — (masc. noun) January

jeudi — (masc. noun) Thursday

jour — (masc. noun) day

jourd'hui — *aujourd'hui, ce jourd'hui* — today

juillet — (masc. noun) July

juin — (masc. noun) June

jusque — (prep.) up to, as far as; *jusqu'au = jusque + au*

l' — (abbreviation of *le*) the; him; (feminine form *la*, plural *les*)

la — (feminine form of *le*) she, her

laquelle — (feminine form of *lequel*) who, which

le — the; him, it

lecture — (fem. noun) reading, perusal

légitime — (adj.) legitimate, lawful

lequel — who, which

les — (plural of *le*) the, them

lesquelles — (feminine plural of *lequel*) — who

lesquels — (plural of *lequel*) who

leur — them, to them, their

lieu — (masc. noun) place, stead; *du lieu* — local

ligne — (fem. noun) line

limité — (from *limiter*) limited

livre — (masc. noun) book, register; (fem. noun) pound

loi — (fem. noun) law

lundi — (masc. noun) Monday

ma → *mon*

maçon — (masc. noun) mason

mai — (masc. noun) May

maire — (masc. noun) mayor

mal — (masc. noun) evil, harm, pain; (adverb) badly

mardi — (masc. noun) Tuesday

marge — (fem. noun) border, edge, margin

mari — (masc. noun) husband

mariage — (fem. noun) marriage

marié — (from *marier*) married

marraine — (fem. noun) godmother

mars — (masc. noun) March

matelas — (masc. noun) mattress

matin — (masc. noun) morning

même — same, self

menuisier — (masc. noun) carpenter

mercredi — (masc. noun) Wednesday

mes — (plural from *mon*) my

mil — (also *mille*) thousand

mille — (also *mil*) thousand

moi — (pronoun) to me

mois — (masc. noun) month

mon — (poss. adj., feminine form *ma*, plural form *mes*) my

monteur — (masc. noun) setter of jewels (in bronze setting: *en bronze*)

moyen — (adj.) middle, mean

moyennant — (prep.) by means of

naissance — (fem. noun) birth

naître — to be born

nationalité — (fem. noun) nationality

né — (from *naître*) born (feminine form *née*)

ne — (adv.) no, not

neuf — nine; *neuf cent* — nine hundred

neuf — (adj.) new (feminine form *neuve*)

neuvième — ninth

nord — (masc. noun) north

notre — our

nourriture — (fem. noun) food, nourishment

nous — (pronoun) we, us

novembre — (masc. noun) November

octobre — (masc. noun) October

officier — (masc. noun) officer

ont — (from *avoir*) [they] have; *ont signé* — they have signed

onze — eleven, eleventh; *onzième* — eleventh

oreiller — (masc. noun) pillow

original — (adj.) original; (masc. noun) original, e. g., *copie conforme à l'original,* the copy conforms to the original

ou — or

ouest — (masc. noun) west; (adj.) west, western

outre — (prep.) beyond; (adv.) further; *en outre* — moreover, in addition

par — (prep.) per, for, through

parcours — (masc. noun) distance covered

paroisse — (fem. noun) parish

parrain — (masc. noun) godfather

passage — (masc. noun) passage; *prix de passage* — fare

passeport — (masc. noun) passport

payé — (from *payer*) paid for

pays — (masc. noun) country, land

perçu — (from *percevoir*) collected

personne — (fem. noun) person

personnel — (adj.) personal

port de destination — port of destination

porteur — (masc. noun) bearer

pour — (prep.) for, on account of

premier — (adj.) first

présent — (adj.) this, present, current; (masc. noun) the present

prêtre — (masc. noun) parish priest, minister

prix — (masc. noun) prize, price

profession — (fem. noun) profession, calling, occupation

quarante — forty; *quarantième* — fortieth

quatorze — fourteen; *quatorzième* — fourteenth

quatre — four, fourth

quatre-vingts — eighty

quatre-vingt-dix — ninety

que — (*qu'* before a vowel): (relative pronoun) who, which, that; (conj.) that, than, as, when; (adv.) how much, how many

quel — (adj.) which, what

qui — (pron.) who, which, that

quinze — fifteen; *quinzième* — fifteenth

raison — (fem. noun) reason, sense, ratio; *à raison de* — at the rate of

reçu — (from *recevoir*) received

registre — (masc. noun) register, record

règlement — (masc. noun) regulation, rule; *règlementaire* — (adj.) regular, prescribed

remplissant — (from *remplir*) fulfilling, carrying out

rend se — (from *se rendre*) is going

république — (fem. noun) republic

respondabilité — (fem. noun) responsibility

restant — (from *rester*) remaining

roi — (masc. noun) king

rue — (fem. noun) street

russe — (adj.) Russian

s' — (abbreviation for *se*) self

sa — (poss. adj.) his, hers, its

samedi — (masc. noun) Saturday

sans — (prep.) without

savoir — to know, know how

se — (pronoun, becomes *s'* before vowels) oneself, himself, herself, themselves, itself

s'effectuera — (from *s'effectuer*) will be carried out

seize — sixteen

s'engagent — (from *s'engager*) [they] undertake, promise

sept — seven, seventh; *septième* — seventh

septembre — (masc. noun) September

sépulture — (fem. noun) burial, tomb

ses — his, hers, its

si — (conj.) if, whether

signé — (from *signer*) signed

signer — to sign (signature)

six — six, sixth

soi — (pron.) (him-, her, it-)self

soir — (masc. noun) evening; *du soir* — p.m.

soixante — sixty

soixante-dix — seventy

somme — (fem. noun) sum, total

son — (poss. adj., fem. form *sa*, plural *ses*) his, her, its

sous — under, below, by; *sous le nom de* — under the name of

soussigné — (from *soussigner*) the undersigned one

sud — (masc. noun) south

Suisse — Switzerland

suivant — (prep.) in accordance with

sur — (prep.) on, upon, onto, over, according to

ta — (feminine form of *ton*) your

tant — (adv.) so much, so many, so far

tante — (fem. noun) aunt

tous — (from *tout*) all

temps — (masc. noun) time

tes — (plural form of *ton*) your

tête — (fem. noun) head, chief

ton — (poss. adj., feminine form *ta*, plural *tes*) your

tout — (pronoun) all, everything; (adj., feminine form *toute*, plural *tous* and *toutes*) all, every

transport — (masc. noun) transport, removal

transporter — to transport, move, convey

treize — thirteen

trente — thirty; *trentième* — thirtieth

très — (adv.) very

trois — three; *troisième* — third

un — (feminine form *une*) a; one

usage — (masc. noun) use

ustensile — (masc. noun) utensil, tool

valable — (adj.) valid

vapeur — (fem. noun) steam

veille — (fem. noun) watch, vigil, eve; *la veille* — the day before

vendredi — (masc. noun) Friday

vigueur — (fem. noun) force, strength, vigor; *en vigueur* — in force

ville — (fem. noun) town, city

vingt — twenty; *vingt-trois* — twenty-three

French Personal Names

It should be remembered that "translating" personal names from one language into another is a tricky business; *Étienne Roi* may translate literally as "Stephen King," but that doesn't mean you should call him that. The English equivalents (some of which are only approximate) are meant to facilitate recognizing names French *emigrés* might adopt in the United States or Canada. Names with asterisks (*) are popular in French-speaking areas of Canada; many have no real English equivalent, and some names popular in Montréal are considered rare or outmoded in Paris.

Alcide *

Adélard *

Alexandre — Alexander

André — Andrew

Antoine — Anthony

Arnaud — Arnold

Céale *

Édouard — Edward

Étienne — Steven

Fleurette *

François — Francis

Françoise — Frances

Frédéric — Frederick

Gautier — Walter

Germaine *

Guillaume — William

Henri — Henry

Jacques — James

Jean — John

Jeanne — Jane, Jean, Joan

Lucien * — Lucian

Mathieu — Matthew

Michel — Michael

Philippe — Philip

Pierre — Peter

Raoul — Ralph

Thérèse — Teresa

Italiano

The Italian Alphabet

Printed	Cursive
A, a	$\mathcal{A}, a$
B, b	$\mathcal{B}, b$
C, c	$\mathcal{C}, c$
D, d	$\mathcal{D}, d$
E, e	$\mathcal{E}, e$
F, f	$\mathcal{F}, f$
G, g	$\mathcal{G}, g$
H, h	$\mathcal{H}, h$
I, I	$\mathcal{I}, i$
J, j	$\mathcal{J}, j$
K, k	$\mathcal{K}, k$
L, l	$\mathcal{L}, l$
M, m	$\mathcal{M}, m$
N, n	$\mathcal{N}, n$
O, o	$\mathcal{O}, o$
P, p	$\mathcal{P}, p$
Q, q	$\mathcal{Q}, q$
R, r	$\mathcal{R}, r$
S, s	$\mathcal{S}, s$
T, t	$\mathcal{T}, t$
U, u	$\mathcal{U}, u$
V, v	$\mathcal{V}, v$
W, w	$\mathcal{W}, w$
X, x	$\mathcal{X}, x$
Y, y	$\mathcal{Y}, y$
Z, z	$\mathcal{Z}, z$

The Italian alphabet offers little to intimidate English-speakers. The letters are the same as in English, and the only special orthographic sign is the accent used to mark stressed vowels at the end of words, e. g., *città* (city), *lunedì* (Monday). The letters *j, k, w,* and *y* are used rarely, appearing only in words borrowed from other languages. The only silent letter in Italian is *h* — all other letters are pronounced, and usually the same way every time.

Obviously space does not suffice for a long discussion of Italian pronunciation, but a few brief comments may be helpful. Most Americans do not find Italian pronunciation that difficult to learn; it's not necessarily easy to develop a truly good accent, but an adequate approximation isn't too hard to attain. Besides, Italians speak their language with gusto, as if enjoying the very act of making the sounds, and that pleasure is contagious.

Italian vowels are purer and pronounced with more tension than English vowels; the vowel in English "meet" lets a slight "y"-sound creep in at the end, but the similar-sounding Italian vowel *i* is spoken with no movement of the tongue and no "y"-sound; and the long Italian *o* has no "w"-sound sneaking in at the end, unlike our long *o*. That said, Italian *a* is pronounced like that in "f<u>a</u>ther"; *i* like the "ee" in "m<u>ee</u>t"; *u* like "oo" in "b<u>oo</u>t", but a little deeper and farther back in the mouth; a long or open *e* like the "a" in "d<u>a</u>te" (but without the "y"-sound, remember!), a closed *e* like that in "met"; and an open *o* sounds like that in "h<u>o</u>tel," and a closed one somewhat like "aw" in "th<u>aw</u>."

Most consonants are pronounced much as in English, but a few are different. One of the most bothersome is *c*, which sounds like "k" except before the vowels *i* or *e* — so *colore* sounds like "koh-LOH-ray" but *cinema* like "CHEE-nay-mah," and *concerto* like "kon-CHAIR-toh." The combination *ch* is used only before *e* or *i* and is pronounced like "k," e. g., *maccheroni* "mah-kay-ROH-nee." Also tough is *g*, which sounds like our "j" in "just" before the vowels *e* and *i*, otherwise like our "g" in "good" (*gh* is also a hard "g" as in "good"). So *regione* sounds like "ray-JOH-nay" but *geografia* like "jay-oh-grah-FEE-ah." The combinations *gl* and *gn* are exceptions: *gl* is pronounced like "lli" in "mi<u>lli</u>on," and *gn* like "ni" in "o<u>ni</u>on." The consonant *h* is always silent: *hanno* (they have) is pronounced as if it were spelled *anno*.

S is worth a paragraph in itself. It sounds like the "s" in "<u>s</u>and" when it precedes *c, f, p, q,* or *t*, when doubled, or when it comes at the start of a word before a vowel (*santo,* for instance). In most other cases it is pronounced like our "z" in "<u>z</u>oo," e. g., *sbaglio,* "ZBAHLL-yoh." An *sc* preceding *e* or *i* sounds like "sh" in "<u>sh</u>ip," in most other cases like "sk" in "<u>sk</u>ip." The combination *qu* always sounds as it does in our word "<u>qu</u>iet." A *z* usually sounds like our combination "ts" in "ge<u>ts</u>," but occasionally like our "dz" in "a<u>dz</u>e."

Another important feature of Italian pronunciation is the doubled consonant: it's held twice as long as a single consonant, really emphasized. The word *hanno* (they have) sounds like "AHN-noh," with each -*n*- pronounced separately. When *cc* or *gg* precede the troublesome vowels *e* and *i*, they sound like "tch" and "dj" respectively: *braccio* (arm) sounds like "BRAHT-choh," and *raggio* (beam, ray) sounds like "RAHD-joh."

Document #1: Steamship Ticket

Many immigrants saved their steamship tickets, which can provide some data regarding the family. The regulations regarding the ship procedures, menus, baggage lists, immigration laws paint a picture for us of our ancestors' passage to America. Below, reproduced and enlarged from a sample ticket, is the section containing information relevant to the passengers.

di TERZA CLASSE di NAPOLI

Biglietto d'imbarco in TERZA CLASSE № 00817 *H*

sul Vapore _____ di bandiera italiana

che partirà da *NAPOLI* il _____21 APR 1916_____

_____ per *NEW YORK*

toccando di scalo il porto di PALERMO _____

PEI PASSEGGIERI

COGNOME E NOME	ETÀ		POSTI E RAZIONI			Cuccette	
	ANNI	MESI					
1. Valente Giuseppa	38		1				
2. Raffaele Salvatore	15						
3. " Ernesto	8		1				
4. " Rosina	7		1				
5. " Ermelinda	4		1				
6. " Alfredo	3		1				
7.							
Totale			2 2 2				

N.° di chiamata _____ da _____ PASSAPORTO } N.°

Vocabulary

biglietto d'imbarco — "embarkation ticket"

in terza classe — "in third class" (*prima classe* is "first class," *seconda classe* is "second class").

sul vapore — "on the steamship"

di bandiera italiana — "under the Italian flag"

che partirà da Napoli — "which will depart from Naples"

per New York — "for New York"

toccando di scalo il porto di Palermo — "touching at the port of Palermo"

pei passeggieri — "for the passengers"

cognome e nome — "surnames and names"

età — "age"

posti i razioni — "reserved seats (or places) and rations" (i. e., food)

cuccette — "berths"

As usual in Italian documents, the surnames are given first, then the Christian names: we would write Giuseppa Valente, followed by Salvatore, Ernesto, Rosina, Ermelinda, and Alfred Raffaele.

Document #2: Civil Family Registration Booklet

PROVINCIA
DI
SIRACUSA

CIRCONDARIO
DI
SIRACUSA

Città di Siracusa

Stato Civile di Famiglia

PROPRIETA LETTERARIA

CHERASCO – TIP. LIBR. F.-RASELLI
1902.

◁

Provincia di Siracusa, Circondario di Siracusa, Città di Siracusa, Stato Civile di Famiglia
  provincia — "province"
  circondario — "district"
  città — "city"
  Stato Civile di Famiglia — "Family Vital Statistics"
Translation: Province of Siracusa, District of Siracusa, City of Siracusa, Family Vital Statistics

▽

Oggi 14 maggio 1903 il Sig[nore] LaRosa, Salvatore, nato in Priolo
Sig.: abbreviation for *Signore* (Mr.), *Signora* (Mrs.), *Signorina* (Miss). [Note: in many Italian documents the surname comes first, as here.]
nato (masc.), *nata* (fem.) — "born"
Translation: Today, May 14, 1903, Mr. Salvatore LaRosa, born in Priolo...

il 27 marzo 1880, figlio di Sebastiano e Marotta, Lucia
  figlio — "son"
  Translation: ...on March 27, 1880, son of Sebastiano and of Lucia Marotta...

e la Sig. Gervasi Santa, nata in Priolo il 1º settembre 1879, figlia di fu Paolo e DiLuciano, Sebastiana
  figlia — "daughter"
  fu — "deceased"
  Translation: ...and Miss Santa Gervasi, born in Priolo, September 1, 1879, daughter of the deceased Paolo and Sebastiana DiLuciano...

hanno celebrato Matrimonio avanti il Sig. Italia Gaetano, Assessore delegato Ufficiale dello Stato Civile di Siracusa.
  celebrare matrimonio — "get married"
  avanti — "before, in the presence of"
  Assessore — "Municipal Magistrate"
  Ufficiale — "official, keeper"
  Translation: ...have been married before Italia [*Italia is his surname*] Gaetano, Municipal Magistrate, delegate Keeper of Vital Statistics of Siracusa.

Oggi 14 Maggio 1903.
il Sig. La Rosa
Salvatore
nato in Priolo il 27 Marzo 1880
figlio di Sebastiano e Marotta Lucia
e la Sig. Gervasi
Santa
nata in Priolo il 1 Settembre 1879
figlia di fu Paolo e si Di Luciano Sebastiana
hanno celebrato Matrimonio avanti il Sig.
Italia sivi Gaetano Assessore delegato
Ufficiale dello Stato Civile di Siracusa.

Stato Civile dei Figli

—:—

(1) Nom *Paolo*

nato il *25 Gennaio 1905 a Priolo*

vaccinato il _____ in _____

sposato in _____ il _____

con _____

morto in _____

—∞—

Stato Civile dei Figli — "Civil Status of Children"

Nom: Paolo — "Name: Paolo"

nato il 25 gennaio 1905 a Priolo — "Born: January 25, 1905 in Priolo"

vaccinato il — "Vaccinated on:"

sposato in — "Married in:"

con — "To:" [literally, "with"]

morto in — "Died in:"

Documents such as these, common in many European nations, recorded all births, deaths, and marriages in the family unit. Changes of address and migrations were also recorded in these documents. They are still required in many countries.

Document #3: Parish Family Registration Documents

Roman Catholic parishes at times issued such family registration documents. Here is a sample of such a record. The first page, reproduced below, specifies the parish where the document was issued. The next two pages are reproduced on pages 84-85, followed by some analysis.

Parrochia di Ispra in Barza

Diocesi di Milano - Pieve di Brozzo

Stato di Famiglia = Pinchetti Pietro di Stefano

Parrochia di Ispra in Barza — Parish of Ispra in Barza

Diocese di Milano – Pieve di Brozzo: Diocese of Milano, Vicarage of Brozzo

Stato di Famiglia: Pinchetti Pietro di Stefano — Status of Family of Pietro Pinchetti, son of Stefano

Cognome	Nome	Genitori	Patria
2 Pinchetti Ponti	Pinchetti Maria Figli Luigia Giuseppe Lenardo Stefano	Pasquale Bassetti Carolina Giuseppe e Andrini Teresa Pietro Ponti Maria " " " " " "	Ispra " Ispra " "

Parroco Ecclesiastico

Ispra li 15 Agosto 1906.

Diocesi Di Milano.

Date delle nascite e Battesimo.	Parr e date del matrimonio religioso.	Osservazioni
6. Aprile 1863.	Brebbia	morto il 5 aprile 1899
1° Maggio 1866.	1 Febb 1890	
7 Dicem. bttz. l'8. 1890.		
9 Febb. „ 12. 1892		
12 agosto „ 15 1897		

This document presents its information in columns headed as follows:

Column 1, *cognome cognome* — indicates the father's and mother's maiden surname.
Column 2, *nome nome* — gives the first names of parents and children.
Column 3, *genitori genitori* — gives the parents' names, including mother's maiden name.
Column 4 gives the parish.
Column 5 gives the dates of birth *nascità (nascità)* and baptism *battesimo (battesimo)*.
Column 6 gives the date and place of religious marriage *matrimonio religioso (matrimonio religioso)*.
Column 7 gives notations, *Osservazioni*; here the father's date of death is given.

Note that the clerk made an error in column 2 and repeated the father's surname, Pinchetti, instead of giving his first name, Pietro. The next name is Maria, followed by *Figli Figli*, "children," whose names were Luigia, Giuseppe, and Leonardo Stefano. Pietro's parents were Pasquale Pinchetti and Carolina née Bassetti, and Maria's parents were Giuseppe Ponti and Teresa née Andrini. Pietro and Maria were married on 1 February 1890, and Pietro died on 5 April 1899.

Document #4: Civil Family Registration Documents

Not all such family registration documents were in the booklet form shown in the samples so far. Some were issued on long sheets of paper, as is shown in the example on the opposite page. Practice deciphering the names and birthdates of the Petrucelli family. Note the following:
— the mother's maiden name is normally provided in such documents;
— the *di* + first name literally means "of" but is best translated as "son/daughter of" followed by the father's first name. As mentioned earlier, *fu* indicates the father is deceased.

To facilitate reading the document, here is a transcription of its contents in standardized script:

MUNICIPIO di CASTELFRANCO in MISCANO

*Situazione di famiglia di Petruccelli
Fedele fu Francesco Saverio*

No. d'ord-ine	Quali-tà	Cognome i nome di ogni membro di famiglia	Comune	Data di nascita			Stato
				giorno	mese	anno	
1	Padre	Petruccelli Fedele fu Fran. Sav.	Castelfranco	26	Dicembre	1858	Italia
2	madre	Nucio M Lucia di Leonard	id.	2	Gennaio	1869	" "
3	figlia	Petruccelli M Nora di Fedele	id.	15	Gennaio	1894	" "
4	figlio	Petruccelli Giovanni di Fedele	id.	20	luglio	1898	" "
5	figlia	Petruccelli M Michela di Fedele	id.	15	aprile	1901	" "
6	figlia	Petruccelli Maria di Fedele	id.	1	maggio	1904	" "

Castelfranco in Miscano 22 febbraio 1913

The column headings are as follows:

1. *Nº d'ordine* — "record number" (sequentially numbered)

2. *Qualità* — "quality, nature," here in the meaning of "relationship."
   padre — father   *figlio* — son
   madre — mother   *figlia* — daughter

3. *Cognome e nome di ogni membro di familia* — "surname and first name of each family member."
   cognome — surname   *ogni* — each
   nome — name   *membro* — member

4. *Comune* — "municipality, town," here *Castelfranco.*

5. *Data di nascità* — "date of birth"
   giorno — day   *mese* — month   *anno* — year

6. *Stato* — here means "nation or citizenship," can also mean "state, status, condition, profession."

PROVINCIÀ DI BENEVENTO CIRCONDARIO DI S. BARTOLOMEO IN GALDO

MUNICIPIO di CASTELFRANCO in MISCANO

Attenzione di famiglia di Petruccelli
Fedele fu Francesco Saverio

N.° d'ordine	Qualità	Cognome e nome di ogni membro di famiglia	Comune	Data di nascita			Stato
				Giorno	mese	anno	
1	padre	Petruccelli Fedele fu Fran. Sav.	Castelfranco	26	Dicembre	1858	Italia
2	madre	Buccio M.ª Lucia di Leonardi	id	2	Gennaio	1869	"
3	figlia	Petruccelli M.ª Rosa di Fedele	id	15	Gennaio	1894	"
4	figlio	Petruccelli Giovanni di Fedele	id	20	luglio	1898	"
5	figlia	Petruccelli M.ª Michela di Fedele	id	15	aprile	1901	"
6	figlia	Petruccelli Maria di Fedele	id	1	maggio	1904	"

Castelfranco in Miscano 22 febbraio 1913

Il Sindaco

A Berina

Document #5: Italian Passport, Booklet Format

Il presente passaporto consta di venti pagine
 Translation: The present passport consists of twenty pages

In nome di sua maestà Vittorio Emanuele III per grazie di Dio e per volontà della nazione Re d'Italia
 Translation: In the Name of His Majesty Vittorio Emanuele III, by the grace of God and the will of the nation, King of Italy

rilasciato a Marino, Angela, moglie di Carta, Francesco
rilasciato a — "issued to"
moglie di — "wife of"
 (If issued to a married female, her married name would appear here. In some cases the passport official entered **maritata,** *married to* or **vedova** *widow.*)
 Translation: Issued to Angela Marino, wife of Francesco Carta...

figlia di fu Carmelo e di fu Garofalo, Maria
 Translation: daughter of the deceased Carmelo and of the deceased Maria Garofalo...

nata a Melilli
il 31 ottobre 1865
residente a Melilli
in provincia di Siracusa
di condizione casalinga
 nata a — "born in"
 residente a — "residing in"

in provincia di — "in the province of"
di condizione — (the occupation appears here)
 Translation: born in Melilli on 31 October 1865, residing in Melilli in the province of Siracusa, by occupation a domestic.

(Page 2)

Connotati del Titolare del Passaporto (Description of the bearer of the passport)

statura m. 1.52	height: 1.52 m.	*baffi* —	moustache: —
età anni: 40	age: 40 years	*colorito naturale*	complexion: natural
fronte regolare	forehead: normal	*corporatura*	physique, body size:
occhi cerulei	eyes: blue	*regolare*	normal
naso affilato	nose: pointed	*segni particolari*	distinguishing
bocca regolare	mouth: normal	*due piccole*	marks: 2 small
capelli castani	hair: brown	*cicatrice*	scars on forehead
barba —	beard: —	*alla fronte*	

Firma del titolare — *signature of the bearer.* (Other possibilities here: *illeterato* or *analfabeta,* which mean "illiterate.")

Connotati del Titolare del Passaporto

Statura m. *1.72*

Età *anni 40*

Fronte *regolare*

Occhi *cerulei*

Naso *affilato*

Bocca *regolare*

Capelli *castani*

Barba *—*

Baffi *—*

Colorito *naturale*

Corporatura *regolare*

Segni particolari *[illegible]*
[illegible] alla fronte

FIRMA DEL TITOLARE

....

Il presente passaporto è rilasciato per (1) *Middletown (New-York) per raggiungere il marito colà residente*

ed è valide (2) *per anni tre*

(3) *Rilasciato gratuitamente a norma dell'articolo 6 comma 4° del R° Decreto 31 gennaio 1901. Siracusa 24 Dicembre 1905. Il Prefetto [signature]*

... ti di destinazione.
...oni; ovvero *fino al 1° aprile* (per gli inscritti
...ra, o *1° gennaio* per gli inscritti di leva ma-
...anno .... (art. 5, comma 2°, del regio decreto
31 gennaio 1901).

(3) Luogo per l'apposizione della marca speciale (o per la dichiarazione che il passaporto viene *Rilasciato gratuitamente a norma dell'art. 6, comma 4°, del regio decreto 31 gennaio 1901*), bollo, data e firma dell'autorità che rilascia il passaporto. Se si tratta di passaporto rilasciato all'estero, in sostituzione della marca speciale l'ufiziale che lo rilascia annoterà, accanto al bollo, l'ammontare della tassa percetta.

(Page 3)

Il presente passaporto è rilasciato per (1) *Middletown/New York per raggiungere il marito colà residente*
  Translation: The present passport is issued for [travel to] Middletown/ New York/ to join her husband, resident there... [The family went to Middletown, Connecticut, by way of New York.]

ed è valide (2) *per anni tre*
  Translation: and is valid for three years.

Item (3) gives the legal basis for issuing the passport, and the date and place of issue are most frequently noted here. In this case the date and place are given on the last line above the provincial stamp, the fourth line of item (3): *Siracusa 24 Dicembre 1905.*

(Pages 4-5)

Persone che accompagnano il Titolare (Persons Accompanying the Bearer)

Surname and Name	Relation to the Bearer	Age	Place of birth	Observations
1. Carta, Maria di Francesco	daughter	6 years	Melilli	8 October 1897
2. Carta, Giovanna di Francesco	daughter	5 years	Melilli	7 January 1900
3. Carta, Salvatore di Francesco	son	3 years	Melilli	1 April 1902
4. Carta, Marianna di Francesco	daughter	1 year	Melilli	14 December 1904

Persone che accompagnano il Titolare (Art. 4 del R. Decreto 31 gennaio 1901).

COGNOME E NOME	Rapporto col Titolare	ETÀ	Luogo di nascita	Osservazioni
1 Carta Maria di Francesco	figlia	anni 6	Melilli	8 Ottobre 1897
2 Carta Giovanna di Francesco	figlia	anni 5	Melilli	7 gennaio 1900
3 Carta Salvatore di Francesco	figlio	anni 3	Melilli	1° Aprile 1902
4 Carta Mariana di Francesco	figlia	anni 1	Melilli	14 Dicembre 1904
5				
6				
7				

If the woman's maiden name is listed on page 1 with no accompanying explanatory details, it is here that her married surname can be discovered via the children's surnames.

Document #6: Long-form Birth Certificate

These documents were issued either on printed forms or totally handwritten in paragraph form. A sample is reproduced on the facing page.

Provincia di *Bari* **Circondario di** *Bari,* **Comune di** *Turi*

Translation: Province of Bari, district of Bari, Town of Turi (sometimes one will see **Municipio di** instead, "Municipality of").

I. Time and Creation of the Document

...**L'anno mill** *novecento quattro* **addì** *ventuno* **di** *Aprile* **a ore** *anti* **meridiane** *dieci* **e minuti — nella casa Comunale.**

addì — this day of

antimeridiane (fem. pl.) — morning, a.m.; *pomeridiane* — afternoon, p.m.

casa Comunale — town hall, local government office

Translation: In the year 1904, on the 21st day of April at ten a.m., at the Town Hall...

Provincia di _Bari_   Circondario di _Bari_

Comune di _Turi_

ATTO DI NASCITA DAL 1875 IN POI

L'anno mille _novecentoquattro_ addi _ventuno_

N. _79_ del Registro   di _Aprile_ a ore _anti_ meridiane _dieci_ e minuti _____

_____ nella casa Comunale.

Atto di nascita
(ESTRATTO)

Massimo
Rosa

Avanti di me _Cosimo Caporizzi Segretario Delegato dal Sinda_
_co ad_

Ufficiale dello Stato Civile del Comune di _Turi_

è compars_a_ _Renato Caterina_ di anni _trentotto_

(1) levatrice domiciliata in _Turi_ _____, la quale

mi ha dichiarato che alle ore _po_ meridiane _cinque_ e mi-

nuti _____ del di _venti_ del mese di _Aprile_ _____ nella

casa posta in _Via Forno Comunale_ al numero _31_

da _Cozzolongo Sebastiana moglie di Massimo Valerio_

ambo contadini domiciliati in Turi

è nato un bambino di sesso _femminile_ che _ella_ mi presenta,

e a cui da i nome di _Rosa_

A quanto sopra e a quest'atto sono stati presenti quali testimoni

Sabatelli Pietro di anni

cinquanta _(1) messo_ e _Renato Vito_

di anni _ventisei_ _(1) messo_

entrambi residenti in questo Comune.

La Dichiarante mi ha annunziata la nascita predetta per aver nella
sua indicata sua qualità prestato i passi dell'arte sua nell'atto del
parto e in luogo del marito della Cozzolongo il quale non ha potuto denun-
ziarla perché assente. Letto il presente atto agl'intervenuti, l'hanno questa meco
sottoscritto. La Dichiarante Renato Caterina, I testimoni Pietro Sabatelli
Vito Renato. L'Ufficiale dello Stato Civile firmato C. Caporizzi

N. _____ del registro d'introito di Segreteria.

Gratis ed in carta libera perché pover _l_ richiedente, giusto

certificato di nullatenenza di _____

Da servire per uso di _Amministrativo_

Rilasciato a richiesta di _R. Console di Hartford Conn_

Turi li _3_ del mese _Aprile_ 191_7_

Per estratto conforme

L'Ufficiale dello Stato Civile

M. Giordano

(1) S'indichi la profes-
sione o la condizione.

VISTO: per la localizzazione della firma
del Sig. _Cosimo Giordano_
Ufficiale dello Stato Civile
della Comune di Turi

Turi
4 Aprile 1917

IL PRETORE
Marchetti

II. Identification of the Town Clerk/Registrar of Vital Records
Avanti di me *Cosimo Caporizzi Segretario delegato dal Sindaco ad* **Ufficiale dello Stato Civile del Comune di** *Turi*

> *avanti di me* — before me
>
> **Translation:** Before me, Cosimo Caporizzi, the Secretary (clerk) delegated by the Mayor to [be] the Registrar of Vital Statistics of the town of Turi...

III. Identification of the Declarant
...è compars*a* *Lenata Caterina* **di anni** *trentotto, levatrice,* **domiciliat***a* **in Turi**

> *è comparso* (masc.), *comparsa* (fem.) — appeared (from *comparire,* to appear). In most cases the father of the child was the primary declarant. If he was unavailable, this duty was assumed by the midwife or by another relative.
>
> **Translation:** Caterina Lenata appeared, age 38 years, a midwife [the declarant's occupation usually appears here], residing in Turi...

IV. Declaration of the Time and Place of Birth
... *la* **quale mi ha dichiarato che alle ore** *po* **meridiane** *cinque* **e minuti —— del dì** *venti* **del mese di** *Aprile* **nella casa posta in** *Via Forno Comunale* **al numero** *31*

> *la quale* — who (if it's a male, the form is *il quale*)
>
> *ha dichiarato che* — has declared that (from the verb *dichiarare*)
>
> *alle ore pomeridiane cinque* — at the hour of 5 p.m. [*antimeridiane* — a. m.]
>
> *e minuti --* — and -- minutes [Some documents fill in the exact time, including minutes; this one does not.]
>
> *del dì venti* — on the twentieth day
>
> *del mese di Aprile* — of the month of April [Some documents have *del mese corrente,* "of the present month," if that is appropriate.]
>
> *nella casa posta in Via Forno Comunale al numero 31* — in the house situated on the Via Forno Comunale at number 31 [*al numero* is followed by the house number]
>
> **Translation:** who declared to me that at five o'clock in the afternoon on the 20th of April in the house situated on the Via Forno Comunale at number 31...

V. Identification of the Mother
...da *Cozzolongo, Sebastiana, moglie di Massimo, Valerio ambo contadini domiciliati in Turi*

> *ambo contadini* — both peasants
>
> *domiciliati in Turi* — residing in Turi [if the father is the declarant, the phrase *seco lui convivente,* "who lives with him," will often appear here]
>
> **Translation:** to Sebastiana Cozzolongo, wife of Valerio Massimo, both peasants residing in Turi...

VI. Identification of the Child's Sex and Name
...è nato un bambino di sesso *femminile* **che** *ella* **mi presenta, e a cui d***a* **il nom***e* **di** *Rosa*

> *è nato un bambino di sesso femminile* — was born a baby of the female sex [*maschile* or *mascolino* — masculine]
>
> *che ella mi presenta* — which she presented to me [if the declarant is male, it's *che egli...*]
>
> *e a cui da il nome di Rosa* — and to which [he/she] gives the name of Rosa [the expression is *dar il nome di -- a --,* "to give the name of -- to --"; if the child has more than one name the text will read *i nomi di --*]
>
> **Translation:** was born a baby of the female sex which she presented to me and to whom the name of Rosa is given...

VII. Identification of the Witnesses
A quanto sopra e a quest'atto sono stati presenti quali testimoni ...

> **Translation:** To the above and to this document the following were present as witnesses:...

The names of the witnesses, their occupations, places of residences, and other identifying information appears here. This is followed by bureaucratic remarks (usually of no genealogical value) by the certifying official.

Document #7: Short-form Birth Certificate

The document on the next page is a short-form Italian birth certificate. Many of the same terms and expressions are used as in the long-form, but the format is different enough to merit study.

Provincia di Siracusa, Circondario di Siracusa, Comune di Canicattini-Bagni
Translation: Province of Siracusa, District of Siracusa, Municipality of Canicattini-Bagni

Certificato di Nascità
Translation: Certificate of birth

Il sottoscritto Ufficiale dello Stato Civile del Comune suddetto CERTIFICA
    sottoscritto — undersigned
    Ufficiale dello Stato Civile — official, registrar of vital records
    del Comune suddetto — of the aforesaid town
    Translation: The undersigned official of vital statistics in the aforesaid town certifies...

Che dal registro degli atti di nascità
    registro degli atti di nascità — the registry of the records [*atto,* plural *atti* — act, record] of birth
    Translation: that from the registry of birth records...

del'anno mille *novecento tre* **serie - volume** *unico* **parte** *prima* *N° 37*
    anno — year   *serie* — series   *unico* — single, only   *parte* — part
    Translation: of the year 1903, series —, volume 1, part 1, No. 37...

risulta che (1) *Cavaliere Lucia* **figli** *a* **di** *Antonio* **e di** *Ciarcia Angela* **è nata**
    risulta che — [it] follows (states) that [from *risultar,* to result, follow, ensue, transpire]
    figlia — daughter ["son" would be *figlio*]
    è nata — was born [*nata* because the subject is feminine; if the child was a son, it would read *è nato*]
    Translation: it states that (1) Lucia Cavaliere, daughter of Antonio of of Angela Ciarcia was born...

il giorno *ventisette del mese di gennaio* **dell'anno mille** *novecentotre*
    il giorno ventisette — [on] the twenty-seventh day
    del mese di gennaio — of the month of January
    dell'anno mille novecentotre — of the year one thousand nine hundred three.
    Translation: ...on 27 January 1903...

Rilascia il presente in carta libera per uso scolastico
    rilascia — issues, is issued [from the verb *rilasciare*]
    in carta libera — on a separate sheet, as a free page
    per uso scolastico — for school usage [other possibilities here: *per uso di emigrazione,* "for use in
        emigration," *per uso di lavoro,* "for employment purposes," *per uso militare,* "for military use"]
    Translation: This document is issued separately for school usage.

PROVINCIA DI SIRACUSA   CIRCONDARIO DI SIRACUSA

COMUNE DI CANICATTINI - BAGNI   *Ca⁔*

Certificato di Nascita

Il sottoscritto Ufficiale dello Stato Civile del Comune suddetto

CERTIFICA

Che dal registro degli atti di nascita dell'anno mille *novecento tre*

_____ serie _____ volume *unico* parte *prima* N. *38*

risulta che (1) *Cavaliere Lucia* _____

figlia di *Antonino* _____ e di *Giarcia Angela* _____

_____ è nato il giorno *ventisette del mese di gennaio*

dell'anno mille *novecentotre* _____

Rilascio il presente in carta libera per uso scolastico _____

Canicattini - Bagni, li *13 Giugno* 1919

L'UFFICIALE DELLO STATO CIVILE

firma

– 94 –

Selected Vocabulary Terms

a — to; *a quanto sopra* — to all of the above; *a quest'atto* — to this document

accompagnato (from *accompagnare*) — accompany, travel with

addì — this day

affilato (from *affilare*) — sharp, sharpened

agosto — August

al — (= *a* + *il*) at, to the; *al numero 31* — at number 31

alla — at, to the (= *a* + *la*)

alla fronte — on the forehead

alle — (= *a* + *le*) at, to the; *alle ore cinque* — at 5 o'clock

ambo — both

analfabeta — illiterate

anno (plural *anni*): year

antimeridiane — a.m., in the morning

aprile — April

assessore — municipal magistrate

atto (plur. *atti*) — document

avanti — before, in the presence of; *avanti di me* — in my presence

baffi — moustache

bambino — baby

bandiera — flag

barba — beard

battesimo — baptism

biglietto — ticket

bocca — mouth

braccio — arm

capelli — hair

carta — card, map, paper

casa — home, house; *casa comunale* — Town Hall

casalinga — domestic (female)

castani — brown (e. g., hair)

celebrat (from *celebrare*) — celebrated

cento — hundred

certifica (from *certificare*) — certifies

certificato — certificate

cerulei — blue

che — which, who, that

cicatrice — scar

cinquanta — fifty

cinque — five

circondario — district

città — city

civile — civil; *stato civile* — Registry of Vital Statistics

classe — class

cognome — surname

col (= *con* + *il*) — with the

colà — with him

colore — color

colorito — coloring, complexion

comparso (from *comparire*) — appeared

comunale — communal, municipal; *casa comunale* — Town Hall

comune — town, community

con — with, by

condizione — condition, status

connotati — identifying marks, description

consta di — consists of

contadino — farmer, peasant

convivente — living with

corporatura — physique

corrente — current

cuccetta — berth

cui — (to) which, (to) whom

d' — abbreviation of *di*

da — from

dà (from *dar*) — gives

dal (= *da* + *il*) — from the; *dal registro* — from the registry

dar — to give; *dar il nome di ... a ...* — to give the name of ... to ...

data — date

decimo — tenth

degli (= *di* + *gli*) — of the; *degli atti di nascità* — from the birth records

del (= *di* + *il*) — from the

delegato — deputy, delegated

della (= *di* + *la*) — of the

dello (= *di* + *lo*) — of the

di — of; *di* contracts to *d'* before vowels

dicembre — December

dichiarato (from *dichiare*) — declared

diciannove — nineteen

diciasette — seventeen

diciotto — eighteen

dieci — ten

Dio — God

dodicesimo — twelfth

dodici — twelve

domenica — Sunday

domiciliato — residing at, in

due — two

due mila — two thousand

duecento — two hundred

e — and (becomes *ed* before vowels)

è — is, was; *è nato* — was born; *è rilasciato* — is issued

ed — and

ella — her

estratto — extract

età — age

famiglia — family

febbraio — February

femminile — feminine

figli — children

figlia — daughter

figlio — son

fronte — forehead; *alle fronte* — on the forehead

fu — deceased, late

genitori — parents

gennaio — January

geografia — geography

giorno — day

giovedì — Thursday

giugno — June

grazie — thanks, grace

hanno (from *avere*) — have; *hanno celebrato* — they have celebrated

il — the (masculine)

il quale — who

illeterato — illiterate

imbarco — embarkation

Italia — Italy

italiano — Italian

la — the (feminine)

la quale — who

letteraria proprietà — copyright

levatrice — midwife

libera — free, separate

luglio — July

lui — him

lunedì — Monday

luogo — place, site
madre — mother
maestà — majesty; *sua maestà* — His Majesty
maggio — May
maritata — married (to)
marito — husband
martedì — Tuesday
marzo — March
maschile — masculine
mascolino — masculine
matrimonio — matrimony, marriage
membro — member
mercoledì — Wednesday
mese — month
mille — thousand
minuti — minutes
moglie — spouse, wife
morte — death
morto — died
nascità — birth
nata — born (feminine)
nato — born (masculine)
naturale — natural, normal
nazione — nation
nell' (= *in* + *l'*) — in the
nella (= *in* + *la*) — in the
No. — (abbreviation of *numero*) — number
nome — name
non — not
nono — ninth
novanta — ninety
nove — nine
novecento — nine hundred; *novecentotre* — nine hundred three
novembre — November
numero — number
occhi — eyes
oggi — today
ogni — each, every
ordine — order; *numero d'ordine* — sequential number
ore — hour; *a ore antimeridiane dieci* — at ten o'clock in the morning
osservazioni — comments, notes
ottanta — eighty
ottavo — eighth
otto — eight
ottobre — October
padre — father

pagine — pages
parrochia — parish
parte — part, section
particolare — individual, particular
partirà (from *partire*) — will leave
passaporto — passport
passeggieri — passengers
per — through, by, via
persona — person (plural *persone*)
piccolo — small
pomeridiane — p.m., in the afternoon
porto — port
posto (fem. *posta*) — positioned, situated, located
presenta (from *presentare*) — presents, shows, introduces
presente — current, the one under discussion, present
primo (fem. *prima*) first
proprieta letteraria — copyright
provincia — province
quali — which, who
qualità — quality, relationship
quaranta — forty
quarto — fourth
quattordici — fourteen
quattro — four
quindici — fifteen
quinto — fifth
raggio — ray, beam
raggiungere — rejoin, catch up with
rapporto — relationship, report
razioni — rations, board
Re — king
regione — region
registro — registry
regolare — regular, normal
religioso — religious
residente a — residing at, living in
rilasciato (from *rilasciare*) — issued
risulta (from *risultar*) — [it] results, is evident, follows
sabato — Saturday
sbaglio — mistake
scalo — port of call
scolastico — scholastic
seco lui convivente — living with him

secondo — second
sedici — sixteen
segni — signs; *segni particolari* — distinguishing marks
sei — six
sessanta — sixty
sesso — sex, gender
sesto — sixth
settanta — seventy
sette — seven
settembre — September
settimo — seventh
signora — Mrs.
signore — Mr.
signorina — Miss
sindaco — mayor
situazione — situation, status
sono — [they] are
sopra — above
sottoscritto — above-written
sposato — married
stato — state, status
stato civile — civil registry
statura — height
sua — his
suddetto — above-mentioned
sul (= *su* + *il*) — on the; *sul vapore* — on the steamship
terzo (fem. *terza*) — third
testimonio — witness
titolare — bearer
toccando — stopping at, calling on
tre — three
tredici — thirteen
trenta — thirty
ufficiale — official
un — one, a
un milione — one million
undicesimo — eleventh
undici — eleven
unico — single, unique
uno — one
uso — use
vaccinato — vaccinated
valide — valid, in force
vapore — steamship
vedova — widow
vedovo — widower
venerdì — Friday
venti — twenty
ventidue — twenty-two
ventisette — twenty-seven
ventuno — twenty-one
via — road, street
volontà — will

Italian Personal Names

Listed below are some common Italian names that may not be readily recognizable to speakers of English. The list is not offered to encourage researchers to change an ancestor named "Giuseppe Verdi" into "Joe Green"; the idea is to present English equivalents of Italian names so that if Giuseppe Verdi had moved to the United States and changed his name for the more American-sounding "Joe Green," his descendants would have a chance at making the connection by seeing that "Joseph" is the English equivalent of "Giuseppe." Of course some Italian names have no real equivalent in English, e. g., equating "Giovanna" with "Joan" is a bit of a stretch.

Alessandro — Alexander
Alfredo — Alfred
Andrea — Andrew
Antonio — Anthony
Aroldo — Harold
Arrigo — Harry
Arturo — Arthur
Carlo — Charles
Carlotta — Charlotte
Corrado — Conrad
Costanza — Constance
Cristoforo — Christopher
Edoardo — Edward
Enrichetta — Henrietta
Enrico — Henry

Erberto — Herbert
Ermanno — Herman
Federico — Frederick
Filippo — Philip
Fiorenza — Florence
Francesca — Frances
Francesco — Francis
Giacobbe — Jacob
Giacomo — James
Giorgio — George
Giovanna — Jane, Jean, Joan
Giovanni — John
Giuliano — Julian
Giuseppe — Joseph
Gualtiero — Walter

Guglielmo — William
Leone — Leo
Luigi — Louis
Matteo — Matthew
Nicola — Nicholas
Orazio — Horace
Ottone — Otto
Paola — Paula
Paolo — Paul
Patrizio — Patrick
Pietro — Peter
Riccardo — Richard
Ugo — Hugo
Vincenzo — Vincent
Vittorio — Victor

The Latin Alphabet

Printed	Cursive
A, a	*A, a*
B, b	*B, b*
C, c	*C, c*
D, d	*D, d*
E, e	*E, e*
F, f	*F, f*
G, g	*G, g*
H, h	*H, h*
I, I	*I, i*
J, j	*J, j*
K, k	*K, k*
L, l	*L, l*
M, m	*M, m*
N, n	*N, n*
O, o	*O, o*
P, p	*P, p*
Q, q	*Q, q*
R, r	*R, r*
S, s	*S, s*
T, t	*T, t*
U, u	*U, u*
V, v	*V, v*
W, w	*W, w*
X, x	*X, x*
Y, y	*Y, y*
Z, z	*Z, z*

It should come as no surprise that the Latin alphabet is so similar to the alphabet used in English, any more than it is surprising when a father and son resemble each other: the alphabet used by the Romans and modified by scholars during the Middle Ages is the one English-speaking writers have used practically since English began to be a written language. A classical scholar will rightly object that Latin originally had a 23-letter alphabet, which only expanded to 26 letters in the Middle Ages when *I* became differentiated into *I* and *J*, and *V* differentiated into *U, V,* and *W.* But for genealogical purposes the distinction is not particularly important because most entries of genealogical significance were written in medieval Latin, after such innovations as separate *I* and *J* and *U, V,* and *W,* and the use of lower-case as well as upper-case letters, had become commonplace.

That *J* began as a variant of *I*, and *V* and *W* as variants of *U*, should be kept in mind, however. A great deal of confusion in the spelling of names has continued for centuries because of those letters; that confusion is partly responsible for variant spellings, for instance, of *Maria* as *Marja* or *Marya* or *Vincent* as *Wincenty* in Polish. Researchers should also be aware that historically the combinations æ and œ were both treated as characters in their own right, whereas in modern times the tendency has been to spell them simply as *ae* and *oe*, respectively, or just as *e*. The standard spelling of "encyclopedia" has still not completely conquered "encyclopædia," and one need not dig back very far in medical books to see not "fetus" but "fœtus."

Two systems of Latin pronunciation have been taught: the classical, based on analysis of ancient Latin, and Church Latin, which sounds more like Italian. The classical may be the more correct, but the Church version was almost certainly the one a clerk or cleric had in mind when filling out personal documents.

In Church Latin the vowels are much the same as in Italian: *a* as in "father," *e* approximately like the "a" in "late," *i* as in "machine," *o* as in "hope," and *u* as in "rude." Short vowels differ from long only in how long they are vocalized, somewhat like the difference between the *u* in "rude" and that in "put." When used as a vowel *y* is pronounced like the German *ü* or French *u*. The diphthongs *ae* and *oe* are pronounced like the "a" in "late," *au* sounds like the "ow" in "cow," *ei* like "ey" in "grey," *eu* like a combination of *e + u*, and *ui* either like "uey" in "Huey" or after *q-* as "wee" (*u* preceding a vowel generally sounds like our "w" — that's how the letters *v* and *w* originated).

Most consonants are pronounced more or less as in English. The *c* is hard as in "car" except before *e, i, ae,* and *oe*, when it's like the "ch" in "child"; *g* is hard as in "go" except before *e* and *i*, when it sounds like the "g" in "gentle" (*gn* is like the "ny" in "canyon"); *j* is pronounced like English "y," and *r* is trilled as in most Romance languages. The *s* is as in "say," but more like a "z" when between two vowels (e. g., *miser*). The combination *cc* sounds like a "ch" before *e* or *i*, otherwise like "-kk-." Latin *ch* is hard, pronounced like our "k"; before *e* or *i* a *gg* is like the "dj" in "adjective," otherwise is a doubled hard "g." The *ph* is pronounced like an "f," *sc* like the "sk" in "skin" except before *e* or *i*, when it sounds like the "sh" in "she."

There are other fine points of pronunciation, and the classical version is quite different; but for this book's purposes these remarks should suffice.

The Use of Latin in Genealogical Records

It might seem unlikely to find family records in Latin, since by the time such records began to be widely kept in most European countries the vernacular had begun to displace Latin as the language for record-keeping. But the Roman Catholic Church still used Latin as a matter of course for most proceedings, and its records of births, baptisms, marriages, and deaths are very often the main source of information available on relatives in the old country. Even when the records were filled out in both Latin and the vernacular, knowledge of Latin can be very handy because its terms are usually easy to figure out (so much of English vocabulary comes from Latin anyway) and undergo far less regional, dialectal, and orthographic variation than those of the native language. The records cited here are Catholic birth and baptismal records from several different countries. Readers can note for themselves the consistency of Latin vocabulary from one area to another, as opposed to the vastly different terms used in Italian or Polish or Ukrainian.

In dealing with Latin, close attention must be paid to the various forms of basic words. Latin is a highly inflected language, like the Slavic languages, and subtractions of endings and other modifications to names will have to be made to arrive at the nominative form of the name, i. e., the form one would find in the dictionary.

Document #1: Slovenian Birth Certificate

The certificate on the next page reflects the sometimes complicated situation of Europe's boundaries and political divisions. Issued by the Roman Catholic Church in Latin and in Italian, the official government language, the document originates in Slovenia, one of the republics of what used to be the country of Yugoslavia. Note the Italian and Slovene variants in the place names involved (e. g., *Vipacco* vs. *Vipava*). The document is not difficult to translate, and a comparison of Latin and Italian terms is instructive (the Italian terms, below enclosed in brackets, can be found under the Italian section).

[Diocesi:] *[illegible]* **Dioecesis:** *Ljubljana*
[Certificato di nascità] — **Testimonium nativitatis**
[Estratto del libro di nascità e di battesimo]
Extractus e libro natorum et baptizatorum *parochiae: Vipava (Vipacco)*
Tom. 17 pag. 137 No 6.
  dioecesis — "diocese"
  testimonium nativitatis — "certificate of birth" (*nativitatis,* from *nativitas*)
  extractus — "extract"
  e libro natorum et baptizatorum — "from the book *(liber)* of those born (*natorum,* from *natus*) and baptized"
    (*baptizatorum,* past passive participle of *baptizare,* "to baptize")
  parochiae — "of the parish" (from *parochia*)
  tom. ... pag. ... No. — abbreviations of *tomus,* "volume," *pagina,* "page," and *numerus,* "number"
  Translation — Diocese: Ljubljana; Birth Certificate; Extract from the book of births and baptisms of Vipava (Vipacco) parish.

[Anno, mese, e giorno della nascita/del battesimo] *Annus, mensis, dies nativitatis/baptismi*
  annus — "year"
  mensis — "month"
  dies — "day"
  baptismi — "of baptism"
  Translation — Year, month, day of birth/baptism: 3/5/1916.

[Luogo e comune della nascita] *Locus et comunitas nativitatis: Vipava, Num. 33*
  locus — "place"
  comunitas — "community"
  Translation — Place and community of birth: Vipava, No. 33.

[Nome e cognome] *Nomen et cognomen: Zofia Premrl*

[Legittimo,illegittimo] *Legitim., illegitim.: legitima*
  nomen — "first name"

Diocesi: ~~Gorizia~~
Dioecesis: *Ljubljana.*   Provincia

Nº *197d.*

Certificato di nascita - Testimonium nativitatis

Estratto dal libro di nascita e di battesimo *parochiae: Vipava (Vipacco)*
Extractus e libro natorum et baptizatorum

Tom. *17;* pag. *137;* Nº *6*

Anno, mese e giorno / Annus, mensis, dies	della nascita / nativitatis	*3./5. 1916.*
	del battesimo / baptismi	*3./5. 1916.*
Luogo e comune della nascita / Locus et comunitas nativitatis		*Vipava, Num. 33.*
Nome e cognome / Nomen et cognomen		*Zofia Premrl,*
Legittimo, illegittimo / Legitim., illegitim.		*legitima*
Nome, cognome, professione, origine	del padre / patris	*Alexander Premrl, possessor -*
Nomen, cognomen, conditio, origo	della madre / matris	*Francisca, nata Petrič.*
Padrini --- Patrini		*Antonius Skala, magister; Aloisia Premrl, uxor magistratus privati;*
Levatrice --- Obstetrix		*Victoria Resek.*
Sac. batt. --- Sac. bapt.		*Rudolf Kaps, Coop. parochialis*
Annotazioni --- Adnotationes		*— · —*

In fede di che, la firma di m. p. e timbro d'ufficio.
In quorum fidem subscriptio manu propria et sigillum officii.

Dall'ufficio parrocchiale *in Vipava, die 23./8. 1928.*
Ex officio parrocchiali

P.C.C.! Parochus: Ignatius Breitenberger

cognomen — "surname"

legitim. — abbrev. of *legitimus,* "legitimate" (*legitima* is the feminine form)

Translation — Given name and surname: Zofia Premrl, legitimate

[Nome, cognome, professione, origine del padre/della madre] Nomen, cognomen, conditio, origo patris/matris: *Alexander Premrl, possessor – Francisca, nata Petrič*

conditio — "profession"

origo — "origin"

patris — "of the father" (from *pater*)

matris — "of the mother" (from *mater*)

possessor — "landowner"

nata — "born, née" (*nata* is the feminine form, *natus* the masculine)

Translation — Name, surname, profession, origin of the father/mother: Alexander Premrl, landowner; Francisca née Petrič

[Padrini] Patrini: *Antonius Skala, magister; Aloisia Prmrl, uxor magistratus privati*

patrini — "godparents" (from *patrinus,* "godfather")

Translation — Godparents: Antonius Skala, teacher; Aloisia Premrl, wife of private magistrate

[Levatrice] Obstetrix: *Victoria Rešek; [Sac. batt.]* Sac. bapt.: *Rudolf Kapš, Coop. parochialis; [Annotazioni]* Adnotationes: —

obstetrix — "midwife"

Sac. Bapt. — presumably an abbreviation of *sacramentum baptismi,* "the sacrament of baptism"

parochialis — "parochial" (adj. formed from *parochia*)

adnotationes — "remarks, observations" (plur. of *adnotatio)*

cooperator — (literally "co-worker") "assistant pastor"

Translation — Midwife: Victoria Rešek; administering the Sacrament of Baptism Rudolf Kapš, assistant pastor.

[In fede di che, la firma di m. p. e. timbro d'ufficio] In quorum fidem subscriptio manu propria et sigillum officii. *[Dall'ufficio parrocchiale]* Ex officio parochiali in *Vipava, die 23/8.1928. Parochus: Ignatius Breitenberger*

in quorum fidem — "in assurance of which things" (*quorum* from *qui, quae, quod,* "who, which, that")

subscriptio — "signature"

manu propria — "[by my] own hand" (from *manus,* "hand")

sigillum officii — "seal of office"

officio — "office" (from *officium*)

parochiali — "parochial" (another form of *parochialis*)

parochus — "pastor"

Translation — In assurance of which [is] the signature in [my] own hand and the seal of office. From the parish office in Vipava, 23 August 1928. Pastor Ignatius Breitenberger.

Document #2: Polish Baptismal Certificate

The document reproduced on the next page is a birth and baptismal certificate filled out by the parish office of a church in Poland; so Latin forms of Polish names are prominent.

Respublica Polonia, **Dioecesis:** *Tarnów,* **Palatinatus:** *Rzeszów,* **Decanatus:** *Mielec* , **Districtus:** *Mielec,* **Parochia:** *Zgórsko* , **Nrus** *336/47,* **Testimonium Ortus et Baptismi**

Respublica Polonia — "the Republic of Poland"

palatinatus — "county"   districtus — "district"   decanatus — "deanery"

nrus — (abbreviation of *numerus*) "number"

testimonium — "deposition, certificate"

ortus — "origin, birth"

Translation — Republic of Poland, Tarnów Diocese, Rzeszów county, Mielec district, Mielec deanery, Zgórsko parish, number 336/47. Certificate of birth and baptism

Respublica Polonia

Palatinatus: _Rzeszów_   Nrus _336/49_   Dioecesis: _Tarnów_

Districtus _Mielec_   Decanatus: _Mielec_

Parochia: _Zgórsko_

TESTIMONIUM ORTUS ET BAPTISMI

Officium parochiale ecclesiae _in Zgórsko_ omnibus et singulis

quorum interest aut interesse poterit, praesentibus testatur, in libro metrices baptisatorum pro

pago Izbiska destinato, tomo _VI_ pag. _4_ Nro ser. _11_ sequentia

reperiri Anno Domini Millesimo ~~octingentesimo nonogesimo primo~~

hoc est _1891_ die _decima prima (11)_ mensis _Augusti (8)_

nat _a_ Platea: ___ et die _12/8 -1891_

ab: ___ R. D-no: _Josepho Lopatowski_ baptisat _a_ est:

Nomen baptisati	Religio	Sexus	Thorus	PARENTES		PATRINI	Adnotatio
				Pater	Mater		
Marianna	Rom-cathol.	femin.	legitim.	Josephus Kosiński et Joanne et Margaretha Deren	Anna et Joanne Midura et Helena Galica	Michael Midura Marianna Deren	Copula ta cum Josepho Lapa.

In quorum fidem hisce litteris sigillo ecclesiae munitis manu propia subscribo.

AB OFFICIO PAROCHIALI.

in Zgórsko die _17 . I_ 194_9_ anni.

Bronislaus Patys

parochus.

Typis T. Druku — Tarnoviae

Officium parochiale ecclesiae in Zgórsko omnibus et singulis quorum interest aut interesse poterit, praesentibus testatur

- *ecclesiae* — "of the church" (from *ecclesia*)
- *omnibus et singulis* — "to all and every [person]"
- *quorum interest aut interesse poterit* — "to whom it is or ever can be of interest" (*interesse* — to be of interest," *poterit* from *possum*, "to be able," and *quorum*, "of whom," from *qui*)
- *praesentibus testatur* — "by [these] presents attests" (from *praesens, praesentis*, "present document" and *testor*, "to attest")

Translation — The parish office of the church in Zgórsko attests by this document to each and all whom it does or will concern, that...

in libro metrices baptisatorum pro pago Izbiska destinato, tomo VI pag. 4 Nro ser. 11 sequentia reperiri Anno Domini Millesimo octingentesimo nonogesimo primo hoc est 1891 die decima prima (11) mensis Augusti (8) nata Platea ... et die 12/8-1891 ab: ... R. D-no: Josepho Łopatowski baptisata est:

- *in libro metrices baptisatorum* — "in the registry book of baptisms"
- *pro pago Izbiska destinato* — "established for the village *(pagus)* of Izbiska"
- *tomo VI pag.4 Nro ser. 11 sequentia reperiri* — "volume *(tomus)* VI, page *(pagina)* 4, number 11, the following [things] *(sequentia)* are to be found *(reperiri)*"
- *Anno Domini Millesimo octingentesimo nonogesimo primo hoc est 1891* — "in the year *(annus)* of the Lord *(dominus)* one thousand eight hundred ninety one, that is, 1891"
- *die decima prima mensis Augusti* — "on the eleventh day of the month of August"
- *nata Platea* — "was born on ... street" (*nata* is the feminine form, referring to a girl born; the street is left blank)
- *ab ... R. D-no Josepho Łopatowski baptisata est* — "was baptized by Rev. Józef (Josephus) Łopatowski"

Translation — ...in the registry book of baptisms designated for the village of Izbiska, vol. VI, page 4, number 11, the following can be found: that on 11 August 1891 on ... street was born, and on 12 August 1891 by Rev. Józef Łopatowski was baptized:... *[The name and other information on the girl born and baptized will be given in the chart following immediately hereafter.]*

Nomen baptisati: Marianna Religio: Rom-cathol. Sexus: femin. Thorus: legitim.
Parentes: Pater Josephus Kosinski ex Joanne et Margaretha Dereń Mater Anna ex Joanne Midura et Helena Galica
Patrini: Michael Midura Marianna Dereń
Adnotatio: Copulata cum Josepho Łapa

- *nomen baptisati* — "name of the baptized"   *sexus* — "sex"   *thorus* — "status"
- *parentes: pater...mater* — "parents: father...mother"
- *ex Joanne et Margaretha Dereń* — "[son of, literally "out of" *(ex)*] Joannus and Margaretha [née Dereń]." Since these names are obviously Polish, in translation they should be rendered in their Polish forms, *Józef, Jan*, etc., rather than these Latinized forms.
- *adnotatio* — "remark, observation"
- *copulata cum Josepho Lapa* — "married to" (literally "with") Josephus Lapa

Translation — Name of the one baptized, Marianna; Religion, Roman Catholic; Sex, female; Status, legitimate; Parents: Father, Józef Kosiński, son of Jan and Małgorzata née Dereń; Mother, Anna, daughter of Jan Midura and Helena Galica; Godparents: Michał Midura, Marianna Dereń; Remarks: married to Józef Łapa

In quorum fidem hisce litteris sigillo ecclesiae munitis manu propia subscribo. AB OFFICIO PAROCHIALI in Zgorsko die 17 I. 1949 anni. Bronislaus Pałys, parochus.

- *in quorum fidem* — "in assurance of which"
- *hisce litteris sigillo ecclesiae munitis* — "this document (literally "these letters"), fortified *(munitis)* with the church's seal"
- *manu propia subscribo* — "I sign with my own hand" (presumably *propia* is a misspelling of *propria*, which means "one's own")
- *ab officio parochiali* — "from the parish office"

Translation — In token of which I sign this document, bearing the church's seal, with my own hand. From the parish office in Zgórsko, date 17 January 1949. Bronisław Pałys, pastor.

Document #3: A Slovak Baptismal Certificate

The baptismal certificate on page 105 deals with Slovak persons living in territory then part of Hungary (now Slovakia, i. e., *Szepes* = is the Spiš [Spisz/Zips] region). You may wish to use it as an exercise in translation: several vocabulary terms are listed with which you should be able to decipher the pertinent facts. A translation follows against which you can check your version.

lecturis salutem in Domino! — "To readers, greeting in the Lord!" It's generally inadvisable to devote much time and energy to deciphering legalese and frills such as this. Concentrate on the facts, which are almost always identifiable because they're written in by hand.

infrascriptus — the undersigned

praesentium vigore — on the strength *(vigore)* of these presents *(praesentium).*

fidem facio — "I certify," literally "I make faith." A similar usage of the word *fides* (accusative *fidem*) appears in the expression "bona fide," literally "of/by good faith."

Hrustinensis — an adjective meaning "of the town of Hruštin." Adjectives are often formed from the names of towns by adding the suffix *-ensis* to the town's name.

Ecclesiae ad S. Joannem Baptistam — "the Church to St. John *(Joannis)* the Baptist." In English this would be "the Church of St. John the Baptist" or just "St. John the Baptist Church."

Comitatu Arvaensi — "Árva county." *Comitatus* is thought to be the Latin word from which English "county" derives. *Arvaensis* is another example of *-ensis* tacked onto a placename.

nongentesimo — nine hundred

Nrus. currens — "sequential number," literally "running number."

nomen baptisati — "name of the baptized one"

col. — abbreviation of *colonus,* "farmer, peasant"

locus originis — "place of origin"

nomen baptisantis — "name of the one performing the baptism"

In cuius plenam fidem — "In full faith of which" (*cuius* from *qui, quae, quod,* "who, which, that")

praesentes, propria manu subscriptas, et officio Ecclesiae Sigillo roboratas, litteras testimoniales — "I have issued (*extradedi,* literally "I have given out") this (*praesentes*) certificate (the plural of *littera* is used to mean "document," and *litteras testimoniales* = "certificate") letters, signed *(subscriptas)* by my own hand and strengthened *(roboratas)* with the Church's official Seal.

Translation

"Readers, Greetings in the Lord!

I, the undersigned, certify by these presents that in the Baptismal Registry of the parochial church of St. John the Baptist in Hruštin, in Szepes diocese, Árva county, the following items are found amid the entries: A.D. 1900, Vol. III, page 93.

Entry No. 43

Year and Day of Birth: 1900, 6 May

Year and Day of Baptism: 1900, 6 May

Name, Sex, Status of the Baptized: Stephanus, masc., leg.

First Name and Surname of the Parents, their Status, Religion, and Place of Origin: Jacobus Marek, Rom. Cath., peasant, Erdödka; Theresia Dymak, Rom. Cath., peasant, Hruštin

Place of Residence, with the House Number: Hruštin, Number 64.

First Name and Surname of the Godparents, their Status, Religion, and Place of Origin: Thomas Smidzsar; Johanna Kutlik, Rom. Cath., peasant, Hruštin

Name of the Baptizer: Eugenius Papp, local parish assistant

In full assurance of which I have issued this certificate, signed with my own hand and validated with the Church's official seal. 5 February 1904, Augustinus Klinovszki, parish priest.

Document #4: A Ukrainian Baptismal Certificate

The document on page 107 was issued by a Greek Catholic parish in the Archdiocese of Lwów, and presents another problem researchers may encounter — that of the use of different languages to identify place names. The archdiocesan city's name, for example, is called *Lvov* in English, *Lwów* in Polish, Львів in Ukrainian,

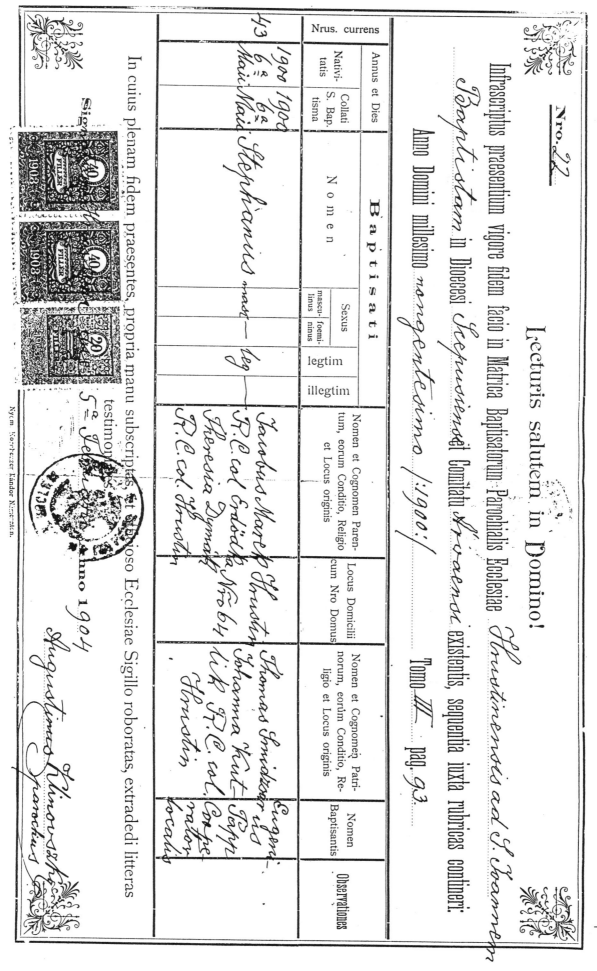

Nro. 22

Lecturis salutem in Domino!

Infrascriptus praesentium vigore fidem facio in Matrica Baptisatorum Parochialis Ecclesiae *Christinensis ad S. Joannem Baptistam* in Dioecesi *Csanadiensi* Comitatu *Torontal* existentis, sequentia iuxta rubricas contineri:

Anno Domini millesimo nongentesimo (:1900:) .... Tomo *III* pag. *93*.

Nrus. currens	Annus et Dies		Baptisati					Nomen et Cognomen Parentum, eorum Conditio, Religio et Locus originis	Locus Domicilii cum Nro Domus	Nomen et Cognomen Patrinorum, eorum Conditio, Religio et Locus originis	Nomen Baptisantis	Observationes
	Nativitatis	Collati S. Baptismatis	Nomen		Sexus		legtim	illegtim					
				masculinus	foemininus							
43	1900 6ᵃ Maii	1900 6ᵃ Maii	Stephanus	masc —		leg		Jacobus Martej Christ. R.C. col Erdödj A/No 64 Theresia Dymaj R.C. col. Christ	Thomas Smrdovszius R.C. col Corte nator localis	Johanna Kut R.C. col Christ	Augustinus Klimovszkÿ Parochus	

In cuius plenam fidem praesentes, propria manu subscriptas, et pioso Ecclesiae Sigillo roboratas, extradedi litteras testimoniales.

Sig... 5ᵃ Februarii Anno 1904

Augustinus Klimovszkÿ
Parochus

Львов in Russian, *Leopolis* in Latin, and was called *Lemberg* under the Austrians, when it was the capital of the province of Galicia. The parish name, "Manajów," is written in Polish orthography, but the stamp at the bottom shows the Ukrainian version, "МАНАЄВ."

While the Latin terminology is surely of primary importance for anyone reading this section of the book, the equivalent Ukrainian terms will be given alongside the Latin ones for the benefit of any readers interested in Ukrainian; they are not translated separately, but there is little need because they are almost all exact literal translations of the Latin terms. There should be no confusing the Latin and Ukrainian terms, since the latter are given in brackets and are written in Cyrillic. All the handwritten material in the certificate is in Latin; Ukrainian words appear only in the printed sections of the form.

Imperium Austriae [Держава Австрийска] — "Empire of Austria"
Regnum Galiciae [королество Галичини] — "Kingdom (or Crownland) of Galicia"
Districtus: [Повіт] *Zborów* — "District: Zborów"
Numerus [Число] — "Number"
Circulus: [Округ] *A[rch]dioecesis: Leopolitana* — "Region: Archdiocese of Lwów"
Decanatus: [Деканат] *Olejoviensis* — "Deanery: Olejów"
Parochia: [Парохия] *Manajów* — "Parish: Manajów"

Testimonium baptismi [СВІДОЦТВО КРЕЩЕНІЯ] — "Baptismal Certificate"

Ex parte Officii parochialis r. gr. cath. *in Manajów* **Ecclesiae** *ad [illegible]* B. V. Mariae
[Від уряду парохияльного гр. кат.] *in Manajów* **[Церкви]** *ad [illegible]* B. V. Mariae
   Translation — On the part of the parish office of the Greek Catholic rite in Manajów, of the church of the Blessed Virgin Mary...

notum testatumque fit in libris metricalibus natorum hujus Ecclesiae, Tom. *V* **pag.** *162* **reperiri sequentia:**
[заявляє ся що в книгах метрик рожденних тоїже Церкви, том *V* **стр.** *162* **находить ся слідуюче:]**
   notum testatumque fit — "it is made known and attested [that]"
   libris metricalibus natorum — ablative case (after the preposition *in*) of *libri metricales natorum*, "registry books of births"
   hujus Ecclesiae — "of this Church"
   Tom. V pag. 162 — "volume V, page 162"
   reperiri sequentia — "[is] to be found the following:"
   Translation — It is announced and attested that in the registry of births of this church, volume V, page 162, the following is to be found: ...

Annus, mensis et dies nativitatis baptismi et cofirmationis [Рік місяць і день рожденія, крещенія і міропомазаня] — "year, month and day of birth, baptism, and confirmation" [*Cofirmationis* is a misprint, it should be *confirmationis*]. Note: unlike Roman Catholics, Greek Catholic and Orthodox practice is to administer baptism and confirmation simultaneously.

Anno Millesimo [Року Божого Тисяць] *nongentesimo quinto (27/3/1905) die 27o Martii nata, baptisata et confirmata* — "In the year [of our Lord] one thousand nine hundred and five, 27th of March, was born, baptized, and confirmed"
Nr. domus [Число дому] *57* — "House number 57"
Nomen [Імя] *Anna* — "Name: Anna"
Religio [Віроисповіданє] *Graeco-catholica* — "Religion: Greek Catholic"
Sexus [Поль] *Feminini* — Sex: female
Thori [Ложа] *Legitimi* — Status: legitimate

Parentes et conditio [Родители і состоянє] — *Pater: Theodorus Jaworski legitimus filius Petri et Mariae Kukurudza agricolarum in Manajów. Mater: Sophia filia legitima Onuphrii Tataryn et Annae Luciw agricolarum in Olejów.*
   parentes et conditio — parents and [their] status (condition/occupation)
   filius Petri et Mariae Kukurudza, agricolarum — son of Peter and Maria Kukurudza, farmers (*Petri* is the genitive of *Petrus*, and *Mariae* the genitive of *Maria*)

Держава Австрийска.
Imperium Austriae.

Королество Галичини.
Regnum Galiciae.

Повіт:
Districtus: Zborów.

Число 120/1914
Numerus /1914.

Округ:
Archidioecesis. Leopoliana.

Деканат:
Decanatus: Olejoviensis.

Парохія:
Parochia: Manajów.

СВІДОЦТВО КРЕЩЕНІЯ.
Testimonium baptismi.

Від уряду парохіяльного гр. кат. в Манаjôw Церкви ad Assumpt. B. V. Mariae
Ex parte Officii parochialis r. gr. cath. Ecclesiae

заявляє ся, що в книгах метрик рождених тоже Церкви, том V стр. находить ся слідуюче:
notum testatumque fit in libris metricalibus natorum hujus Ecclesiae. Tom V. pag. 162. reperiri sequentia:

Рік місяць і день рожденія, крещенія і мірономазанія / Annus, mensis et dies nativitas baptismi et cofirmationis	Число дому / Nr. domus	ІМЯ / Nomen	Віроісповідане / Religio	Поль / Sexus	Ложа / Thori	Родителі і состояне / Parentes et conditio	Куми и состояне / Patrini et conditio
Року Божого Тисяч.	57.	Анна	Graeco-catholica	Feminini	Legitimi	Pater: Theodorus Jaworski legitimus filius pd. Petri et Mariae Kukurudza agricolarum in Manajów. Mater: Sophia, filia legitima Onuphrii Tataryn et Annae Eneir, agricolarum in Olejów. Agricolae.	☩ Nicolaus Kucharyszyn. ☩ Anna Cosmae Bodnar uxor. Agricolae loci.
Anno Millesimo nongentesimo quinto /27/3 1905./ die 27ª Martii nata, baptisata et confirmata.							

Obstetrix: Tatianna Budny K. — Baptisavit et confirmavit: Rev. Dom. Gregorius Kosar, parochus e Ratyszcze. Inscripsit: Rev. Dom. Philemon Ternawski, parochus in Manajów.

Котре свідоцтво власною рукою підписую і печатію церковною ствёрджую.

Quas testimoniales manu propria subscribo sigilloque Ecclesiatico corroboro.

Manajów дня 22ª Julii Р. Б. 1914.
die А. D. 1914.

S. Spiszerun
parochus loci. —

filia Onuphrii Tataryn et Annae Luciw — daughter of Onuphrius Tataryn and of Anna Luciw

Translation — Parents and status: Father, Teodor Jaworski, legitimate son of Piotr and Maria Kukurudza, farmers in Manajów; Mother: Sophia, legitimate daughter of Onufry Tataryn and Anna Luciw, farmers in Olejów. [Notice that names given in Latin are converted to a vernacular language to arrive at an individual's proper given name. Thus "Teodor Jaworski" surely was never known as "Teodorus" except in these Latin documents; the same is true of Onufry Tataryn, surely never called "Onuphrius" outside of a church.]

Patrini et conditio [Куми и состоянє] † *Nicolaus Kucharyczyk* † *Anna Cosmae Bodnar uxor Agricolae loci. Obstetrix Tatianna Budnyk*

    patrini — godparents
    uxor — wife
    agricolae loci — farmers of the area (*loci* from *locus* — place, site, area)
    obstetrix Tatianna Budnyk — midwife Tatianna Budnyk
    Translation — Godparents and status: Mikołaj Kucharczyk; Anna, wife of Kosma Bodnar; local farmers.

Baptisavit et confirmavit: Rev. dom. Gregorius Kosar, parochus e Ratyszcze. Inscripsit: Rev. dom. Philemon Tarnawski, parochus in Manajów.

    baptisavit ... confirmavit ...inscripsit — baptized ... confirmed ...entered (or "wrote the entry")
    Translation — Baptism and confirmation administered by: Rev. Grygori Kosar, parish priest from Ratyszcze. Entry made by: Rev. Philemon Tarnawski, parish priest in Manajów.

Quas testimoniales manu propria subscribo sigilloque Ecclesiatico corrobro. *Manajów*
[Котре свідоцтво власною рукою підписую і речатню церковною срверджую.]
die [/дня] *22o Julii* **A.D. [Р. Б.]** *1914*.

    quas testimoniales — which certificate (accusative, i. e., this is the direct object of a subsequent verb, *subscribo*) [in Ukrainian, the verb is *підписую*], "I sign," and *котре свідоцтво*, "which certificate," is the direct object]
    manu propria — by [my] own hand (*manu* from *manus,* "hand"; in Ukrainian *рукою* is the instrumental of the word for hand and *власною* the adjective "[my] own").
    sigilloque Ecclesiastico — *-que* is a suffix that means "and," and the ablative of *sigillum,* "seal," is used instrumentally: "with the seal [*Ecclesiastico* — "of the church"]
    corrobro — I corroborate, I certify
    Translation — Which certificate I sign with my own hand and certify with the Church's seal.

Selected Vocabulary Terms

It is simply beyond the scope of this book to acquaint the reader with the complexities of grammar in highly inflected languages such as Latin; to do so would fill a thick volume, and many such volumes already exist. But changes in words' endings and forms play such an important role in translating Latin that grammatical considerations cannot be completely ignored. The most reasonable compromise is to suggest just enough of the grammar to allow readers to decipher pertinent facts, but not so much as to overwhelm people who have no interest in learning Latin. Fortunately, context often aids a researcher; it is generally not too difficult to guess whether a given word or phrase has something to do with a name, a date, a place, an occupation, a birth, a marriage, or a death, which cuts down the number of possible interpretations to a manageable number.

Latin nouns, adjectives, and pronouns change their endings to reflect changes in meaning, and there are a number of different patterns to these changes. Many textbooks on Latin indicate the pattern a given noun follows by showing the noun's nominative form (used when the word is the subject of a predicate) and genitive form (that used to show possession). This approach has much to recommend it — especially since it will acquaint readers with a convention they'll encounter in other reference works — and it is used in this word-list; for example, the entries for *pater*, "father," and *liber*, "book," read:

    pater, patris — (masc. noun) father   *liber, libri* — (masc. noun) book

This means that the first word's form is *pater* when it is used as the subject of a predicate, and that other forms are made by adding suffixes to the root *patr-* (some of those other forms are *patri, patrem, patres, patrium, patribus*). Similarly, the nominative of the word for "book" is *liber*, "of the book" is *libri*, "in the book" is *in libro*, and so on.

If one sees both the nominative and genitive singular forms of a noun, one can usually recognize almost any other form one comes across; and context will usually suggest exactly how the noun is used.

Adjectives also are easy to translate once their basic form is recognized. Most Latin adjectives follow different patterns of change depending on whether the noun they modify is masculine, feminine, or neuter in gender (gender is not the same as sex; the Latin names of many inanimate objects are masculine or feminine in gender); "my father" is *meus pater,* "my mother" is *mea mater,* "the new book" is *novus liber,* and so on (for simplicity's sake, only nominative forms are given here, but different forms are used for different grammatical cases). In the word list, adjectives are given in the nominative masculine singular form; in a few cases the genitive singular is also given when that form is helpful, e. g. *currens, currentis.*

As for pronouns, they, too, follow declensional patterns, but in this list the forms most frequently encountered are simply given with reference to the nominative form under which they're to be found in dictionaries.

Verbs cannot be summarized simply, but a few instructive points can be made. Latin verbs, like English verbs, have "principal parts," words regarded as different forms of the same verb from which one constructs various tenses; just as English has "write, wrote, written," Latin has *scribeo, scribere, scripsi, scriptus.* The form one will usually find in the dictionary is the second, the infinitive, usually ending in *-are, -ere,* or *-ire.* This word-list gives a number of verb forms most often encountered — especially participles such as *scriptus,* "written," or *baptisans,* "baptizing" — but there is not enough room for much more than that. Fortunately, the format of many documents is a chart or list, and these generally feature nouns or adjectives, with relatively little usage of verb forms.

This short summary should suffice to let readers use the word-list profitably. Of course those wishing to develop a fuller comprehension of Latin should acquire a good dictionary and a book on grammar.

7bris — in September

8bris — in October

9bris — in November

10bris — in December

ab — (prep.) from

ad — (prep.) to

adnotatio, adnotationis — (fem. noun) remark

aetas, aetatis — (fem. noun) age

agricola, agricolae — (masc. noun) farmer

annus, anni — (masc. noun) year; *anno* — in the year

apothecarius, apothecarii — (masc. noun) shopkeeper

Aprilis, Aprilis — April

Augustus, Augusti — August

auster, austri — (masc. noun) South; the south wind

australis — (adj.) southern

aut — (conj.) or

avia, aviae — (fem. noun) grandmother

avunculus, avunculi — (masc. noun) maternal uncle

avus, avi — (masc. noun) grandfather

baptisans, baptisantis — (masc. noun) the one performing baptism

baptismus, baptismi — (masc. noun) baptism

baptizatus — (part. from *baptizare*) baptized

baptizavit — he has baptized

barba, barbae — (fem. noun) beard

caelibis — (adj.) unmarried

caelum, caeli — (neut. noun) heaven

catholicus — (adj.) Catholic

caupo, cauponis — (masc. noun) innkeeper

centesimus — (adj.) one hundredth

centum — (numeral) one hundred

circulus, circuli — (masc. noun) region (administrative division)

civis, civis — (masc. or fem. noun) citizen

civitas, civitatis — (fem. noun) citizenship

cognomen, cognominis — (neut. noun) surname

colonus, coloni — (masc. noun) peasant

color, coloris — (masc. noun) color

comitatus, comitatus — (masc. noun) county

comunitas, comunitatis — (fem. noun) community

conditio, conditionis — (fem. noun) condition, occupation

confirmatio, confirmationis — (fem. noun) confirmation

confirmatus — (part.) confirmed

confirmavit — [he, she] has confirmed

coniugatus — (part.) married, spouse

cooperator, cooperatoris — (masc. noun) parish assistant, priest

copulatus — (part.) married (*cum* = to)

coram — (prep.) before, in the presence of

corrobro — I corroborate, confirm, strengthen

cuius — of which (from *qui*)

cum — (prep.) with

currens, currentis — (part.) running, current, sequential

decanatus — (masc. noun) deanery

decem — (numeral) ten

December, Decembris — December

decimus — (adj.) tenth; *decimus primus* — eleventh

defunctus — (adj.) deceased

destinatus — (part.) prescribed, established

Deus, Dei — (masc. noun) God

dies — (masc. or fem. noun) day, date; *die* — on the day

dioecesis, dioecesis — (fem. noun) diocese

districtus — (masc. noun) district

domicilium, domicilii — (neut. noun) residence

dominus, domini — (masc. noun) lord, landlord

domus, domus or *domi* — (fem. noun) home, house

duo, duae — (numeral) two

duodecim — (numeral) twelve

duodevicesimus — (adj.) eighteenth

duodeviginti — (numer.) eighteen

e — (prep.) from (same as *ex*)

ecclesia, ecclesiae — (fem. noun) church

ego — (pron.) I

ejus — (pron.) his, her, its

ejusdem — the same day (literally "of the same," from *idem*)

et — (conj.) and

ex — (prep.) from; *ex loco* — from the place, from the area

extractus — extract

faber — (adj.) skilled; (as a noun) smith; *faber ferra[rius]* — blacksmith; *faber tignarius* — carpenter; *faber muranus* — bricklayer, mason

facere — (v.) to make, do; *facio* — I make

familia, familiae — (fem. noun) family

famula, famulae — (fem. noun), or *famulus, famuli* — (masc. noun) farm worker, servant

Februarius, Februarii — February

femininus — (adj.) feminine

fides, fidei — (fem. noun) faith, guarantee, assurance

filia, filiae — (fem. noun) daughter

filius, filii — (masc. noun) son

fit — it became (from verb *fieri*)

flumen, fluminis — (neut. noun) river

frater, fratris — (masc. noun) brother

graecus, graeci — (adj. also used as noun) Greek; *graeco-catholicus* — Greek Catholic

haec — (adj. or pron.) this (from *hic*)

hic — (adj. or pron.) this

hisce — (form of *hic*) [to, by] these

hoc — this (from *hic*)

hora, horae — (fem. noun) hour

hujus — of this (from *hic*)

idem — (adj. or pron.) the same

illegitimus — (adj.) illegitimate

imperium, imperii — (neut. noun) empire

in — (prep.) in, to

infrascriptus — (part.) undersigned

inquilinus, inquilini — (masc. noun) farm laborer, resident, inhabitant

inscripsit — [he, she] has inscribed, made this entry

interest — (from *interesse*) is of interest

Januarius, Januarii — January

Judaeus, Judaei — (masc. noun) Jew

Julius, Julii — July

Junius, Junii — June

juvenis, juvenis — (adj.) youth; (noun) groom

laborus — (masc. noun) laborer

lanius, lanii — (masc. noun) butcher

legitimus — (adj.) legitimate

levantes — (plur. noun) godparents

lex, legis — (fem. noun) law

liber, libri — (masc. noun) book; *e libro* — from the book; *in libro* — in the book, record; *liber baptizatorum* — baptism register; *liber matrimoniorum* — marriage register

liberi, liberorum — (masc. plur. noun.) children

libertus, liberti — (masc. noun) freedman

lignarius, lignarii — (masc. noun) carpenter

littera, litterae — (fem. noun) letter; *litterae, litterarum* (plur.) document, epistles, books, literary works

localis — (adj.) local

locus, loci — (masc. noun) place; *locus nativitatis* — place of birth; *locus originis* — place of origin

magister, magistri — (masc. noun) teacher, master

magnus — (adj.) great, large

Maius, Maii — May

manus, manus — (fem. noun) hand; *propria manu* — by [my, his, etc.] own hand

maritus, mariti — (masc. noun) husband

Martius, Martii — March

masculus — (adj.) male, masculine

mater, matris — (fem. noun) mother

matrica, matricae — (fem. noun) registry

matrimonium, matrimonii — (neut. noun) marriage

matrina, matrinae — (fem. noun) godmother

me — (pron., from *ego*) me

mensis, mensis — (masc. noun) month

mercator, mercatoris — (masc. noun) merchant

meridianus — (adj.) noon; southern

meridies, meridiei — (fem. noun) midday; south; *post meridiem* — in the afternoon

metricalis — (adj.) registry

metrices — (plur. noun) registry

meus — (poss. adj.) my

mihi — (pron., from *ego*) to me

miles, militis — (masc. noun) soldier

mille — (numeral) one thousand

millesimus — (adj.) one thousand

molitor, molitoris — (masc. noun) builder, miller

mons, montis — (masc. noun) mountain

morbus, morbi — (masc. noun) sickness, disease

mors, mortis — (fem. noun) death

mortuus — (part. from *mori*) dead; *mortuus est* — died, has died

munitus — (part.) provided, fortified

nativitas, nativitatis — (fem. noun) birth; *locus nativitatis* — place of birth

natus — (part. from *nasci*) born; *natus est* — was born

nepos, nepotis — (masc. noun) grandson

neptis, neptis — (fem. noun) granddaughter

nobis — (pron., < *nos*) [to, by] us

nomen, nominis — (neut. noun) first name

non — (adv.) not

nonagesimus — (adj.) ninetieth

nonaginta — (numeral) ninety

nongentesimus — (adj.) nine hundred

nongenti — (numeral) nine hundred

nonus — (adj.) ninth

nos — (pron.) we, us

noster, nostra, nostrum — (poss. adj.) our; *Pater Noster* — Our Father

notus — (part. from *nosco*) known

novem — (numeral) nine

November, Novembris — November

novus — (adj.) new

nox, noctis — (fem. noun) night

nrus, abbrev. of *numerus*, q. v.

numerus, numeri — (masc. noun) number

observatio, observationis — (fem. noun) observation

obstetrix, obstetricis — (fem. noun) midwife

occidens, occidentis — (masc. noun) West

occidentalis — (adj.) western

octagesimus — (adj.) eightieth

octavus — (adj.) eighth

octingentesimus — (adj.) eight hundredth

octingenti — (numeral) eight hundred

octo — (numeral) eight

October, Octobris — October

octoginta — (numeral) eighty

oculus, oculi — (masc. noun) eye

officium, officii — (neut. noun) office

omnibus — (adj., from *omnis*) to, by all

omnis — (adj.) all

operarius, operarii — (masc. noun) laborer, worker

opilio, opilionis — (masc. noun) shephered

oppidanus, oppidani — town resident

oriens, orientis — (masc. noun) East

orientalis — (adj.) eastern

origo, originis — (fem. noun) origin

ortus, ortus — (masc. noun) birth, origin

os, oris — (neut. noun) mouth

pagina, paginae — (fem. noun) page

pagus, pagi — (masc. noun) village; canton

palatinatus — (masc. noun) county

parentes — (plur. noun) parents

parochia, parochiae — (fem. noun) parish

parochialis — (adj.) parochial, of the parish

parochus, parochi — (masc. noun) parish priest

pars, partis — (fem. noun) part; *ex parte* — on behalf of, on the part of

pastor, pastoris — (masc. noun) shepherd

pater, patris — (masc. noun) father

patrina, patrinae — (fem. noun) godmother

patrini, patrinorum — (plur. noun) godparents

patrinus, patrini — (masc. noun) godfather

patruus, patrui — (masc. noun) paternal uncle

pedagogus — (masc. noun) teacher

pictor, pictoris — (masc. noun) painter

piscator, piscatoris — (masc. noun) fisherman

pistor, pistoris — baker, miller

platea, plateae — (fem. noun) street

plenus — (adj.) full

possessor, possessoris — (masc. noun) landowner

post — (prep.) after

potere — (v.) to be able; *poterit* — it might be

praesens, praesentis — (adj.) present, this; *praesentes, praesentium* — (plur. noun) presents (legal term, = "this document", e. g., "by these presents be it known...")

primus — (adj.) first

privatus — (adj.) private, personal

proprius — (adj.) [my, your, his, her, their, our] own

publicus — (adj.) public

puella, puellae — (fem. noun) girl

puer, pueri — (masc. noun) boy

quadragesimus — (adj.) fortieth

quadraginta — (numeral) forty

quartus — (adj.) fourth; *quartus decimus* — fourteenth

quas — which (fem. plur., from *qui*)

quattuor — (numeral) four

quattuordecim — (numeral) fourteen

qui — (relative pron.) who, which, that

quindecim — (numeral) fifteen

quinquagesimus — (adj.) fiftieth

quinquaginta — (numeral) fifty

quinque — (numeral) five

quintus — (adj.) fifth; *quintus decimus* — fifteenth

quod — (neut. relative pron., from *qui*) which, that

quorum — (rel. pron., from *qui*) of which

regnum, regni — (neut. noun) kingdom

religio, religionis — (fem. noun) religion

reperiri — (passive infinitive) [is] to be found

res, rei — (fem. noun) thing, matter, issue

respublica, reipublicae — (fem. noun, from *res* + *publica*) republic, commonwealth

ritus, ritus — (masc. noun) rite, ceremony

romanus — (adj.) Roman

rusticus, rustici — (masc. noun) farmer

sacerdos, sacerdotis — (masc. noun) priest

saeculum, saeculi — (neut. noun) century, age, generation

salus, salutis — (fem. noun) health, greeting, welfare

sanctus — (adj.) holy; *Sanctus* — Saint

sartor, sartoris — (masc. noun) tailor

se — (pron.) oneself, himself, herself, themselves

secundus — (adj.) second

sedecim — (numeral) sixteen

septem — (numeral) seven

September, Septembris — September

septendecim — (num.) seventeen

septentrionalis — (adj.) northern

septentriones, septentrionum — (plur. noun) North

septimus — (adj.) seventh; *septimus decimus* — seventeenth

septingentesimus — (adj.) seven hundredth; *septingenti* — (numeral) seven hundred

septuagesimus — (adj.) seventieth

septuaginta — (numeral) seventy

sepultura, sepulturae — (fem. noun) burial

sepultus — (part. from *sepelio*) buried

sequens, sequentis — (part.) the following (plural *sequentia, sequentium*)

sex — (numeral) six

sexagesimus — (adj.) sixtieth

sexaginta — (numeral) sixty

sextus — (adj.) sixth; *sextus decimus* — sixteenth

sexus, sexus — (masc. noun) sex, gender

si — (conj.) if

sibi — (pron., from *se*) to himself [herself, themselves]

sigillum, sigilli — (neut. noun) seal

singulus — (adj.) each; *singulis* — to each

soror, sororis — (fem. noun) sister

subscribo — (v., infinitive *subscribere*) I sign

subscriptio, subscriptionis — (fem. noun) signature

subscriptus — (part. from *subscribere*) signed

sutor, sutoris — (masc. noun) shoemaker

suus — (poss. adj.) one's own

tabula, tabulae — (fem. noun) list, slate

te — (pron., from *tu*) you

tempus, temporis — (neut. noun) time, date

tertius — (adj.) third; *tertius decimus* — thirteenth

testatur — [he, she, it] attests (from *testor*); *testatus* — (part. from *testor*) attested

testis, testis — (masc. noun) witness (plur. *testes*)

testimonium, testimonii — (neut. noun) certificate

textor, textoris — (masc. noun) weaver

thorus, thori — (masc. noun) status (especially of legitimate or illegitimate birth)

tibi — (pron., from *tu*) to you

tomus, tomi — (masc. noun) volume

tredecim — (numeral) thirteen

tres, tria — (numeral) three

tricesimus — (adj.) thirtieth

triginta — (numeral) thirty

tu — (pron.) you, thou

tuus — (poss. adj.) your, thy

undecim — (numeral) eleven

undevicesimus — (adj.) nineteenth

undeviginti — (numeral) nineteen

unus — (adj.) one

urbs, urbis — (fem. noun) city, town

uxor, uxoris — (fem. noun) wife

vesper, vesperis — (masc. noun) evening; West

vester (fem. *vestra*, neut. *vestrum* — (poss. adj.) your

vicesimus — (adj.) twentieth; *vicesimus primus* — twenty-first

vicinus — (adj.) nearby, neighboring

vicus, vici — (masc. noun) village

vidua, viduae — (fem. noun) widow

viduus, vidui — (masc. noun) widower

viginti — (numeral) twenty; *viginti unus* — twenty-one

vigor, vigoris — (fem. noun) strength; *praesentium vigore* — by virtue of these presents

vir, viri — (masc. noun) man, husband

virgo, virgonis — (fem. noun) maiden, bride

vobis — (pron., from *vos*) you; *vobiscum = cum vobis* — with you

vos — (pron.) you

Xbris — in December

Selected Personal Names

Since virtually all documents written in Latin were written in places where some other language was the vernacular, the Latinized names of people and places that appear in the documents usually differ from the name the people and places were known by. Personal names in Europe were most often saints' names anyway, and the saints were known through the Latin church, so a person's "church" name would be Latin while his everyday name would be German or Polish or Italian or whatever. Use these English (approximate) equivalents to cross-reference names in the relevant vernacular; so recognize that *Joannis* may be "John" in English, but in Polish it's probably *Jan*, in German *Hans* or *Johann*, in French *Jean*, and so forth. This is a tricky procedure, with plenty of opportunity to go wrong, but with luck one may recognize a name that would have otherwise passed by undetected.

Amadeus — (= German *Gottlieb*, in Polish *Bogumił*, in Russian the root of *Bogolyubov*)

Andreas — Andrew

Carolus — Carl, Charles

Ceslaus — (Polish) Czesław, Česlav (Czech)

Felicia — Phyllis

Franciscus — Francis

Guillelmus — William

Henricus — Henry

Hieronymus — Jerome

Hyacinthus — Jacek (Polish)

Joannis — John

Johanna — Joan, Jane

Ludovicus — Louis, Ludwig

Marcus — Mark

Mateus — Matthew

Petrus — Peter

Stanislaus — (Polish) Stanisław

Stepania — Stefanie

Stephanus — Steven

Timoteus — Timothy

Vincentus — Vincent

Português

Printed	Cursive
A, a	𝒜, a
B, b	ℬ, b
C, c	𝒞, c
D, d	𝒟, d
E, e	ℰ, e
F, f	ℱ, f
G, g	𝒢, g
H, h	ℋ, h
I, I	ℐ, i
J, j	𝒥, j
K, k	𝒦, k
L, l	ℒ, l
M, m	ℳ, m
N, n	𝒩, n
O, o	𝒪, o
P, p	𝒫, p
Q, q	𝒬, q
R, r	ℛ, r
S, s	𝒮, s
T, t	𝒯, t
U, u	𝒰, u
V, v	𝒱, v
W, w	𝒲, w
X, x	𝒳, x
Y, y	𝒴, y
Z, z	𝒵, z

The Portuguese Alphabet

The Portuguese alphabet is the same as the English, in the same order, but the letters *k, w,* and *y* appear only in words borrowed from other languages. A number of diacritical marks are used with Portuguese vowels, and a *c* with cedilla *(ç)*, always sounded like the *s* in English *sin,* is distinct from *c* — but the *ç* and the accented vowels do not represent separate characters affecting alphabetical order.

People who don't know better are tempted to think of Portuguese as mispronounced Spanish, but Portuguese is a fully developed language in its own right. Portuguese and Spanish evolved from the same basic Romance descendant of Latin, and both languages share a similar grammatical structure and lexical base; but Portuguese has many features and sounds that distinguish it from Spanish. It is the language of Portugal and Brazil and former Portuguese colonies such as Angola, Mozambique, and Macao.

In general, vowels are pronounced roughly as in most Romance languages: *a* as in "f<u>a</u>ther," *e* as in "l<u>e</u>t," *i* as in "mach<u>i</u>ne," *o* as in "thr<u>o</u>ne," and *u* like the *oo* in "t<u>oo</u>t." Such a statement, however, is enormously over-simplified, as one sees vowels with acute accent *(á, é, í, ó, ú),* circumflex *(ê, ô),* grave accent *(à, è),* and tilde *(ã, ẽ, õ, ũ).* In general the acute accent (e. g., *é, ó*) signifies an "open" vowel sound and the circumflex (e. g., *ê, ô*) a "closed" one, and the tilde (e. g., *ã, ẽ*) marks a nasal vowel, as in the name of the city "São Paulo." Syllables marked with acute accents, the circumflex, or the tilde are always stressed. The diacritical marks are not merely cosmetic — they represent different pronunciations which can signify different meanings.

The nasal vowels deserve a few more words. These vowels — usually marked with a tilde, but *am, en, im, om,* and *um* are also nasalized — add a nasal ending to the pronunciation of the vowel, almost as if the final sound of "fang" is coming but is never quite completed. The meaning of words featuring nasalized vowels is sometimes easier to remember if one knows that they usually correspond to a dropped *-n-* in Latin or Spanish, e. g., *mãos* "hands" = Spanish *manos* and Latin *manus,* or *nações* = Spanish *naciones.* Persons familiar with French or Polish will have an advantage in pronouncing nasal vowels correctly because such vowels are also prominent in those languages.

Vowel combinations are fairly standard for Romance languages. The *ou* sounds somewhat like *ow* in English "thr<u>ow</u>" (but in dialectal variation can sound like the *ow* in English "c<u>ow</u>"); the *ai* like *i* in "l<u>i</u>me," and the *ei* like *a* in English "l<u>a</u>me." The combination *eu* is a brief combination of *e* as in "g<u>e</u>t" with *u* as in "p<u>u</u>t."

Most of the consonants are pronounced roughly as in English, but as any student of languages knows, any statement that simple has to be followed by the listing of a number of exceptions. The *ch* combination is always pronounced like the *sh* in English "<u>sh</u>in," and *j* sounds like the *z* in English "a<u>z</u>ure" — *g* sounds the same way when it precedes *e* or *i.* As noted earlier, the *ç* is always pronounced like the *s* in English "<u>s</u>in"; *s* sounds the same except when between vowels, when it sounds like the *z* in English "<u>z</u>ip." The *lh* combination is pronounced like the *lli* in "mi<u>lli</u>on," and *nh* like the *ni* in "o<u>ni</u>on." A *qu* is pronounced like *k* when followed by *e* or *i,* but like *kw* when followed by *a, o,* or *u.* Similarly, *gu* is a hard *g* as in "gamble" when it precedes *e* or *i,* but sounds like *gw* before *a, o,* or *u.*

Document #1: An Identity Card from the Azores

On the opposite page is an identity card issued in the Azores [Açores]. The handwriting on this is less than ideal, but the document contains a number of terms one encounters frequently in research.

República Portuguesa: Ministério do Interior
   república — "republic"
   portuguesa — "Portuguese" (adjective, feminine form modifying the feminine noun *república*)
   do ministério — "ministry" (*do = de + o,* "of the")
   Translation — Republic of Portugal, Ministry of the Interior

Govêrno Civil de Ponta Delgada
   govêrno — "government, administration"
   civil — "civil, civilian"
   Ponta Delgada — a town on the island of São Miguel in the Azores
   Translation — Civil Government of Ponta Delgada

BILHETE DE IDENTIDADE
   bilhete — "card"
   identidade — "identity"
   Translation — Identity card

Nome: Gabriela Vasconcellos Gomes
   nome — "name"
   Translation — Name: Gabriela Vasconcellos Gomes

Filiação: José Maria Gomes e de Maria José Vieira de Carvalho e Vasconcellos
   filiação — "descent, parentage"
   Translation — Descent: [daughter of] José Maria Gomes and of Maria José Vieira de Carvalho e Vasconcellos

Naturalidade (conc. e freq.): Vila Franco do Campo, S. Miguel
   naturalidade — "birthplace"
   conc. — abbreviation of *concelho,* "district" (composed of several villages)
   freq. — abbreviation of *frequezia,* "parish"
   Vila Franco do Campo — a town on the island of São Miguel
   S. Miguel — abbreviation of *São Miguel* (*São,* "saint", is the equivalent of *San* in Spanish)
   Translation — Birthplace (district and parish): Vila Franco do Campo, S. Miguel

Idade: 6 anos. Data do nascimento: 22-7-1913
   idade — "age"
   anos — "years" (plural of *ano*)
   data do nascimento — "date of birth"
   Translation — Age: 6 years. Date of birth: 22 July 1913.

Estado: -- Profissão: -- Observações --
   estado — "(civil) status" (presumably in the case of an adult the standard answer would be *casado* [masc.] or *casada* [fem.], "married")
   profissão — "profession"
   observações — "observations, remarks"
   Translation — Status: — Profession: — Observations: — [In view of the bearer's age, no answer was to be expected.]

Fórmula Dactiloscópica. Impressões do dedo ... da mão ... do identificado.
   dactiloscópica — "dactyloscopic" (adj. meaning "of fingerprints," with feminine ending *-a* because the noun it modifies, *fórmula,* is feminine in gender)

REPÚBLICA PORTUGUESA: Ministério do Interior

Govêrno Civil de *Pont. Delgada*

N.º *55*

BILHETE DE IDENTIDADE

Nome: *Gabriela Vasconcellos Gomes*

Filiação: *José Maria Gomes e de Maria José*
Vieira de Cabral e Vasconcellos

Naturalidade (conc. e freg.): *Vila Franca do Campo*
S. Miguel

Idade: *6* anos. Data do nascimento: *22-7-1913*

Estado: Profissão:

Observações:

FÓRMULA DACTILOSCÓPICA
Série
Secção

Retrato tirado em *19* de *Março* de 19*19*

Côr da pele:
Altura:
Olhos:
Cabelo:
Barba:
Sinais particulares:

Assinatura do identificado:

Residência: *S. Miguel*

Assinatura do identificador:

AÇORES

Data: *19 de Março de 1919*

O Governador Civil,

SEGURANÇA PUBLICA
Sêlo a tinta
1850

- $08 -
ADICIONAL DE 5%

impressões — "impressions"

do dedo ... da mão ... — "of the ... finger of the (*da = de + a*) ... hand" *do identificado* — "of the one being identified"

Translation — Dactyloscopic formula. Impressions of the ... finger on the ... hand of the bearer.

Retrato tirado em 19 *de Março de* 1919 [caption under photograph]

    retrato — "photograph"

    tirado — "shot, taken"

    março — "March"

    Translation — Photograph taken on 19 March 1919.

Côr da pele ... Altura ... Olhos ... Cabelo ... Barba ... Sinais particulares...

    côr da pele — "color (côr) of skin (pele)"

    altura — "height"

    olhos — "eyes"

    cabelo — "hair"

    barba — "beard"

    sinais particulares — "distinguishing marks"

    Translation — Skin color ... Height ... Eyes ... Hair ... Beard ... Distinguishing marks ...

Assinatura do identificado ... Residência S. Miguel

    assinatura — "signature"

    residência — "residence"

    Translation — Signature of the bearer ... Residence: Saõ Miguel

Assinatura do identificador: ... Data: 19 *de Março de* 1919

    identificador — "the identifier" (note the contrast between *identificado*, the one being identified, and the *identificador*, the one doing the identifying)

    Translation — Signature of the identifier *[illegible]* Date: 19 March 1919.

Pel O Governador Civil, O Oficial Manuel...

    pelo — "for the, on behalf of the" (*pelo = por,* "for," + *o*, "the")

    o governador civil — "the civil governor" (*o* is the definite article "the" in the masculine singular; *os* is masculine plural, *a* feminine singular, *as* feminine plural)

    Translation — For the civil governor, the official Manuel ... *[the rest of the signature is illegible]*

Impressões do dedo ... da mão direita do identificador.

    da mão direita do identificador — "of the identifier's right hand" ("left" hand would be *esquerda*; the word specifying which finger was used is illegible)

    Translation — Impressions of the ... finger on the identifier's right hand.

Segurança Publica ... Sêlo a tinta

    segurança — "safety"

    sêlo a tinta — "stamped in ink"

    Translation — Public Safety ... Stamped in ink.

Document #2: A Birth Certificate from the Azores

On the following two pages is a full-size reproduction of a birth certificate from the Azores (notice "Açores" in the ornate seal at the upper left of the document's first page). The handwriting is no better than that in the preceding document, but the vocabulary and format of this certificate are so typical and useful that it is worth the effort to decipher it. Accordingly, in the next few pages each section of the original will be reproduced directly above a rendering in standardized script, followed by analysis and translation of that section.

José Velho Quintanilha de Sousa Caroço, Bacharel Formado em Direito, pela Universidade de Coimbra, Oficial do Registo Civil do Concelho da Ribeira Grande

Certifico, que no L.º dos assentos de batismos do arquivo paroquial da freguesia da Conceição deste concelho, se acha exarado a fl.ª 4 v. e sob o n.º 9, o assento do teor seguinte:

Aos nove dias do mez de Ferreiro do ano de mil novecentos e dois, nesta egreja paroquial de Nossa Senhora da Conceição, concelho da Vila da Ribeira Grande, diocese d'Angra, batizei solenemente um individuo do sexo masculino a quem dei o nome de "Manuel", e que nasceu nesta freguezia ás duas horas da manhã do dia vinte e tres do mez de janeiro do corrente ano de mil novecentos e dois; filho legitimo de José Corrêa Janeiro, camponez, natural da freguezia de Nossa Senhora da Estrela, deste concelho e diocese, e de Maria do Rosario Batista, de compaixão domestica, natural desta freguezia, onde foram recebidos e de que são paroquianos moradores na rua dos Apostolos; netos pa-

I. Identification of the Keeper of Vital Records

José Velho Quintanilho de Sousa Larocq.
Bacharel (Formado em Direito pela Univer-
sidade de Coimbra, Oficial do Registo
Civil do Concelho da Ribeira Grande,

Bacharel — "graduate, holder of bachelor's degree"
formado — "educated"
em Direito — "in law"
pela Universidade de Coimbra — "by the University of Coimbra"
oficial do Registo Civil — "official of the Civil Registry" (*Registro* is the standard spelling of this word)
do concelho da — "of the district of"

Translation — [I,] José Velho Quintanilho de Sousa Larocq., Graduate (educated in Law at the University of Coimbra), Official of the Civil Registry of the District of Ribeira Grande ...

II. Identification of Entry's Location

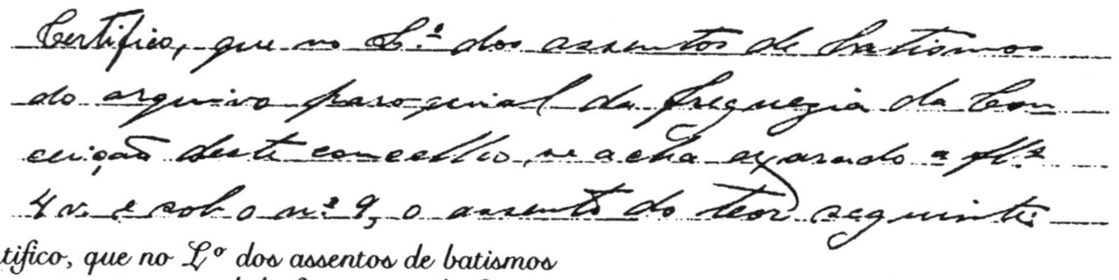

[handwritten cursive lines]

Certifico, que no *L°* dos assentos de batismos
do arquivo paroquial da frequezia da Conceição deste concelho se acha exarado a fl°
4 v. e sob o n° 9 o assento do teor seguinte:

certifico que — "I certify that"

no L° dos assentos de batismos — "in the book (*Livro*, here abbreviated) of the (*dos = do + os*) records *(assentos)* of baptisms" *(batismos)*

do arquivo paroquial — "of the parish archives"

frequezia da Conceição — "parish of the [Immaculate] Conception"

deste concelho — "of this (*deste = de + êste*) district"

se acha exarado — "is found imprinted" (*achar*, "to find"; *exarar*, "to engrave, imprint")

fl° — abbreviation of *folio*

4 v. e sob o n° 9 — "volume 4, under the number *(o número)* 9"

do teor seguinte — "of the following contents"

Translation — I certify that in the book of baptismal records of the parish archives of Immaculate Conception parish, of this district, is to be found, in volume 4, number 9, the record of the following contents...

III. Verbatim Extract from the Register

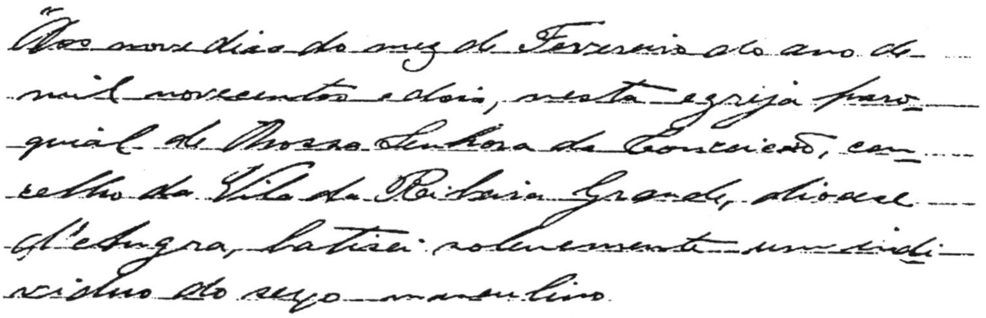

[handwritten cursive lines]

" *Aos* nove dias do mez de Fevereiro do ano de
mil novecentos e dois, nesta egreja paroquial de *Nossa Senhora da Conceição*, concelho da *Vila da Ribeira Grande*, diocese
d'*Angra* batisei solenemente un individuo do sexo masculino

aos nove dias do mez de Fevereiro — "on the ninth *(nove)* day *(dias)* of the month (*mez*, modern standard spelling *mês*) of February *(Fevereiro)*"

mil novecentos e dois — "one thousand *(mil)* nine hundred *(novecentos)* and two *(dois)* (1902)"

nesta egreja paroquial — "in the (*nesta = em + esta*) parish church" (*egreja*, standard spelling *igreja*)

Nossa Senhora da Conceição — "Our Lady of the [Immaculate] Conception"

concelho da Vila da Ribeira Grande — "district of Vila da Ribeira Grande"

batisei — "I baptized"

solenemente — (adv.) "solemnly"

un individuo do sexo masculino — "an individual of the male sex"

Translation — On February 9, 1902, in the parish church of Our Lady of the Conception, district of Vila da Ribeira Grande, diocese of Angra, I solemnly baptized an individual of the male sex...

IV. Extract (cont'd): Name of Child

... a quem dei
o nome de " Manuel" e que nasceu nesta
frequezia as duas horas da manhã do di-
a vinte e tres do mez de Janeiro do corr-
ente ano de mil novecentos e dois, filho

  a quem dei o nome — "to whom I gave *(dei)* the name"
  que nasceu — "who was born"
  as duas horas da manhâ — "at two *(duas)* o'clock *(horas)* in the morning *(manhâ)*"
  vinte e três do mêz de Janeiro — "on the 23rd of the month of January"
  do corrente ano — "of the present year"
  filho — "son" (this word goes with *legitimo* in the next section)
  Translation — to whom I gave the name of Manuel and who was born in this parish at two o'clock in the morning on the 23rd of January of the current year of 1902...

V. Extract (cont'd): Identification of Parents

legitimo de José Corrêa Janeiro campo-
nez, natural da frequezia de Nossa Senho-
ra da Estrela, deste concelho e diocese, e
de Maria do Rosario Batista docupação
domestica, natural desta frequezia, onde
foram recebidos e de que são paroquianos
moradores na rua dos Apostolos;

  filho legitimo — "legitimate son"
  camponez — "farmer, peasant" (modern standard spelling *camponês*)
  natural — "native"
  docupação domestica — "of domestic occupation" (standard usage would be *de ocupação*, not *docupação*; this is probably just an error or dialectal variant)
  onde foram recebidos — "where they were accepted"
  são paroquianos — "they are parishioners"
  moradores — "inhabitants, residents"
  rua dos Apostolos — "street *(rua)* of the Apostles"

Translation — ... legitimate son of José Corrêa Janeiro, farmer, a native of the parish of Nossa Senhora da Estrêla [literally, Our Lady of the Star], of this district and diocese, and of Maria de Rosario Batista, occupied domestically, a native of this parish, where they were accepted and where they are parishioners, residing on the Rua dos Apostolos...

VI. Extract (conclusion): Grandparents and Godparents

... *neto pa-*
terno de Manuel Corrêa Janeiro e de Juli-
a Emilia e materno de José Pacheco e de
Maria Augusta. Foi padrinho Antonio
Pacheco Batista, casado, camponez, e ma-
drinha Carolina Julia, casada;

    neto paterno — "paternal grandson"
    materno — "maternal [grandson]"
    foi padrinho — "[the] godfather was"
    casado — "married" (masculine form modifying the masculine nouns *padrinho Antonio Pacheco Batista*)
    madrinha — "godmother"
    casada — "married" (feminine form modifying feminine nouns, *madrinha Carolina Julia*)

    Translation — ... paternal grandson of Manuel Corrêa Janeiro and of Julia Emilia, and maternal grandson of José Pacheco and of Maria Augusta. The godfather was Antonio Pachecho Batista, married, a farmer, and the godmother Carolina Julia, married.

The remainder of the document contains the usual legalistic attestations that this is a true copy of the original and so on. As it is of minimal importance for genealogical purposes, it is not analyzed or translated here — although some readers may find it useful practice to try to identify some of the key phrases.

Selected Vocabulary Terms

Portuguese originally derived its grammatical structure and lexical base from the same source as Spanish, and most Americans do not find it too difficult to deal with Spanish, at least on the superficial level necessary to decipher documents; so it is reasonable to assume Portuguese will not cause most readers much trouble. The most difficult aspect of Portuguese — and perhaps the one in which it differs most from Spanish — is its verb system; fortunately most vital records can be interpreted without detailed knowledge of verbs, so this list gives only a few forms of some verbs most commonly encountered in documents.

Many Portuguese words are enough like their Latin or Spanish counterparts that one can recognize them once two simple linguistic patterns are grasped. Where Latin or Spanish had intervocalic -l- (i. e., an -l- between vowels), Portuguese often dropped the -l- and lengthened or accented the second vowel: saída ("exit") vs. Spanish salida, Port. saúde ("health") vs. Latin salus, salute. Similarly, intervocalic -n- in Latin or Spanish tends to be dropped in Portuguese, but the preceding vowel is nasalized: Spanish mano becomes Portuguese mão. Portuguese has the same -li- sound as Italian, but it is spelled -lh- in Portuguese, e. g., Italian figlio (son) vs. Portuguese filho. The -ni- sound common in Spanish and represented by the -ñ- exists in Portuguese but is spelled -nh-, e. g., Spanish señora (lady) vs. Portuguese senhora. Familiarity with these tendencies will often enable one to recognize words that initially look unfamiliar.

Portuguese nouns are either masculine or feminine in gender, and adjectives modifying a noun must be of the same gender and number. The simplest way to remember that is to remember the forms of the definite article: o is masculine singular, os is masculine plural, a is feminine singular, as is feminine plural. Adjectives are listed in their masculine singular form, but one should understand that when an adjective like casado ("married") modifies a feminine noun, its ending will change to casada.

a — the (feminine)
abaixo — below
abril — April
acha — (from *achar*) finds; *se acha* — is found
advogado — lawyer
agôsto — August
aldeia — village
alfaiate — tailor
alí — there, in that place
altura — height
amarelo — (adj.) yellow
ano — year
apostolo — Apostle
aqui — here
arquivo — archives
as — (fem. plur. form of *o*) the
assento — record
assinatura — signature
até — until
azul — (adj.) blue
bachare — (noun) graduate
barba — beard
barco — boat
batisei — (verb form) [I] baptized
batismo — baptism
bilhete — card
bôca — mouth
braço — arm
branco — white
cabeça — head
cabelo — hair

camponês — farmer, peasant (also spelled *camponêz*)
capitão — captain
carimbo — (noun) stamp, seal
carniceiro — (noun) butcher
carpinteiro — carpenter
carta — letter
casa — house
casado — (adj.) married
casamento — wedding
catorze — fourteen
cego — (adj.) blind
cem — one hundred
cemitério — cemetery
certifico — (verb form) [I] certify
chegada — arrival
cidade — town
cididão — citizen
cinco — five
cinquenta — fifty
cinzento — grey
civil — civil, civilian
clero — clergy
comerciante — merchant
conceição — conception
concelho — district
contra — against
côr — color; *côr da pele* — skin color
corpo — body
corrente — (adj.) current, present

cozinheiro — (noun) cook
criança — child
custo — cost
da — (from *de + a*) of the, from the
dactiloscópico — (adj.) of fingerprints
das — (from *de +as*) of the, from the
data — date
de — (prep.) of, from
debaixo — (adv.) down
dedo — (noun) finger
dei — (verb form, from *dar*) [I] gave
delgado — (adj.) thin
depois — (prep.) after
desta — (from *de + esta*) of this
deste — (from *de + êste*) of this
Deus — God
dez — ten
dezembro — December
dezenove — nineteen
dezesseis — sixteen
dezessete — seventeen
dezoito — eighteen
dia — day
dinheiro — money
diocese — diocese
direito — (adj.) right; (noun) law
do — (from *de + o*) from the, of the

doença — disease
dois — two
domestico — domestic
domingo — Sunday
dos — (from de + os) from the, of the
doze — twelve
duas — two (fem.)
e — and
egreja — church (→ igreja)
em — (prep.) in, at, on
enderêço — address
enfermeira — (fem. noun) nurse
engenheiro — (noun) engineer
escola — school
esquerda — left
esta — (demonstr. pron./adj., fem.) this
estado — status
este — east
êste — (demonst. pron./adj., masc.) this
estrada — highway
estrangeiro — (adj.) foreign
estrêla — star
estudante — student
exarado — carved, imprinted
fazenda — farm
fevereiro — February
filha — (fem. noun) daughter
filho — (masc. noun) son
filição — parentage, descent
foi — (verb form, from ser) was
foram — (verb form, from ser) they were
formado — (adj.) educated
frequezia — parish
governador — governor
govérno — government, administration
grande — large
guerra — war
hoje — (adv.) today
homem — man
hora — hour, o'clock
idade — age
identidade — identity
identificado — the one being identified, bearer
identificador — one identifying
igreja — church (also spelled egreja)
ilha — island
impressões — impressions
individuo — individual

informação — information
inverno — winter
irma — sister
irmão — brother
janeiro — January
jovem — (adj.) young
julho — July
junho — June
lago — lake
legitimo — (adj.) legitimate
língua — language
livro — book
louro — (adj.) blond
madrinha — godmother
mãe — mother
maio — May
manhã — morning
mão — hand
mar — sea
março — March
marido — husband
marinheiro — sailor
marrom — (adj.) brown
masculino — (adj.) masculine
materno — (adj.) maternal
matrimônio — marriage
médico — doctor
meio dia — midday, noon
menina — girl
menino — boy
mês — month (older variant spelling mez)
mez — (see mês)
mil — thousand
ministério — ministry
montanha — mountain
morador — inhabitant, resident
morte — death
mulher — woman
na — (from en + a) in the, on the, at the
não — (adv.) no
nariz — nose
nasceu — (verb form) was born
nascimento — birth
natural — (noun) native
naturalidade — birthplace
negócio — business
nesta — (from em + esta) in this
neto — grandson
no — (from en + o) in the, on the, at the
noite — night
noiva — bride
nome — (masc. noun) name

norte — north
nossa — (poss. adj.) our
nove — nine
novecentos — nine hundred
novembro — November
noventa — ninety
o — (masc. sing. form) the
observações — observations
ocupação — occupation
oeste — west
oficial — (noun) offical
oitenta — eighty
oito — eight
ôlho — eye
onde — (adv.) where
ontem — (adv.) yesterday
onze — eleven
os — (masc. plur. form) the
outro — (adj.) another
outubro — October
padeiro — baker
padrinho — godfather
pai — (noun) father
pais — parents
país — country
paroquial — parochial
paroquino — parishioner
partida — departure
passaporte — passport
paterno — paternal
pela — (por + a) for the, by the, at the
pele — skin
pelo — (por + o) for the, by the, at the
pergunta — question
perna — leg
pêso — weight
por — (prep.) for
porque — because
pôrto — port, harbor
português — (adj.) Portugese; (fem. form portuguesa)
preço — price
prêto — black
primavera — spring
primo — (noun) cousin
profissão — profession
próximo — near
publico — (adj.) public
quarenta — forty
quarto-feira — Wednesday
quatro — four
que — (conj.) that; (pronoun) who, which, that, who? what?

queixo — chin

quem — (pron., from que) whom

quinta-feira — Thursday

quinze — fifteen

rainha — queen

recebido — (adj.) received, accepted

registro — registry; Registro Civil — Registry of Vital Statistics

rei — king

religião — religion

república — republic

residência — residence

retrato — (noun) photograph

rio — river

rosto — (noun) face

rua — (fem. noun) street

sabado — Saturday

saída — exit

são — Saint

são — (verb form, from ser) they are

saúde — health

se — [him, her, it]self

século — century

seguinte — (adj.) following

segunda-feira — Monday

segurança — safety

seio — (noun) breast

seis — six

semana — week

senhor — gentleman, Mr.

senhora — lady, Mrs.

sessenta — sixty

ser — to be

sete — seven

setembro — September

setenta — seventy

sexo — sex, gender

sexta-feira — Friday

sim — (adv.) yes

sinais — signs, marks; sinais particulares — distinguishing marks

sobre — (prep.) on, at

soldado — soldier

solenemente — (adv.) solemnly

sul — south

tarde — afternoon

tardinha — evening

tempo — (masc. noun) time

teor — contents

têrca-feira — Tuesday

tia — aunt

tio — uncle

tirado — (participle) shot, taken

três — three

treze — thirteen

trinta — thirty

tudo — (adj.) all

um — one (fem. uma)

universidade — university

velho — (adj.) old

verão — summer

verde — green

vinte — twenty

Selected Portuguese First Names

Most Portuguese names do not differ greatly in form from their Spanish counterparts, but there are some significant differences. A few of the most popular first names are listed here so that researchers can have the opportunity to see how they are spelled and can recognize them in texts. Approximate English equivalents are listed beside them, but not all have close English equivalents — those names are marked with asterisks.

Amelia — Amelia
Anabela — Annabelle
Antonio — Anthony
Armindo — Armand
Celeste — Celeste
Cristina — Christine
Dulce *
Elisa — Elise
Fatima *
Fernanda *

Fernando — Ferdinand
Florinda — Florinda
Francisco — Francis
Gracinda *
Henrique — Henry
João — John
Joaquim — Joachim
Jorge — George
José — Joseph
Marco — Mark

Maria — Mary
Miguel — Michael
Ofelia — Ophelia
Paulo — Paul
Pedro — Peter
Ricardo — Richard
Rosa — Rose
Suzete — Susan
Vicente — Vincent
Zulmira *

The Romanian Alphabet

Printed	Cursive
A, a	$\mathcal{A}$, a
Ă, ă	$\mathcal{\breve{A}}$, ă
Â, â	$\mathcal{\hat{A}}$, â
B, b	$\mathcal{B}$, b
C, c	$\mathcal{C}$, c
D, d	$\mathcal{D}$, d
E, e	$\mathcal{E}$, e
F, f	$\mathcal{F}$, f
G, g	$\mathcal{G}$, g
H, h	$\mathcal{H}$, h
I, I	$\mathcal{I}$, i
Î, î	$\mathcal{\hat{I}}$, î
J, j	$\mathcal{J}$, j
L, l	$\mathcal{L}$, l
M, m	$\mathcal{M}$, m
N, n	$\mathcal{N}$, n
O, o	$\mathcal{O}$, o
P, p	$\mathcal{P}$, p
R, r	$\mathcal{R}$, r
S, s	$\mathcal{S}$, s
Ş, ş	$\mathcal{S}$, ş
T, t	$\mathcal{T}$, t
Ţ, ţ	$\mathcal{T}$, ţ
U, u	$\mathcal{U}$, u
V, v	$\mathcal{V}$, v
W, w	$\mathcal{W}$, w

Printed	Cursive	Printed	Cursive
X, x	$\mathcal{X}$, x	Z, z	$\mathcal{Z}$, z

Romanian uses the Roman alphabet, modified for the phonetic needs of the language. The Romanian language has undergone a series of spelling reforms, the most recent in 1967, so older documents may well contain orthographic renditions which conflict with a current dictionary (as is evident in the sample documents). The letters k, q, w, x, and y can be considered part of the alphabet but appear only in foreign words and certain surnames. The alphabet as shown at the left is given in a form to acquaint readers with the various letters one sees, but generally ă, â, ê, ş and ţ are not considered separate letters in their own right. Some letters not normally seen at the beginning of words are shown here in upper- as well as lower-case forms because documents often capitalize entire words for emphasis and one might see upper-case forms of those letters in that context. In addition to the cedilla under ş and ţ, Romanian uses two other diacritical marks, a caret over the vowels â and î and a breve over the vowel ă. In older documents other possibilities may be seen; for instance, ḑ and ĕ appear in sample Document #1.

Many people have the notion that Romanian is a Slavic language, perhaps because Romania is located in southeastern Europe and was long a Communist state. In fact Romanian is a Romance language, specifically, a representative of the eastern Romanic branch of the Romance language family; it exhibits the most complicated grammar of any of the Romance literary languages. As the only survivor of the Latin language as spoken in the Eastern Roman Empire, whose evolution was not as influenced by medieval Latin as its western cousins, Romanian conserves more of the features of the Romance mother language.

The evolution of Romanian was influenced by the Slavic and other languages spoken by its immediate neighbors. Thus one finds Serbian, Turkish, Hungarian, Albanian, and Greek influences in the language; but a significant chunk of its core vocabulary remains of Latin origin.

The vowels e, o and u resemble the sounds in the English words "ten," "home," and "moon"; a and i without diacriticals are similar to English "father" and "deep." The other vowel sounds are more complicated and may vary depending on the position in which they're found. The ă epresents a central mid vowel close to the English sound in "dental," and â and î are also central vowels somewhat like the sound in "bottom."

Many Romanian consonants require no special remarks, but several deserve attention. Usually c is pronounced as in English "cool" but ce is pronounced as in English "chain" and ci as in "cheek." To conserve the k-sound with these consonants an -h- is inserted, so that che sounds like the sound in "kept" and chi like that of "key" (much as in Italian). The g behaves the same way; normally it is pronounced as in "gold" but ge and gi are pronounced much like the je sounds in "jet" and "jeep," respectively, while ghe and ghi resemble the sounds in "gay" and "geese." The letter j is pronounced like the si in English "collision," and the r is trilled as in Spanish. The s is like the sh in "ship" and t is rendered as the ts sound heard in "cats."

Document #1: A Romanian Birth Certificate

On the opposite page is a reproduction of a Romanian birth certificate. The key words and phrases are analyzed and translated below. A number of the words appear in spellings no longer considered standard, but seeing these forms may actually be helpful in reconciling the spellings you see in real documents with the spellings to be found in modern, standardized dictionaries.

REGATUL ROMÂNIEI. PRIMARIA COMUNEĬ BUCURESCI. OFICIUL STĂREĬ CIVILE. No. 950. BULETIN DE NASCERE.

>   *regatul* — "the kingdom." This illustrates Romanian's use of the postposited article; that is, instead of putting the article before the noun (as in English, "<u>the</u> kingdom"), Romanian adds the suffix *-ul* to *regat*, "kingdom." The article has different forms, all deriving ultimately from the Latin pronoun *ille*. A few other examples are *numele* (from *nume*, "name"), *casa* (from *casă*, "house"), and *cartea* (from *carte*, "book"), so often a word that seems unfamiliar is actually one in the dictionary but with the ending modified by the definite article.
>   *primaria* — "Town Hall" (from *primărie*)
>   *Bucuresci* — "Bucharest"
>   *Oficiul Stăreĭ Civile* — "The Office of Vital Statistics" (modern standardized spelling *Oficiul Starii Civile*)
>   *Nascere* — "Birth"
>   **Translation:** — The Kingdom of Romania. Town Hall of the Community of Bucharest. The Office of Vital Statistics. No. 950. Certificate of Birth.

Numele de familie Faerberg

>   *numele* — "the name"; *numele de familie* — "the family name, surname"
>   **Translation** — Surname: Faerberg

Numele de botez Hana, de sex feminin.

>   *botez* — "baptism, christening"
>   **Translation** — Baptismal name: Hana, of the female sex

Născut*ă la ora 1 a.m. în ziua de 3 ale luneĭ Februarie,*
strada Sfinti No. 58 inscrisă astă-ḑĭ 6 ale
luneĭ Februarie anul una mie opt sute nouĕ ḑecĭ și 8
Fica a Dei Mendel Faerberg, de ani 39,
* croitor de dame.*
și a Dei Rosa născută Aron Rotman,
de ani 34, casnica

>   *născută* — "born"
>   *oră* — "hour, o'clock"
>   *ziua* — "the day" (from *zi*)
>   *luneĭ* — "the month of" (from *lună*)
>   *strada* — "street" (from *stradă*)
>   *astă-ḑĭ* — "today" (archaic form; acceptable modern standard forms are *astăzi* or *azi*)
>   *anul* — "the year" (from *an* + *-ul*)
>   *una mie opt sute nouĕ ḑecĭ și 8* — "one thousand eight hundred ninety and eight" (standard spelling of "ninety" now is *nouăzeci*)
>   *fica* — "the daughter" (or *fiică*; alternative: *fiu*, "son")
>   *de ani 39* — "of 39 years," i. e., "age 39"
>   *croitor de dame* — "ladies' tailor"
>   *și* — "and"
>   *casnică* — "domestic"
>   **Translation** — Born at 1 a.m. on the third day of the month of February, at 58 Sfinti Street, registered today, the sixth of the month of February, 1898, the daughter of Mendel Faerberg, age 39, a ladies' tailor, and Rosa, daughter of Aron Rotman, age 34, a domestic.

REGATUL ROMÂNIEI

PRIMARIA COMUNEĬ BUCURESCI

OFICIUL STĂREĬ CIVILE

No. 950

BULETIN DE NASCERE

Numele de familie *Faerberg*

Numele de botez *Hana*, de sex fe-
menin.

Născut ă la ora *1 a.m.* în ziua de *3* ale luneĭ *Februarie*
strada *Sfinți* No. *58* înscris ă astă-ḑi *6* ale
luneĭ *Februarie* anul una mie opt sute nouě ḑecĭ *și 8*
Fi ca a D. lui *Mendel Faerberg, de ani 39,*
croitor de dame.
și a D. *Rosa născută Aron Rotman*
de ani 34, casnică.

Spre credinţă s'a liberat acest certificat spre a servi la
ceremonia religioasă

OFICIAR

Șeful Serviciuluĭ

— 127 —

Document #2: A Romanian Passport

IN NUMELE MAJESTĂŢEI SALE
FERDINAND I
REGELE ROMANIEI

PASPORT

Liberat D...
Ghinda Brener

Născut la 1883 la Alexandreni
Jud. Bălţi in Basarabia
Domiciliat la Alexandreni-Bălţ

De profesiune casnica
Călătorind in America

Semnătura titularului:
(Signature du porteur)

Semnalmente:

Etatea: 37 ani
Talia: mijlocie
Părul: carunt
Fruntea: normale
Sprâncenile: castanii
Ochii: căprii
Nasul: } normale
Gura:
Barba:
Bărbia: } ovale
Faţa (obrazul):
Tenul: smead
Semne particulare: nu are

In numele Majestăţei sale Ferdinand I, Regele Romaniei — "In the name of His Majesty Ferdinand I, the King of Romania"

Liberat Dnei Ghinda Brener — "Issued to Mme. Ghinda Brener"

Născut la 1883 la Alexandreni — "Born in 1883 in Alexandreni"

Jud. Bălţi in Basarabia — "Băltă district [*Judeţ* — "district"] in Bessarabia." Bessarabia is one of the regions historically comprising Romania (the others: Wallachia, Moldavia, Crisana-Maramures, Transylvania, Dobrudja, the Banat, and part of Bucovina). Since 1940 large parts of these regions have been incorporated into Bulgaria, Hungary, and Ukraine; Băltă, for instance, is now Balta, a city north and west of Odessa in Ukraine.

Domiciliat la Alexandreni- Bălţi — "Residing in Alexandreni, Băltă"

De profesiune casnica — "Of profession: domestic"

Călătorind in America — "Traveling in America" (*călătorind* is from the verb *călători*).

Semnătura titularului — "Bearer's signature"

Semnalmente — "Description"
Etatea: 37 ani — "Age: 37 years"
Talia: mijlocie — "Stature: medium"
Părul: carunt — "Hair: greying"
Fruntea: normale — "Forehead: normal"
Sprâncenile: castanii — "Eyebrows: light brown"
Ochii: căprii — "Eyes: brown"
Nasul: normale — "Nose: normal"
Gura: normale — "Mouth: normal"
*Barba: -- * — "Beard: —"
Bărbia: ovale — "Chin: oval"
Faţa (obrazul): ovale — "Face (cheek): oval"
Tenul: smead — "Complexion: pale"
Semne particulare: nu are — "Distinguishing marks: none"

The handwriting makes it impossible to be sure of some of the answers above, but those given appear to be correct (we cheated by checking answers given in French on accompanying pages, omitted here to save space). Note that most of the nouns here have the definite article — *părul = păr + -ul, faţa = faţă + -a, nasul = nas + -ul*, and so on.

– 128 –

Selected Vocabulary Terms

Compiling a useful vocabulary list for Romanian is a difficult task; reliable and comprehensive reference sources are hard to find, and variations in spelling are confusing — one pre-1967 dictionary shows that "Romanian" is *Român* and "word" is *cuvânt*, but a post-1967 source gives *Romîn* and *cuvînt*. Most documents family researchers encounter will probably use those older spellings, so they are emphasized here. The terms listed are those likely to appear in documents, but the treatment here is greatly simplified to minimize confusion for casual students of the language.

Words are listed here in as simple a form as possible, with the basic Romanian form followed by the English meanings that make sense in the context of documents; parts of speech are indicated when ambiguity could easily cause confusion. Nouns are given in the singular, usually without the definite article, but readers need to remember that the article is often added to the noun and will change the ending somewhat. The few verbs necesssary are generally given in their infinitive form (the form under which they would normally be found in a dictionary); the formats of most documents require relatively little knowledge of verbs.

No separate listing of Romanian first names is given because Romanian names are generally either easy to recognize as like their counterparts in other languages, or else unique, without counterparts in other languages.

acolo — (adv.) there
afacere — affair, business
aici — here
alb — white
albastru — blue
alta — another
amiaza, amiazi — noon
an — year
aprilie — April
apropiat — near
armată — army
astă-ḑĭ (astăzi) — today
august — August
autoritate — authority
avea — to have
avocat — lawyer
azi — today
bagaj — luggage
băiat — boy
bani — money
barbă — beard
bărbie — chin
barcă — boat
bilet — ticket
birou — office
biserică — church; *bisericaş* — priest
boală — disease
bogat — rich
bolnav — sick
botez — baptism, christening
brun — brown
brutar — baker
bucătar — (noun) cook
buletin — certificate
bun — good
bunic — grandfather; *bună, bunică* — grandmother
călători — to travel

cantitate — amount
cap — head
carte — book
carunt — gray
casă — house
căsătorie — marriage
casnica — domestic
castaniu — chestnut, light brown
cetăţean — citizen
chitanţă — receipt
cimitir — cemetery
cinci — five; *cincisprezece* — fifteen; *cincizeci* — fifty
cine — who?
comerciant — merchant
comună — parish, community
contra — against
copil — child; *copilă* — girl
corp — body
credinţă — belief
croitor — tailor; *croitor de dame* — ladies' tailor
cuvânt — word
da — yes; (verb) to give
dată — date
de — from, of
deasemenea — also
decemvrie — December
dedesubt — below
departe — far
diferit — different
dimineaţă — morning
doi — two; *doisprezece* — twelve
domiciliat — residing, living
douăsprezece — twelve
douăzeci — twenty
drept — (adj.) right; (n.) law
drum — way
dulgher — carpenter

duminică — Sunday
dumnezeu — God
după — after; *după amiazi* — afternoon
el — he
est — east
etateă — age
Evreu — Jew
fabrică — factory
face — to make; *făcut* — made, done
fată — girl
faţă — face
februarie — February
femeie — woman
fi — to be
fiică — daughter
fiu — son
foarte — very
frate — brother
frunte — forehead
gardă — guard
graniţă — border
greş, greşală — mistake
greşit — (adj.) wrong
greutate — weight
gri — grey
gură — mouth
guvern — government
hârtie — paper
ianuarie — January
iar — again
ieri — yesterday
ieşire — exit
impozit — (noun) tax
împreună — together
înalt — tall
inginer — engineer
inimă — heart

însoţì — to accompany
insulă — island
înţelege — to understand
interzice — forbidden
intrare — entrance
între — between
întrebare — (noun) question
întunecat — dark
învăţător — teacher
ipotecă — mortgage
iulie — July
iunie — June
joi — Thursday
judeţ — district
jumătate — half
la — at, in
lac — lake
liber — free
liberat — issued
limbă — language, tongue
lună — month; moon
lung — long
luni — Monday
măcelar — butcher
mai — May
mamă — mother
mare — (adj.) large; (noun) sea
marinar — sailor
martie — March
marţi — Tuesday
mătuşă — aunt
meserie — profession
mic — small
mie — thousand
miercuri — Wednesday
mijlociu — average, medium
mînă — hand
mireasă — bride
moarte — death
mult — much
muncă — (noun) work
munte — mountain
nas — nose
nascere, născare — birth
născut — born
naştere — birth
negru — black
niciodată — never
noapte — night
noemvrie — November
noră — daughter-in-law
nord — north
nou — new
nouă — nine; *nouăsprezece* — nineteen; *nouăzeci* — ninety
nu — no

nume — name; *numele de familie* — surname; *numele de botez* — given name
nuntă — wedding
obraz — cheek
ochi — eye
octomvrie — October
oficiul — office; *oficiul stăreĭ civile* — the Office of Vital Statistics
om — man
opt — eight; *optsprezece* — eighteen; *optzeci* — eighty
oră — hour, o'clock
oraş — town
orb — blind
păr — hair
părinţi — parents
paşaport — passport
patru — four; *patrusprezece* — four teen; *patruzeci* — forty
permis — permitted
plecà — to leave; *plecare* — departure
preţ — (noun) cost, price
primărie — town hall
proprietate — property
prunc — baby
răsboi — war
răspunde, răspuns — (noun) answer
regat — kingdom
rege — king; *regină* — queen
religie — religion
rîu — river
roş, roşiu — red
şaisprezece — sixteen
şaizeci — sixty
sâmbătă — Saturday
sănătate — health
şaptămână — week
şapte — seven; *şaptesprezece* — seventeen; *şaptezeci* — seventy
şase — six
sat — village
şcoală — school
scrie — to write
scrisoare — letter
scurt — short
seară — evening
secol — century
semnalment(e) — description
semnătură — signature
semne particulare — distinguishing marks

septemvrie — September
servitoare — (chamber)maid
sfat — advice
sfert — quarter
şi — and
sigil — seal, stamp
siguranţă — safety
singur — alone
soldat — soldier
soră — sister
sosire — arrival
soţ — husband
sprâncenile — the eyebrows
stâng — left (opposite of right)
stare — state, condition
staţiune — station
stradă — street
străin — foreign; *în străinătate*, abroad
sub — under
subţire — thin
sud — south
surd — deaf
sută — hundred
talie — height, stature
tânăr — young
ţară — (noun) country
ţăran — peasant
târziu — late
tată — father
tenul — the complexion
timp — time
tot — all
traduce — to translate
trei — three; *treisprezece* — thirteen; *treizeci* — thirty
tren — (noun) train
un — one; *unsprezece* — eleven
unchiu — uncle
unde — where
ureche — ear
valoare — value
vamă — duty, toll
văr — cousin
vârstă — age
vechi — old
vecin — neighbor
venì — to come
verde — green
vest — west
viaţă — life
vineri — Friday
vinovat — guilty
vitreg- — step- (mother, etc.)
vorbì — to speak, to talk
zi — day

Español

The Spanish Alphabet

Printed	Cursive
A, a	*A, a*
B, b	*B, b*
C, c	*C, c*
Ch, ch	*Ch, ch*
D, d	*D, d*
E, e	*E, e*
F, f	*F, f*
G, g	*G, g*
H, h	*H, h*
I, i	*I, i*
J, j	*J, j*
K, k	*K, k*
L, l	*L, l*
Ll, ll	*Ll, ll*
M, m	*M, m*
N, n	*N, n*
Ñ, ñ	*Ñ, ñ*
O, o	*O, o*
P, p	*P, p*
Q, q	*Q, q*
R, r	*R, r*
Rr, rr	*Rr, rr*
S, s	*S, s*
T, t	*T, t*
U, u	*U, u*
V, v	*V, v*

Printed	Cursive	Printed	Cursive
W, w	*W, w*	Y, y	*Y, y*
X, x	*X, x*	Z, z	*Z, z*

The only unfamiliar letter in the Spanish alphabet is *ñ*, which sounds like the "ni" sound in the English word "onion." The letters *k* and *w* appear only in words of foreign origin. *Ch, ll, ñ* and *rr* are considered distinct characters in the alphabet and are so listed in the dictionary.

One often sees vowels marked with an acute accent, as in the word *habló*, "spoke," but the accented letters do not represent separate alphabetical characters. The accent (1) indicates the syllable is accented when normal rules of stress would not call for it, (2) shows that words such as *donde* "where" or *cuando* "when" are being used as interrogatives, *¿dónde?* "where?" or *¿cuándo?* "when?", and (3) distinguishes words spelled alike but different in meaning, e. g., *el* "the" as opposed to *él* "he." The first point is of some importance, because as a rule Spanish words ending in a consonant are accented on the last syllable but those ending in a vowel are stressed on the penultimate. *Hablo*, "I speak," ends in a vowel and so the first syllable is stressed. *Habló*, stressed on the last syllable, means "he [she, it] spoke," and the acute accent signals a departure from normal stress and a change in meaning.

Most Americans find it easy to learn to pronounce Spanish passably. The vowels, like those of Italian, are clear and pure; *a* is pronounced as in our word "father," *e* more or less as in our word "let," *i* as in "machine," *o* as in "hotel," *u* as in "rule," and *y*, alone or at the end of a word, acts just like, and is pronounced the same as, Spanish *i*. Vowel combinations are not too tough: *ai* sounds much like our long *i* in "ice," *au* sounds like the *ow* in "cow," *ei* like our *a* in "late," and *oi* like the diphthong in "boy." The *i* combined with another vowel generally sounds like our *y* (e. g., *bien* sounds like "byen," *gracias* like "grahs-yas"), and the *u* combined with a vowel sounds like our *w* except after a *q*, in which case it's silent (e. g., *quien* sounds like "kyen").

Pronunciation of consonants varies considerably in different areas, but some general guidelines can be given. The *b* and *v* are pronounced the same, somewhat like English *b* but unaspirated; *c* is hard as in "car" except before *e* or *i*, when it sounds like the *c* in "century" (in some areas more like the *th* in "thin"). The *ch* is pronounced as in "chair"; *g* sounds like a rather guttural *h* before *e* and *i*, otherwise like the *g* in "go." The *h* is silent, *j* is a sound somewhat more guttural than our *h*, and the *ll* in many instances sounds like the *y* in "yarn". The *r* is trilled with the tip of the tongue, especially at the beginning of a word; *s* usually sounds like the *s* in "sin" (or *th* in "thin") but resembles the *z* in "zone" when it precedes *m* or *n*. *X* sounds like the *s* in "sin" when it follows an *e-*, otherwise it sounds like *ks* (except for words like *Texas* and *Mexico*, where it is pronounced like Spanish *j*). Consonantal *y* (i. e., followed by a vowel at the beginning of a word or syllable) is like the *y* in "yarn," and *z* is pronounced like the *s* in "sin" or, in some areas, like the *th* in "thin." The lisping sound of *c* and *z* typifies Castillian pronunciation, considered the most classical and correct.

Document #1: Civil Birth Certificate

Reproduced at full size on the next two pages is a Spanish civil birth certificate. The handwriting is clear (once you get used to it), and the terminology used is typical of that found in such documents — so this certificate is worth close study.

[handwritten text]

Don Cristino Sanchez Moreno, Juez Municipal y encargado del Registro Civil de esta Capital

> Don — title of respect used before names
> Juez — "judge"
> encargado — "person in charge, keeper"
> Registro Civil — "Civil Registry, Vital Statistics"
> **Translation:** Don Cristino Sanchez Moreno, Municipal Judge and Keeper of the Capital's Vital Records...

[handwritten text]

Certifico: Que en el tomo ochenta y cinco de la Sección
primera de nacimientos al folio ciento noventa y cinco
vuelto y bajo el número tres mil setecientos setenta y
nueve, aparace la siguiente

> certifico — "I certify" (from certificar, to certify)
> tomo ochenta y cinco — "volume eighty-five"
> la Sección primera — "the first section"
> nacimientos — "births" (plural)
> al folio ciento noventa y cinco — "on page one hundred ninety-five"
> bajo el número — "under number"
> tres mil setecientros setenta y nueve — "three thousand seven hundred seventy-nine"
> aperece — "appears" (from aperecer, to appear)
> la siguiente — "the following"
> **Translation:** ...I certify that in volume 85 in the First Section regarding births, on page 195, certificate #3779, the following appears:

[handwritten text]

En la ciudad de Almería a treinta y uno de Diciembre de mil novecientos dos ante D. José Comarco y Reyes
Juez Municipal y D. Eduardo Morcillo, Secretario.

> ciudad — "city"
> treinta y uno — "thirty-one"
> Diciembre — "December"

A.4.414.098 ✱

Don Cristino Sánchez Moreno, Juez Municipal y encargado del Registro Civil de esta Capital _____

Certifico: Que en el tomo ochenta y cinco de la Sección primera de nacimientos al folio ciento noventa y cinco vuelto y bajo el número tres mil, setecientos setenta y nueve, aparece la siguiente _____

En la ciudad de Almería, a treinta y uno de Diciembre de mil novecientos dos, ante D. José Carrasco y Reyes Juez Municipal y D. Eduardo Morcillo, Secretario, compareció D. Andrés Guilliano Macías, natural de Gibraltar término municipal de id. provincia de id. de 42 años, del comercio, domiciliado en esta Ciudad en la calle de Beloy nº 3 presentando con objeto de que se inscriba en el Registro Civil un niño y al efecto, como padre declaró: Que dicho niño nació en esta Ciudad, a las diez y siete horas del día veinte y nueve en dicho domicilio = Que es hijo legítimo del compareciente y de Da. Amalia Naval Alba, natural de Gibraltar, de 32 años, casados, que es nieto por línea paterna de D. Eugenio y de Da. Adela naturales de Gibraltar y por la materna de D. Francisco, de Córdoba y de Da. Josefa, de Gibraltar = I, que, a el

expresado niño se le puso el nombre de Eugenio = Todo
lo cual presenciaron como testigos D. Indalecio Gassinello Vivas y D. José Murcia Moreno, naturales de Almería, mayores de edad, y de estos vecinos = Leída ín-
tegramente este acta e invitadas las personas que deben suscribirla, a que la leyeran por sí mismas, si
así lo creían conveniente, se estampó en ella el sello del
Juzgado Municipal, y la firmaron el Sr. Juez, declarante y los testigos, y de todo ello como Secretario certifico =
José Carrasco y Reyes = Andrés Guilliano Macías = Indalecio Gassinello = José Murcia = Eduardo Morcillo ————

Así, aparece de su original, a que me remito. I para que cons-
te, a petición de parte interesada, expido la presente en Almería
a ocho de Mayo de mil novecientos diecisiete..

I hereby certify that the foregoing signature
is that of Cristino Sanchez, Municipal Judge of
this City, and I further certify that the person
named Eugene Guillano in the foregoing Municipal
certificate was entered in the Register of British
Subjects by his father Andrew Sebastian Guillano,
British Colonial subject, on the thirtieth day of
March one thousand nine hundred and three.-
              British Vice Consulate,
          ALMERIA 9th   May   1917.

              British Vice Consul.

– 134 –

mil novecientos dos — "one thousand nine hundred two"

ante — "before, in the presence of"

Translation: In the city of Almería on the thirty-first of December of 1902 before Don José Comarco y Reyes, Municipal Judge, and Don Eduardo Morcillo, Secretary...

[handwritten text]

com-

pareció D. Andres Guilliano Macías, natural de Gibraltar
término municipal de id. provincia de id. de 42 años
del comercio, domiciliado en esta Ciudad en la calle de Beloy Nº 3, presentando con objeto de que se inscriba en el
Registro Civil un niño y al efecto, como padre declaró:

del comercio — literally "of the commerce," means the declarant's occupation, a merchant

compareció — "appeared" (preterite tense, from *comparecer,* to appear)

natural de — "native of"

id. [idem] — "the same, the aforementioned"

año — "year"

domiciliado — "residing, domiciled"

calle — "street"

presentando — literally, "presented" (from *presentar*), but the passive or reflexive *(presentarse)* can mean "appearing, presenting himself"

con objeto de que — "with the goal that..."

se inscriba — "be registered" (from *inscribirse,* to be registered)

niño — "boy, male child"

al efecto que — "to the effect that"

como padre declaró — "as the father declared" (from *declarar,* to declare)

Translation: ...Don Andres Guilliano Macías appeared, a native of Gibraltar, city of Gibraltar and Province of Gibraltar, 42 years of age, a merchant residing in this city on 3 Beloy St. who has appeared with the intention of registering in the Civil Registry [the birth of] a male child, and, as the father stated...

[handwritten text]

Que dicho niño nació en esta Ciudad a las diez y siete
horas del día veinte y nueve en dicho domicilio: Que es
hijo legítimo del compareciente y de Da. Amalia Naval
Alba, natural de Gibraltar, de 32 años, casados,

dicho — "the aforesaid"

nació — "was born" (from *nacer,* to be born)

hora — "hour, o'clock"; *a las diez y siete horas* — "five p.m." ("at 17 o'clock")

día — "day"

– 135 –

veinte y nueve — "twenty-nine"
domicilio — "home, residence, domicile"
hijo legítimo — "legitimate son"
compareciente — "the party who appeared, the declarant"
Da [Doña] — "Mrs." (feminine equivalent of *Don*)
casados — "married" (plural)

Translation: ...that the aforesaid child was born in this city at 17⁰⁰ hours on the 29th day in said residence and that he is the legitimate son of the declarant and Doña Amalia Naval Alba, a native of Gibraltar, 32 years of age, both married...

nieto por linea paterna de D. Eugenio y de Da. Adela (que es)
naturales de Gibraltar y por la materna de D. Francis-
co de Córdoba y de Da. Josefa, de Gibraltar:

es — "[he] is" (from the irregular verb *ser*, to be)
nieto — "grandson"
por linea paterna — "on the father's side" (literally "through paternal line")
la [linea] materna — "on the mother's side"

Translation: ...and that he is the grandson on his father's side of Eugenio and Adela, natives of Gibraltar, and on the mother's side of Francisco of Córdoba and of Josefa of Gibraltar...

Y que a el
expresado niño se le puso el nombre de Eugenio: Todo
lo cual presenciaron como testigos D. Indalecio Cami-
nello Vivas y D. José Murcia Moreno, naturales de Al-
mería mayores de edad y de estos vecinos:

a el expresado niño — literally, "to the aforesaid boy"
se le puso — literally, "to him was put, placed," (*puso* from *poner*), but here is better translated as "on the aforesaid boy was placed" or "to the aforesaid boy was given"
el nombre de — "the name of"
todo lo cual — "all of which"
presenciaron — "witnessed, saw, were present at" (from *presenciar*)
testigos — "witnesses"
mayores de edad — "of age" (*edad* means "age")
vecinos — "area, vicinity" (archaic expression)

Translation: ...and that the aforementioned child was given the name of Eugenio. All this was attested to by the witnesses Indalecio Caminello Vivas y José Murcia Moreno, natives of Almería of legal age and from this area.

Leida ín-
tegramente este acta e invitadas las personas que de-
ben suscribirla a que la leyeran por sí mismas, sí
así lo creían conveniente, se estampó en ella el sello del
Juzgado Municipal, y la firmaron el Sr. Juez, decla-
rante y los testigos y de todo ello como Secretario certifico:

Leida in-
tegramente este acta e invitadas las personas que de-
ben suscribirla a que la leyeran por si mismas, si
así lo creian conveniente, se estampó en el sello del
Juzgado Municipal, y la firmaron el Sr. Juez, decla-
rante y los testigos y de todo ello como Secretario certifico:

leida integramente este acta — "this document [was] read (from *leer*) in its entirety"

invitadas — "[were] invited" (from *invitar*)

que deben suscribirla — "who are supposed to sign it"

la leyeran por si mismas — "they had read it for themselves"

si así lo creian conveniente — "if they think it suitable" (*creian* from *creer,* to believe, think)

se estampó en ella el sello del Juzgado Municipal — "the seal of the Municipal Court was stamped on it" (*estampó* from *estampar,* to stamp).

firmaron — "they signed it" (from *firmar*)

declarante — "the declarant"

y de todo ello certifico — "and I certify all this"

Translation: This document was read in its entirety and all the persons who were to sign it if they found it to be correct were invited to read it for themselves, and the seal of the Municipal Court was affixed to it, and it was signed by the Judge, the declarant, and the witnesses, and I, as Secretary, certify all of this...

[The remainder of the document simply lists the names of those signing it and gives a little legalese of no genealogical significance.]

Document #2: Identity Card

Consejo Superior de Emigración — "Upper (Superior) Emigration Council"

Cartera de Identidad — "Identification Card"

del Emigrante — "of the emigrant"

D. Angelino Caselles Más— "Don Angelino Caselles Más"

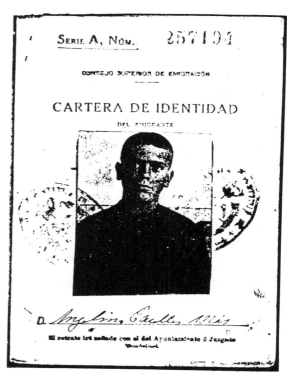

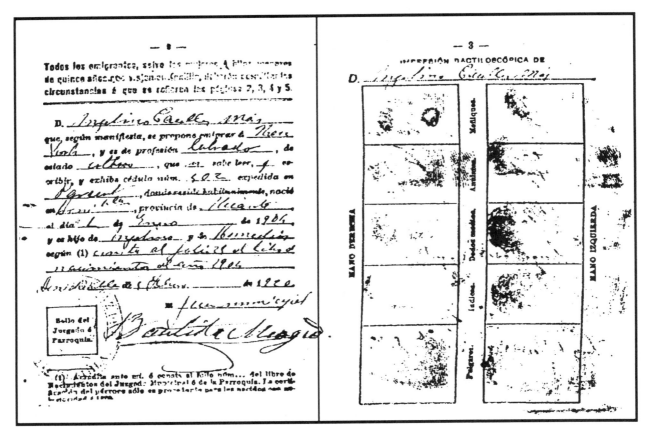

D. *Angelino Caselles Más* que según manifiesta, se propone emigrar a *New York*, y es de profesión *labrador* de estado *soltero* que no sabe leer y escribir y exhibe cédula núm. *502* expedida en *Parcent* nació en *Benichembla* provincia de *Alicante* al día *1* de *enero* de *1904* y es hijo de *Angelino* y *Remedios*, según consta al folio *29* al libro de nacimientos del año *1904*.

según manifiesta — "according to statements made"

se propone — "intends, proposes" (from *proponerse*)

emigrar a — "emigrate to"

profesión — "profession"

labrador — "farmer, peasant"

estado — "status"

soltero — "single"

sabe — "knows" (from *saber*)

leer — "to read"

escribir — "to write"

exhibe — "bears, shows, has" (from *exhibir*)

cédula — "identification papers"

expedida — "issued"

nació — "was born" (from *nacer*)

enero — "January"

consta — "is on record" (from *constar,* to be clear or evident, to consist of, to be on record)

folio — "page, folio"

libro de nacimiento — "birth register"

Translation: Mr. Angelino Caselles Más, according to statements made, proposes to emigrate to New York, and is a laborer by profession, single, who cannot read or write, and who has identification document #502, issued in Parcent. He was born in Benichembla, Province of Alicante, on January 1, 1904, and is the son of Angelino and Remedios, according to the information recorded on folio 29 in the Register of Births for the year 1904.

page 4 *[page 3 bears only Angelino's Impresión Dactiloscópica, i. e., fingerprints.]*

CARACTERISTICOS QUE CONCURREN EN
D. *Angelino Caselles Más*

estatura: *baja*   ojos: *[illegible]*
corpulencia: *regular*   nariz: *regular*
pelo: *negro*   boca: *id*
cejas: *al pelo*   labios: *id*
bigote: —   orejas: *id*
barba: —   cutis: *fino*
frente: *regular*   color: *pálido*

SEÑAS PARTICULARES

Pecas: —   Calvas: —
Cicatrices: *[illegible]*   Imperfecciones: *Ningún*
Lunares: *[illegible]*   Otras señas: —

Although these blanks are often filled in with illegible scrawls (as in some instances here), a knowledge of the terms involved and the possible answers can often help one decipher the scrawl. Here are some of the unfamiliar words used in this description:

estatura — height   ojos — eyes
corpulencia — weight   nariz — nose
pelo — hair*   boca — mouth
cejas — eyebrows   labios — lips
bigote — moustache   orejas — ears
barba — beard   cutis — skin
frente — forehead   color — color, complexion
pecas — freckles   calvas — bald spots
cicatrices [singular   imperfecciones — imperfections
     cicatriz] — scars   otras señas — other marks
lunares — moles   ningún — none

*(an alternative word for "hair" is cabello)

Possible responses for some of the abovenamed categories:

pelo (hair) — negro (black), castaño (brown), rubio (blonde), pellirojo (red)

ojos (eyes) — azules (blue), negro (black)

estatura (height) — baja (short), alta (tall)

In many cases the word regular (normal) will be recorded in places where a color is not required, i. e., forehead, nose, mouth, etc.

Here is a translation of the information given on page 4:

CHARACTERISTICS APPEARING IN
D. Angelina Caselles Más

Height: short	*Eyes:* [illegible]
Weight: normal	*Nose:* normal
Hair: black	*Mouth:* same
Eyebrows: like the hair	*Lips:* same
Moustache: none	*Ears:* same
Beard: none	*Skin:* fine
Forehead: normal	*Color:* pale

DISTINGUISHING MARKS

Freckles —	*Bald Spots* —
Scars: [illegible]	*Imperfection:* None
Moles: [illegible]	*Other marks* —

The other items on pages 4 and 5 are basically legalities which give no useful information in this particular case; but since they could conceivably give useful clues in some cases, a very brief analysis and translation of them may be of value.

Declaramos conocer al individuo a que se hace referencia en esta hoja y en la anterior, así como que es la suya la fotografía unida a esta Cartera y sellado con el sello oficial de este Ayuntamiento.

conocer — "to know, be acquainted with"

a que se hace referencia — "to whom reference is made" (*se hace* from *hacerse*, "to be made, to become, get")

hoja — page, sheet, leaf

en la anterior — "on the previous [page]"

la suya — "his"

unida — "joined, attached" (from *unir*, to join, attach)

sellada — "sealed" (from *sellar*, to seal, derived from *sello*, seal)

Ayuntamiento — "Municipal Government, Town Hall"

Translation: We declare that we know the individual to whom reference is made on this and on the preceding page, so that his is the photograph attached to this card and stamped with the official seal of this Municipal Government.

ANTECEDENTES PENALES — *Del emigrante D. Angelino Caselles Más hasta esta fecha no aperecen en este Registro antecedentes penales, según los que est sujeto a condena...*

del emigrante — "of the, regarding the emigrant" (from *de + el*)

hasta esta fecha — "up to this date"

aperecen — "appear" (from *aperecer*, to appear)

antecedentes penales — "criminal antecedents" (i. e., previous crimes)

según los — "according to those"

est...sujeto a condena — "is subject to punishment"

Translation: Regarding the emigrant D. Angelino Casalles Más, to this date there do not appear in this Registry any previous crimes [the rest is crossed out as inapplicable].

PROCESAMIENTO — *Examinados los antecedentes oportunos, no consta que D. Angelino Caselles Más esta sujeto a procesamiento.*

examinados — "having been examined" (from *examinar*, to examine)

oportunos — "at hand"

no consta — "it does not appear" (from *constar*, to appear, be evident, consist of)

procesamiento — "prosecution"

Translation: Upon examination of the antecedents at hand, it does not appear that D. Angelino Casalles Más is subject to prosecution.

Document #3: A Consular Record

The following consular record is bilingual and self-explanatory. Studying and comparing the Spanish and English texts carefully will give useful insight into official Spanish terminology.

CONSULADO GENERAL DE ESPAÑA EN NUEVA YORK

CONSULATE GENERAL OF SPAIN AT NEW YORK

Cédula de Nacionalidad para transeuntes No. *6758*

Certificate of Nationality for transients No.

Don *Presentacion Sastre Guitart*
Mrs.

natural de *Pego, Alicante* edad *17* años
native of years old

estado *Soltera* profesion *Su casa*
condition *Single* occupation *house-wife*

residente en *77 Canton st., Hartford, Conn.*,
resident at

se halla empadronado en el Registro de españoles transeuntes
is entered in the Register of Spanish transients
de este Consulado.
of this Consulate.

Y á fin de que el interesado pueda acreditar su
And in order that the above interested party may have his
nacionalidad, le expido la presente cédula en Nueva York á
nationality established, the present certificate is issued to him at
17 de *Noviembre* de 19 *20*
New York, N.Y., this 17 day of November 19 20.

El Cónsul General

Alfonso Bun

The Consul General

VALE POR UN AÑO
VALID FOR A YEAR

NUEVA YORK
No. *6758*
Articulo 66 — *37*
Derechos$ *1.25*
Fecha *17–11–20*

_____
(Firma del interesado.)
(*Signature of interested party.*)

– 141 –

Selected Vocabulary Terms

Spanish vocabulary does not usually cause American students a great deal of trouble. One factor contributing to this may be the large pool of words Spanish and English share from Latin, which assures that in any document one might reasonably expect at least half the words to resemble English words enough to give a clue to their meaning (although that clue does not **always** turn out to be trustworthy). Another contributing factor is the presence of a large Spanish-speaking populace in the United States, which has acquainted even the least gifted, linguistically, with more than a few Spanish words. In any case, this word-list probably does not need extensive explanation.

The parts of speech are specified only when needed to prevent confusion, e. g., *bajo* can be an adjective meaning "low, short," and it can also be a preposition meaning "below," so each set of meanings is identified by "(adj.)" and "(prep.)" Verb parts are given cautiously, most often by infinitive, because verbs are the most complicated part of Spanish grammar, and it is unwise to dabble much with them; if you need more on verbs than is given here, consult a textbook or competent teacher.

Note that adjectives in Spanish take endings appropriate to the nouns they modify, i. e., a married man is *casado,* but a married woman is *casada,* and married people are *casados.* Adjectives are generally given in the masculine singular form because that is how they will generally be listed in dictionaries; but readers should understand that just because *alta* is not listed separately is no cause for despair: it is merely the feminine form of *alto.*

Please remember that these words are given in the forms and with the meanings most commonly seen in documents. Thus *alto* can be the command *¡Alto!* ("Stop!"), but only its meaning as an adjective is given here because that is the only usage you are likely to encounter in documents.

a — (preposition) to; it precedes nouns or pronouns used as direct objects of verbs

a fin de que — toward the end that, in order that

abril — April

acreditar — establish, accredit

acta — document, record

agosto — August

al — to the (=*a* + *el*)

alto — tall

año — year

ante — before, in the presence of

antecedente — antecedent, preceding

anterior — previous

aparecer — to appear, show up

así — thus

ayuntamiento — municipal government, town hall

azul — blue

bajo — (adj.) low, short; (prep.) below

barba — beard

bigote — moustache

boca — mouth

calle — street

calva — bald spot

característica — (noun) characteristic, trait

característico — (adj.) characteristic

cartera — card; *cartera de identidad* — identity card

casado — married

castaño — (adj.) brown

catorce — fourteen

cédula — certificate, slip of paper

ceja — eyebrow

certificar — to certify, register

cicatriz — scar (pl. *cicatrices*)

cien — one hundred

ciento — hundred; *ciento uno* — one hundred one (101)

cinco — five

cincuenta — fifty

ciudad — city

color — color, complexion

comercio — commerce, trade

como — like, as, how

comparecer — to appear (before a judge, official, etc.)

compareciente — the one appearing, the declarant

con — with

concurrir — to meet, appear, be evident

condena — prison term, sentence

conocer — to know

constar — to be evident, appear, consist of (*consta* — [it] appears, consists of)

consulado — consulate

conveniente — convenient, suitable

corpulencia — weight

creer — to believe, think

cual — which; *cuál* — which?; *todo lo cual* — all that which

cuarenta — forty

cuarto — fourth

cuatro — four

cutis — skin; complexion

Da. — (abbreviation of *Doña*)

dactiliscópico — of fingerprints

de — of, from, about

deber — to owe, to have to (*deben* — they are supposed to)

décimo — tenth

declarante — declarant

declarar — to declare, state; (*declaramos* — we state; *declaro* — I state)

del — of the (abbrev. of *de* + *el*)

día — day

dicho — said, e. g., *el dicho niño* — the aforesaid boy

diciembre — December

diecinueve — nineteen

dieciocho — eighteen

dieciséis — sixteen

diecisiete — seventeen

diez — ten

doce — twelve

domiciliado — residing in

domicilio — home, residence

domingo — Sunday

Don — Don (title used before men's first names)

Doña — Doña (title used before women's first names)

dos — two

duodécimo — twelfth

edad — age

efecto effect, result — *al efecto que* — to the effect that

el — the

él — he

ella — she

ello — it

emigrante — emigrant

emigrar — to emigrate (*a Nueva York* — to New York)

empadronado — entered, registered

en — in

encargar — to put in charge; *encargado* — in charge

enero — January

escribir — to write

España — Spain

español — Spanish

esta — this

está — is (from *estar*)

estado — state, condition, rank, marital status

estampar — to stamp

estatura — height

este — this

estos — those (pl. of *este*)

examinar — to examine

exhibir — to show, display, bear

expedir — to dispatch, issue; *expedido* — issued; *expido* — I issue

expresar — to express; *expresado* — the one mentioned

febrero — February

fecha — date (*hasta esta fecha* — to this date)

firma — signature

firmar — to sign (*firmaron* — they signed)

folio — page

frente — forehead

hacer — to make, do (this verb is used many ways in many different idiomatic expressions, including *hacerse,* to make oneself, become)

hallar — to find; *hallarse empadronado* — to find oneself entered, to be entered/registered

hasta — until, up to

hermana — sister

hermano — brother

hija — daughter

hijo — son

hoja — page, sheet, leaf

hora — hour; *a las diez y siete horas* — at seventeen (hundred) hours = 5:00 p.m.

id. — (abbreviation of *idem*) the same, ditto

identidad — identity

imperfección — imperfection, flaw

impresión — impression; *impresión dactiliscópica* — fingerprints

inscribir — to inscribe, register; *inscribirse* — to be registered

integramente — in its totality

interesado — the one interested, concerned

invitar — to invite; *invitado* — invited

jueves — Thursday

juez — judge

julio — July

junio — June

juzgado — court, tribunal

labio — lip

labrador — farmer, peasant

le — [to] him, [to] her, [to] it

leer — to read; *leido* — [it was] read; *leyeron* — they read

legítimo — legitimate, real

libro — book

linea — line; *por linea paterna* — by the paternal line

lo — it

lunar — (noun) mole, blemish

lunes — Monday

madre — mother

martes — Tuesday

marzo — March

materno — (adj.) maternal

mayo — May

mayor — larger, greater; *mayor de edad* — of legal age

miércoles — Wednesday

mil — thousand

mismo — self; *por sí mismas* — for themselves

nacimiento — birth, origin

nacer — to be born; *nació* — was born

nacionalidad — nationality

nariz — nose, nostril; *narices* (plur.) — nostrils

natural — native (*de* — of)

negro — black

nieto — grandson, grandchild; *nieta* — granddaughter

ningún — no, none

niño — child, boy; *niña* — girl

no — not, no

nombre — name

novecientos — nine hundred

noventa — ninety

noviembre — November

nueve — nine

nuevo — new

núm. — abbreviation of *número*

número — number

objeto — object, purpose

ochenta — eighty

ocho — eight

octavo — eighth

ojo — eye

once — eleven

oportuno — at hand, convenient

oreja — ear

otro — other

padre — father

para — (prep.) for

particular — particular, special

paterno — (adj.) paternal

peca — freckle

pellirojo — red (hair)

pelo — hair

penal — penal, criminal

persona — person, individual

peso — peso; weight; hair

poner — to place, put; *ponerse* — to be placed, put

por — for

presenciar — to be present at, witness; *presenciaron* — they witnessed

presentado — presented, introduced

presente — present, this

primero — first

procesamiento — prosecution

profesión — profession

proponer — to propose; *proponerse* — to intend

provincia — province

poder — to be able

puede — is able, can (from *poder*)

puso — [he, she, it] placed (from *poner*)

qué — what?, which?

que — which, who; *á que* — to whom, to which

quince — fifteen

quinto — fifth

referencia — reference; *a que se hace referencia* — to whom reference is made

registro — registry

regular — normal, regular

rubio — blonde (hair)

sábado — Saturday

saber — to know; *sabe* — [he, she, it] knows

se — (reflexive pron.) himself, herself, itself

sección — section

secretario — secretary

según — according to; *según los* — according to them

segundo — second

seis — six

sellado — sealed

sello — seal

seña — sign, mark; *señas particulares* — distinguishing characteristics

Señor — Señor, Mr.

Señora — Señora, Mrs.

Señorita — Señorita, Miss

septiembre — September

séptimo — seventh

sesenta — sixty

setecientos — seven hundred

setenta — seventy

sexto — sixth

si — (conj.) if

sí — self; *por sí mismas* — for themselves

sí — yes

siete — seven

siguiente — (the) following

soltero — single, unmarried

Sr. — abbreviation of *Señor*

sujeto a — subject to

suscribir — to subscribe, sign

suya — his own, her own

tercero — third

término — end, completion, boundary, limit

testigo — witness

todo — all

tomo — volume

transeuntes — transients

trece — thirteen

treinta — thirty

tres — three

undécimo — eleven

unir — to join, unite; *unida* — join attached

uno — one

valer — to be valid; *vale por un año* — is valid for one year

veinte — twenty; *veintiuno* — twenty-one; *vientidós* — twenty-two

viernes — Friday

vuelto — turned (from *volver*)

Selected Personal Names

It should be remembered that "translating" personal names from one language into another is a dubious business; "José Verde" may translate literally as "Joe Green," but that doesn't mean it would be right to call him that. These equivalents (some of which are only approximate equivalents) are given mainly to facilitate research; if one realizes that *Guillermo* is a rough equivalent of "William," he may not be confused to find that his grandfather got on the boat "Guillermo Sanchez" but left Ellis Island as "Bill," or will not be fooled into thinking Christopher Columbus and Cristóbal Colón were two different people.

Adán — Adam

Alejandro — Alexander

Andrés — Andrew

Arturo — Arthur

Carlos — Charles

Cristóbal — Christopher

Eduardo — Edward

Enrique — Henry

Esteban — Steven

Federico — Frederick

Felipe — Philip

Francisco — Francis

Germán — Herman

Gualterio — Walter

Guillermo — William

Heriberto — Herbert

Inés — Agnes, Inez

Isabela — Elizabeth

Jaime — James

Jorge — George

José — Joseph

Juan — John

Luis — Louis

Marcos — Mark

Mateo — Matthew

Miguel — Michael

Pablo — Paul

Pedro — Peter

Ricardo — Richard

Tomás — Thomas

Vicente — Vincent

The Slavic Languages

Spoken largely in Eastern Europe and in emigré colonies in North and South America as well as Australia, the Slavic languages are generally subdivided into three groups: East, West, and South.

East Slavic
    Byelorussian (also known as "White Russian"), spoken in Belarus and portions of
        Eastern Poland
    Russian, spoken throughout the former Soviet Union
    Ukrainian, spoken in Ukraine and portions of eastern Poland and Czechoslovakia

West Slavic
    Polish, spoken in Poland and nearby areas in Lithuania, Belarus, and Ukraine
    Czech, spoken primarily in the Czech Republic (the western part of former Czechoslovakia)
    Slovak, spoken primarily in Slovakia (the eastern part of former Czechoslovakia)
    Lusatian, spoken in areas of eastern Germany, notably near Kottbus and Batuzen

South Slavic
    Bulgarian
    Macedonian
    Serbian   all, with the exception of Bulgarian, spoken in the area
    Croatian   that used to be Yugoslavia
    Montenegrin
    Slovenian

The Slavic languages written in the Roman alphabet are Polish, Czech, Slovak, Lusatian, Croatian, and Slovenian. The remainder employ Cyrillic script.

The Slavic languages are closely related in both their phonological and morphological structures. In many respects the lexical bases of the languages in this family are very similar. The researcher should not assume, however, that they are so similar as to be mutually intelligible. Distinct and significant differences exist and must be taken into consideration.

One feature of the Slavic languages shared by all except Bulgarian and Macedonian is a rather complex system of attaching grammatical endings to word stems, also called "inflection." (This has nothing to do with the variation in vocal tone also denoted by that word.) A typical noun, adjective, or pronoun, for example, can have up to fourteen forms, and it is the task of the researcher to recognize these different forms and deduct the endings to arrive at the base form of the word as found in the dictionary. The system of endings is referred to by many as "grammatical case." Each case has a distinct grammatical function; in very general terms, the functions of the cases are as follows:

Nominative — the dictionary form of the word, used primarily when a word is the subject of a predicate
Genitive — indicates possession, much like 's in English; also required in many languages after negatives, certain prepositions, some verbs, and expressions of quantity
Dative — used for the indirect object, and as the object of certain prepositions and verbs
Accusative — used for the direct object of a verb and as the object of certain prepositions
Locative or **Prepositional** — always accompanied by a preposition, most frequently indicating location (in, on, at, etc.)
Instrumental — expresses the means or instrument by which some activity is performed; the object of certain prepositions and other expressions
Vocative — used for direct address (absent in some languages)

It is essential to realize that cases are not theoretical devices proposed by language professors; they are an integral feature of most Slavic languages, whether spoken by scholars or peasants. To illustrate the system of case endings, the word for "wife" (or, in some languages, "woman") is given in the singular below. Note the different endings.

	Polish	*Russian*	*Serbocroatian*
Nominative	żona	жена	žena
Genitive	żony	жены	žene
Dative	żonie	жене	ženi
Accusative	żonę	жену	ženu
Locative	(o) żonie	(o) жене	(o) ženi
Instrumental	żoną	женой	ženom
Vocative	żono!	*[non-extant]*	ženo!

One can readily observe that an English speaker attempting to decipher a document in a Slavic language may become confused by the profusion of endings words can exhibit. The standard rendition of a birthplace or other proper name is mandatory in conducting further research; several examples (from Polish) of how endings must be deleted are illustrated below:

Examples: On urodził się w Stawiskach. = "He was born in Stawiski." Here a plural locative ending, *-ach,* required after the preposition *w,* is added to the root of the name of the town Stawisk*i* after the nominative plural ending *-i* has been deleted.

Similarly, *córka Jana Andruszkiewicza* = "the daughter of Jan Andruszkiewicz." Here the genitive ending, frequently used as a possessive "of...," is attached to the first name and surname. The researcher might erroneously conclude that the ancestor's name was "Jana Andruszkiewicza" rather than the correct "Jan Andruszkiewicz." This point is especially important because the nominative form of many Slavic feminine names is identical to the genitive/accusative of similar masculine names; so a mistake on this score can switch your ancestors' sex rather drastically. If your grandfather Andrzej is described as in a document as "Andrzej, syn Bronisława i Marty," it's desirable to realize that this means "Andrzej, son of Bronisław and Marta," **not** "Andrzej, son of Bronisława and Marty."

Names

Some basic observations on names may assist in clarifying their proper rendition. Names, either nominal (nouns in form) or adjectival (adjectives in form), are inflected for gender. In other words there may be a masculine and feminine version of the same surname. Adjectival surnames, ending most frequently in *-ski/-cki* in Polish, *-ský/-cký* in Czech, and -ский in Russian, have feminine forms in *-ska/-cka, -ska/-cka,* and -ская, respectively. Nominal surnames may add a suffix denoting the gender and, in some cases, the marital status of the bearer. One of the most common Slavic suffixes of this type is *-owa* (Polish), *-ová* (Czech), -ова in Russian. In the U.S. the feminine versions of surnames were often dropped. Note the following:

	Polish	*Czech*	*Russian*
Adjectival Type Surname			
Masc.	Mierzejewsk<u>i</u>	Rybnick<u>ý</u>	Маяковск<u>ий</u>
Fem.	Mierzejewsk<u>a</u>	Rybnick<u>á</u>	Маяковск<u>ая</u>
Noun Type Surname			
Masc.	Mikłosz	Sedlák	Александров
Fem.	Mikłosz<u>owa</u>	Sedlák<u>ová</u>	Александров<u>а</u>

Thus as integral parts of the language under study, the surnames and names will not only contain grammatical endings for case but gender markers as well. In short, the researcher needs at times to deduct both a gender marker as well as a case ending to arrive at the form of the surname (usually masculine) that came to be used in the United States. Researchers not familiar with the Slavic tongues hold the misconception that the two gender versions constitute two distinct surnames. This is a false premise. The feminine version is merely an inflected form of the same surname reflecting changes required by the language's structure.

In the pages that follow we have indicated in many instances what case is employed. Dates also require special attention in the various Slavic languages for several reasons. One reason for this is the fact that different calendars were in use in various nations. In the Russian Empire, the Julian calendar was used until the time of the 1917 Revolution, whereas in most other European countries the transition to the Gregorian calendar had been made long before then. Thus Russian-language documents issued in Poland or Lithuania will have two dates, the Julian followed by the Gregorian. There is approximately a twelve- or thirteen-day difference between the two.

In many of the Slavic languages dates are recorded in the genitive case. A researcher would need to know that in Polish, for example, *grudnia,* the form usually seen in dates, is the genitive of *grudzień,* which is the nominative singular and the form under which a dictionary would list the word.

Verbs in the Slavic languages also exhibit a high incidence of inflected forms, which means that they will have endings marking tense as well as person.

In conclusion, the Slavic languages are morphologically complex, and a researcher needs to be aware that many words will exhibit a wide range of forms and that these forms need to be modified in order to search for the lexical meaning in a dictionary or to determine the standard spelling of a place name. A researcher aware of those facts, however, should have positive results in interpreting any given document.

The map below is far from complete — it does not show Lusatian, Slovak, or any of the South Slavic languages, due to lack of space — and one must recognize that the regions overlap. Russian has long been the first or second language for anyone living in areas governed by the Russian Empire and then the Soviet Union, so in the area shaded for Byelorussian or Ukrainian, for instance, Russian is widely understood. Poland historically ruled much of Ukraine and Polish is still spoken there and in Byelorussia, and so on. And of course any comprehensive map of regions where Slavic languages are spoken would have to represent the emigré communities in North and South America. But if the map helps researchers visualize the native lands where these languages originated, it will have served its purpose.

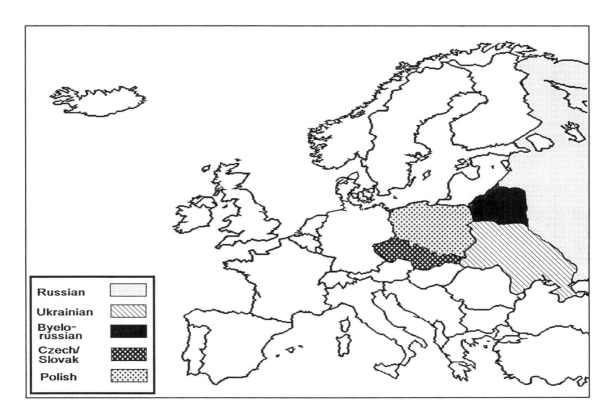

Český

The Czech Alphabet

Printed	Cursive
A, a	*A, a*
B, b	*B, b*
C, c	*C, c*
Č, č	*Č, č*
D, d	*D, d*
Ď, ď	*Ď, ď*
E, e	*E, e*
F, f	*F, f*
G, g	*G, g*
H, h	*H, h*
Ch, ch	*Ch, ch*
I, i	*I, i*
J, j	*J, j*
K, k	*K, k*
L, l	*L, l*
M, m	*M, m*
N, n	*N, n*
Ň, ň	*Ň, ň*
O, o	*O, o*
P, p	*P, p*
R, r	*R, r*
Ř, ř	*Ř, ř*
S, s	*S, s*
Š, š	*Š, š*
T, t	*T, t*
Ť, ť	*Ť, ť*

Printed	Cursive	Printed	Cursive
U, u	*U, u*	Z, z	*Z, z*
V, v	*V, v*	Ž, ž	*Ž, ž*
Y, y	*Y, y*		

Czech is one of the West Slavic languages, like Polish, and it uses the Roman alphabet, with some modifications. The letters *q*, *w*, and *x* appear only in unassimilated words borrowed from other languages. Diacritical marks are used to represent phonetic differences in vowel and consonant pronunciation. All letters, incidentally, are given here in upper and lower case, even though some seldom occur initially, because documents often highlight words by printing them in all caps — so it seems best to familiarize researchers with all upper-case forms, even those rarely encountered.

In the vowels *á, é, í, ó, ú, ý* the accent *(čárka)* simply indicates that they are pronounced longer than *a, e, i, o, u, y*. The *kroužek* seen over *ů* is used when a *ú* appears in the middle or at the end of a word. The consonants marked with the hook or *háček* —*č, ď, ň, ř, š, ť*, and *ž* — are considered "soft," as are *c* and *j*. The vowels *i* and *ý* are the same sound, but Czech spelling has *ý/y* following hard consonants and *í/i* following soft ones; so the consonants just named can only be followed by *i* or *í*, while *h, ch, k, r*, and non-softened *t, d*, and *n* can only be followed by *y* or *ý*. The other consonants can be either hard or soft and may precede either vowel.

The *á* is like the *a* in "f<u>a</u>ther," *é* like the *e* in "m<u>e</u>n," *í/ý* halfway between the vowels in "f<u>ee</u>t" and "f<u>i</u>t," *ó* somewhere between the different *o* sounds in "<u>O</u>ct<u>o</u>ber," and *ú* like the *u* in "r<u>u</u>de." The short versions of the vowels are truly "shorter" — the same sound but not held as long. Czech vowels are pure, i. e., an *i* does not have the slight *y*-sound that creeps in at the end when an American says "see." The diphthongs *au, eu* and *ou* are simply combinations of their component vowels, *a + u*, etc. (*ou* approximates the sound in English "sn<u>ow</u>"). *Aj/áj* sounds much like the *i* in "r<u>i</u>de," *ej/éj* like the *ay* in "d<u>ay</u>," *ij/yj/íj/ýj* like the *ee* in "f<u>ee</u>t," *oj* like the *oi* in "n<u>oi</u>se," and *uj/új* like a *y* added to the *u* sound.

Pronounced much as in English are *v*, *f*, and *g* (always hard, like that in "<u>g</u>o"); likewise *b, p*, and *k*, but without the aspiration (a slight "h" sound) English-speakers add to these sounds. *M* and *n* are as in English, but *ň* is somewhat like *ni* in "o<u>ni</u>on." *L* resembles the *l*-sound in "<u>l</u>eaf" more than in "midd<u>l</u>e," *s* is like the *s* in English "<u>s</u>un" but a bit sharper, and *z* is like the *z* in "<u>z</u>ebra." *H* is like English *h* but voiced (the vocal cords sound while pronouncing it); *ch* is like *ch* in German *Ba<u>ch</u>*. *C* and *dz* sound like *ts*, *š* like *sh* in "<u>sh</u>ip," and *ž* like the *s* in "plea<u>s</u>ure." The *č* sounds like *ch* in "chur<u>ch</u>," and *dž* like the *j* in "<u>j</u>udge." The *j* sounds like *y* in "<u>y</u>es" (initial *j* before consonants is usually not pronounced). The *r* is trilled, much as in Spanish; *ř* is trilled and voiced and sounds a little like a combination of the Czech *r* and *ž*. The palatized *ť* and *ď* are hard to describe, like a light *t* or *d* followed quickly by a *y* sound (without aspiration). The *háček* of *ď* and *ť* disappears when either is followed by *i* or *í*, and when *ě* follows a soft consonant the *háček* appears over the vowel only (exceptions: *č, ř, š*, and *ž* carry the "hook" instead of the *ě*, e. g., *řeka*, "river," *město*, "town").

Czechs, Bohemians, Moravians, Slovaks, and Their Languages

The tangled history of the peoples of eastern Europe still confuses their descendants. Some Czech-Americans insist that their ancestors were from Bohemia, not Czechoslovakia, or that they emigrated from Hungary but were Slovaks, and so on. All this can be true, and it may be helpful to define a few terms before proceeding to the study of documents.

By the 9th century the regions of Bohemia, Moravia, and Slovakia, each peopled with closely related but distinct Slavic tribes, were parts of the powerful kingdom of Moravia; Slovakia lay to the south and east, Silesia to the north, Bohemia to the west, and Moravia was between Bohemia and Slovakia. Moravia was simply named for the Morava river, and in German the name appears as *Mähren*. Bohemia's name originally came from Latin and meant "land of the Boii," a tribe the Romans identified as living in the area; this name also appears in the German term for the area, *Böhmen*. Slovakia took its name from the Slovak tribe that lived there. Eventually Slovakia fell under the control of Hungary, and from the 11th century to 1918 remained part of Hungary and later the Austro-Hungarian Empire. Bohemia, in the meantime, grew closer and closer to the Holy Roman Empire; it prospered under the Przemyslid dynasty — from the 14th to the 17th centuries the Kingdom of Bohemia included Silesia and Moravia, and Prague was perhaps the major cultural center of eastern Europe. Close contacts with Poles and Germans led to a certain amount of ethnic mixing, so that one finds Czechs who lived near Kraków and Germans who lived in Moravia and so on. The term "Czech" *(Čech)* came to be applied to Bohemians as well; the name is that of one of three mythical brothers who founded Slavic nations, Czech (Bohemia), Lech (Poland), and Rus (Ruthenia and or Russia), but the actual origin of the name is uncertain.

Eventually the kingdom of Bohemia declined and came under control of the Hapsburgs, and thus became part of Austria-Hungary until the end of World War I. At that point Czechs and Slovaks decided to form a federal union, the Republic of Czechoslovakia, which lasted until Hitler entered the Sudetenland in October of 1938 (his pretext for doing so was that the many ethnic Germans living there were being oppressed and deserved to be part of the Reich). Eventually Hitler took over Czechoslovakia and the country disappeared until it was reborn after World War II as a Communist-controlled federation in which the Czech and Slovak republics each had an assembly. On January 1, 1993 long-standing tensions between Czechs and Slovaks led to the peaceful division of Czechoslovakia into two independent nations, the Czech Republic and Slovakia.

In practice, "Czech" is a synonym for "Bohemian," and the primary distinction to be drawn is between Czech and Slovak; Moravia has not really been a major factor in the struggle for identity. There was no "Czechoslovakia" before 1918, so emigrants from before that year could rightly say that was not their country of origin. Czech was (and is) the national language of Bohemia and Slovak of Slovakia, and though patriots and idealists have long tried to establish "Czechoslovak" as the one official language for both groups — and in fact Czech and Slovak are very similar languages — the differences and the sense of ethnic identity have been strong enough to maintain a distinction. While two World Wars have shuffled the ethnic mix considerably, many ethnic Germans, Poles, and Magyars trace their origins to Czechoslovakia; and since the whole country was at one time or another under control of the Austro-Hungarian Empire, tracing records of families can easily involve deciphering documents in Latin, German, Czech or Slovak (to say nothing of Polish, Ukrainian, Romanian, etc.)

The Slovak language has several features that distinguish it from Czech, to the extent that a person familiar with the differences can usually tell from a fairly small selection of text which language it is in. Slovak has a flat vowel *ä* (Slovak *pät* = Czech *pět*, "five"), a palatized *l* (written as *l'*), and diphthongs *ia, ie, io* and *iu* which do not appear in Czech. It developed *dz* and *dž* as separate phonemes, and does not have the *ř* of Czech. Still — if it may be said without given offense to fervent Czech and Slovak nationalists — the languages are so similar that the differences should not cause serious problems for researchers who need only comprehend enough to extract a few facts.

Document #1: A Czech Birth and Baptismal Certificate

On the next two pages is a reproduction of a Czech birth and baptismal certificate. It dates from 1898 and therefore was issued when the area was under the control of the Austro-Hungarian Empire, and as such the place of issue is identified by "crownland" (*Kronland* in German, *korunní země* in Czech), political district *(polit. okres)*, diocese *(diecése)*, deanery *(děkanství)* and parish *(fara)*. Obviously the *korunní země* and *polit. okres* are political divisions and the *diecése, děkanství* and *fara* are ecclesiastical.

Číslo 232.

Korunní země _Morava_

Polit. okres _Uh. Brod_

(Samosprávné město.)

Diecése _Olomouc_

Děkanství _Val. Klobouky_

Fara _Vlachovice_

Rodní a křestní list.

zdejší rodné a křestní knihy Sv. _V._ list _175_ dosvědčuje se tímto úředně, že

v obci (místo, ulice, číslo) _Vlachovicích čís. 42._

dne (vypiš) _osmého září_ tisíc

osm set _devadesát osm_ (číslicemi) _8/9 1898_

se narodil-(a), a dne (i rok) _10. září 1898_ důst. pánem

Petrem Leharem, kooperátorem ve _farním_

chrámu Páně ad Sct. _Michaelem_ dle římskokatolického obřadu

pokřtěn-(a) byl-(a) manželská syn — (dcera):

(křestní a rodné jméno) _Anna Bětíková_

Otec*) _Bětík Josef, pacholek ve dvoře vlachovkém, syn Jiřího Bětíka, polníka z Lužné a jeho manželky Marianny, dcera Josefa Urubka, polníka z Lužné._

Matka*) _Terezie, dcera Josefa Polácha, polníka z Lužné a jeho manželky Terezie, dcery Jana Hyžáka, podsedníka z Lužné_

Kmotři: _Josef Polách, polník z Lužné a jeho manželka Kateřina_

Babka: Anna Zvonkova z Vlachovic čís. 143.

Poznámka:

Potvrzuje vlastnoručním podpisem a razítkem úředním:

Farní úřad ve Vlachovicích dne 7. října 1913.

František Svacina

kooperátor

n křestní jméno, náboženství, čas narození atd. jako v matrice.

Kniž. arcib. knih- a kamenotiskárna v Olomouci. — Čís. skl. 105-a

I. Identification of the political and ecclesiastical divisions of the locality where the document was created

Číslo 232 Korunní země *Morava* Polit. okres *Uh. Brod* (samosprávné město)
Diecése *Olomouc* Děkanství *Val. Klobouky* Fara *Vlachovice*
Rodní a křestní list.

číslo — "number"

korunní země — "crown land" (German *Kronland*), here "Morava" (Moravia)

polit. okres — "political district," here "Uherský Brod"

diecése — "diocese," here "Olomouc" (German name "Olmütz") in central Czechoslovakia

děkanství — deanery, here "Valašské Klobouky"

fara — "parish"

rodní — "birth" (adj.; the standard spelling of this is *rodný*, and this may be a misprint).

a — "and"

krestní — "baptismal" (adj.)

list — "certificate"

Translation — Number 232, Crown land of Moravia, Political District of Uherský Brod (self-ruled city), Diocese of Olomouc, Deanery of Valašské Klobouky, Parish of Vlachovice. A Birth and Baptismal Certificate.

II. Identification of volume from which the extract was taken and the date of the event

Dle zdejší rodné a křestní knihy Sv. *V.* list *175*, dosvědčuje se tímto úředně, že v obci (místo, ulice, číslo) Vlachovicích čís. *42* dne (vypiš) *osmého září* tisíc osmset devadesát osm (číslicemi) *8/9/1898*

dle — "according to"

zdejší — "local," adjective formed from *zde,* "here."

knihy — "book, register." This form is the genitive singular of *kniha.*

dosvědčuje se tímto úředně, že — "it is hereby officially certified, that..." *Dosvědčuje se* is literally "it certifies itself"; *tímto* is instrumental of *tento* and means literally "by means of this."

v obci (místo, ulice, číslo) Vlachovicích čís. *42* — "in the municipality (place, street, number) Vlachovice, number 42." The suffix *-ích* is the locative plural, the case that follows *v* showing "location where," namely, in Vlachovice.

dne (vypiš) osmého září — "on the day (written out) the eighth of September." This is in the genitive as an expression of "time when." Note that *(vypiš)* means the date is to be written out in words here, and will be given in numerals *(číslicemi)* subsequently.

tisíc osmset devadesát osm — "thousand eight hundred ninety eight"

číslicemi — "in numerals" (an instrumental plural form with *-emi*)

Translation — From the local book of births and baptisms, Vol. V, leaf 175, it is hereby officially certified that in the municipality of Vlachovice, number 42, on (in writing) the eighth of September, eighteen hundred ninety-eight (in numbers) 8/9. 1898...

III. Date, place, and performer of baptism

se narodila, a dne (i rok) 10. září 1898 důst. pánem Petrem Leharem, kooperatorem ve fárním chrámu Páně ad Sct. Michaelem dle římskokatolického obřadu pokřtěna byla manželska dcera

> *se narodila* — "was born." Since (as becomes clear later) it was a daughter that was born, and this predicate's subject, *dcera* "daughter," is a feminine noun — which may seem obvious but actually cannot be taken for granted, as the word for "girl," *děvče,* is neuter in gender! — the priest who filled out this document drew a line to connect the ending *(a)* to the verb and thereby make it feminine. In the case of a son *(syn)* the form would be simply *se narodil* and the *(a)* would be crossed out.

> The structure of this whole clause is *že ... se narodila a ... pokřtěna byla manželska dcera,* "that was born and was baptized the legitimate daughter," but before the verbs and finally the subject come phrases saying where, when, and how it all happened.

> *a dne (i rok) 10 září 1898* — "and on the day (and in the year) 10 September 1898"

> *důst. pánem Petrem Leharem, kooperatorem* — "by the Rev. Petr Lehar, assistant pastor." This whole phrase is in the instrumental case because the baptism was performed *by* Rev. Lehar.

> *ve fárním chrámu Páně ad Sct. Michaelem* — "in the parish of the church of St. Michael" (*ad Sct. Michaelem* is Latin, *ad Sanctum Michaelem,* literally "to St. Michael" but in English the usage is "of St. Michael").

> *dle římskokatolického obřadu* — "according to the Roman Catholic rite." *Dle* is followed by the genitive case, and the endings *-ého* and *-u* are typical of masculine adjectives and nouns in the genitive.

> *pokřtěna byla manželská dcera* — "was baptized the legitimate daughter" (her name follows in the next section). A *manželé* is a married couple, so *manželská* means "[born to] a married couple," i. e., legitimate. *Pokřtěna* is a past passive participle meaning "baptized," formed from a verb with the same root as the adjective *křestní* and the noun *křesťan* "Christian" (somewhat like the verb "christen" in English).

Translation — ... there was born, and on 10 September 1898 by the Rev. Petr Lehar in the parish church of St. Michael according to the Roman Catholic rite there was baptized the legitimate daughter...

IV. Name of child

(křestní a rodné jméno) Anna Bětíkova

> *jméno* — "name" (from the same root, originally, as Latin *nomen,* Polish *imię/imiona,* and English *name*).

> *Anna Bětíkova* — "Anna Bětík." Note the feminine ending on the surname, which should probably be dropped when translating to avoid confusion as to why a female doesn't have the same surname as her husband or father. Czech distinguishes a feminine form of the surname, much as Russian and Polish do, and as in those languages the feminine form is considered merely a separate form of the same surname, not a distinct surname in itself. If the surname is adjectival in origin, i. e., ends in *-ý,* the ending changes to *-á,* so that the wife of *pan* (Mr.) *Černý* would be *paní* (Mrs.) *Černá,* and their daughter would be *slečna* (Miss) *Černá.* If the surname is a noun in form or origin the suffix *-ová* is added to it, e. g., *pan Novák, paní Nováková, slečna Nováková.* Surnames with *-e-* in the final syllable drop the *-e-* to add the suffix, i. e., *pan Novaček → paní Novačková. Pan, paní* and *slečna* are capitalized only at the start of a sentence; in writing *paní* is usually abbreviated *pí,* and *slečna* as *sl.*

> *Translation* — "(given name and surname) Anna Bětík."

V. Parents' names and identification

Otec: Bětík Josef, pacholek ve dvoře vlachovském, syn Jiřího Bětíka, rolníka z Lužné a jeho manželky Marianny, dcera Josefa Urubka, rolníka z Lužné.

Matka: Terezie, dcera Josefa Polácha, rolníka z Lužné a jeho manželky Terezie, dcery Jana Hyžáka, podsedníka z Lužné.

otec — "father"

pacholek — "farm servant." In many European languages there are a variety of terms for "farmer, peasant" that cannot be adequately translated into English because they refer to various kinds of farms, different kinds of workers on them, or the terms under which one worked: Did the peasant own the land he worked? Did he hold it on terms of recompensing the lord with money, portion of the crop, or other service? Was he just a hired hand? Modern American English has no terms to describe these nuances, so one can only translate words such as *pacholek, rolnik, sedlák,* etc. with approximations.

ve dvoře vlachovském — "at the Vlachové estate." It is unclear from context whether *vlachovský* is the adjectival form for *Vlachovice* (with the *-ice* ending simply dropped before the *-ský* suffix was added), or if this refers to another, nearby place of similar name (a phenomenon not unknown in eastern European research), perhaps an estate named *Vlachovo* or *Vlachové*. The latter seems the most likely possibility, but one would need a really detailed map of the area, as it existed in 1898, to settle this for sure. We can translate this as "at *Vlachové** estate" provisionally, but with an asterisk to remind us that this name for a village or estate near Vlachovice, in Uherský Brod district, needs to be confirmed by subsequent research.

syn Jiřího Bětíka — "son of Jiří Bětík." The name *Jiří* is adjectival in origin, so its genitive ending is the typical masculine genitive singular *-ho,* while the surname *Bětík,* in origin a noun, has the *-a* which is one of the two typical genitive singular endings for masculine nouns (the other: *-u*).

rolníka — "farmer" (genitive singular, as a noun in apposition to *Jiřího Bětíka*)

z Lužné — "from Lužná." *Z,* or *ze* in some instances, is a preposition taking the genitive case, and *Lužné* is the genitive form of *Lužná.*

a jeho manželky — "and of his wife." *Manžel* is a husband, a *manželka* is a wife (*manželky* is the genitive singular of *manželka*), and *manželé* is a married couple.

dcera Josefa Urubka — "daughter of Josef Urubek." When nouns ending in *-ek* add declensional endings the *-e-* drops out; when reconstituting the nominative form, as here (from the genitive), one must remember to add it back in again. Czechs, who find it simple to pronounce things like *Strč prst skrz krk* ("Push your finger through the neck"), recoil in horror at the difficulty of saying something like "Urubk" and insert the *-e-* to make it easier to pronounce: *Urubek.*

matka...podsedník —*Matka* is "mother," and a *podsedník* is the owner of a small farm.

Translation — Father: Josef Bětík, a farm servant at the Vlachové* estate, the son of Jiří Bětík, a farmer from Lužná, and his wife Marianna, the daughter of Josef Urubek, a farmer from Lužná. Mother: Terezie, the daughter of Josef Polách, a farmer from Lužná, and his wife Terezie, the daughter of Jan Hyžak, a *podsedník* from Lužná.

VI. Godparents, midwife, and legalese

Kmotři: Josef Polách, rolník z Lužné a jeho manželka Kateřina
Babka: Anna Zvonkova z Vlachovic čís. 143.
Poznámka: —
Potvrzuje vlastnoručním podpisem a razítkem úředním: Farní úřad ve Vlachovicích dne 7. října 1913. František Svačina, kooperator.

kmotři — "godparents"
babka — "midwife"
poznámka — "notation, comment"
potvrzuje — "confirms, certifies"
vlastnoručním podpisem — "with a signature in [his] own hand" (instrumental case)
a razítkem úředním — "and [with] the seal (nominative *razítko*) of the office"
farní úřad ve Vlachovicích — "the parish office in Vlachovice"
7 října 1913 — "7 October 1913

Translation — Godparents: Josef Polách, a farmer from Lužná, and his wife, Kateřina. Midwife: Anna Zvonkova, from Vlachovice, number 143. [The undersigned] certifies [this] with his signature in his own hand and with the official seal: The parish office in Vlachovice, 7 October 1913. František Svačina, assistant pastor.

Document #2: Parish Family Registration Document

Documents such as the one reproduced below listed members of a given family. As more children were born, their names were added. Note that the document was issued in Moravia, but is in Czech and German.

Vedle výnosu c. k. minist. obchodu ze dne 1. července 1886 čís. 7335|516 bez kolku.
Laut hohen k. k. Ackerbau-Ministerial-Erlasses vom 1. Juli 1886, Z. 7335|516 stempelfrei.

Výpis z farních knih.
Auszug aus den Pfarrbüchern.

Závod :
Betrieb :

Výpis z farních knih — Extract from the parish books.

Ludvik Břenek naroz. 3 tého -5- 1878 v Hrabově— Ludvik Břenek, born 3 May 1878 in Hrabová
oddaný 26 tého -2- 1906 s Annou Zizka— married 26 February 1906 to Anna Zižka
naroz. 28 tého -6- 1883 Račkovicích— born 28 June 1883 in Račkovice

Dítky — children
Augustina naroz. 28 tého srpna 1905 v Ostravě— Augustine, born 28 August 1905 in Ostrava
Emil " 5 tého dubna 1907 v. Hrabově— Emil, born 5 April 1907, in Hrabová
V Mor. Ostravě, dne 4 tého -2- 1908 — In Ostrava, Moravia, 4 February 1908

Note these points worth remembering:
naroz., abbreviation of *narozený,* "born"
-tého — Just as English ordinals generally end in *-th,* most Czech ordinals end in the suffix *-tý.* The genitive masculine/neuter ending is *-tého,* and the genitive is used in expressions meaning "on such-and-such a day of such-and-such a month." Thus *-tého* marks the date.
oddaný, term meaning "married" ("to" = *s* with the instrumental case: *Annou*)

Document #3: A Slovak Passport

This passport, issued in the Slovakia portion of the Republic of Czechoslovakia (1918-1938) proves that the differences between Slovak and Czech need not intimidate researchers (especially when the document is bilingual and has French equivalents to check against).

— 1 —

Tento cestovný pas obsahuje
32 stránok
Ce passeport contient
32 pages

Okresný úrad vo Vyšnom Swidniku

VYSTAHOVALECKY
EMIGRANT
CESTOVNÝ PAS
PASSEPORT

REPUBLIKA ČESKOSLOVENSKÁ

RÉPUBLIQUE
TCHÉCOSLOVAQUE

Číslo cestovného pasu }
No du passeport }   *50/923*

Méno majitel'a }   *Kovalova Mária*
Nom du porteur }

Doprevádzaný svojou manželkou }   *1.*
Accompagné de sa femme }

a svojmi *2* detmi.
et de   enfants.

ŠTÁTNA PRÍSLUŠNOSŤ }
NATIONALITÉ }

— 2 —

OSOBNÝ POPIS
SIGNALEMENT

Manželka — Femme

Zamestnanie }   *domaca*
Profession }   *femme l menage*

Rodisko a datum }   *Šandal*
narodenia }   *18 okt. 1891*
Lieu et date }
de naissance }

Bydlisko }   *Hoča*
Domicile }

Obličaj }   *kulata —*
Visage }

Barva oči }   *hnede — blond*
Couleur des yeux }

Barva vlasov }   *kaštanové — châtain*
Couleur des cheveux }

Zvláštné znamenie }
Signes particuliers }

DETI — ENFANTS

Meno / Nom	Vek / Age	Pohlavie / Sexe
Maria	*9*	*dievče*
Anna	*7*	

Tento cestovný pas obsahuje 32 stránok. — This passport contains 32 pages.

Okresný úrad vo Vyšnom Swidniku — District Office in Vyšný Swidnik

Vystahovalecký Cestovný Pas — Emigrant Passport

Republica Československá — Republic of Czechoslovakia

Číslo cestovného pasu — Passport Number

Méno majitel'a } *Kovalova María* — Bearer's name María Koval[ova]

Doprevádzaný svojou manželkou — Accompanied by his wife } —

a svojmi 2 detmi — and by his/her 2 children

Štátna Príslušnosť' — Nationality [it appears to say that she was a citizen *(obč.* = *občanka)* of the République Tchécoslovaque].

Osobný Popis — Personal description

Manželka — Wife

Zamestnanie } *domaca*— Occupation: housewife

Rodisko a datum narodenia } *Šandal* — Birthplace and date of birth: Šandal, 18 October 1891

Bydlisko } *Hoča* — Residence: Hoča

Obličaj } *kulata* — Face: round

Barva oči } *hnede* — eye color: brown

Barva vlasov } *kaštanové* — Hair color: chestnut

Zvláštné znamenie } — Distinguishing marks

Deti — Children

Meno — name

Vek — age

Pohlavie — sex

[The children are *María,* a girl *(dievče)* age 9, and Anna, a girl, age 7]

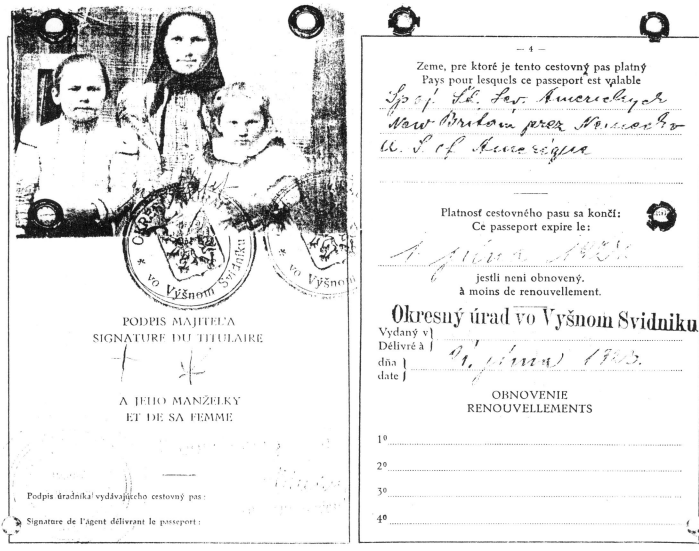

PODPIS MAJITEL'A
SIGNATURE DU TITULAIRE

A JEHO MANŽELKY
ET DE SA FEMME

Podpis úradníka vydávajúceho cestovný pas :

Signature de l'agent délivrant le passeport :

Zeme, pre ktoré je tento cestovný pas platný
Pays pour lesquels ce passeport est valable

Platnosť cestovného pasu sa končí:
Ce passeport expire le:

jestli neni obnovený.
à moins de renouvellement.

Okresný úrad vo Vyšnom Svidniku

Vydaný v }
Délivré à }
dňa }
date }

OBNOVENIE
RENOUVELLEMENTS

1⁰ ....

2⁰ ....

3⁰ ....

4⁰ ....

Podpis Majitel'a — Bearer's signature
A jeho manželky — and of his wife
Podpis úradníka vydávajúceho cestovný pas —
 Signature of the official issuing the passport

A few notes on Czech vs. Slovak

Slovak uses the diphthongs *ia, ie, io, iu,* and Czech doesn't: Slovak *zamestnanie* vs. Czech *zaměstnání* (employment, job), Slovak *dievče* vs. Czech *děvče* (girl). Slovak does not have *ř*, Czech does (Slovak *úrad* vs. Czech *úřad* [office]) but Slovak has *l'* and Czech doesn't (Slovak *majitel'a* vs. Czech *majitele* [bearer's]). Contrast Slovak *méno* and Czech *jméno* (first name) and Slovak *obličaj* and Czech *obličej*. But compare the Czech words in the vocabulary with most of the Slovak terms seen here and the similarities are obvious.

Zeme, pre ktoré je tento cestovný pas platný: Spoj. St. Sev. Amerických New Britain prez Nemecko U. S. of Amerique — "Country for which this passport is valid: United States of North America, New Britain, by way of Germany, U. S. of Amerique" [There appears to be some confusion on the official's part as to exactly which languages this passport is being written in!]

Platnosť cestovného pasu sa končí: 1. júna 1923 — "Validity of this passport expires on 1 June 1923"

jestli neni obnovený — "unless it is renewed."

Vydaný v} Okresný úrad vo Vyšnom Svidniku dňa 21. júna 1923. — "Issued at the District Office in Vyšný Svidnik, 21 June 1923." [Note that in Czech the date would be *dna 21. června 1923.*]

Obnovenie — Renewals.

Selected Vocabulary Terms

As with Latin and the other Slavic languages, there is not enough space to present all the information a student of this language would want to know; but presumably most readers of this book do not need or want a comprehensive study of Czech vocabulary. Instead, about 500 common words are given here, identified by part of speech, in the forms and with the definitions as most commonly encountered in the context of family history documents. Most of these words are Czech, but for comparison a sampling of Slovak words is given, each identified as such.

Words are listed in alphabetical order according to Czech order, not English; this should cause few problems, as the only really major departures from English order are that *ch* comes after *h,* not after *c,* and *č* follows *c* and *š* follow *s*. Nouns appear in the nominative singular (except for nouns that are plural in form), and in a few instances where declensional oddities might prove confusing the genitive singular or nominative plural are indicated in parentheses. Listings of prepositions include the case used with each preposition. Verb forms are simply listed as usually seen, with no effort to discuss conjugational complexities which must either be studied in depth or not at all. Some of the most frequently seen case forms of pronouns such as *co* and *ten* are listed with an arrow indicating the nominative form under which the pronoun is defined, e. g., *čeho → co* means that *čeho* is a form of the pronoun *co.*

a — (conj.) and
aby — (conj.) in order to
ale — (conj.) but
anglický — (adj.) English
ani — (conj.) neither...nor
ano — (adv.) yes
armáda — (fem. noun) army
atd. — (abbreviation of *a tak dále*) and so forth, etc.
až — (conj.) until
babička — (fem. noun) grandmother
babka — (fem. noun) midwife
barva — (fem. noun) color
bez — (prep. with genitive) without
bílý — (adj.) white
blízký — (adj.) near
bohatý — (adj.) rich
bratr — (masc. noun) brother
bratranec — (masc. noun) cousin
březen — (masc. noun, gen. *března*) March
bydlisko — (Slovak, neut. noun) residence
byl(a) — (v., from *byti*) he (she) was
byli — (v., from *byti*) [they] were
byt — (masc. noun) apartment
byti — (v.) to be
celnice — (fem. noun) custom house
cena — (fem. noun) cost
cesta — (fem. noun) way, road
cestovní — (adj., in Slovak *cestovný*), travel-; *cestovní pas* — passport

cizina — (fem. noun) foreign country, abroad
co — (pron.) what, which
čas — (masc. noun) time
část — (fem. noun) part
částka — (fem. noun) amount
čeho, čem, čemu → co
Čech — (masc. noun) Czech (plur. *Česi*)
Čechoslovák — (masc. noun) a Czechoslovak
Čechy — (fem. pl.) Bohemia
černovlasý — (adj.) black-haired
černý — (adj.) black
červen — (masc. noun, gen. *června*) June
červenec — (masc. noun, gen. *července*) July
červený — (adj.) red
Československo — (neut. noun) Czechoslovakia
český — (adj.) Czech
Češka — (fem. noun) Czech (woman)
čím → co
číslo — (n.) number; *číslicemi* — in numbers
člověk — (masc. noun) man (plural *lidé*)
čtení — (neut. noun) reading
čtrnáct — (num.) fourteen
čtrnáctý — (adj.) fourteenth
čtvrt — (fem. noun) quarter
čtvrtek — (masc. noun) Thursday
čtvrtý — (adj.) fourth
čtyři — (num.) four
čtyřicátý — (adj.) fortieth
čtyřicet — (num.) forty

čtyřista — (num.) four hundred
čtyřstý — (adj.) four hundredth
daleko — (adv.) far
dama — (fem. noun) lady
dcera — (fem. noun) daughter
děd — (masc. noun) grandfather (nom. plur. *dědové*)
děkanství — (neut. noun) deanery
den — (masc. noun, genitive *dne*) day
desátý — (adj.) tenth
deset — (num.) ten
devadesát — (num.) ninety
devatenáct — (num.) nineteen
devátý — (adj.) ninth
děvče — (Czech, neut, noun; gen. sing. *děvčete*) girl
devět — (num.) nine; *devětset* — (num.) nine hundred; *devítistý* — (adj.) nine hundredth
diecése — (n.) diocese
dieťa — (Slovak noun) child
dievče — Slovak → *děvče*
dítě — (neut. noun, gen. sing. *dítěte*, plur. *děti*) child
dle — (prep. with genitive) according to, by
dlouhý — (adj.) long
dnes — (adv.) today
do — (prep. with genitive) to, until, up to
doba — (fem. noun) time, period
dobrý — (adj.) good; *dobře* — well, good
dole — (adv.) below
doma — (adv.) at home → *dům*
domov — (masc. noun) homeland
dopis — (masc. noun) letter

dopoledne — (neut. noun) morning, a.m.

dosvědčuje se — (v.) it is certified, attested

dovolená — (fem. noun) leave

druhý — (adj.) another; second

duben — (masc. noun, gen. *dubna*) April

dům — (masc. noun, gen. sing. *domu*) house

dva — (num.) two

dvacet — (num.) twenty

dvacátý — (adj.) twentieth

dvanáct — (num.) twelve

dvanáctý — (adj.) twelfth

dvěstě — (num.) two hundred

dviustý — (adj.) two hundredth

dvůr — (loc. *ve dvoře*) farm, estate

fara — (n.) parish

farní — (adj.) of the parish

francouzský — (adj.) French

hlava — (fem. noun) head

hlavní — (adj.) chief, main; *hlavní město* — capital

hluchý — (adj.) deaf

hnědý — (adj.) brown

hodina — (fem. noun) hour

holič — (masc. noun) barber

hora — (fem. noun) mountain

hospodářství — (neut. noun) small farm

hostinský — (adj. used as noun, gen. sing. *hostinského*) inn-keeper

hrabě — (masc. noun, gen. sing. *hraběte*) count (nobleman)

hraběnka — (fem. noun) countess

hranice — (fem. noun) border

hrob — (masc. noun) grave

hrobař — (masc. noun) grave-digger

hřbitov — (masc. noun) cemetery

chalupa — (fem. noun) hut, cottage

chlapec — (masc. noun) boy

choroba — (fem. noun) illness

chrám — (masc. noun) church

chudý — (adj.) poor

i — (conj.) and, and also (*i...i* both...and)

inženýr — (masc. noun) engineer

já — (pers. pron.) I (gen./acc. *mne* or *mě*, dat. *mi* or *mně*, instr. *mnou*, loc. *mně*)

jak — (adv.) how; *jakoby* — as if

jaký — (adj.) what kind of

jaro — (neut. noun) spring

jazyk — (masc. noun) language

je — (v., from *byti*) [he, she, it] is

jeden — (num.) one

jedenáct — (num.) eleven

jeho — (pron.) his, its

jej → *ona*

její — (pron.) her

jejich — (pron.) their

jemu → *on, ono*

jenž, jež — (pron.) who, whom, which

jestli(že) — (conj.) if

jezero — (neut. noun) lake

jih — (masc. noun) south

jim → *oni*

jižní — (adj.) southern

jméno — (neut. noun) first name

jsem — (v., from *byti*) I am

jsou — (v., from *byti*) they are

k — (sometimes *ke* or *ku*, prep. with dative) to, toward

kde — (adv.) where

kdo — (pron.) who

kdy — (conj.) when

kmotr — (masc. noun) godfather; *kmotři* — godparents

kniha — (fem. noun) book

kníže — (masc. noun, gen. sing. *knížete*) prince

kooperator — (masc. noun) assistant pastor

korunní — (adj.) of the crown; *korunní země* — crownland

kostel — (masc. noun) church

kovář — (masc. noun) smith

král — (masc. noun) king

královna — (fem. noun) queen

krátký — (adj.) short

krejči — (adj. used as masc. noun, gen. *krejčího*) tailor

krk — (masc. noun) neck

křesťan — (masc. noun) Christian

křestní — (adj.) baptismal

který — (rel. pron.) which, who, that

kuchař — (masc. noun) cook

kulatý — (adj.) round

květen — (masc. noun, gen. *května*) May

leden — (masc. noun, gen. *ledna*) January

lékař — (masc. noun) doctor

léto — (neut. noun) summer

levý — (adj.) left

lidé — (masc. plur.) people

list — (masc. noun) page, sheet, certificate

listina — (fem. noun) document

listopad — (masc. noun, gen. *listopadu*) November

loď — (fem. noun) ship

loďka — (fem. noun) boat

macecha — (fem. noun) stepmother

Maďar — (masc. noun) Hungarian; *Maďarsko* — (neut. noun) Hungary

maďarský — (adj.) Hungarian

maj — (masc. noun, gen. *maja*) May

majitel — (masc. noun, in Slovak *majiteľ*) owner, bearer

malý — (adj.) small

manžel — (masc. noun) husband

manželka — (fem. noun) wife

manželský — (adj.) legitimate

matka — (fem. noun) mother

matrika — (Czech or Slovak noun) registry, record

meno — (Slovak noun) name

mezi — (prep. with acc. or instr.) between

měsíc — (masc. noun) month

město — (neut. noun) city

mimo — (prep. with accusative) outside, besides

místo — (neut. noun) place

mladý — (adj.) young

mlynář — (masc. noun) miller

mne, mně, mnou → *já*

moc — (fem. noun) authority

modrý — (adj.) blue

Morava — (fem. noun) Moravia

Moravan — (masc. noun) Moravian

moravský — (adj.) Moravian

moře — (neut. noun) sea

mrtvý — (adj.) dead

můj — (poss. adj.) my

muž — (masc. noun) man

mužský — (adj.) male

my — (pers. pron.) we

na — (prep. with acc. or loc.) on, at, to

náboženství — (neut. noun) religion

nad — (prep. with acc. or instr.) above, over, upon

nádraží — (neut. noun) station

nami → *my*

námořník — (masc. noun) sailor

naproti — (prep. with dative) opposite

narodenie — Slovak → *narození*

narodil(a) se — (v.) was born

národní — (adj.) national

narození — (neut. noun) birth

nas → *my*

nazdar — hello, goodbye

ne — (adv.) no

něco — (pron.) nothing

neděle — (fem. noun) Sunday

nemanželský — (adj.) illegitimate

nemluvně — (neut. noun) baby

nemoc — (fem. noun) illness

nemocnice — (fem. noun) hospital

nemocný — (adj.) ill

Němec — (masc. noun) German

Německo — (neut. noun) Germany

Němka — (fem. noun) German (woman)

není — (negative verb) is not

nepřítel — (masc. noun) enemy

nesprávný — (adj.) wrong

neudané — (Slovak participle) not given

nevěsta — (fem. noun) bride

nikdy — (adv.) never

noc — (fem. noun) night

nos — (masc. noun) nose

noviny — (fem. plur. noun) newspaper

nový — (adj.) new

nula — (fem. noun) zero

nyní — (adv.) now

o — (prep. with locative) about, on, concerning

občan — (masc. noun) citizen

obec — (fem. noun) municipality

obchodník — (masc. noun) merchant

obličej — (fem. noun) face (Slovak *obličaj*)

obnovenie — (Slovak, neut. noun) renewal

obnovený — (Slovak, part.) renewed

obřad — (masc. noun) rite

obuvník — (masc. noun) shoemaker

od, ode — (prep. with genitive) from, of

oddaný — (part.) married (to: s)

odjezd — (masc. noun) departure

odpoledne — (neut. noun) afternoon, p.m.

oko — (neut. noun) eye; *barva oči* — color of eyes

okres — (masc. noun) district; *okresný* — (adj.) district

omulva — (fem. noun) excuse

on — (pers. pron.) he, it

ona — (pers. pron.) she, it

ono — (pers. pron.) it

opět — (adv.) again

opis — (masc. noun) copy

osm — (num.) eight

osmdesát — (num.) eighty

osmistý — (adj.) eight hundredth

osmnáct — (num.) eighteen

osmset — (num.) eight hundred

osmý — (adj.) eighth

osobný — (adj.) personal

otázka — (fem. noun) question

otčim — (masc. noun) stepfather

otec — (masc. noun; nom. plur. *otcové*) father

padesát — (num.) fifty

pacholek — (masc. noun) farm servant

pan — (title) Mr.

pán — (masc. noun) gentlemen, sir, lord

paní — (fem. noun) lady, Mrs.

pasažér — (masc. noun) passenger

pät — (Slovak) five

pátek — (masc. noun) Friday

patnáct — (num.) fifteen

pátý — (adj.) fifth

pekař — (masc. noun) baker

peníze — (masc. plur. noun) money

pět — (num.) five

pětistý — (adj.) five hundredth

pětset — (num.) five hundred

platnost' — (Slovak, fem. noun) validity

platný — (Slovak, adj.) valid

po — (prep. with locative) on, about, after

pod — (prep. with acc. or instr.) under

podpis — (masc. noun) signature

podsedník — (masc. noun) owner of a small farm

podzim — (masc. noun) fall, autumn

pohlaví — (neut. noun) sex (Slovak *pohlavie*)

pohřeb — (masc. noun) funeral

pokrstený — (Slovak, adj.) baptismal

pokřtěn — (participle) baptized

Polák — (masc. noun) Pole

Polsko — (neut. noun) Poland

pondělí — (neut. noun) Monday

poněvadž — (conj.) because

popis — (masc. noun) description

poslední — (adj.) last

postel — (fem. noun) bed

potvrzuje — (v.) [he, she, it] confirms, certifies

povolání — (neut. noun) profession

práce — (fem. noun) work

pracovník — (masc. noun) worker

pradlena — (fem. noun) washerwoman

Praha — (fem. noun) Prague

praotec — (masc. noun) forefather, ancestor

právník — (masc. noun) lawyer

pravý — (adj.) right

Pražan — (masc. noun) citizen of Prague

pre — (Slovak, prep.) for

priezvisko — (Slovak noun) surname

pro — (prep. with accusative) for

proč — (interrog.) why?

prosinec — (masc. noun, gen. *prosince*) December

proti — (prep. with dative) against

protože — (conj.) because

první — (adj.) first

před — (prep. with acc. or instr.) in front of, before

přes — (prep. with accusative) across

při — (prep. with locative) at, near, by

příchod — (masc. noun) arrival

příjmení — (noun) surname

přísta — (noun) harbor

přitomnost — (fem. noun) presence

přitomný — (adj.) present

radnice — (fem. noun) town hall

Rakousko — (neut. noun) Austria

rakouský — (adj.) Austrian

ráno — (neut. noun) morning

razítko — (neut. noun) seal, stamp; *úředním razitkem* — with the official seal *rodiče* — (masc. plur. noun) parents (Slovak form *rodičia)*

rodina — (fem. noun) family

rodisko — (Slovak, neut. noun) birthplace

rodný — (adj.) birth, family

rok — (masc. noun, gen. *roku)* year

rolník — (masc. noun) farmer

ruka — (fem. noun) hand

různý — (adj.) different

Rus — (masc. noun) Russian

Rusko — (neut. noun) Russia

rybář — (masc. noun) fisherman

řeka — (fem. noun) river

řezník — (masc. noun) butcher

říjen — (masc. noun, gen. *října)* October

římskokatolický — (adj.) Roman Catholic

s — (sometimes *se*, prep. with instrum.) with, along with

sa konči — (Slovak, v.) ends, expires

sám — (pron. and adj., fem. *sama*, neut. *samo)* [my, your, him, her, it]self

se — (refl. pron., used with many verbs) [one]self

sedlák — (masc. noun) farmer, peasant

sedm — (num.) seven

sedmdesát — (num.) seventy

sedmistý — (adj.) seven hundredth

sedmnáct — (num.) seventeen

sedmset — (num.) seven hundred

sedmý — (adj.) seventh

sestra — (fem. noun) sister

sestřenice — (fem. noun) female cousin

sever — (masc. noun) north

silný — (adj.) strong

skrz — (prep. with accusative) through

slečna — (fem. noun) young lady, Miss

slepý — (adj.) blind

slobodný — (Slovak, adj.) single, unmarried

Slovák — (masc. noun) Slovak

Slovensko — (neut. noun) Slovakia

slovník — (masc. noun) dictionary

slovo — (neut. noun) word

sluha — (masc. noun, nom. plur. *sluhové)* servant

smrt — (fem. noun) death

snacha — (fem. noun) daughter-in-law

sobáš — (Slovak noun) wedding

sobota — (fem. noun) Saturday

soudce — (masc. noun) judge

soused — (masc. noun) neighbor

spojený — (adj.) united

správce — (masc. noun) manager

správný — (adj.) correct

srdce — (neut. noun) heart

srpen — (masc. noun, gen. *srpna)* August

stalo se — (v.) it happened

starosta — (masc. noun) mayor

starý — (adj.) old

stát — (masc. noun) state

sto — (num.) hundred

stý — (adj.) hundredth

strana — (fem. noun) party

stráž — (noun) guard

strážník — (noun) policeman

strýc — (masc. noun) uncle

středa — (fem. noun) Wednesday

svatba — (fem. noun) wedding

svobodný — (adj.) free

svá, své → *svůj*

svůj — (poss. adj.) [my, your, his, her, its, our, their] own

syn — (masc. noun, nom. plur. *synové)* son

šedesát — (num.) sixty

šedivý — grey

šest — (num.) six

šestistý — (adj.) six hundredth

šestnáct — (num.) sixteen

šestset — (num.) six hundred

šestý — (adj.) sixth

škola — (fem. noun) school

šlechtic — (masc. noun) nobleman

štátna príslušnosť — (adj. and fem. noun, Slovak) nationality

šťastný — (adj.) happy

švagr — (masc. noun) brother-in-law

ta → *ten*

tak — (adv.) thus

také — (adv.) also

tam — (adv.) there

Tatry — (fem. plur. noun) the Tatra Mountains

těch → *ten*

tedy — (adv.) then, therefore

tělo — (neut. noun) body

těm, těmi → *ten*

ten — (pron.) that

tenký — (adj.) think

tento — (demonstr. adj.) this

tentýž — (pron.) the same

teta — (fem. noun) aunt

těžký — (adj.) heavy, hard, difficult

ti → *ten*

tím → *ten*

tisíc — (num.) thousand

tkáč — (masc. noun) weaver

tlumočník — (masc. noun) interpreter

tlustý — (adj.) thick

tmavý — (adj.) dark

to — (pron., neut. of *ten)* that

toho, tomu, tom, tou → *ten*

truhlář — (masc. noun) carpenter

třetí — (adj.) third

tři — (num.) three

třicátý — (aadj.) thirtieth

třicet — (num.) thirty

třináct — (num.) thirteen

třista — (num.) three hundred

třistý — (adj.) three hundredth

tu — (adv.) here

tucet — (masc. noun) a dozen

tvář — (fem. noun) face

ty → *ten*

ty — (pers. pron.) you

týden — (masc. noun) week

u — (prep. with genitive) at, near

účet — (masc. noun) bill

učitel — (masc. noun) teacher

ucho — (neut. noun) ear

údaj — (Slovak noun) datum, information

ukazatel — (masc. noun) index

ulice — (fem. noun) street

únor — (masc. noun, gen. *února)* February

úřad — (masc. noun, Slovak *úrad)* office; *úředním razitkem* — with the official seal

úředník — (masc. noun, Slovak *úradník)* clerk, official

ústa — (neut. plur. noun) mouth

ústně — (adv.) orally

úterý — (neut. noun) Tuesday

v — (sometimes *ve*, prep. with acc. or loc.) in, into, to

váha — (fem. noun) weight

válka — (fem. noun) war

váš — (poss. adj.) your

vážený — (adj.) honored, "dear" (as in "Dear Sir")

včera — (adv.) yesterday
vdova — (fem. noun) widow
vdovec — (masc. noun) widower
večer — (masc. noun) evening
vedle — (prep. with genitive) next to, by
věk— (masc. noun) age
velký — (adj.) large
velmi — (adj.) very
ves — (fem. noun) village
vesnice — (fem. noun) village
vězení — (neut. noun) prison
vchod — (masc. noun) entrance
Vídeň — (masc. noun, gen. Vídně) Vienna
vláda — (fem. noun) government
vlak — (masc. noun) train
vlas — (masc. noun) hair; barva vlasov — hair color
vlast — (fem. noun) homeland
vlastní — (adj.) one's own
vlastnoruční — (adj.) with one's own hand[s]
vnouče — (neut. noun, gen. sing. vnoučete) grandchild
voják — (masc. noun) soldier
volný — (adj.) free
vousy — (plur. noun) beard
vše — (pron.) all, everything

všechen — (adj.) all
vy — (pers. pron) you
vydaný — (part.) issued
východ — (masc. noun) east; exit
výchova — (fem. noun) education
vypiš — (noun used adverbially) written out
výpis — (masc. noun) extract
vysoký — (adj.) tall
výška — (fem. noun) height
vzdálenost — (fem. noun) distance
z — (sometimes ze, prep. with genitive) from, of
za — (prep.): (with gen.) on, during; (with acc.) for, in place of, beyond, behind; (with instr.) behind, beyond
zahradnik — (masc. noun) gardener
zahraniční — (adj.) foreign
zakázaný — (adj.) forbidden
zákonný — (adj.) legal
zaměstnání — (neut. noun) job, occupation (Slovak form zamestnanie)
západ — (masc. noun) west
zápis — (Slovak noun) entry
září — (neut. noun, gen. září) September

zástupce — (masc. noun) representative
záznam — (Slovak, noun) record, registry
zde — (adv.) here
zdejší — (adj.) local, of here
zdravý — (adj.) healthy
zelený — (adj.) green
země — (fem. noun) land, earth
zima — (fem. noun) winter
zítra — (adv.) tomorrow
znamienie — (Slovak, neut. noun plur.) marks
známý — (adj.) known, acquainted
zomrel(a) — (v.) he (she) died
zvláštni — (adj.) special, distinguishing
žádný — (adj.) no, not any
že — (conj.) that
žena — (fem. noun) woman
ženatý — (adj.) married
ženích — (Slovak, noun) groom
ženský — (adj.) female
židovský — (adj.) Jewish
živý — (adj.) living

Selected Personal Names

As is evident from this list, many Czech names have no real equivalent in English. Those names that have a rough counterpart are listed with those equivalents. Czech names with no real English counterpart are simply listed so that researchers trying to decipher documents can have a little help separating personal names from other lexical items, so that they will not waste time trying to figure out what a *Jarmila* is — it's a girl!

Note that Czech is rich in diminutive names that may be used by family and friends, e. g., *Evička* = "little Eva," *Boženka* = "little Božena." It is unlikely that many such names will be found on official documents — bureaucrats generally have little use for terms of endearment — but if one is using family sources such as a Bible or oral history from family members it can be important to remember Czech's tendency to form diminutives. It may save a great deal of time searching for an ancestor named *Pavliček* if one realizes that that is a diminutive of *Pavel,* "Paul." Of course *Pavliček* long since developed into a surname in its own right, but then very little in family history is simple and straightforward!

Aleksandr — Alexander
Alena — Alena
Alžběta — Elizabeth
Antonin — Anthony
Bohumil — Theophil
Božena — Božena
František — Francis
Jan — John
Jana — Jana
Jarmila — Jarmila
Jaroslav — Jaroslav

Jiří — George
Josef — Joseph
Karel — Charles
Kašpar — Casper
Kateřina — Catherine
Květa — Květa
Ladislav — Ladislaus
Lukáš — Luke
Matěj — Matthew
Mikuláš — Nicholas
Miroslav — Miroslav

Ondřej — Andrew
Pavel — Paul
Petr — Peter
Řehoř — Gregory
Tomáš — Thomas
Václav — Vaclav
Vilém — William
Vlasta — Vlasta
Vitězslav — Vitězslav
Vojtěch — Vojtek
Zdeňka — Zdenka

Polski

The Polish Alphabet

Printed	Cursive
A, a	*A, a*
Ą, ą	*Ą, ą*
B, b	*B, b*
C, c	*C, c*
Ć, ć	*Ć, ć*
D, d	*D, d*
E, e	*E, e*
Ę, ę	*Ę, ę*
F, f	*F, f*
G, g	*G, g*
H, h	*H, h*
I, i	*I, i*
J, j	*J, j*
K, k	*K, k*
L, l	*L, l*
Ł, ł	*Ł, ł*
M, m	*M, m*
N, n	*N, n*
Ń, ń	*Ń, ń*
O, o	*O, o*
Ó, ó	*Ó, ó*
P, p	*P, p*
R, r	*R, r*
S, s	*S, s*
Ś, ś	*Ś, ś*
T, t	*T, t*

Printed	Cursive	Printed	Cursive
U, u	*U, u*	**Z, z**	*Z, z*
W, w	*W, w*	**Ź, ź**	*Ź, ź*
Y, y	*Y, y*	**Ż, ż**	*Ż, ż*

Polish is one of the Slavic languages that use the Roman alphabet, not the Cyrillic, largely because writing came to the Poles by way of Roman Catholic rather than Greek Orthodox clergy. The letters *q, v,* and *x* are not used in Polish, and the distinctly Polish characters *ą, ć, ę, ł, ń, ó, ś, ż* and *ż* are considered letters of the alphabet, each following its unmodified counterpart (*ą* after *a, ć* after *c,* and so on). The *ą, ę, ń,* and *y* never appear initially and thus are seldom capitalized; but since documents sometimes highlight words by spelling them out in upper-case letters, it seems best to show researchers all upper-case forms, even those rarely seen.

The basic vowels of Polish are much as in the Romance languages: *a* is like the *a* in "father," *e* like that in "let," *i* like that in "machine," *o* somewhat like that in "hotel," *u* like the *oo* in "book," and *y* like the short *y* sound in "very." The vowel *ó* is pronounced exactly the same as Polish *u,* and some words are spelled either way (*Jakób* vs. *Jakub,* for example). The nasal vowel *ą* usually sounds like English "own" with the *n*-sound never quite finished, but before *b* or *p* it sounds more like *om* in "home." The nasal *ę* is generally pronounced like *en* in "men," again without quite finishing the *n*-sound; before *b* or *p* it sounds more like *em* in "memory," and in some positions it loses its nasal quality. But generally pronouncing *ą* like *on (om)* and *ę* like *en (em)* will approximate the correct sound.

The *i* is special because it often follows consonants as a sign of softening; thus Poles pronounce *ne* as somewhat like "neh," but *nie* more like "nyeh." The consonants *ć, ń, ś,* and *ż* are spelled that way only when they precede other consonants; before vowels they're spelled *ci, ni, si,* and *zi.* In either case they are pronounced, respectively, more or less like soft *ch* (as in "cheese"), *ni* (as in "onion"), *sh* (as in "sheep") and the sound of the *s* in "pleasure." In a word like *cicho* (quiet, quietly) the *i* not only softens the *c* to a *ch*-sound, it also supplies the first syllable's vowel.

Many consonants are pronounced much as in English, but the *l* is more like that in "leaf" than that in "hill," and the *r* is lightly trilled, as in Italian. Polish *h* and *ch* are pronounced the same, a little harsher than an initial *h* in English but not quite so guttural as German *ch* in *Bach.* Polish *w* is pronounced like English *v* and Polish *ł* is pronounced like English *w* (all of which explains how "Lech Wałęsa" can come out sounding like "Lekh Vawensa"). The *c* is pronounced like a combined *ts* (e. g., English "knights"), the *g* is always as in "gone" (never as in "gym"), and the *j* is always pronounced like *y* in "yield." The *s* is pronounced as it is in English "soon," and *z* is pronounced as in "zebra" (but remember the softened pronunciation of *ci, ni, si,* and *zi*).

The *cz, rz, sz* combinations are similar to *ć, ż,* and *ś,* respectively, but are articulated differently; *ż* is pronounced the same as *rz.* The combination *dż* or *dzi* sounds like an English *j* in "jail."

The Polish Language

Polish, a West Slavic language spoken in Poland and border areas of neighboring nations, is also spoken by over twelve million persons in the United States. It is the most widely spoken Slavic language in North America. Like Russian and Latin, Polish is a language in which meaning is highly dependent on endings added to the stem forms of nouns, adjectives, and verbs. The addition of endings often modifies the form of the stem, e. g., "to write" is *pisać*, "he wrote" is *pisał*, but "he writes" is *pisze* — in the present tense the *-s-* sound of the root is modified to *-sz-* (pronounced, according to English phonetic values, as an "sh" sound). This makes recognizing verb forms more difficult, as most dictionaries would not give a separate entry for *pisze*, mentioning it, if at all, only under the listing of the infinitive form, *pisać*. The answer — short of taking a course in Slavic linguistics — is to maintain a certain flexibility of mind when looking up words.

The Format of Long-Form Documents

Although only two so-called "long-form" documents are included in this book (Documents #1 and #4), so many of the birth, marriage, and death certificates one finds are in this format that devoting a few pages to studying it seems well worthwhile. After the reader becomes familiar with the general features of the format, analysis of two sample documents should suffice to make any long-form document comprehensible.

19th-century Polish-language vital records generally appeared either in a columnar format or in the "long-form" or "Napoleonic" format. The columnar type presents fewer difficulties because data was simply filled into appropriate columns with standard headings; the columnar arrangement actually provides a visual context that facilitates translation. The long-form documents are harder to decipher because they consist of blocks of hand-written text, and the names and dates, appearing as they do in sentences, are fully exposed to the complexities of Polish grammar. Fortunately, the long-form documents also followed set patterns, and once one recognizes the patterns it is easier to pick out the data and ignore the legalese. Spotting a few key phrases will establish which sort of record it is, then one can concentrate on using the expressions that typically appear in that sort of record as handwriting samples that give clues as to what the non-standard parts say.

The standard pattern of these documents is summarized as templates on the next page. For a more complete treatment of this subject, see Judith Frazin's book, listed in the Bibliography.

In the templates, items appearing in *cursive* are the Polish words that usually appear in the records; *italicized words* represent Polish expressions that vary according to context, i. e., the pertinent data; and [bracketed] items, with or without italics, are words appearing sometimes but not always.

Before looking at the templates, however, two standard elements of these records deserve attention. The first and last sentences of these documents varied very little, whether for birth, marriage, or death records. The first sentence usually ran more or less as follows:

Działo się w [mieście/wsi] (name of town/village) dnia (day/month/year) roku o godzinie (hour) (time of day — przedpołudniem/popołudniu/rano/wieczorem/w nocy)

Translation — This occurred in *(town)* on *(day/month/year)* at *(—)* o'clock *(time of day)*.

That is the typical opening for documents drawn up after 1826; before that time the standard opening formula was:

Roku (year) dnia (date) miesiąca (month). Przed nami (position of registrar [often proboszczem, "pastor" of the town's Catholic church]) Urzędnikiem Stanu Cywilnego Gminy (name of district) powiatu (name of county) w województwie (name of province).

Translation — In the year *(year)* on the day *(date)* of the month of *(month)*. Before us *(name of official)* Civil Registrar for the district of *(district)*, county of *(county)*, province of *(province)*.

Sometimes instead of *Urzędnikiem Stanu Cywilnego* one sees *sprawującym obowiązki urzędnika Stanu Cywilnego*, "fulfilling the duties of the Civil Registrar").

The typical closing, for pre- or post-1826 documents, consists of some variation of this:

Akt ten stawiącemu [sometimes instead of *stawiącemu* it's *oświadczącemu*) *i świadkom przeczytany [został], przez (signing witnesses and/or registrar) podpisany.*

Translation: This document was read aloud to the declarant and witnesses and was signed by ....

When the witnesses could not read or write — as was often the case in rural areas — the clerk would insert words indicating their illiteracy — e. g., *niepiśmienny* or *nieumiejący pisać* or *czytać nie umieją*, and would go on to say the document was "signed only by us," *tylko przez nas podpisany.*

Another standard feature of these records is the typical assembly of phrases used to identify individuals. As a rule the document gives these facts for any person mentioned: name, occupation, age, place of residence; if the person was a minor his/her parents were usually identified, and a married woman's maiden name was also usually given (*z Grabowskich* = "née Grabowska," *z Nowaków* = "née Nowak"). Thus a typical witness might be *Jan Nowacki, gospodarz, lat trzydzieści trzy mający [liczący], we wsi Grabowo zamieszkały* — "Jan Nowacki, farmowner, age 33, living in the village of Grabowo." In the following summary of document formats, [**name:** witness] means that what follows would be the name, occupation, age, and residence of a witness; [**name:** groom] means the same facts for a bridegroom; and so on. Sometimes the order of these items will vary slightly, sometimes they'll be combined for two persons if applicable to both, and sometimes if one or more was unknown it was omitted.

In fact, there was considerable variance in the exact wording of these records, but they usually followed fairly closely along these lines. If one is struggling to decipher the handwriting, it helps a great deal to know "Now the word *zapowiedzi* (banns) ought to appear here somewhere." Deciphering these records is much like working a crossword puzzle — filling in the familiar words will help enormously in making out the unfamiliar ones.

Template for Birth Records

Działo się w (town) dnia (day, month, year) roku o godzinie (time of day). Stawił się [osobiście] [**name:** child's father, or occasionally an uncle, neighbor, or midwife] *w obecności* [**name:** witness] *i* [**name:** witness] *i okazał nam dziecię płci (sex) urodzone (where born) (day of birth,* usually day/month and *bieżącego roku* "of the current year") *o godzinie (hour of birth) (time of day) z małżonki jego* [**name:** mother, often with maiden name *z —ów* or *z —ich*]. *Dziecięciu temu na chrzcie świętym udzielonym/odbytym (date baptized) przez (by whom baptized) nadano imię (child's first name),* * *a rodzicami chrzestnymi byli* [**name:** godfather] *i* [**name:** godmother]. *Akt ten oświadczającemu i świadkom przeczytany i przez ... podpisany.*

Translation — This happened in *(town)* on *(day/month/year)* at *(hour)* o'clock *(time of day)*. There appeared [in person] *(child's father or uncle, midwife)* in the presence of *(witnesses)* and showed us a child of the *(male, męskiej, or female żeńskiej)* sex, born *(where born)* *(when born)*, at *(time born)* *(date born)* to his wife *(mother's name)*. To this child in Holy Baptism, administered *(day baptized)* by *(baptizer)* was given the name *(child's name),* * and the godparents were *(godparents)*. This document was read to the declarant and to the witnesses and was signed by *(whoever signed)*.

*Very often the child's name or names appear as the most clearly written words in this kind of record, preceded by *imię* or *imiona* (name/names). This can help you get your bearings as to what appears where.

Template for Death Records

Działo się w (town) dnia (day, month, year) roku o godzinie (time of day). Stawili się [**name:** witness] *i* [**name:** witness] *i oświadczyli, że dnia (date of death) o godzinie (hour of death) umarł (place of death)* [**name:** deceased], *syn/córka* [**name:** deceased's father] *i* [**name:** deceased's mother] *małżonków, zostawiwszy po sobie* [**name:** surviving relatives, usually spouse first, then children]. *Po przekonaniu się naocznem o zejściu (deceased,* in the genitive case), *akt ten oświadczającemu i świadkom przeczytany i przez ... podpisany.*

Translation — This happened in *(town)* on *(day/month/year)* at *(hour)* o'clock *(time of day)*. *(Witness)* and *(witness)* appeared and stated that on *(day of death)* at *(time of death)* died at *(place of death) (deceased)* son/daughter of *(parents' names)*, survived by *(names of relatives surviving the deceased)*. After an eyewitness identification of the death of *(deceased)*, this document was read to the declarant and to the witnesses and was signed by *(whoever signed)*.

Template for Marriage Records

Działo się w (town) dnia (day, month, year) roku o godzinie (time of day). Stawił się [**name:** priest, rabbi, groom's father, or some other responsible witness] *oraz z* [**name:** groom] *i [tudzież z panną]* [**name:** bride] *i w przytomności świadków* [**names:** witnesses] *oświadczył, że przed nim na dniu (date of marriage) między (groom) i (bride) zawarte zostało małżeństwo religijne które poprzedziły trzy zapowiedzi (3 dates* when the banns were read, usually a week apart) *(place of the banns' reading). Na to małżeństwo nastąpiło zezwolenie ustnie obecnych tu* [**names:** parents], *ojców nowo zaślubionych i tamowanie małżeństwa nie zaszło. Małżonkowie nowi oświadczyli przy tym, iż pomiędzy sobie żadnej umowy nie zawarli. Akt ten oświadczającemu i świadkom przeczytany i przez ... podpisany.*

Translation — This happened in *(town)* on *(day/month/year)* at *(hour)* o'clock *(time of day)*. *(Priest, rabbi, whoever)* appeared along with *(groom)* and *(bride)* and in the presence of witnesses *(witnesses)* stated, that before him on *(date of wedding)* between *(groom)* and *(bride)* was contracted a religious marriage which was proceeded by three readings of the banns *(when banns read)* at *(where banns read)*. To this marriage permission was given orally by the parents, who were present, *(parents)* and no objection was made to the marriage. The newlyweds testified on this occasion that no premarital agreements were made between them. This document was read to the declarant and to the witnesses and was signed by *(whoever signed)*.

Document 1: A Long-Form Polish Birth Certificate

Now a specific document may profitably be studied. Note that it does not conform exactly to the template given above, but is reasonably similar. The handwriting is not too easy to read, so what follows is a rendering of the handwritten body of the document in a standardized (and presumably more legible) cursive. Analysis of the document follows.

Rzeczpospolita Polska

Województwo *Białostockie*   Powiat *Suwalski*

Proboszcz Rzymsko-Katol. Parafii *św. Aleksandra w Suwałkach*

niniejszym zaświadcza, że w księgach metrykalnych tejże parafii za rok *1886* pod. Nr. *259*

znajduje się następujący:

AKT URODZENIA I CHRZTU

Mało-

Pijawne

akt

urodzenia

Jana

Kozicza

W języku rosyjskim który w przekładzie na polski brzmi:

"Działo się w mieście Suwałkach dnia dziewiątego Maja tysiąc osiemset osiemdziesiątego szóstego roku o godzinie trzeciej po południu. Stawił się osobiście Antoni Kozicz, rolnik zamieszkały we wsi Małe-Pijawne trzydzieści osiem lat mający, w obecności Antoniego Tarleckiego i Adama Kulbackiego po pięćdziesiąt lat mających rolników zamieszkałych we wsi Małe-Pijawne i okazał nam dziecię płci męskiej urodzone we wsi Małe-Pijawne drugiego Maja bieżącego roku o godzinie dziesiątej rano z jego prawnej małżonki Józefy z Kopiczków, trzydzieści lat mającej. Dziecięciu temu na chrzcie świętym udzielonym w dniu dzisiejszym przez księdza Wincentego Gryketysa nadano imię Jan, a rodzicami chrzestnymi byli: Piotr Kujałowicz i Anna Tarlecka. Akt ten oświadczającemu i świadkom niepiśmiennym przeczytany, przez nas tylko podpisany.

Ks. A. Makowski G. S. par.

Zgodność niniejszego odpisu z oryginałem zaświadczam

Suwałki, dnia *10 września* 19 47 roku

Proboszcz: *Ks. B.* [illegible]

Rzeczpospolita Polska

Województwo *Białostockie*   Powiat *Suwalski*

Proboszcz Rzymsko - Katol. Parafii *św. Aleksandra w Suwałkach*

niniejszym zaświadcza, że w księgach metrykalnych tejże parafii za rok *1886* pod Nr. *259*

znajduje się następujący:

AKT URODZENIA I CHRZTU

w języku rosyjskim który w przekładzie na polski brzmi:

Mało-Pijawne akt urodzenia Jana Kozicza

„ Działo się w mieście Suwałkach dnia dziewiątego Maja tysiąc ośmset osiemdziesiątego szóstego roku o godzinie trzeciej po południu. Stawił się osobiście Antoni Kozicz, rolnik zamieszkały we wsi Mało-Pijawne trzydzieści osiem lat mający w obecności Antoniego Gasleckiego i Adama Kulbackiego po pięćdziesiąt lat mających rolników zamieszkałych we wsi Mało-Pijawne i okazał nam dziecię płci męskiej urodzone we wsi Mało-Pijawne drugiego Maja bieżącego roku o godzinie dziesiątej rano z jego prawnej małżonki Józefy z Kasperków, trzydzieści lat mającej. Dziecięciu temu na chrzcie świętym udzielonym w dniu dzisiejszym przez księdza Wincentego Grykotysa nadano imię Jan, a rodzicami chrzestnymi byli: Piotr Kujałowicz i Anna Gaslecka. Akt ten świadczącemu i świadkom niepiśmiennym przeczytany, przez nas tylko podpisany.

(—) Ks. A. Makowski P. S. par.

Zgodność niniejszego odpisu z oryginałem zaświadczam

Suwałki dnia *10 września* 19*47* roku

Proboszcz *Ks. B. Gumowski*

– 167 –

Rzeczpospolita Polska — "The Republic of Poland"

województwo Białostockie — "Białystok province." A *województwo* is an administrative division in Poland, roughly equivalent to a province; *białostocki* is the adjectival form of *Białystok,* and the *-e* ending is the neuter nominative singular, agreeing with the noun it modifies.

powiat Suwalski — "Suwałki county." *Suwalski* is the adjectival form of *Suwałki,* and a *powiat* was a smaller administrative division, roughly equivalent to a county, within a *województwo.* The *powiaty* were eliminated in the 1970's, but for research purposes they are still important in pinpointing the origin of records.

proboszcz — "pastor"

Rzymsko-Katol. Parafii św. Aleksandra — "of the Roman Catholic parish (from *parafia*) of St. Alexander." *Św.* is the abbreviation for *święty,* "holy," or, used with a person's name, "Saint."

w Suwałkach — "in Suwałki." The ending *-ach* is locative plural for nouns and adjectives, and *Suwałki* is plural in form; *-ach* is a common ending after prepositions such as *w,* "in."

niniejszym — "hereby" (a word commonly seen in Polish documents and letters)

zaświadcza, że — "attests, certifies that" (from *zaświadczać*)

w księgach metrykalnych tejże parafii — "in the registry books of that parish"

za rok 1886 pod Nr. 259 — "for the year *(rok)* 1886 under number 259"

znajduje się następujący — "is found (from *znajdować się*) the following" (from *następować*)

akt urodzenia i chrztu — "certificate *(akt)* of birth (genitive of *urodzenie,* "birth") and baptism" (*chrztu* is the genitive form of *chrzest*)

Translation — Republic of Poland. Białystok Province. Suwałki county. The pastor of the Roman Catholic church of St. Alexander attests that in the registry books of that parish for the year 1886, under number 259, is found the following: A birth and baptismal certificate.

w języku rosyjskim który w przekładzie na polski brzmi:

w języku rosyjskim — "in the Russian language." *Rosyjskim* is the locative singular masculine of *rosyjski,* "Russian." *Języku* is the masculine locative singular of *język,* "tongue, language."

który — "who, which, that"

w przekładzie na polski — "in translation *(przekład)* to Polish"

brzmi — "translates, reads" (from *brzmieć*)

Translation — ...in the Russian language, which in translation reads as follows...

[from the column on the left side]

Małe-Pijawne akt urodzenia Jana Kozicza

Małe-Pijawne — "Małe-Pijawne" (the village in which the birth took place)

akt urodzenia Jana Kozicza — "certificate *(akt)* of birth *(urodzenia)* of Jan Kozicz" (the *-a* endings are typical of the genitive case of masculine and neuter nouns)

Translation — Małe-Pijawne, birth certificate of Jan Kozicz

[Registry documents often have a brief notation of this sort in a column on the left or as a notation on the top of the document; when this notation is legible, it tells the name of the person with whom the document deals and his/her home town or village. Since these towns or villages were often rather small, the place where the document was drawn up will often be different, i. e., the nearest larger town or parish center where the local registry clerk was located.]

Działo się w mieście Suwałkach, dnia dziewiątego Maja tysiąc osiemset osiemdziesiątego szóstego roku o godzinie trzeciej po południu.

Działo się — "[This] happened, took place" (from *dziać się*)

w mieście Suwałkach — "in the town of Suwałki." *Mieście* is the locative singular case of *miasto,* "town, city." Also possible here: *we wsi,* "in the village," *w miasteczku,* "in the small town."

dnia dziewiątego maja — "on the ninth day of May," literally "of the ninth day," from *dzień.*

tysiąc osiemset osiemdziesiątego szóstego roku — "of the 1886th year," i. e., 1886.

o godzinie trzeciej — "at the third *(trzeciej)* hour" (locative singular of *godzina,* "hour, o'clock." Time is indicated by the expression *o godzinie* plus the **ordinal** number in the locative case)

po południu — "in the afternoon," literally "after midday." Also possible here are *rano,* "in the morning, *wieczorem,* "in the evening," *po północy,* "after midnight," *przed południem* "before noon."

Translation — This took place in the city of Suwałki, on 9 May 1886, at 3 p.m.

Stawił się osobiście Antoni Kozicz, rolnik zamieszkały we wsi Małe-Pijawne, trzydzieści osiem lat mający, w obecności Antoniego Tarleckiego i Adama Kulbackiego, po pięćdziesiąt lat mających rolników zamieszkałych we wsi Małe-Pijawne...

Stawił się — "presented himself, appeared" (from *stawić się*)

osobiście — "personally" (from *osoba*, "person," *osobisty*, "personal")

rolnik — "a farmer"

zamieszkały — "residing." The same word appears later in the genitive plural masculine, *zamieszkałych*, modifying *rolników*.

we wsi — "in the village." The preposition *w* (in) adds an *-e* before some consonant clusters to make it easier to pronounce. *Wsi* is the locative singular of *wieś*, "village."

trzydzieści lat mający — literally, "thirty *(trzydzieści)* years *(lat)* having," i. e., "age 30 years." The participle *mający* comes from the verb *mieć*,"to have."

w obecności — "in the presence [of]." The names and occupations of the witnesses follow, in the **genitive** case. To arrive at the proper version of their names, the genitive endings must be deleted: Antoni/ego Tarlecki/ego → Antoni Tarlecki, and Adam/a Kulbacki/ego → Adam Kulbacki.

po pięćdziesiąt lat mających — "each age 50 *(pięćdziesiąt)* years." The preposition *po* is often used in such constructions in the idiomatic sense of "[to] each."

rolników zamieszkałych we wsi Małe-Pijawne — "farmers living in the village of Małe-Pijawne." Both *rolników* and *zamieszkałych* are genitive plural forms because they are in apposition to the names of the men, which are genitive following *w obecności*.

Translation — Antoni Kozicz appeared in person, a farmer living in the village of Małe-Pijawne, age 38; in the presence of Antoni Tarlecki and Adam Kulbacki, each age 50, farmers living in the village of Małe-Pijawne...

...i okazał nam dziecię płci męskiej urodzone we wsi Małe-Pijawne drugiego Maja bieżącego roku o godzinie dziesiątej rano z jego prawnej małżonki Józefy z Kopiczków, trzydzieści lat mającej.

i okazał nam — "and showed us..." *Okazał* is the past tense of *okazać*, "to show," and *nam* is the dative of *my*, "we."

dziecię płci męskiej — "a child *(dziecię)* of the male *(męskiej)* sex *(płci).*" The other possibility here is *dziecię płci żeńskiej*, "a child of the female sex."

urodzone ... drugiego Maja bieżącego roku — "born... on May 2nd of the current year." *Urodzone* is the past passive participle of *urodzić*, "to give birth."

z jego prawnej małżonki — "of *(z)* his *(jego)* lawful *(prawnej)* spouse *(małżonki).*" *Małżonki* is the genitive of the feminine noun *małżonka*.

Józefy z Kopiczków — The noun *Józefy* is in the genitive, because it is in apposition to *małżonki*, so one must delete the feminine genitive ending *-y* and replace it with the feminine nominative ending *-a:* so her proper name is *Józefa*. *Z* plus the genitive plural is one way of rendering a maiden name (it means literally "of the ——-s"), so *z Kopiczków* means her maiden name was "Kopiczek" (or "Kopiczko" — grammatically either form is possible). Thus this phrase translates as "Józefa née Kopiczek."

Translation — ...and showed us a child of the male sex, born in the village of Małe-Pijawne on May 2nd of the current year at 10 o'clock in the morning of his lawful wife Józefa née Kopiczek, age 30.

Dziecięciu temu na chrzcie świętym udzielonym w dniu dzisiejszym przez księdza Wincentego Gryketysa nadano imię Jan, a rodzicami chrzestnymi byli: Piotr Kujałowicz i Anna Tarlecka.

Dziecięciu temu — dative case, meaning "to this child."

na chrzcie świętym — "at Holy Baptism" (nominative case *chrzest święty*)

udzielonym w dniu dzisiejszym — "administered on this day." *Udzielonym* (locative case, like the noun it modifies, *chrzcie*) is the past passive participle of *udzielić*, "to administer, confer, share."

przez księdza Wincentego Gryketysa — "by Rev. Wincenty Gryketys." In passive expressions the preposition *przez* means "by," and it always takes the accusative case. The priest's name is composed of a first name declined as an adjective and a surname declined as a noun; the *-ego* ending is typical of masculine adjectives in the genitive or accusative cases, and the nominative ending would be *-y* or *-i*. The typical accusative ending of masculine nouns is *-a*, and the nominative would be formed by simply removing the ending. So the nominative form of *Wincentego Gryketysa* would be *Wincenty Gryketys*.

nadano imię — "the name *(imię)* was given" *(nadano*, from *nadać*).

rodzicami chrzestnymi byli — In Polish forms of the verb *być,* "to be," are often followed by nouns with instrumental case endings; *-ami* is the plural instrumental for nouns, and *-ymi* for adjectives. So this means "The godparents were:"

Translation — At Holy Baptism, administered on this date by Rev. Wincenty Gryketys, the child was given the name of Jan. And the godparents were: Piotr Kujałowicz and Anna Tarlecka.

Akt ten oświadczającemu i świadkom niepiśmiennym przeczytany, przez nas tylko podpisany.

oświadczającemu i świadkom — "to the one making the declaration and to the witnesses." Both are dative forms; the nominative singular of *świadkom* is *świadek,* "witness," and the nominative form of *oświadczającemu* (a participle form from *oświadczać*) is *oświadczający.*

niepiśmiennym — "illiterate, not knowing how to write." The form is dative plural, in agreement with the noun *świadkom.*

przeczytany — "[was] read aloud," from *przeczytać,* "to read through."

przez nas tylko podpisany — "[was] signed by us *(nas)* only *(tylko)."* Podpisany is the passive participle of *podpisać,* "to sign" (literally, "to write *[pisać]* under *[pod]*").

Translation — This act was read to the declarant and to the illiterate witnesses and was signed by us alone.

Zgodność niniejszego odpisu z oryginałem zaświadczam.

Translation — I certify *(zaświadczam)* the conformity *(zgodność)* of this copy with the original.

Document #2: A Short-Form Polish Birth Certificate

Document #2 is an extract taken from a record like Document #1 (this reproduction has been reduced in size slightly to make it fit onto the preceding page). After studying the long-form certificate a researcher should have no problem in translating the short form.

z roku 1906 — "from the year 1906." The preposition *z* can mean several things; with a genitive form (e. g., *roku*) it means "of, from." With an instrumental form it means "with," e. g., *z oryginałem* "with the original" (see last line of Document #1).

świadectwo metryczne — "a registry certificate." *Metryczne* is an adjective formed from *metryka*, the generic Polish term for registries of vital documents (*metryka* comes originally from the same Greek root as the English word "metric").

imię i nazwisko — "first name and surname"

urodziła się — "was born." The masculine is *urodził się*, and the feminine ending is written in to show that the person born was female. Notice the other options which have been crossed out, *Zmarł* "he died," and *ślubowali* "they were wed." This is an all-purpose form, to be hand-modified as appropriate.

w Folwarku Nowopol — "in the Nowopol *folwark*." Some translate *folwark* as "grange," which was the residence and central area of a gentleman farmer's estate.

imiona rodziców — "parents' names." *Imiona* is plural nominative of *imię*, and *rodziców* is the genitive of the plural noun *rodzice*, "parents."

Anna Rydzewska — "Anna Rydzewska." The *-ska* ending of her surname is a feminine form; the corresponding masculine would be *Rydzewski*. Poles automatically recognize this and don't even think of *Rydzewski* and *Rydzewska* as being separate surnames — the latter is simply the feminine variant of the former.

kwietnia — "April." Obviously the names of months normally appear in dates, but the form used is the genitive, such as *kwietnia*, not the nominative form, *kwiecień*, that one would usually see in a dictionary. So the date is: "2 April 1906."

córka — *córka*, "daughter." Obviously "daughter" implies "daughter *of*," and that's why the names of Anna's parents are given in the genitive case: *Adama, Franciszki z Cimochowskich*. The father's name was *Adam* (the *-a* is the genitive ending) *Rydzewski* and the mother's *Franciszka* (*-i* is the feminine genitive ending and must be replaced with nominative *-a*) *Rydzewska née Cimochowska*.

Wyraźnie tysiąc dziewięćset szóstego roku — Literally, "Expressly, one thousand nine hundred sixth year." *Wyraźnie* indicates that the year, already given once in numerals, is now to be written out in words. As usual, general time is expressed in the genitive case, thus the endings on *szóstego roku*.

Za zgodność niniejszego z oryginałem świadczę: Bakałarzewo dnia 1 Września 1919 roku. Urzędnik Stanu Cywilnego. "I certify the conformity of this [document] with the original." (Compare this clause with the similar one at the end of Document #1.) Then the place and date this certificate was filled out are written in: "Bakałarzewo, 1 September 1909." The document is signed by the Civil Registrar *(Urzędnik Stanu Cywilnego),* in this case a priest. Note the Latin seal, *Sigillum Ecclesiae Bakałarzewiensis,* "Seal of the Bakałarzewo Church."

Document #3: A Jewish Birth Certificate (Hebrew and Polish)

Poland's ethno-cultural minorities often necessitated that certificates be issued in Polish and another language. To illustrate this point, a birth certificate of an individual of the Jewish faith appears on pages 172-173. Until the Nazi Holocaust decimated the Jewish communities in Poland, Jews comprised a significant portion of Poland's population. In the earlier part of the 19th century Jews at times went to Roman Catholic parishes to register their births, deaths, and marriages because in most areas the nearest Catholic church served as the local registry of vital statistics for all faiths.

This document may be particularly interesting for descendants of Polish Jews because the right-hand side is a Hebrew-language equivalent of the left-hand, Polish version. The Hebrew contents are functionally the same as the Polish, although they are not always literal translations of the Polish terminology; e. g. the column heading *Kto dokonał obrządku religijnego,* "Who performed the religious ceremony," is שם המוהל, "name of the *mohel*," in Hebrew. The column headings correspond from left to right, in both sections, even though the individual Hebrew entries, of course, are written from right to left within each column.

Wileński

RABIN NACZELNY

WYCIĄG

z ksiąg metrycznych o izraelitach
urodzonych w m. Wilnie
w r. tysiąc *dziewięćset czter-*
nastym 1914

№ 215

m. Wilno.

№		Kto dokonał obrządku religijnego	Miesiąc i data urodzenia i obrz. rel.		Gdzie się urodził	Stan ojca, imię ojca i matki.	Kto się urodził i jakie dano mu lub jej imię.
Żeńskiej płci	Męskiej płci		Chrześci-jańska	Żydow-ska			
	8	Icyk Bukat-man	urodz. 3 obrzez. 10	18 25	Wilno	Ojciec: Wiszew-ski mieszczanin Efraim-Lejba syn Hirsza-Jankiela Gurwicz Matka: Basia córka Newacha	Syn

Z oryginałem zgodne

Wileński Rabin Naczelny

Rabin

Druk. I. Neless i S. Szwallicha, Wilno

Wileński Rabin Naczelny [הרב דעדת וילנה] — "Wilno's Chief Rabbi." The city called "Wilno" in Polish is the historic capital of Lithuania; in Lithuanian it is "Vilnius," in Russian Вильнюс, and it has sometimes been called "Vilno" in English. Multiple names in various languages for geographical places are a circumstance with which one must be prepared to deal when doing research connected with eastern Europe.

Wyciąg [תעודת לדה] *z ksiąg metrycznych o izraelitach urodzonych w m. Wilnie w r. tysiąc dziewięćset czternastym 1914* — "Excerpt from the registry books *[z ksiąg metrycznych]* of Jews born in the city of Wilno in the year one thousand nine hundred fourteen 1914."

[בספר הנולדים של יהודי וילנה לשנת חמשת אלפים ושש מאות 1914 נמצא כתוב:]

№. Żeńskiej płci/Męskiej płci 8 [8 זכרים / נקבות מספר] — "Sequential # of the female gender/ of the male gender 8," i. e., number eight under the listing of males.

Kto dokonał obrządku religijnego [שם המוהל] *Icyk Bukatman*— "Who performed the religious ceremony." The *mohel* was Icyk Bukatman.

Miesiąc i data urodzenia i obrz. rel. [חודש ויום הולדת ויום המילה] — "Month and day of birth and religious ceremony *(obrz[ądku] rel[igijnego])*." (Actually, since the Polish word for circumcision, *obrzezanie*, could also conceivably be abbreviated *obrz.*, that could be what is meant here; the Hebrew word המילה means "the circumcision" rather than just "ceremony.") The two columns under this heading are *Chreścijańska* [העמים למספר] (Christian) and *Żydowska* [ישראל למספר] (Jewish). The Polish reads that on January *(Stycznia)* 3rd, or the 18th of Tevet *(Tew.)*, the child was born (*urodz. urodz.*), and he was circumcised *(obrzez.)* on the 10th (the 25th of Tevet).

– 172 –

הרב דעדת
וילנה.

№

תעודת לדה

בספר הגולדים של יהודי וילנה לשנת חמשת אלפים ושש מאות

1944

נמצא כתוב:

מספר		שם המוהל	חודש ויום הולדת ויום המילה.		איה נולד	שם האב והאם של הילד ומזמדם	מי נולד ואיזה שם נתן לו
			למספר העמים	למספר ישראל			

הרב דעדת וילנה

MIASTA WILNA ZAŚWIADCZA, IŻ NINIEJSZY
...SKI) JEST ZGODNYM Z DANYMI KTÓRE ZAWI?
ARCHIWUM. WILNO, Dnia 9. LUT. 1928

Gdzie się urodził [איה נולד] *Wilno* — "Where *(gdzie)* he was born: Wilno."

Stan ojca, imię ojca i matki [שם האב והאם של הילד ומעמדם] — "Father's standing, name of father and mother." The word *stan* means "state, condition, level, status," and in the society of the time one's standing was the same as one's occupation, so the answer to this is usually a profession. *Ojca* is the genitive of *ojciec*, "father," and *matki* the genitive of *matka*, "mother."

Ojciec: Święcianski mieszczanin Efraim-Lejba syn Hirsza-Jankiela Gurwicz — "Father: burgher of Święciany Efraim-Lejba, son of Hirsz-Jankiel Gurwicz."

Matka: Gitla Basia córka Newacha — "Mother: Gitla Basia, daughter of Newach."

Kto się urodził i jakie dano mu lub jej imię [מי נולד ואיוה שם נתן לו] *Syn Jona* — "Who was born and what name was given him or her: a son, Jona."

Z oryginałem zgodne, Za Wileński Rabin Naczelny — "In conformance with the original, for the Chief Rabbi of Wilno." The handwritten *Za* inserted before *Wileński Rabin Naczelny* means that the rabbi signing this did so on behalf of the Chief Rabbi. Grammatically it should be *Za Wileńskiego Rabina Naczelnego*, but the necessary point is made.

Archwium Miejskie miasta Wilna zaświadcza, iż niniejszy wyciąg (tekst polski) jest zgodnym z danymi które zawiera metryczna księga Archiwum. Wilno, Dnia 9 Lut. 1928. Archiwariusz... "The Municipal Archive of the city of Wilno certifies that this extract (the Polish text) is in conformance with the data which the Archive's Registry Record contains. Wilno, 9 February 1928. The archivist."

Document #4: A Polish/German Birth and Baptismal Certificate

On the opposite page is reproduced a copy of a bilingual birth and baptismal certificate, with Polish on the left and German on the right (in addition, the original document from which this was copied was in Russian!). It is a long-form certificate, and is instructive because of its format and vocabulary, and because it illustrates the value of bi- or trilingual documents: one can check the different translations against each other and thus improve the chances of comprehending the whole. This document also shows how the spelling of proper names varies from one language to another, as "Matylda Szewe" (Polish) turns into "Mathilda Schewe" (German.)

Below is a rendering of both sections in standardized script, to facilitate reading of the document. Much of this is already familiar from the first three documents; you may be able to decipher the relevant facts for yourself and check them against the analysis and translation.

Odpis	*Abschrift*

z ksiąg aktów stanu cywilnego parafii ewan-
gelicko-augsburskiej w Sierpcu, sub No 123
z roku 1907.

Akt urodzenia i chrztu
Działo się w Sierpcu, dnia dwudziestego szóstego
sierpnia
/ósmego września/, tysiąc dziewięćset
siódmego roku,
o godzinie drugiej popołudniu. Stawił się Juljusz
Sierp*, rolnik z Zurawieńca, lat trzydzieści
trzy mający, w obecności rolników Henryka
Rossol z Ossówki, lat czterdzieści siedem i Gottliba
Jabs z Zurawieńca, lat czterdzieści pięć i okazał nam dziecię płci żeńskiej oświadczając,
że urodziło się ono w Zurawieńcu, dnia siedem-
nastego /trzydziestego/ sierpnia, roku bieżącego,
o godzinie dziewiątej wieczorem, z małżonki
jego Matyldy z domu Szewe lat dwadzieścia osiem mającej. Dziecięciu temu
na chrzcie świętym, w dniu dzisiejszym
odbytym, nadane zostało imię Emma,
a rodzicami chrzestnymi jego byli: pierwszy świadek z Pauliną Blank. Akt
ten obecnym, pisać nieumiejącym przeczytany i przez nas tylko podpisany został. —/Podpisany:/ Pastor R. Gundlach.

*Poprawiony wyraz czytać "Sierp."

Zgodność tłumaczenia niniejszego odpisu z oryginałem rosyjskim zaświadczam. —

Sierpc, d. 13 września 1921 r.
Urzędnik Stanu Cywilnego. J. Bachman

---

aus den Zivilstandesaktenbüchern der evangelisch-
augsburgischen Pfarrgemeinde zu Sierpc
sub No 123 vom Jahre 1907.

Geburts und Taufakt
Geschehen zu Sierpc, den sechsundzwanzigsten
August /achten September/, des Jahres neunzehnhun-
dert sieben, zwei Uhr nachmittags. Es erschien der
Land-
wirt Julius Sierp, aus Zurawienice, dreiunddreißig Jahre alt, im Gegenwart der Land-
wirte Heinrich Rossol aus Ossówka, siebenund-
vierzig Jahre alt und Gottlieb Jabs aus Zurawienice,
fünfundvierzig Jahre alt und zeigte uns ein
Kind weiblichen Geschlechts vor, ausgebend, daß
dasselbe in Zurawienice, am siebzehnten /drei-
ßigsten/ August, des laufenden Jahres, neun Uhr
abends, von seiner achtundzwanzig Jahre alten
Ehefrau Mathilda geboren Schewe
geboren wurde. Diesem Kinde ist in der am
heutigen Tage vollzogenen heiligen Taufe
der Name Emma beigelegt worden, als
Paten waren der erste Zeuge mit Pauline Blank.
Dieser Akt ist den des Schreibens unkündigen An-
wesenden vorgelesen und nur von uns unter-
schrieben worden.
/Gezeichnet/ Pastor R. Gundlach.

Die Übereinstimmung der Übersetzung dieser
Abschrift mit dem rußischen Original
wird hiermit bescheinigt. —

Sierpc, d. 13. September 1921.
Der Standesbeamte J. Bachman

Odpis

z księgi aktów stanu cywilnego parafji ewan-
gelicko-augsburskiej w Sierpcu, sub. № 123
z roku 1907.

Akt urodzenia i chrztu:

Działo się w Sierpcu, dnia dwudziestego szóstego sierpnia
/ósmego września/ tysiąc dziewięćset siódmego roku,
o godzinie drugiej popołudniu. Stawił się Juljusz
Sierp, rolnik z Żurawieńca, lat trzydzieści
trzy mający, w obecności rolników Henryka
Rossol z Osówki, lat czterdzieści siedem i Gottliba
Fabs z Żurawieńca, lat czterdzieści pięć, okazał nam dziecię płci żeńskiej, oświadczając,
że urodziło się ono w Żurawieńcu, dnia siedem-
nastego /trzydziestego sierpnia, roku bieżącego,
o godzinie dziewiątej wieczorem, z małżonki
jego Matyldy z domu Szewe lat dwadzieścia osiem mającej. Dziecięciu temu
na Chrzcie świętym, w dniu dzisiejszym
odbytym, nadano zostało imię Emma,
a rodzicami chrzestnymi jego byli: sier-
wszy świadek z Pauliną Blank. Akt
ten obecnym, pisać nieumiejącym, przeczytany i przez nas tylko podpisany został. -/: Podpisano:/ Pastor R. Gundlach.

× poprawiony wyraz czytać: „Sierp."

Zgodność tłumaczenia niniejszego odpisu z oryginałem rosyjskim zaświadczam. —

Abschrift

aus der Zivilstandsaktenbüchern der evangelisch
augsburgischen Pfarrgemeinde zu Sierpc
sub № 123 vom Jahre 1907.

Geburts- und Taufakt:

Geschehen zu Sierpc, den sechsundzwanzigsten
August /achten September/ des Jahres neunzehnhun-
dert sieben, zwei Uhr nachmittags. Es erschien der Landwirt Julius Sierp aus Żurawieniec, drei-
und dreißig Jahre alt, in Gegenwart der Land-
wirte Heinrich Rossol aus Osówka, siebenund-
vierzig Jahre alt und Gottlieb Fabs aus Żurawieniec,
fünfundvierzig Jahre alt und zeigte uns ein
Kind weiblichen Geschlechts vor, angebend, daß
dasselbe in Żurawieniec, am siebzehnten /drei-
ßigsten/ August, des laufenden Jahres, neun Uhr
abends, von seiner achtundzwanzig Jahre alten
Ehefrau Mathilda geborenen Schewe
geboren wurde. Diesem Kinde ist in dem am
heutigen Tage vollzogenen heiligen Taufe
der Name Emma beigelegt worden, als
Paten waren der erste Zeuge mit Pauline Blank.
Dieser Akt ist den des Schreibens unkundigen An-
wesenden vorgelesen und nur von uns unter-
schrieben worden. ————
/: Gezeichnet:/ Pastor R. Gundlach.

Die Übereinstimmung der Übersetzung dieser
Abschrift mit dem russischen Original
wird hierum bescheinigt. ————

Sierpc, d. 13 Września 1921 r.
Urzędnik Stanu Cywilnego

Sierpc, d. 13 September 1921.
Der Standesbeamte

F. Bachman

- 175

Unfamiliar Words Appearing in this Document

Stan Cywilny — *Stan Cywilny*, genitive *Stanu Cywilnego*, means "The Civil Registry," as seen in the next-last line of the document in the expression *Urzędnik Stanu Cywilnego*, literally "The Offical of the Civil Registry."

ewangelicko-augsburski — an adjective describing the Evangelical Lutheran church.

dnia dwudziestego szóstego sierpnia — "on the 26th *(dwudziesty szósty)* day of August *(sierpnia).*"

/ósmego września/ — "eighth of September." The parts of Poland under Russian control were required to reckon time by the Old Style calendar, and this date was followed by a parenthetical insertion of the date as reckoned in the West, usually 12-13 days later than the Old Style date. When the difference involved different months, as it does here, both days and months were specified, e. g., "26 August/ 8 September." As seen in a date later in the document, the different dates often fell within the same month and only the dates were specified, e. g., "17th/30th of August."

tysiąc dziewięćset siódmego roku — "one thousand nine hundred seventh year," i. e., in 1907.

z Żurawieńca — "from Żurawieniec." The Polish and German versions of the name differ slightly, but to find the proper Polish spelling one must recall that the preposition *z* is followed by the genitive case; so to find the standard, nominative-case form of this name one must remove the genitive *-a* ending (Żurawieńca → Żurawieńc), remember that *-ń-* is spelled *-ni* before consonants (Żurawieńc → Żurawienic), and recall that Polish has a tendency to prefer a nominative form ending in *-iec* rather than *-ic* (compare the name *Wawrzyniec*, genitive *Wawrzyńca*, and the month July, *lipiec*, genitive *lipca*). So the proper Polish name of this town is "Żurawieniec." This form differs from the undeclined form that appears in the German translation, "Zurawienice," but the German names of Polish towns usually differed, at least somewhat, from the Polish ones.

Matylda Szewe/ Mathilda Schewe, Juljusz Sierp/ Julius Sierp, Henryk Rossol/ Heinrich Rossol, Gottlib Jabs/ Gottlieb Jabs, Paulina Blank/ Pauline Blank — It's instructive comparing the Polish versions of these names to the German ones. Sometimes the Polish version of a name will differ greatly from the German, e. g., *Wawrzyniec* vs. *Laurenz*, but usually the spellings reflect the different ways languages represent the same sounds. A Pole would pronounce *Matylda Szewe* almost exactly the same as a German would pronounce *Mathilda Schewe* (something like "mah-TILL-dah SHAVE-uh"). One could argue at length over which is the "correct" version of the name — a Pole might answer to Polish, German, Russian, Ukrainian, Czech, Byelorussian, and Yiddish versions of his name. But if all indications suggest that a given person considered himself or was considered a Pole, then the Polish form of his name would be the most appropriate.

odbyty — "done, taken place," from *odbyć się,* "to happen, occur, take place"

pierwszy świadek — "the first witness," i. e., Henryk/Heinrich Rossol.

obecnym, pisać nieumiejącym — "[to those] present, not knowing how to write." This construction is in the dative case, which can often be translated with the English prepositions "to" or "for." *Nieumiejącym* is a participle of the verb *umieć,* meaning "to know how," with the negative *nie-* prefixed. The point is that the document was signed only by the clerk because he was the only one who knew how to write, and this was often the case.

*Poprawiony wyraz czytać: "Sierp." — "Corrected expression to read: Sierp." The clerk had made an error in writing the declarant's name on the Polish side, and noted the error and this correction.

Translation

Copy from the records of the civil registry of the Evangelical-Lutheran parish in Sierpc, under #123 from the year 1907.

<u>Certificate</u> of <u>Birth</u> and <u>Baptism</u>: This happened in Sierpc on the 26th of August /8th of September/ 1907, at two p.m. <u>Juliusz Sierp</u> appeared, a farmer from Żurawieniec, age 33, in the presence of the farmers Heinrich Rossol from Ossówka, age 47, and of Gottlieb Jabs from Żurawieniec, age 45, and showed us a child of the female gender, stating that [the child] was born in Żurawieniec, on the 17th/30th of August of the current year, at 9 p.m., of his wife <u>Matylda</u> <u>née</u> <u>Szewe</u>, age 28. At Holy Baptism, performed on this day, this child was given the name of <u>Emma</u>, and the godparents were: the first witness with Paulina Blank. This certificate was read to those present, unable to write, and was signed only by us. /Signed:/ Pastor R. Gundlach.

I certify the conformity of this copy with the Russian original.

Sierpc, 13 September 1921, the Civil Registrar, J. Bachman.

Document #5: A Passport Application

Many nations required a passport application which was issued only after officials determined that the applicant owed no taxes or had fulfilled all military obligations. The application for passports was not always made to a national administrative agency but sometimes to provincial or district officials. The form on the following page was issued by local district officials.

All the words in this document are included in the vocabulary at the end of this section, and the analysis of the preceding documents should have given a rudimentary sense of Polish grammar. Therefore only words of particular interest or relevance are given here, and the various sentences and phrases are simply translated.

Gmina Radgoszcz (Gmina Radgoszcz) — "The District of Radgoszcz." A *gmina,* literally "community," was a governmental administrative district, lower than a *powiat* (county).

Poświadczenie celem uzyskania paszportu do podróży — "Statement for the purpose of obtaining a passport to travel"

Niżej wymienione osoby w tutejszej gminie stale mieszkają, do służby wojskowej nie należą pod śledztwem karnem nie zostają procesu o długi nie mają, podatków państwowych ani gminnych nie są winne, w obowiązku służbowym nie zostają, że przeto przeciw wydaniu paszportu do podróży nie zachodzą przeszkody. — "The persons enumerated below are permanent residents of this district, are not serving in the military, are not under criminal investigation, are not being sued for debt, do not owe any government or district taxes, and have no military obligations, and for this reason there are no obstacles to issuing them a passport to travel."

[Columnar Headings:]

Imię i nazwisko starającego o paszport: Władysław Moskal — "Name and surname of passport applicant: Władysław Moskal." *Starającego o paszport* literally means "of the one trying for a passport," from the verb *starać się,* "to attempt, try."

Czy gospodarz lub wyrobnik: Wyrob. — "Is [he] a farmowner or a laborer? Laborer." *Czy* is an introductory particle that indicates an upcoming question; sometimes it can be translated as "whether?"

Czy popisowy rezerwista lub landwerzysta z którego roku: — "Is he a conscripted reservist or a member of the *Landwehr* (militia), from what year?" [No answer]

Miejscowość w której urodzony i do której przynależny: Radgoszcz — "Place where born and where officially registered (*przynależny,* literally, "belonging to"): Radgoszcz."

Konskrybowany pod Nr. ... — "Conscribed under No." [No answer]

O jaki paszport stara się i na jaki czas: Do Prus na 8 miesiący — "What sort of passport applied for, and for what time [period]? To Prussia for 8 months"

Czy taksę wojskową zapłacił i za który rok — "Has he paid military tax and for which year" [No answer]

Czy brał już pierwej opis na paszport, kiedy i pod którą liczbą protokołu paszportowego gminnego: Nie — "Were the specifications for a passport taken earlier? When and under what file number in the District Passport Records? No."

Rysopis — "Description"

    liczy lat: 17 — "Age: 17"

    wzrost: średnio-mierny — "Height: mid-average"

    twarz: okrągła — "Face: oval"

    włosy: blond — "Hair: blond"

    oczy: siwe — "Eyes: grey"

    usta: mierne — "Mouth: average"

    nos: mierny — "Nose: average"

    znaki szczególne: ... — "Distinguishing marks: ..."

Uwaga — "Observation, Notation"

Naczelnik gminy — "District chief" [signature illegible]

Zwierzchność gminna — "District authority"

Radgoszcz dnia 17 lutego 1913 — "Radgoszcz, 17 February, 1913."

Poświadczenie celem uzyskania paszportu do podróży.

Niżej wymienione osoby w tutejszej gminie stałe mieszkają, do służby wojskowej nie należą pod śledztwem karnem nie zostają pod procesu o długi nie mają, podatków przewozowych ani gminnych nie są winne, w obowiązku służbowym nie zostają, że przeto przeciw wydaniu paszportu do podróży nie zachodzą przeszkody

Imię i nazwisko starającego się o paszport	Czy gospodarz lub wyrobnik	Czy popisowy rezerwista lub landwerzysta z którego roku	Miejscowość w której urodzony i do której przynależny	Konskrybowany pod Nr.	O jaki paszport stara się i na jaki czas	Czy taksę wojskową zapłacił i za który rok	Czy brał już pierwej opis na paszport, kiedy i pod którą liczbą protokółu paszportowego gminnego	liczy lat	wzrost	twarz	włosy	oczy	usta	nos	znaki szczególne	UWAGA
Władysław Mathal wyrobnik	—		Radgoszcz		Do Prus na 8 miesięcy		nie	17	średniego wzrostu	okrągła	blond	siwe	mierne	mierny		

ZWIERZCHNOŚĆ GMINNA

Radgoszcz dnia 17 Lutego 1913.

Piotr Pikul
Naczelnik gminy

L. skł. 170.

Document #6: A Republic of Poland Passport

Passports exhibited various formats over the last decades of the last century and the early decades of this one. On this and the following page is a full-size reproduction of a passport issued by the Republic of Poland during the interwar period (1918-1939). Note that it is bilingual, with all entries given both in Polish and French.

[Photograph]

Identyczność Józefa Kota oraz jego własnoręczny podpis potwierdza się

13 /4 1921

[Seal of Cieszanów Starostwo]

identyczność — "identity, identification photo"
    Józefa is genitive case, so *identyczność Józefa Kota* minus the genitive ending *-a* shows that this means "identity photo of Józef Kot." Note also that he signed his name "Juzef."
oraz — "and, as well as"
jego — "his, its"
własnoręczny — "by his own hand"
podpis — "signature"
podtwierdza się — "is confirmed"
starostwo — an administrative division, the area under the administration of a *starosta*

Rzeczpospolita Polska
M. S. W.

Republique Polonaise
M. I.

Paszport —Passeport

dla/pour Józefa Kot

zatrudnienie/profession —

miejsce zamieszkania/domicile Ostrowiec

M.S.W. (Ministerstwo Spraw Wewnętrznych) — Ministry of the Interior
dla — for (+ genitive case, so *Józefa = Józef*)
zatrudnienie — profession
miejsce zamieszkania — place of residence

Rysopis Właściciela / Signalement du porteur:
Rok urodzenia / Date de naissance} 1906
Wzrost / Stature} mały / petite
Twarz / Visage} owalna / ovale
Włosy / Cheveux} blond / blonde
Oczy / Yeux} siwe / gris
Usta / Bouche} mierne / moyenne
Nos / Nez} prosty / droit
Znaki szczególne / Distinctions spec.} żadne / nulles
Mówi językami / Parle} polskim / polonais
Własnoręczny podpis posiadacza / Signature propre
   Juzef Kot

rysopis właściciela — "description of bearer"

rok urodzenia — "year of birth: 1906"

wzrost: mały — "height: small"

twarz: owalna — "face: oval"

włosy: blond — "hair: blond"

oczy: siwe — "eyes: grey"

usta: mierne — "mouth: average"

nos: prosty — "nose: straight"

znaki szczególne: żadne — "distinguishing marks: none"

mówi językami: polskim — "speaks languages: Polish"

własnoręczny podpis posiadacza — "bearer's signature in his own hand: Juzef [or Józef] Kot"

udaje się z / se rend de Ostrowca
powiat / district Cieszanów
do / à Ameryki / Amerique
Paszport ten jest ważny / Ce passeport est valable:
sześć miesiące / 6 mon
Cieszanów d. 13 / 4 1921
W imieniu... [illegible]

udaje się z ... — "comes from, hails from." From udać się), with the preposition z + the genitive case (the masculine genitive ending -a is added to Ostrowiec → Ostrowieca and the -ie drops out to give the form Ostrowca) to show from where.

powiat — "district" or "county"

do Ameryki — "to America." Do takes the genitive case, and the genitive of Ameryka is Ameryki.

Paszport ten jest ważny: sześć miesiące — "This passport is valid (ważny — "valid, in force") six months." Ten, the demonstrative pronoun or adjective "this, that," takes different forms in different cases, e. g., tego, temu, tym, tych, temu, tymi.

Cieszanów d. 13/4 1921 — "Cieszanów, 13 April 1921"

w imieniu — "in the name of." Apparently an official signed on behalf of the starosta.

Document #7: A Polish/German Passport from the Austrian Sector

Passports issued by the Austrian-ruled portion of Poland (1772-1918) were frequently printed in German and Polish. The answers in this passport are in German, and reference to the section on German may prove instructive for researchers, since anyone tracing Polish roots will probably have to deal with records in German (and/or Russian) sooner or later. As the format of this document differs very little from the previous one, it should be fairly easy to decipher the Polish.

(Containing 16 pages)

No. 14435609

In the Name of His Majesty

FRANZ JOSEPH I

Kaiser of Austria, King of Bohemia, and
Apostolic King of Hungary

Passport

for} Johann Hałuszka
character/occupation} Taglöhner (day-laborer)
residing at} Dąbrówka Starzeńska
in county} Brzozów
crownland} Galizien (Galicia)

Description of the bearer's person

Year of birth} 1870
Height} mittel (medium)
Face} länglich (elongated)
Hair} dunkel (dark)
Eyes} grau (grey)
Mouth} mässig (average)
Nose} lang (long)
Distinguishing Marks} keine (none)
Signature in his own hand}

(In case the Polish words are hard to read, they are: *rok urodzenia, wzrost, twarz, włosy, oczy, usta, nos, szczególne znamiona, własnoręczny podpis*)

Dieselbe reist von **Dąbrówka**

Tenże (Taż) podróżuje **Starzeńska**

nach / do **Amerika**

Dieser Pass ist gültig:
Paszport ten ważny:

auf drei Jahre

Brzozów am 26. Mai 1913.

In Namen Sr Exzellenz
des Herrn k. k. Statthalters
Der k. k. Bezirkshauptmann:

Mit ihm reist:
Z nim (z nią) podróżuje:

Namen und Vornamen / Nazwisko i imię	Charakter / Charakter	Geburtsort / Miejsce urodzenia	Alter / Wiek	Stand / Stan	Statur / Wzrost	Gesicht / Twarz	Haare / Włosy	Augen / Oczy

-3-

-4-

This same person is traveling} *von* 𝒟ąbrówka 𝒮tarzeńska *(from Dąbrówka Starzeńska)*

to 𝒜merika *(America)*

This passport is valid: *auf drei Jahre* *(for three years)*

Brzozów am 26. Mai 1913 *(Brzozów, 26 May 1913)*

In the name of His Excellency the royal imperial Governor, the royal imperial county chief: [signature illegible]

With him/her is traveling:

Surname and First Name:	*Helene Haluszka*	*Kazimir Haluszka*
Character:	*Ehefrau* (wife)	*Sohn* (son)
Birthplace:	*Dąbrówka Starzeńska*	
Age:	*41 Jahre* (41 yrs.)	*13 Jahre* (13 yrs.)
Status:	*verehe- ratet* (married)	*ledig* (single)
Height:	*mittel* (medium)	*klein* (small)
Face:	*länglich* (long)	*rund* (round)
Hair:	*braun* (brown)	*dunkel blond* dark blond
Eyes:	*grau* (grey)	*grau* (grey)

Document #8: A German/Polish/Ukrainian Employment Booklet

Nr. 28

Arbeitsbuch
Książka robotnicza
Книжка робітнича

für dla для

Vor- und Zuname:
Imię i nazwisko:
Имя і наввиско: } *Jan Marut*

Geburtsort:
Miejsce urodzenia:
Місце уродженя: } *Wola raniżowska*

Geburtsjahr:
Rok urodzenia:
Рік уродженя: } *1895*

Heimatsgemeinde (politischer Bezirk):
Gmina przynależności (Powiat polityczny):
Громада приналежности (Политичний повіт): } *Wola raniżowska Kolbuszowa*

Stand (ob ledig oder verheiratet):
Stan (wolny lub żonaty):
Женатий або неженатий: } *wolny*

Religion:
Religia:
Віросповідане: } *rzym. kat.*

Beschäftigung:
Zatrudnienie:
Занятє: } *wyrobnik*

Statur: Wzrost: Рiст: *średni*

Gesicht: Twarz: Лице: *okrągła*

Haare: Włosy: Волосье: *ciemno-blond*

Augen: Oczy: Очи: *bure*

Mund: Usta: Уста: *mierne*

Nase: Nos: Hic: *mrykły*

Besondere Kennzeichen:
Szczegółowe znaki:
Особенні признаки: } *żadne*

Marut Jan.

Namensfertigung des Hilfsarbeiters:
Własnoręczny podpis robotnika pomocniczego:
Підпис робітника помічничого (челядника): } *umie*

Fertigung der ausstellenden Gemeindebehörde:
Podpis wystawiającej zwierzchności gminnej: *Wola* ...

Zusätze Dodatki Дописки
für jugendliche Hilfsarbeiter beziehungsweise Lehrlinge
dla młodocianych pomocników względnie uczniów
дотично нелітних помочничих робітників (челядників), вглядно учеників.

Auskunft über die Schulverhältnisse und die erworbene Schulbildung:
Wyjaśnienia co do stosunków szkolnych i uzyskanego wykształcenia szkolnego:
Дані о шкільних відношенях і о степени шкільного образованя: *umie czytać i pisać*

Name und Wohnort des Vaters oder Vormundes:
Imię i miejsce zamieszkania ojca lub opiekuna:
Имя і місце замешканя отця або опікуна: } *Wola raniżowska Jan Marut*

Die Zustimmung zur Eingehung des Arbeits- oder Lehrverhältnisses ist erfolgt*)
Zezwolenie do zawarcia stosunku robotniczego, względnie naukowego nastąpiło*)
Призволене до вступленя до роботи або на науку послідовало*)

n Seite des Vaters:
strony ojca:
сторони отця: } *Tak*

n Seite des Vormundes:
strony opiekuna:
сторони опікуна: }

n Seite der Aufenthaltsgemeinde:
strony gminy pobytu:
сторони громади перебуваня: } *Wola raniżowska*

Anmerkung: Hier ist ersichtlich zu machen, ob das Arbeitsbuch mit Zustimmung des Vaters oder des Vormundes, oder wenn eine solche nicht zu beschaffen ist, nach § 80 al. 2 Gewerbeordnung mit Zustimmung der Aufenthaltsgemeinde erfolgt ist.
Uwaga: Należy tu uwidocznić, czy książka robotnicza została

Arbeitsbuch/ *Książka robotnicza*/ Книжка робітнича — "Employment booklet"

für/ *dla*/ для — "for"

Vor- und Zuname/ *Imię i nazwisko*/ Имя і наввиско: *Jan Marut*— "First name and surname: Jan Marut"

Geburtsort/ *Miejsce urodzenia*/ Місце уродженя: *Wola raniżowska* — "Place of birth: Wola Raniżowska"

Geburtsjahr/ *Rok urodzenia*/ Рік уродженя: *1895* — "Year of birth: 1895"

Heimatsgemeinde (politischer Bezirk)/ *Gmina przynależności (Powiat polityczny)*/ Громада приналежности: *Wola Raniżowska Kolbuszowa* — "District of affiliation (Political county): Wola Raniżowska, Kolbuszowa"

Stand (ob ledig oder verheiratet)/ *Stan (wolny lub żonaty)*/ Женатий або неженатий: *wolny*— "Status (single or married): single"

Religion/ *Religia*/ Віросповідане: *rzym. kat.* — "Religion: Rom. Cath."

Beschäftigung/ *Zatrudnienie*/ Занятє: *wyrobnik* — "Occupation: farm-worker"

Statur/ *Wzrost*/ Рiст: *średni*— "Height: medium"

Gesicht/ *Twarz*/ Лице: *okrągła*— "Face: round"

Haare/ *Włosy*/ Волосье : *ciemno-blond*— "Hair: dark blond"

Augen/ *Oczy*/ Очи: *bure*— "Eyes: dark grey"

Mund/ *Usta*/ Уста: *mierne*— "Mouth: average"

– 183 –

𝕽𝖆𝖘𝖊/ *Nos*/ Hic: *zwykły* — "Nose: normal"

𝖁𝖊𝖘𝖔𝖓𝖉𝖊𝖗𝖊 𝕶𝖊𝖓𝖓𝖟𝖊𝖎𝖈𝖍𝖊𝖓/ *Szczegółowe znaki*/ Особенні признаки: *żadne* — "Distinguishing marks: none."

𝕹𝖆𝖒𝖊𝖓𝖘𝖋𝖊𝖗𝖙𝖎𝖌𝖚𝖓𝖌 𝖉𝖊𝖘 𝕳𝖎𝖑𝖋𝖘𝖆𝖗𝖇𝖊𝖎𝖙𝖊𝖗𝖘/ *Własnoręczny podpis robotnika pomocniczego*/ Підпис робітника помічничого (челядника): *umie* — "Signature of worker giving assistance: Knows how" (in other words, the bearer knows how to write and needed no one to help him fill out the form).

𝕱𝖊𝖗𝖙𝖎𝖌𝖚𝖓𝖌 𝖉𝖊𝖗 𝖆𝖚𝖘𝖘𝖙𝖊𝖑𝖑𝖊𝖓𝖉𝖊𝖓 𝕲𝖊𝖒𝖊𝖎𝖓𝖉𝖊𝖇𝖊𝖍𝖔̈𝖗𝖉𝖊/ *Podpis wystawiającej zwierzchności gminnej: Wola ra...* — "Signature of the community authority issuing [this document]: Wola ..." (The bottom of the document is cut off, so the Ukrainian text and the rest of the community's name are missing; but it appears that the name of the community is "Wola Raniżowska."

𝖅𝖚𝖘𝖆̈𝖙𝖟𝖊/ Dodatki/ Дописки

𝖋𝖚̈𝖗 𝖏𝖚𝖌𝖊𝖓𝖉𝖑𝖎𝖈𝖍𝖊 𝕳𝖎𝖑𝖋𝖘𝖆𝖗𝖇𝖊𝖎𝖙𝖊𝖗 𝖇𝖊𝖟𝖎𝖊𝖍𝖚𝖓𝖌𝖘𝖜𝖊𝖎𝖘𝖊 𝕷𝖊𝖍𝖗𝖑𝖎𝖓𝖌𝖊/ *dla młodocianych pomocników względnie uczniów*/ дотично нелітних помочничих робітників (челядників) взглядно учеників. — Supplements for young assistants as regards apprentices."

𝕬𝖚𝖘𝖐𝖚𝖓𝖋𝖙 𝖚̈𝖇𝖊𝖗 𝖉𝖎𝖊 𝕾𝖈𝖍𝖚𝖑𝖛𝖊𝖗𝖍𝖆̈𝖑𝖙𝖓𝖎𝖘𝖘𝖊 𝖚𝖓𝖉 𝖉𝖎𝖊 𝖊𝖗𝖜𝖔𝖗𝖇𝖊𝖓𝖊 𝕾𝖈𝖍𝖚𝖑𝖇𝖎𝖑𝖉𝖚𝖓𝖌/ *Wyjaśnienia co do stosunków szkolnych i uzyskanego wykształcenia szkolnego*/ Дані о шкільних відношенях и о степени шкільного образованя: *umie czytać i pisać* — "Information on relations with school and on education received: Can read and write."

𝕹𝖆𝖒𝖊 𝖚𝖓𝖉 𝖂𝖔𝖍𝖓𝖔𝖗𝖙 𝖉𝖊𝖘 𝖁𝖆𝖙𝖊𝖗𝖘 𝖔𝖉𝖊𝖗 𝖁𝖔𝖗𝖒𝖚𝖓𝖉𝖊𝖘/ *Imię i miejsce zamieszkania ojca lub opiekuna*/ Імя і місце замешканя отця або опікуна: *Wola raniżowska Jan Marut* — "Name and place of residence of the father or guardian: Wola Raniżowska, Jan Marut"

𝕯𝖎𝖊 𝖅𝖚𝖘𝖙𝖎𝖒𝖒𝖚𝖓𝖌 𝖟𝖚𝖗 𝕰𝖎𝖓𝖌𝖊𝖍𝖚𝖓𝖌 𝖉𝖊𝖘 𝕬𝖗𝖇𝖊𝖎𝖙𝖘 - 𝖔𝖉𝖊𝖗 𝕷𝖊𝖍𝖗𝖛𝖊𝖗𝖍𝖆̈𝖑𝖙𝖓𝖎𝖘𝖘𝖊𝖘 𝖎𝖘𝖙 𝖊𝖗𝖋𝖔𝖑𝖌𝖙*/ *Zezwolenie do zawarcia stosunku robotniczego, względnie naukowego nastąpiło/* Призволенє до вступленя до роботи або на науку послідовало:* — "Agreement to entry into a work or schooling relationship has been obtained..."

𝖛𝖔𝖓 𝕾𝖊𝖎𝖙𝖊 𝖉𝖊𝖘 𝖁𝖆𝖙𝖊𝖗𝖘/ *ze strony ojca*/ со сторони отця: *tak* — "...on the part of the father: yes."

𝖛𝖔𝖓 𝕾𝖊𝖎𝖙𝖊 𝖉𝖊𝖘 𝖁𝖔𝖗𝖒𝖚𝖓𝖉𝖊𝖘/ *ze strony opiekuna*/ со сторони опікуна: — "...on the part of the guardian" (not filled in, apparently not applicable).

𝖛𝖔𝖓 𝕾𝖊𝖎𝖙𝖊 𝖉𝖊𝖘 𝕬𝖚𝖋𝖊𝖓𝖙𝖍𝖆𝖑𝖙𝖘𝖌𝖊𝖒𝖊𝖎𝖓𝖉𝖊/ *ze strony gminy pobytu*/ со сторони громади перебуваня: *Wola raniżowska* — "...on the part of the district of residence: Wola Raniżowska."

𝕬𝖓𝖒𝖊𝖗𝖐𝖚𝖓𝖌: 𝕳𝖎𝖊𝖗 𝖎𝖘𝖙 𝖊𝖗𝖘𝖎𝖈𝖍𝖙𝖑𝖎𝖈𝖍 𝖟𝖚 𝖒𝖆𝖈𝖍𝖊𝖓, 𝖔𝖇 𝖉𝖆𝖘 𝕬𝖗𝖇𝖊𝖎𝖙𝖘𝖇𝖚𝖈𝖍 𝖒𝖎𝖙 𝖅𝖚𝖘𝖙𝖎𝖒𝖒𝖚𝖓𝖌 𝖉𝖊𝖘 𝖁𝖆𝖙𝖊𝖗𝖘 𝖔𝖉𝖊𝖗 𝖉𝖊𝖘 𝖁𝖔𝖗𝖒𝖚𝖓𝖉𝖊𝖘, 𝖔𝖉𝖊𝖗 𝖜𝖊𝖓𝖓 𝖊𝖎𝖓𝖊 𝖘𝖔𝖑𝖈𝖍𝖊 𝖓𝖎𝖈𝖍𝖙 𝖟𝖚 𝖇𝖊𝖘𝖈𝖍𝖆𝖋𝖋𝖊𝖓 𝖎𝖘𝖙, 𝖓𝖆𝖈𝖍 §80 𝖆𝖑. 2 𝕲𝖊𝖜𝖊𝖗𝖇𝖊𝖔𝖗𝖉𝖓𝖚𝖓𝖌 𝖒𝖎𝖙 𝖅𝖚𝖘𝖙𝖎𝖒𝖒𝖚𝖓𝖌 𝖉𝖊𝖗 𝕬𝖚𝖋𝖊𝖓𝖙𝖍𝖆𝖑𝖙𝖘𝖌𝖊𝖒𝖊𝖎𝖓𝖉𝖊 𝖊𝖗𝖋𝖔𝖑𝖌𝖙 𝖎𝖘𝖙/ *Uwaga: Należy tu uwidocznić, czy książka robotnicza została...* — "Note: It is to be shown here whether the employment booklet has been issued with the agreement of the father or of the guardian or, if such can not be procured, whether, according to § 80 al. 2 of the Trade Regulations, with that of the community of residence." (The Polish and Ukrainian texts have been cut off, but clearly this explains the legal requirement that some competent authority has signed off on this young man's employment.)

Selected Vocabulary Terms

It is difficult to know exactly how much material to present in this vocabulary. Simply giving a Polish word and an English equivalent is not adequate — words in different languages are not interchangeable parts, one cannot translate by pulling out the Polish module and snapping in an English one. But exhaustive information on gender, number, declensional or conjugational variations, and lexical nuances will almost surely overwhelm most readers of this book — who, after all, did not buy it expecting a comprehensive treatment of the Polish language.

So, vital as considerations of gender and inflection are to Polish, this list generally ignores such considerations. It gives the most commonly encountered forms of the most commonly encountered Polish words (including some forms seen in documents but no longer considered correct); indicates grammatical forms that might trip up the unwary; indicates the word's part of speech (noun, verb, etc.); and gives its standard English translation in the context of genealogical research. Thus *zawiera* can mean a great deal more than just "contains," but in context that is the meaning researchers are most likely to need. Imperfective and perfective aspects of verbs are ignored, genitive or other case forms of tricky nouns are given when necessary, and grammatical gender is generally not given. The words are listed by Polish alphabetical order, which differs somewhat from English, for the sake of compatibility with dictionaries and other reference works.

Of course, anyone wanting to acquire a deeper understanding of the Polish language is most welcome to buy a good dictionary, find a good book on grammar, or better yet sign up for Polish lessons!

akt — (n.) record, document, certificate

akuszerka — (n.) midwife

angielski — (adj.) English

ani — (conj.) nor

archiwariusz — (n.) archivist

archiwum — (n.) archive

asystencja — assistance

austryacki — (adj.) Austrian

babcia — (n.) grandmother

barwa — (n.) color

bez — (prep. + genitive) without

bezdzietny — (adj.) childless

bezimienny — (adj.) nameless

bierzmowanie — (n.) confirmation (sacrament)

bieżący — (adj.) current, present; *bieżącego roku* — this year, the current year

biskup — (n.) bishop

bożnica — (n.) synagogue

blond — (adj.) blond

brał — (verb, from *brać*) took

brat — (n.) brother

bratowa — (n.) sister-in-law

broda — (n.) beard

brzeg — (n.) shore, coast

brzmi — (verb, from *brzmieć*) it sounds, reads

być — (verb) to be; *był* — he was; *byli* — they were

cel — (n.) goal, aim; *celem* — for the purpose of

cena — (n.) price, cost

chłop — (n.) peasant

chłopiec — (n.) boy

chrzcie → *chrzest*

chrzest — (n., genitive *chrztu*, locative *chrzcie*) baptism

chrzestny — (adj.) baptismal; (n.) godfather; *chrzestna* — godmother

chrześcianin — (n.) Christian

chwilowy — (adj.) temporary

ciotka — (n.) aunt

cmentarz — (n.) cemetery

co — (pronoun) what, what?; *co do* — (plus genitive) as far as … is concerned, as regards

córka — (n.) daughter

cyrkuł — (n., Austrian term) district

cyrulik — (n.) barber

czas — (n.) time; *na jaki czas* — for how long?

czasowy — (adj.) temporary

czego → *co*

czemu — why (→ *co*)

czerwiec (gen. *czerwca*) — June

czeski — (adj.) Czech

część — (n.) part

często — (adv.) often

człowiek — (n.) man, person

czterdzieści — (num.) forty

czterdziesty — (adj.) fortieth

czterechsetny — (adj.) four hundredth

czternaście — (num.) fourteen

czternasty — (adj.) fourteenth

cztery — (num.) four

czterysta — (num.) four hundred

czwartek — (n.) Thursday

czwarty — (adj.) fourth

czy — (particle) whether

czynszownik — renter

czytać — (verb) to read

dane — (plur. n., adjectival in form) data, information (instrumental case *danymi*)

dano — (part. from *dać*) given

data — (n.) date

dekanat — (n.) deanery

dla — (prep. with genitive) for

długi — (n.) debts; (adj.) long

dnia → *dzień*

dniu — (locative of *dzień*) day

do — (prep. with genitive) to, for

dochód — (n.) income

dodatek — (n.) supplement, addition

dokonał — (verb, from *dokonać*) performed, carried out

dom — (n.) house

dotąd — (adv.) to this point

drewniany — (adj.) wooden

drobny — (adj.) fine, small; retail

drugi — (adj.) second; other

drukowany — (adj.) printed

duński — (adj.) Danish

dwa — (num.) two

dwadzieścia — (num.) twenty

dwanaście — (num.) twelve

dwieście — (num.) two hundred

dwudziesty — (adj.) twentieth; *dwudziesty pierwszy* — twenty- first

dwunasty — (adj.) twelfth

dwusetny — (adj.) two hundredth

dziadek — (n.) grandfather

działo się — (verb, from *dziać się*) it happened, took place

dziecię — (n.) child

dziecko — (n.) child

dzień — (n.) day (genitive *dnia*, locative *dniu*)

dziennik — (n.) newspaper

dziesiąty — (adj.) tenth

dziesięć — (num.) ten

dziewczyna — (n.) girl

dziewiąty — (adj.) ninth

dziewięć — (num.) nine; *dziewięćdziesiąt* — (num.) ninety; *dziewięćdziesiąty* — (adj.) ninetieth; *dziewięćset* — (num.) nine hundred; *dziewięćsetny* — (adj.) nine hundredth

dziewiętnaście — (num.) nineteen; *dziewiętnasty* — (adj.) nineteenth

dzisiejszy — (adj.) today's

dziś — (adv.) today

ewangelicko-augsburski — (adj.) Lutheran

folwark — (n.) manor, grange

fornal — (n.) carter

francuski — (adj.) French

furman — (n.) wagon driver

Galicja, Galicya — (n.) Galicia

gdy — (conj.) when

gdzie — (adv.) where

głęboki — (adj.) deep

gmina — (n.) community, district

gminny — (adj.) of the community

godzina — hour; *o trzeciej godzinie* — at three o'clock

gospodarz — (n.) farmowner

góra — (n.) mountain

górnik — (n.) miner

grecki — (adj.) Greek

grecko-katolicki — (adj.) Greek Catholic

grudzień (genitive *grudnia*) — (n.) December

gubernia — (n.) gubernia (an administrative division under the Czarist government)

handel — (n.) trade

hrabia — (n.) count

i — (conj.) and

identyczność — (n.) identity, identity papers, proof of identity

imię — (n.) [first] name; *w imieniu* — in the name [of]; *imiona* — names

iż — (conj.) that

izraelit — (n.) Jew

ja — (pron.) I

jaki — (adj.) what kind of, which

jeden — (num.) one

jedenaście — (num.) eleven

jedenasty — (adj.) eleventh

jego — (pron., from *on* or *ono*) his, its

jej — (pron., from *ona*) her

jest — (verb, from *być*) is

jezioro — (n.) lake

język — (n.) language, tongue

już — (adv.) already

kaplica — (n.) chapel

kapłan — (n.) priest

karny — (adj.) penal, criminal

karta — (n.) page, card, sheet

kawaler — (n.) bachelor

kiedy — (conj.) when

kobieta — (n.) woman

koło — (prep. with genitive) near

komornik — (n.) bailiff

koronny — (adj.) of the crown, royal

kościół — (n.) church

kowal — (n.) blacksmith

kraj — country, land, Poland; *stary kraj* — the old country; *kraj koronny* — Kronland (Austrian Empire division, "crownland")

kramarz — (n.) stallkeeper

krawiec (genitive *krawca*) — (n.) tailor

król — (n.) king

królestwo — (n.) kingdom

ksiądz (genitive *księdza*) — (n.) priest, Father

książę (genitive *księcia*) — (n.) prince

książka — (n.) booklet

księga — (n.) book; *w księgach metrykalnych* — in the registry books

księstwo — (n.) Duchy

kto — (pron.) who

które, którego, któremu, których, którzy → *który*

który — (rel. pron., adj.) who, which, that; *z którego roku* — from what year

ku — (prep. with dative) towards

kupiec (genitive *kupca*) — (n.) merchant

kuśnierz — (n.) furrier

kuzyn, kuzynka — (n.) cousin

kwartał — (n.) quarter of a year

kwiecień (genitive *kwietnia*) — (n.) April

landwerzysta — (n.) member of the *Landwehr* (militia)

lat — (plur. n., genitive plural form of *rok*) years

legitymacja — (n.) identity, identity card; process of verifying membership in the aristocracy

liczący — (participle from *liczyć*) counting; *26 lat liczący* — age 26

liczba — (n.) number, numeral

liczy — (verb, from *liczyć*) numbers, counts; *liczy lat 17* — age 17

lipiec (genitive *lipca*) — (n.) July

list — (n.) letter

listopad (gen. *listopada*) — (n.) November

litewski — (adj.) Lithuanian

lub — (conj.) or

luty (genitive *lutego*) — (n.) February

łaciński — (adj.) Latin

łotewski — (adj.) Latvian

łoże — (n.) bed; *z nieprawego łoża* — illegitimate

macocha — (n.) stepmother

maj (genitive *maja*) — (n.) May

mają — (verb, from *mieć*) they have

mający — (verb, from *mieć*) having; *17 lat mający* — age 17

majątek — (n.) estate

malarz — (n.) painter

małoletni — (adj.) underage; (n.) minor (feminine *małoletna*)

mały — (adj.) small

małżeństwo — (n.) marriage

małżonka — (n.) wife

marka — (n.) German mark (money)

marzec (genitive *marca*) — (n.) March

matka — (n.) mother

mąż (genitive *męża*) — husband, man

metryka — (n.) certificate, vital records

metryczny, metrykalny — (adj.) registry, of the vital records

męski — (adj.) male

mężczyzna — (n.) man

miasteczko — (n.) small town

miasto — (n.) town, city; *w mieście* — in the town [of]

miejsce — (n.) place, site; *miejsce zamieszkania* — residence

miejscowość — (n.) locality

miejscowy — (adj.) local

miejski — (adj.) urban, municipal

mierny — (adj.) average

miesiąc — (n.) month

mieszczanin — (n.) burgher

mieszkają — (verb, from *mieszkać*) they live, reside

mieszkaniec (genitive *mieszkańca*) — (n.) inhabitant

mieście → *miasto*

między — (prep. with instrumental) between, among

mimo — (prep. with genitive) in spite of

ministerstwo — (n.) ministry

młodociany — (adj.) juvenile, adolescent, youthful

młodszy — (adj.) younger, junior

młody — (adj.) young

młodzian — (n.) young man

młynarz — (n.) miller

mojżeszowy — (adj.) Jewish

morga — (n.) measure of land (varies, but generally about 5600 m²)

mówić — (verb) to speak; *mówi językami* — to speak ... languages

mu — (pron., dative of *on*) to/for him, it

murowany — (adj.) brick, stone

my — (pron.) we

na — (prep. with locative or accusative) in, on, to, upon

naczelnik — (n.) chief

naczelny — (adj.) chief, head

nad — (prep. with instrumental) upon, on

nadano — (part. from *nadać*) given, bestowed, conferred

najemnik — (n.) day-laborer, hired man, mercenary

należą — (verb, from *należyć*) they belong

należy — (verb, from *należyć*) should be, it is fitting to, belongs to

nam — (dative of *my*) to/for us

nami — (instrumental of *my*) us

naocznie — (adv.) with one's own eyes

naoczny — (adj.) visual, evident

narzeczona — (adj. used as noun) fiancée)

narzeczony — (adj. used as noun) fiancé

nas — (pron., from *my*) us

nastąpiło — (verb, from *nastąpić*) it followed, happened

następujący — (participle from *następować*) the following

natychmiast — (adv.) at once, immediately

nauczyciel — (n.) teacher

nauka — (n.) science, learning

naukowy — (adj.) scientific, scholarly, research

nazwisko — (n.) surname

nie — (adv.) not

niedaleko — (adv.) not far

niedziela — (n.) Sunday; week

Niemcy — (n.) Germany, Germans; *w Niemczech* — in Germany

niemiecki — (adj.) German

niepiśmienny — (adj.) illiterate

nieprawy — unlawful; *z nieprawego łoża* — illegitimate

nieślubny — (adj.) illegitimate

nieumiejący pisać — (adj.) illiterate

niewiadomy — (adj.) unknown

niezamężna — (adj.) unmarried (used only of women)

nim → *on* or *ono*

niniejszy — (adj.) this, the present; *niniejszego* — of the present (e. g., document); *niniejszym* (instrumental singular) hereby

niżej — (adv.) lower, below

noc — (n.) night

nos — (n.) nose

nowi małżonkowie — (plur. noun) newlyweds

nowy — (adj.) new

numer — (n.) number, issue

o — (prep.) about, on, for

obecność — (n.) presence; *w obecności* — in the presence

obecny — (adj.) present

obowiązek — (n.) duty, obligation

obrządek — (n.) rite, ceremony

obrzezanie — (n.) circumcision

obrzęd — (n.) ceremony, custom

obwód — (n.) district

obywatel — (n.) citizen

obywatelstwo — (n.) citizenship

oczy → *oko*

od — (prep. with genitive) from

odbyty — (participle from *odbyć*) occurred, taken place

odległy — (adj.) distant, far-off

odpis — (n.) copy

odpowiedź — (n.) answer, reply

ogrodnik — (n.) gardener

ojciec (genitive: singular *ojca*, plural *ojców*) — father

ojczym — (n.) stepfather

okazał — (verb, from *okazać*) showed

oko (plural *oczy*) — (n.) eye

okrąg — circumference, circle, district

okrzęg — (n.) district

okupnik — (n.) tenant-farmer

on — (pron.) he

ona — (pron.) she

ono — (pron.) it

opiekun — (n.) guardian

oraz — (conj.) and, as well as

oryginał — (n.) original

osada — (n.) settlement, colony

osiem — (num.) eight; *osiemdziesiąt* — (num.) eighty; *osiemdziesiąty* — (adj.) eightieth; *osiemnaście* — (num.) eighteen; *osiemnasty* — (adj.) eighteenth; *osiemset* — (num.) eight hundred; *osiemsetny* — (adj.) eight hundredth

ósmy — (adj.) eighth

osoba — (n.) person

osobiście — (adv.) personally

oświadczać/oświadczyć — (v.b) to declare; *oświadczając* — declaring; *oświadczy* — declares; *oświadczyli* — they declared

owalny — (adj.) oval

owszem — (adv.) yes

ów — (pron.) that

pamiętnik — (n.) memorial

pan — (n.) lord, gentleman, Mr. (also used in polite speech as "you")

pani — (n.) woman, lady, Mrs. (also used in polite speech as "you")

panieński — maiden's

panna — maid, Miss

państwo — (n.) nation, state

państwowy — national

parafia — (n.) parish

parafialny — (adj.) parochial

parobek — (n.) farm helper, hired hand

paszport — (n.) passport

październik (genitive *października*) — (n.) October

piątek — (n.) Friday

piąty — (adj.) fifth

pięć — (num.) five; *pięćdziesiąt* — (num.) fifty; *pięćdziesty* — (adj.) fiftieth; *pięćset* — (num.) five hundred; *pięćsetny* — (adj.) five hundredth

piekarz — (n.) baker

pierwej — (adv.) previously

pierwszy — (adj.) first

piętnaście — (num.) fifteen

piętnasty — (adj.) fifteenth

pisać — (verb) to write; *pisał* — he wrote; *pisze* — [he, she, it] writes

pisarz — (n.) clerk

płeć (genitive *płci*) — (n.) sex, gender

po — (prep.) after, according to, by, to; *po południu* — afternoon; *po-polsku* — in Polish

pod — (prep.) under, near (i. e., *pod Lublinem* — near Lublin); *kościół pod wezwaniem św. Jana* — St. John's Church

podatek — (n.) tax

podczas — (prep. with genitive) during

podług — (prep. with genitive) according to

podpis — (n.) signature

podpisany — (participle from *podpisać*) signed

podróż — (n.) travel, journey

podróżuje — (verb, from *podróżować*) is traveling

pogrzeb — (n.) burial

polityczny — (adj.) political

polski — (adj.) Polish

południe — noon, midday; south

pomiędzy — (prep. with instrumental) among

pomocniczy — (adj.) auxiliary, assistant

pomocnik — (n.) assistant, helper

poniedziałek — (n.) Monday

poprawiony — (participle, from *poprawić*) corrected

poprzedziły — (verb, from *poprzedzić*) preceded

posiadacz — (n.) bearer

poświadczenie — (n.) statement

powiat — (n.) county; *w powiecie* — in the county

pół — (num.) half

północ — (n.) midnight; North

półtora — (num.) one and a half

prawny — (adj.) legal

prawo — (n.) law, right

prawosławny — Orthodox

proboszcz — (n.) pastor

proces — (n.) trial, suit

prosty — (adj.) straight, simple

protokół — (n.) protocol, official record

pruski — (adj.) Prussian

Prusy — (plur. n.) Prussia

przeciw — (prep.) against

przeczytany — (participle, from *przeczytać*) read through

przed — (prep.) before, in front of

przekład — (n.) translation; *w przekładzie* — in translation

przekonanie się — (n.) persuading oneself

przemysł — (n.) industry

przeszkoda — (n.) obstacle, hindrance

przeszły — (participle, from *przejść*) past, bygone, last (as in "last week")

przeto — (conj.) therefore, accordingly

przez — (prep. with accusative) by, through, across

przy — (prep. with locative) near, at, by

przyczyna — (n.) cause

przynależny — (adj.) belonging to, affiliated with

przytomność — (n.) presence; *w przytomności* — in the presence [of]

przywilej — (n.) privilege, grant, prerogative

rabin — (n.) rabbi

rano — (n.) morning; (adv.) early, in the morning

religia — (n.) religion

religijny — (adj.) religious

ręka — (n.) hand

robota — (n.) work, labor

robotniczy — (adj.) workers', laborers'

robotnik — (n.) worker

rodzeństwo — (n.) brothers and sisters

rodzice — (plur. n., genitive *rodziców*) parents

rodzina — (n.) family

rok — (n.; plural is *lata*) year; *roku* — in, of the year

rolnik — (n.) farmer

rosyjski — (adj.) Russian

ród — (n.) clan, family

rysopis — (n.) description [of document bearer]

rzecz — (n.) thing, matter, affair

rzeczpospolita — (n.) republic, commonwealth

rzeka — (n.) river

Rzesza — (n.) Reich

rzeźnik — (n.) butcher

rzymsko-katolicki — (adj.) Roman Catholic

sam — (pron.) self, same

są — (verb, from *być*) they are

sąd — (n.) court

setny — (adj.) one hundredth

siebie — (pron. from *się*) -self (myself, yourself, etc.)

siedem — (num.) seven; *siedemdziesiąt* — (num.) seventy; *siedemdziesiąty* — (adj.) seventieth; *siedemnasty* — (adj.) seventeenth; *siedemnaście* — (num.) seventeen; *siedemset* — (num.) seven hundred; *siedemsetny* — (adj.) seven hundredth

sierota — (n.) orphan

sierpień (genitive *sierpnia*) — (n.) August

się — (reflexive pron.) -self (myself, yourself, etc.)

siostra — (n.) sister

siódmy — (adj.) seventh

siwy — (adj.) grey

sklep — (n.) shop, store

skorowidz — (n.) index

słownik — (n.) dictionary

słowo — (n.) word

służący — (adj. used as masc. noun) servant (fem. *służąca*)

służba — (n.) service

sobie — (pron.) -self (myself, yourself, etc.)

sobota — (n.) Saturday

spekulant — (n.) money-lender

spłodzone — (participle of *spłodzić*) begotten

sprawa — (n.) matter, affair

sprawujący — (participle of *sprawować*) carrying out, fulfilling

stacja (stacya) — (n.) station; *stacja drogi żelaznej* — railway station; *stacja pocztowa* — post office

stale — (adv.) steadily, consistently, permanently

stan — (n.) state, condition, occupation, status; *stan cywilny* — civil registry; *Stany Zjednoczone* — United States

starający — (participle of *starać*) trying, striving; *starający o paszport* — applicant for a passport

starostwo — (n.) region governed by a *starosta*

starozakonny — (adj. used as noun) [Orthodox] Jew

starszy — (adj.) older, senior

stary — (adj.) old

stawić — (verb) to place, put; *stawiący* — the one appearing, the declarant; *stawił się* — [he] appeared, presented himself

stelmach — (n.) cartwright

sto — (num.) hundred

stolarz — (n.) carpenter

stolica — (n.) capital (city)

stosunek — (n.) relationship

strona — (n.) page, side; *ze strony* — on the part [of]

stryj — (n.) paternal uncle

stulecie — (n.) century

styczeń (genitive *stycznia*) — (n.) January

swego → *swój*

swój — (adj.) [my, your, his, her, its, our, their] own

swym → *swój*

syn — (n.) son

synowa — (n.) daughter-in-law

szczególny — (adj.) special, particular, distinguishing

szczegółowy — (adj.) detailed, particular

szeroki — (adj.) wide, broad

szesnaście — (num.) sixteen

szesnasty — (adj.) sixteenth

sześć — (num.) six; *sześćdziesiąt* — (num.) sixty; *sześćdziesiąty* — (adj.) sixtieth; *sześćset* — (num.) six hundred; *sześćsetny* — (adj.) six hundredth

szewc — (n.) shoemaker

szkolny — (adj.) school —

szkoła — (n.) school

szlachcic — (n.) nobleman

szlachecki — (adj.) noble

szlachta — (n.) nobility

szmuklerz — (n.) haberdasher

szósty — (adj.) sixth

szwagier — (n.) brother-in-law

szynkarz — (n.) innkeeper

śledztwo — (n.) inquiry, investigation

ślub — (n.) marriage, wedding; vow

śmierć — (n.) death

środa — Wednesday

świadczę — (verb, from *świadczyć*) I vouch

świadectwo — (n.) certificate

świadek — (n.) witness, deponent

święty — (adj.) holy, sacred; (noun) Saint

ta → *ten*

tak — (adv.) so, yes

taksa — (n.) tax

tam — (adv.) there

tamowanie — (n.) objection

tego, tej, temu → *ten*

ten — (pron. & adj.) this

ten że — (pron.) the same one

tkacz — (n.) weaver

tłumaczenie — (n.) translation

to — (pron., neut. of *ten*) this, that

tokarz — (n.) turner, lathe-worker

trzechsetny — (adj.) three hundredth

trzeci — (adj.) third

trzy — (num.) three; *trzydziesty* — (adj.) thirtieth; *trzydzieści* — (num.) thirty; *trzynasty* — (adj.) thirteenth; *trzynaście* — (num.) thirteen; *trzysta* — (num.) three hundred

tu — (adv.) here

tudzież — (adv.) also

tutejszy — (adj.) local, of this place

twarz — (n.) face

tydzień (genitive tygodnia) — (n.) week

tylko — (adv.) only

tym → *ten*

tysiąc — (num.) thousand

tysięczny — (adj.) thousandth

u — (prep. with genitive) among, at, with

ubogi — (adj.) poor

uczeń (genitive plural *uczniów*) — students, pupils

udaje się — (verb, from *udać się*) to go or come (*z* from, *do* to)

udzielony — (participle from *udzielić*) imparted, dispensed, administered

umarł — (verb, from *umrzeć*) [he] died

umieć — (verb) to know how; *umie pisać* — can write

umowa — (n.) contract, agreement

umrzeć — (verb) to die

uroczystość — (n.) ceremony

urodzenie — (n.) birth

urodził się — (verb, from *urodzić*) was born

urodzone — (participle from *urodzić*) born

urząd — (n.) office, department

urzędnik — (n.) official

usta — (plur. n.) mouth

ustnie — (adv.) orally

utrzymanie — (n.) living, livelihood

utrzymując się — (participle from *utrzymywać się*) making one's living

uwaga — (n.) attention, notice

uwidocznić — (verb) to show

uzyskanie — (n.) obtaining, acquisition

uzyskany — (participle from *uzyskać*) obtained, acquired

w (before some consonant clusters *we*) — (prep.) in, to

ważny — (adj.) valid, important

wąsy — (plur. n.) moustache

wczoraj — (adv.) yesterday

wdowa — (n.) widow

wdowiec (genitive *wdowca*) — (n.) widower

we → *w*

według — (prep. with genitive) according to

wesele — (n.) wedding

wewnętrzny — (adj.) interior

węgierski — (adj.) Hungarian

wiadomy — (adj.) known

wieczór — (n.) evening; *wieczorem* — in the evening

wiek — (n.) age

wieś (genitive *wsi*) — (n.) village

winny — (adj.) guilty

władza — (n.) authority, power

właściciel — (n.) owner

własnoręczny — (adj.) with one's own hands

Włochy (locative *Włoszech*) — (plur. n.) Italy

włóka — (n.) measure of area (16.8 hectares)

włościanin — peasant

włoski — (adj.) Italian

włosy — (plur. n.) hair

wnuczka — (n.) granddaughter

wnuk — (n.) grandson

województwo — (n.) province

wojskowy — (adj.) military

wolny — (adj.) single, free

wtorek — (n.) Tuesday

wrzesień (genitive *września*) — (n.) September

wschód — (n.) east

wsi → *wieś*

wszystko — (n.) all, everything

wuj — (n.) maternal uncle

wyciąg — (n.) extract

wydanie — (n.) issuance, edition

wydany — (participle from *wydać*) issued

wyjaśnienie — (n.) explanation

wykształcenie — (n.) education

wyłącznie — (adv.) exclusively

wymienione — (participle from *wymienić*) mentioned, named

wyraz — (n.) term, word, expression

wyraźnie — (adv.) explicitly, distinctly

wyrobnik — (n.) workman, day-laborer (fem. *wyrobnica*)

wystawiający — (adj. from *wystawiać*) exhibiting, issuing

wytwórca — (n.) manufacturer

wyznanie — (n.) religion, denomination

wyżej — (adv.) higher, above

względem — (prep. with genitive) with regard to, concerning

względnie — (adv.) relatively, in respect to

wzrost — (n.) height, stature

z — (prep. with genitive) out, of, from, (with instrumental) with; *z domu* — (prep. phrase) née

za — (prep. with genitive) in, in the time of, during; (with instrumental) for, after, behind

zachód — (n.) west

zachodzą — (verb, from *zachodzić*) happen, occur

żadny — (adj.) no, none

zagrodnik — (n.) cottager

zajęcie — (n.) occupation

zamężna — (adj.) married (woman)

zamiast — (prep. with genitive) instead of

zamieszkały — (adj.) residing

zamieszkanie — (n.) residence

zapłacił — (verb, from *zapłacić*) paid

zapowiedź — (n.) wedding bann

zaślubiony — (participle from *zaślubić*) married, wedded

zaświadcza — (verb, from *zaświadczyć*) testifies, attests

zaszło — (verb, from *zajść*) happened

zatrudnienie — (n.) employment, occupation

zawarcie — (n.) conclusion (of a transaction), contracting (marriage)

zawarli — (verb, from *zawrzeć*) they transacted, contracted; *żadnej umowy nie zawarli* — they made no agreement

zawarty — (participle from *zawrzeć*) made, concluded, transacted

zawiera — (verb, from *zawierać*) contains

zawód — (n.) occupation

zejście — (n.) death, demise

zeszły — (adj.) past, preceding

zezwolenie — (n.) permission

zgodność — (n.) conformance

zgodny — (adj.) agreeing, in conformity

zgon — (n.) death; *świadectwo zgonu* — death certificate

złoty — (n.) Polish złoty (money)

zmarły — (adj.) dead

znajduje się — (verb, from *znajdować się*) is found

znak — (n.) sign, mark

zostają — (verb, from *zostać*) they become, are, get; *został* — was, became

zostawiwszy — (part. from *zostawić*) having left behind, survived by

zwierzchność — (n.) authority

źródło — (n.) source

że — (conj.) that

żeński — (adj.) female, feminine

żona — (n.) wife

żonaty — (adj.) married

życie — (n.) life

Żyd — (n.) Jew

żydowski — (adj.) Jewish

żyjący — (adj.) living

Selected Personal Names

It is misleading to give American or English equivalents of Polish personal names, because *Czesław* is *not* the same as "Chester," and *Stanisław* is *not* the same as "Stanley." These equivalents are meant primarily to help trace what names Polish immigrants to America may have taken as they became Americanized — especially the ones in quotations, which are definitely *not* equivalents but are names that were sometimes used in America because of a similarity in sound. One must remember, however, that just because George Bush's name translates literally to *Jerzy Krzak* doesn't mean it's right to call him that!

Andrzej — Andrew
Bartłomiej — Bartholomew
Bolesław — Bolesław, "Bill"
Czesław — Ceslaus, "Chester"
Elżbieta — Elizabeth
Feliks — Felix
Filip — Philip
Franciszek — Francis
Franciszka — Frances
Fryderyk — Frederick
Genowefa — Genevieve
Grzegorz — Gregory
Hieronym — "Harry," Jerome
Jacek — Hyacinth, Jack
Jadwiga — Hedwig
Jakub — Jacob, James
Jan — John

Janina — Jane
Jędrzej — Andrew
Jerzy — George
Józef — Joseph
Karol — Charles
Katarzyna — Catherine
Kazimierz — Casimir
Krzysztof — Christopher
Ksawery — Xavier
Leokadia — Leocadia, "Lucy"
Ludwik — Louis
Łukasz — Luke
Marek — Mark
Michał — Michael
Mikołaj — Nicholas
Paweł — Paul
Piotr — Peter

Rafał — Raphael
Rozalia — Rose
Ryszard — Richard
Stanisław — Stanislaus, "Stanley"
Szczepan — Stephen
Szymon — Simon
Tadeusz — Thaddeus
Tomasz — Thomas
Walenty — Valentine
Wawrzyniec — Lawrence
Wincenty — Vincent
Władysław — Ladislaus
Wojciech — Adalbert
Zdzisław — "Zachary"
Zofia — Sophie
Zuzanna — Susan
Zygmunt — Sigmund

Русский

The Russian Alphabet

Printed	Cursive	English
А,а	*А, а*	*a*
Б,б	*Б, б*	*b*
В,в	*В, b*	*v*
Г,г	*Г, г*	*g*
Д,д	*Д, g*	*d*
Е,е	*Е, е*	*ye*
Ё,ё	*Ё, ё*	*yo*
Ж,ж	*Ж, ж*	*zh*
З,з	*З, з*	*z*
И,и	*И, и*	*i*
Й,й	*Й, й*	*y*
К,к	*К, к*	*k*
Л,л	*Л, л*	*l*
М,м	*М, м*	*m*
Н,н	*Н, н*	*n*
О,о	*О, о*	*o*
П,п	*П, п*	*p*
Р,р	*Р, р*	*r*
С,с	*С, с*	*s*
Т,т	*Т, m*	*t*
У,у	*У, у*	*u*
Ф,ф	*Ф, ф*	*f*
Х,х	*Х, х*	*kh*
Ц,ц	*Ц, ц*	*ts*
Ч,ч	*Ч, ч*	*ch*

Printed	Cursive	English	Printed	Cursive	English
Ш,ш	*Ш, ш*	*sh*	**-,ь**	*-, ь*	—
Щ,щ	*Щ, щ*	*shch*	**Э,э**	*Э, э*	*e*
-,ъ	*-, ъ*	—	**Ю,ю**	*Ю, ю*	*yu*
-,ы	*-, ы*	—	**Я,я**	*Я, я*	*ya*

Russian is one of several Slavic languages that use the Cyrillic alphabet (others are Bulgarian, Byelorussian, Ukrainian, Serbian, and Macedonian). There are minor variations in the form of the Cyrillic alphabet used in other Slavic languages; the alphabet shown here is that used in modern Russian. A few archaic characters relevant to genealogical research are discussed under "The Russian Language," on the next page.

Even a superficial glance at the Cyrillic alphabet reveals that it is not totally foreign. When Cyril tried to devise a way of writing Slavic sounds, he borrowed extensively from the Greek alphabet and also modified some characters to re-present distinctively Slavic phonemes. A few sounds were so foreign to Greek that characters were borrowed from other sources, e. g., ש and צ from Hebrew to make ш and ц, representing the *sh* and *ts* sounds.

Besides the printed and cursive forms, italic letters appear in documents. Even after one becomes familiar with the normal printed forms, a few italic forms can be puzzling, e. g., *m, д, г*, but the answer is simple: some italic forms are derived from their cursive equivalents. So *m* = т, *д* = д (*g* and *д* are both acceptable cursive forms of д), *г* = г, and so on.

Russian vowels are like those of other European languages — "a" = *a* as in "father," "e" = *e* as in "let," "и" = *i* as in "machine," "o" = a sound somewhere between the *o*'s in "October," and "y" = *u* as in "rude" — but a, э, ы, o and y follow what are termed "hard" consonants, while the forms я, е, и, ё and ю follow consonants that are "softened" or palatalized. The basic distinction is illustrated by the word нет ("no"), pronounced "nyet" because the *e* vowel follows a palatalized н — a word pronounced like English "net," with a hard н, would be spelled нэт. This is why one often sees я transcribed as *ya,* ё as *yo,* and so on; the vowels are written differently to reflect the hard or soft quality of the consonants they follow. Standard Russian pronunciation gives full value only to vowels in accented syllables, and the farther the vowel is from the stress the less distinctly it is pronounced: молоко (milk), accented on the last syllable, is not pronounced like "mo-lo-KO" but more like "muh-lah-KO."

The table at left shows approximate English equivalents of the sounds represented by Russian consonants, but more must be said. The letter г does generally sound like the English *g* in "go," but at the end of words it can sound like *k,* and in the declensional suffixes -ого, -его, and archaic -яго and -аго it sounds like English *v.* The letter ж sounds like *s* in English "pleasure." The ч sounds like the *ch* in "church," the ш sounds like the *sh* in "sheet," and щ is *sh* and *ch* run together, as in the name "Khrushchev."

Of the letters with no English equivalents given, the х is pronounced like *ch* in German "Bach" or Scottish "loch," ъ signifies that the preceding consonant is not softened or palatalized, ь shows that it is softened or palatalized, and ы represents a unique sound somewhat like the *y* in "very."

The Russian Language

Russian, as the official government language, was used in the recording of all vital records in the multi-ethnic Russian Empire. However, local officials were likely to issue bilingual documents. Record-keeping in Imperial Russia was in most instances the duty of clergymen of the numerous religious congregations in the Empire. Offered here are sample documents from several major religious groups: Roman Catholic, Russian Orthodox, Jewish, and Moslem.

The documents, largely handwritten, employ the pre-Revolution orthographical system and as such contain symbols such as "ѣ" (cursive form *ѣ*), no longer used and generally replaced by the letter "e," and "i" (cursive form *i*), also obsolete and replaced by "и." They also follow certain spelling conventions — i. e., the letter "ъ" at the end of words after a hard consonant, e. g., паспортъ, now spelled simply паспорт — which have been eliminated through orthographic reform. To arrive at the modern spelling of words with those characters, simply replace the archaic characters with their modern counterparts or delete those which are no longer required.

Like most other Slavic languages, Russian employs a complex system of inflection, and one must often delete declensional endings from names to arrive at the "real" surname or place name. There simply is no adequate way to summarize these complexities; a researcher should either study Russian in earnest and tackle the problem head-on, or else try to get by with a superficial grasp of what the more common endings sometimes mean. In the analysis of these documents the sentences are not exhaustively parsed, but typical usage cases and representative endings are noted; many readers will have no interest in those notes and should ignore them, simply concentrating on the translation. But some readers may derive from those notes an inkling of how Russian cases work, and that will enhance their ability to make sense of documents they encounter.

The transcription employed here is a hybrid of several systems currently in use. The academic transcription is perhaps the most precise. However, most readers are more likely to recognize transliteration systems used by journalists and many libraries, so we have chosen forms on the basis of their more widespread use. (We only hope that none of our former professors read this page!)

Readers may notice and find it odd that so many of these Russian-language records deal not with ethnic Russians but with Poles or Jews or Muslims, but anyone who has tried to research Russian roots will understand immediately. Until the fall of the Soviet Union it was almost impossible to get authorities to cooperate with or even acknowledge requests for researching family records; so most Russian-language documents available in the West either came over with immigrants from Russia or, if obtained since 1917, originated in regions formerly under Soviet control that now permit researchers access to records (Poland is an obvious example). As of this writing Russian archival authorities have begun to cooperate with efforts to acquire documents of genealogical importance, and research into Russian roots has become a real possibility.

One cannot study Russian documents without a basic knowledge of how Russian names work; generally Moscow has forced even non-Russians under its control to comply with Russian customs regarding names. A Russian generally has three: a given name (имя), a patronymic (отчество), and a surname (фамилия). A patronymic is a name formed from one's father's name; *Johnson* (John's son) and *Davidson* (David's son) are examples of English names that began as patronymics. A Russian named Ivan (Иван) who had a son Boris (Борис) and a daughter Anna (Анна) would name the son Boris Ivanovich (Борис Иванович) and the daughter Anna Ivanovna (Анна Ивановна); so a Russian's second name almost always ends in -ович/-евич (male) or -овна/-евна (female). A female's surname is usually slightly different from her father's or husband's, in that the feminine suffix -a is added, so that the wife of someone name *Krylov* (Крылов) would be called *Krylova* (Крылова). In Russian it is standard procedure to call someone by his/her first name and patronymic rather than by some title prefixed to the surname; if someone addresses a man named "Boris Ivanovich Ivanov" as "Boris Ivanovich," he is not being friendly or familiar, but simply polite. There are further subtleties regarding names, but familiarity with the ones outlined should suffice for the purposes of this book.

Researchers should familiarize themselves with the alphabet as the first step in mastering a Russian-language document. This can be done by carefully reading the documents in this section, trying first to identify individual letters and then working up to deciphering whole words. To ease this task slightly, handwritten parts of documents are rendered in a standardized cursive or in italic type (much like the cursive but perhaps easier to read) in the analyses of the records. The hope is that readers can compare the original with the standardized cursive and thus gradually develop the capacity to recognize the admittedly difficult Russian script.

Document #1: A Russian Orthodox Birth Certificate

The Russian Orthodox Church has employed standard forms for the keeping of its sacramental registers for much of the past century. The register is columnar in format; a series of questions is posed and answers are entered in the appropriate spaces. The following record serves as a good introduction to Russian-language records; the top and bottom margins of the first page have been cropped to save space, but the second and third pages are reproduced at full size on the following pages.

Note that the printed column headings capture the antiquity and tradition of the Russian Orthodox Church by employing a style of type patterned after the Old Church Slavonic language (which is a fascinating and involving study in itself!). The letter "Ѧ" is used instead of modern Russian "Я," and the letter "ѡ," based on the Greek omega ω, is used for "o." The other characters may be hard to identify at first, but they are merely variants of the characters in the standard alphabet.

This first page, the cover page, identifies the type of extract, the place of issue, and the identity of the person issuing the document.

ВЫПИСЬ ИЗЪ МЕТРИЧЕСКОЙ КНИГИ

ЧАСТЬ ПЕРВАЯ

О РОДИВШИХСЯ

за *1915* годъ.

Выданная _____

_____

ВЫПИСЬ ИЗЪ МЕТРИЧЕСКОЙ КНИГИ. ЧАСТЬ ПЕРВАЯ О РОДИВШИХСЯ за *1915* годъ.

выпись изъ — "Extract from."

метрической книги — Literally, "Registry Book," or in English one might just as well call it "Vital Statistics Records." The adjective and noun appear in the genitive because the preposition изъ takes that case.

часть первая — "first part." Russian registers were frequently divided into часть первая, "first part," the baptismal register; часть вторая, "second part," the matrimonial register; and часть третья, "third part," the death register.

о родившихся — Literally "for those born," but "of births" sounds smoother in English and fits the usage of the Russian term. Родившихся is the prepositional plural of a participle from the verb родиться, "to be born."

за *1915* годъ — "for the year 1915."

Translation — Extract from the Vital Statistics Record, Part One, Births for 1915.

Счетъ родившихся.		Мѣсяцъ и день		Имена родившихся	Званіе, имя, отчество и фамилія родителей, и какого вѣроисповѣданія.
Мужеска пола.	Женска пола.	рожденія.	крещенія.		
2		11	17	Январь Владимиръ	Виленской губерніи, Виленскаго уѣзда, деревни Пакомово крестьянинъ Феодоръ Антоновичъ Силявка и его законная жена Анастасія Георгіевна. Оба православные

Что сія ко[...]ымъ актомъ вѣрна, въ томъ подписомъ и приложеніемъ церковной печ[...]

г. Antonio form. U.S.A.; мѣсяца Января 24го дня, 19 17 года.

Званіе, имя, отчество и фамилія воспріемниковъ.	Кто совершалъ таинство крещенія.
Александръ Михайловичъ Микулинъ и Сусанна Матвеевна Карданъ	Священникъ Евгеній Крыловскій со псаломщикомъ Александромъ Спириным Священникъ Евгеній Крыловскій

вѣряю.

Выданная *Настоятелемъ Трехъ Святительской Церкви въ городѣ Ansonia, Conn. Священникомъ Евгениемъ Крышановскимъ.*

> выданная — "issued." This is a participle from the verb выдать, "to issue," and is feminine singular nominative in form because it modifies the noun выпись (which is feminine in gender, singular in number, and nominative in case).
>
> настоятелемъ — "by the dean [of such-and-such a church]."
>
> Трехъ Святительской Церкви — "of Three Saints' Church"
>
> въ городѣ Ansonia, Conn. — "in the city of Ansonia, Connecticut." Въ (modern spelling в) is a preposition taking either the accusative or prepositional case; here the ending in городѣ is prepositional, indicating location rather than destination.
>
> Священникомъ Евгениемъ Крышановскимъ — "Rev. Evgeniy Kryshanovsky." The case endings are instrumental (-ом/-ем for a masculine or neuter noun, -им/-ым for the adjective, and names ending in -ский [-ski or -sky] are adjectival in origin) because the Rev. Kryshanovsky is the means or agency of this document's being issued.

Pages 2-3

It is hard enough to begin trying to translate Russian documents without the added complication of deciphering non-standard characters and scrawled handwriting; so here is a rendering of the material on pages 2 and 3 of the document in standardized typeface and cursive.

ВЫПИСЬ ИЗЪ МЕТРИЧЕСКОЙ КНИГИ. ЧАСТЬ ПЕРВАА ѡ РОДИВШИХСА за *1915* годъ.							
Счетъ родившихся		Мѣсяцъ и день		Имена Родившихса	Званіе, имя, ѡтчество и фамиліа родителей, и какого вѣроисповеданіа	Званіе, имя, отчество и фамиліа воспріемниковъ	Кто соверсшилъ таинство крещеніа
Мужеска пола	Женска пола	рожденіа	крещеніа				
2		*Января* *11*	*17*	*Владиміръ*	*Виленьской губерніи, Виленьскаго уѣзда, деревни Нахомова крестьянинъ Феодоръ Антоновичъ Силявка и его законная жена Анастасія Георгіевна оба православные*	*Александръ Михайловичь Микуличь и Сусанна Матфеевна Кордикъ*	*Священникъ Евгеній Крышановскій съ псаломщикомъ Димитріемъ Слуцкиэъ*
Что сія коп[ія съ подлиннымъ] актомъ вѣрна, бъ томъ подписомъ и приложеніемъ церковной печати удостовѣряю. Г. *Ansonia, Conn. U.S.A.*, мѣсяца *Января 24го* дня, *1917* года. № *4*.							

The top line, ВЫПИСЪ ИЗЪ МЕТРИЧЕСКОЙ КНИГИ, ЧАСТЬ ПЕРВАА, ѡ РОДИВШИХСА, ЗА *1915* ГОДЪ, says exactly the same thing as the first line on the cover page, but the Old Church Slavonic type-style may make it hard to recognize. Remember that the "А" is the same as modern "Я," and "ѡ" is the same as modern "О." So this simply means "Extract from the Registry Book, Part One, of Births, for the Year 1915."

Here is a breakdown of the contents of the entry by columnar heading.

Счетъ родившихса: Мужеска пола 2 / женска пола — "Number of the births: Male sex, 2 / Female sex —." The number of births for each sex was recording in this column. In this case the bearer of the document was the second male baptized in this parish in 1915. Incidentally, this usage is not standard Russian, by which "of the male sex" would be мужского пола and "of the female sex" would be женского пола.

Мѣсяцъ и день рожденіа/крещеніа: *Января 11 /17*— "Month and day of birth/baptism: January 11/17." Note the standard modern spelling of this phrase: месяц и день рождения/крещения.

Имена родившихсѧ: *Владиміръ* — "Names of the persons born: Vladimir." Имена is the plural nominative form of the word имѧ, which means "first name."

Званіе, имѧ, ѿчество, и фамилія родителей, и какого вѣроисповѣданіѧ: *Виленской губерніи Вилейскаго уѣзда, деревни Нахомово крестьянинъ Феодоръ Антоновичъ Силявка и его законная жена Анастасія Георгіевна. Ѻба православные* — "Occupation, name, patronymic, and surname of the parents, and their religion (literally "of what religion"): Of the Province of Vilno, County of Vilejka, village of Nahomovo, the peasant Feodor Antonovich Silyavka and his legal wife, Anastasiya Georgiyevna, both Orthodox." Виленской and Вилейскаго are genitive-case adjectives formed from the towns' names, Vilno and Vilejka.

Званіе, имѧ, отчество, и фамилія воспріемниковъ: *Александръ Михайловичъ Микуличъ и Сусанна Матѳеевна Кордикъ* — "Occupation, name, patronymic, and surname of the godparents: Aleksandr Mihailovich Mikulich and Susanna Matfeyevna Kordik."

Кто совершилъ таинство крещенія: *Священникъ Евгеній Крышановскій съ псаломщикомъ Димитріемъ Слуцкичъ* — "Who administered the sacrament of baptism: The priest Yevgeniy Kryshanovsky and the psalm-reader Dimitri Slutskich."

Что сія коп[ія съ подлиннымъ] актомъ вѣрна, въ томъ подписомъ и приложеніемъ церковной печати удостовѣряю. — "That this copy is faithful to the [original] documents, to this I attest with [my] signature and the affixing of the seal." The material in brackets is that portion of the text covered by the seal, but it is fairly certain that the obscured words are as read or something very similar. The priest certifies the copy **by means of** his signature and the affixing of the church's seal, so the nouns подписомъ and приложеніемъ are in the **instrumental** case; the phrase съ подлиннымъ актомъ is another example of the instrumental, employed not because of instrumentality but because it follows a preposition that takes the instrumental. The **genitive,** frequently signaled by of in English, appears in церковной печати, "of the church's seal." Сія копія is an example of the **nominative** case (here feminine singular), used generally for the subject of a predicate. The phrase въ томъ literally means "in this" and is an example of the **prepositional** case, a case that always follows a preposition (but not every preposition is followed by the prepositional case!). So this one sentence gives concise examples of much of the Russian case system!

Г. *Ansonia, Conn., U.S.A.,* мѣсяца *Января 24го* дня, *1917* года. № *4*. — "The city of Ansonia, Conn., U.S.A., the month of January, the 24th day, the year 1917." The abbreviation "г." is usually short either for "город," "city," or for some form of the word for "year," "год." It is generally simple to tell from context which is appropriate, as it is in this case. Also, the literal translation of the date shown here is helpful for beginners to decipher, but this is a standard way of stating a date in Russian, so its more appropriate translation in English is simply "January 24, 1917."

Священникъ Евгеній Крышановскій — "Father Yevgeniy Kryshanovsky."

Here is a translation of the whole document.

Extract from the Registry Book, Part One, of Births, for the Year 1915					
Birth number		Month and day of		Names of Those Born	Occupation, name, patronymic, and surname of parents, and of what faith	Occupation, name, patronymic and surname of the godparents	Who performed the sacrament of baptism
Male	Female	birth	baptism				
2		January 11	17	Vladimir	The peasant Feodor Antonovich Silyavka of the Province of Vilno, County of Vilejka, Village of Nahomovo, and his legal wife Anastasiya Georgievna, both Orthodox	Aleksandr Mihailovich Mikulich and Susanna Matfeevna Kordik	The priest Yevgeniy Kryshanovsky and the psalm-reader Dimitri Slutzkich
That this copy is faithful to the original documents, I certify with [my] signature and the affixing of the church's seal. The city of Ansonia, Conn., U.S.A., the month of January, the 24th day, the year 1917. *Father Evgeniy Kryshanovsky.*							

Document #2: Long-Form Roman Catholic Birth Record

Here is a rendering in italic type of the document on the opposite page:

Кози Боркъ
№ 23.

Состоялось въ деревнѣ Щутово шетого (девятнад-
цатого) марта тысяча девятьсотъ пятого года
въ десять часовъ утра Явился Станиславъ Заборовски
(Stanisław Zaborowski) крестьянинъ изъ Козяго Бор-
ка двадцати четырехъ лѣҗъ отъ роду въ присутсҗвіи
Яна Каминьскаго сорока трехъ и Францишка Тлу-
ховскаго тридцати трехъ лѣтъ отъ роду обоихъ —
крестьян изъ Боруховъ и предъявилъ Намъ младенца
женскаго пола, объявляя что онъ родился въ Козимѣ
Боркѣ перваго (четырнадцатаго) марта сего года
въ десять часовъ утра отъ законной его женѣ Леокадіи
урожденной Тыбурской (Leokadyi z Tyburskich) двад-
цати лѣтъ отъ роду. Младенцу этому при святомъ
крещеніи совершенномъ сего числа дано имя Чеслава
(Czesława) воспріемниками были Францишекъ Тлу-
ховски и Кажаржина Чижевска. Актъ сей объявляющему
и свидѣтелямъ неграможнымъ прочитанъ Нами только
подписанъ. Администраторъ прихода Щутово содержа-
щій акты гражданскаго соҗҗоянія. (-) Кс. В. Киньски.

Readers with very sharp eyes may have noticed a couple of odd letters in this document. Several times the priest who filled out this certificate used *җ* instead of *m*, the standard cursive form of т (for instance line 5, word 4, *лѣҗъ* instead of *лѣтъ*, and line 16, word 3, *Кажаржина* instead of *Катаржина*). Also word 2 of line 8, *изъ*, has з, a variant form of *җ*. Either form is used, *җ* or з, but fortunately they both look enough like the English letter *z* in cursive to cause little confusion. As for *җ*, it is an alternative form for *m* (which is т in non-italic type) and is encountered frequently; one also sees a form that looks much like a crossed *t* as used in English, but it is not regarded as correct and is more likely to be seen in letters rather than official documents. Sometimes Russians write *m* with a line drawn over it, and *ш* with a line drawn under it, to distinguish these letters; but these forms, too, will not normally appear in anything official. The cursive forms shown in the alphabet chart on page 191 may be regarded as the correct ones, and anything else as an exception.

Состоялось въ деревнѣ Щутово шетого/девятнадцатаго марта тысяча девятьсотъ пятого года въ десять часовъ утра.

   состоялось — "it happened" (past tense, neuter, from состоиться)

   в деревнѣ Щутово — "in the village of Szczutowo." В is a preposition followed by the accusative or prepositional case; деревнѣ (modern spelling деревне) is the prepositional case of деревня. Another possibility here is в городѣ, "in the city [of]." The people and places in this document are from the regions of Poland taken over by the Russian Empire, and that is why all proper names should be given in their Polish spelling (English phonetic spelling of the town's name would be "Shchutovo").

Состоялось въ деревнѣ Шутово шестого (девятнад-цатого) марта тысяча девятьсотъ пятого года въ десять часовъ утра Явился Станиславъ Заборовскій (Stanisław Zaborowski) крестьянинъ изъ Козягоро-жа двадцати четырехъ лѣтъ отъ роду въ присутствіи Яна Каминьскаго сорока трехъ и Францишка Тху-ловскаго тридцати трехъ лѣтъ отъ роду обоихъ = крестьянъ изъ Боруховъ и предъявилъ Намъ младенца женскаго пола, объявляя, что онъ родился въ Козихъ Борокъ перваго (четырнадцатого) марта сего года въ десять часовъ утра отъ законной его жены Леокадіи урожденной Тыбурской (Leokadji z Tyburskich) двад-цати лѣтъ отъ роду. Младенцу этому при святомъ крещеніи совершенномъ сего числа дано имя Чеслава (Czesława) воспріемниками были Францишекъ Тху-ловскій и Казимира Чижневска. Актъ сей объявляющему и свидѣтелямъ неграмотнымъ прочитанъ Нами только подписанъ. Администраторъ прихода Шутово содержа-щій акты гражданскаго состоянія (-) Кс. В. Концки.

шетого / девятнадцатого марта— "on the sixth/nineteenth of March." General time is expressed by the genitive case, and this means literally "of the sixth/nineteenth of March." "Sixth" in Russian is шестой, genitive шестого, and it appears the priest who wrote up this record misspelled the word as шетого. The difference in the dates is that between the Julian calendar, used in the Russian Empire and therefore required in records, and the Gregorian calendar, the standard in the West; records in regions traditionally Russian, of course, would give only the Julian date, but Russian-language records in formerly Polish regions give both. The Gregorian date is generally 12 to 13 days later than the Julian; so when one sees double dates in this form, the second date is the one Westerners would consider correct.

тысяча девятьсотъ пятого года — Literally, "of [the one] thousand nine hundred and fifth year." In dates the year is expressed with cardinal numbers and the final element (here *пятого*) as an ordinal, agreeing in gender, number, and case with the next word, which is a form of the word for "year," *год*.

въ десять часов утра — "at ten o'clock in the morning."

Translation — This occurred in the village of Szczutowo on the 6th/19th of March, 1905, at 10 a.m.

Явился Станиславъ Заборовски (Stanisław Zaborowski) крестьянинъ изъ Козяго Борка двадцати четырехъ лѣтъ отъ роду

явился — "[he] appeared," past tense masculine, from *явиться*.

Станиславъ Заборовски (Stanisław Zaborowski) — "Stanisław Zaborowski," the name of the declarant who appeared to testify. The name is given in Russian and Polish spelling, presumably for the sake of legal precision.

крестьянинъ изъ Козяго Борка — "a peasant from Kozi Borek."

двадцати четырехъ лѣтъ отъ роду — Literally "of 24 years from birth." *Лѣтъ* (modern spelling *лет*) is considered the genitive plural of *год*, and the whole expression *двадцати четырехъ лѣтъ* is genitive. *Отъ* (modern spelling *от*) is a preposition followed by the genitive, and *роду* is the genitive of *род*, a word meaning "family, birth, origin, sort."

Translation — Stanisław Zaborowski appeared, a peasant from Kozi Borek, age 24...

въ присутствіи Яна Каминьскаго сорока трехъ и Францишка Тлуховскаго тридцати трехъ лѣтъ отъ роду обоихъ крестьян изъ Боруховъ

въ присутствіи — "in the presence [of]." *Присутствіи* (modern spelling *присутствии*) is the prepositional case of *присутствие*, "presence." The sense of this phrase suggests "in the presence of" and that explains why the names that follow are in the genitive case.

Яна Каминьскаго — "of Jan Kamiński." Note the archaic genitive ending *-аго*. The genitive singular for masculine adjectives (and *Kamiński*, though a proper name, is adjectival in form), had two variants, *-аго* and *-яго*. Orthographic reforms in this century deleted those endings and replaced them with *-ого* and *-его*, respectively.

сорока трехъ — Literally, "of forty-three." Rather than repeat the word *лѣтъ* here and after Franciszek Tłuchowski's age, the word is given only there.

и Францишка Тлуховскаго тридцати трехъ лѣтъ отъ роду — "and of Franciszek Tłuchowski, 33 years from birth"

обоихъ крестьян изъ Боруховъ — "both peasants from Boruchy." *Обоихъ крестьянъ* is genitive plural, as a noun phrase in opposition to "Jan Kamiński... and Franciszek Tłuchowski." *Боруховъ*, a genitive plural form in Russian, corresponds to *Boruchów* in Polish, and the nominative form of *Boruchów* in Polish is *Boruchy*. Since these names are Polish anyway, "Boruchy" is the correct way to transliterate this word.

Translation — ...in the presence of Jan Kamiński, age 43, and of Franciszek Tłuchowski, age 33, both peasants from Boruchy...

и предъявилъ Намъ младенца женскаго пола, объявляя что онъ родился въ Козимъ Боркѣ перваго (четырнадцатаго) марта сего года въ десять часовъ утра

и предъявилъ Намъ — "and [he] showed us." *Предъявилъ* (modern spelling *предъявил*) is the past tense, masculine (the subject of this predicate is still "Stanisław Zaborowski"). *Нам* is the dative case of the pronoun *мы*, "we."

младенца женскаго пола — "a child of the female sex." *Младенца* is the genitive/accusative case of *младенец*, "baby, infant," in the accusative because it is the direct object of *предъявилъ*. Obviously the alternative to "of the female sex" is "of the male sex," *мужскаго* (modern spelling *мужского*) *пола*.

объявляя что — "stating, declaring that." This is a participial form of the verb *объявить*, "to declare, announce, state." It is still Stanisław Zaborowski who is doing all the appearing, showing, and now declaring.

онъ родился въ Козимъ Боркѣ — "it [the child] was born in Kozi Borek." Although the child in question is a girl, the grammatical antecedent of the pronoun is *младенец*, a masculine noun, so the pronoun referring to it is masculine, *он*, "he," not *она*, "she." *Въ* shows location where by taking a noun in the prepositional, and *Козимъ Боркѣ* (modern spelling would be *Козим Борке*) is the prepositional form of that place name.

перваго (четырнадцатаго) марта сего года — "of the first/fourteenth of March of this year." *Сего* is masculine genitive singular of *сей*, a pronoun meaning "this." This pronoun is not used much any more, but this form is seen in the common word *сегодня*, "today," literally "of this day."

въ десять часовъ утра — "at ten o'clock in the morning."

Translation — ...and showed us a child of the female sex, stating that it was born in Kozi Borek on the first/fourteenth of March of this year at ten o'clock in the morning...

отъ законной его жены Леокадіи урожденной Тыбурской (Leokadyi z Tyburskich) двадцати лѣтъ отъ роду.

отъ законной его жены Леокадіи — "of his legal wife Leokadia." *Жены* is the genitive form after the preposition *отъ*, which means "from, of." *Законной* is the genitive singular feminine declensional ending of the adjective *законный*, "legal, lawful," agreeing with *жены* and *Леокадіи*. *Его* is a pronoun, "his, its."

урожденной Тыбурской (Leokadyi z Tyburskich) — Literally, "born Tyburska," this is one way of saying "née Tyburska." Another is like the Polish expression seen here in parentheses: the first name + the preposition *с* + the maiden name in the genitive plural: *Леокадия с Тыбурских.* Note that again the Polish spelling of the name is given.

двадцати лѣтъ отъ роду — "twenty years from birth."

Translation — ...of his legal wife Leokadia née Tyburska, age 20.

Младенцу этому при святомъ крещеніи совершенномъ сего числа дано имя Чеслава (Czesława)

младенцу этому — "to this child." This is a dative masculine singular, used for an indirect object. *Этому* is the dative singular masculine of *этот*, "this."

при святомъ крещеніи — "at Holy Baptism." *При* is a preposition meaning "at, with, by" and takes the prepositional case, which is the case *святомъ* (holy) *крещеніи* (baptism) is in. The nominative of *крещеніи* is *крещеніе* (modern spelling *крещение*).

совершенномъ сего числа — "performed on this date." *Совершенномъ* is the prepositional neuter singular case (modifying *крещеніи*) of the past passive participle from the verb *совершить*, "to perform, do, complete." The phrase *сего числа* is a genitive expression of time when, "on this date."

дано имя Чеслава (Czesława) — "was given the name of Czesława." *Дано* is the neuter past passive participle from the verb *дать*, "to give." *Имя* means "first name," it is a neuter noun (thus the neuter ending on *дано*).

Translation — At Holy Baptism, administered on this day, this child was given the name of Czesława...

воспріемниками были Францишекъ Тлуховски и Казаржина Чижевска.

воспріемниками — "the godparents," from *воспріемникъ* (modern spelling *восприемник*). The word is in the instrumental case (the *-ами* ending is standard instrumental plural for nouns) because the instrumental is often used when a form of the verb *быть*, "to be," is used to identify, as here: "The godparents were ..."

были — "[they] were," past tense plural of *быть*.

Францишекъ Тлуховски и Катаржина Чижевиска — "Franciszek Tłuchowski and Katarzyna Czyżewska." A literal transliteration would be *Frantsishek Tlukhovski* and *Katarzhina Chizhewska,* but these are Polish names and should properly be given Polish spellings.

Translation — The godparents were Franciszek Tłuchowski and Rozalia Czyżewska.

Актъ сей объявляющему и свидѣтелямъ неграмоэнымъ прочитанъ Нами только подписанъ. Администраторъ прихода Щутово содержащій акты гражданскаго состоянія. (-) Кс. В. Киньски.

Актъ сей — "This document." The genitive form of *сей, сего,* appeared in line 10 *(сего года)* and line 14 *(сего числа).*

объявляющему — "to the declarant." *Объявляющему* is the dative masculine singular of the present active participle *объявляющий*, "the declaring one," which comes from the verb *объявлять*, "to declare, state." Dative constructions can generally be translated with the English prepositions "to" or "for," and the sense of this will be clear from context.

и свидѣтелямъ неграмотнымъ — "and to the illiterate witnesses." Both the noun and adjective are dative plural in form, for the same reason *объявляющему* was dative singular: as indirect objects of the verb *прочитанъ*.

прочитанъ — "[was] read," the past passive participle of the verb *прочитать,* "to read."

Нами только подписанъ — "[and] by us only signed." *Нами* is the instrumental of *мы,* "we," and *подписанъ* (from *подписать,* "to sign") is a past passive participle, like *прочитанъ.*

администраторъ прихода Щутово — "Administrator of the parish of Szczutowo."

содержащій акты гражданскаго состоянія — "the keeper of vital records," literally "The one keeping *(содержащій)* the documents *(акты)* of the civil state *(гражданскаго состоянія)."* *Содержащій* (modern spelling *содержащий*) is the present active participle of the verb *содержать,* "to keep, maintain," and *состояніе* (modern spelling *состояние*) is a noun meaning "state, status, condition."

Кс. В. Киньски — "Rev. W. Kiński." *Кс.* is an abbreviation of *Ксендз,* the Russian spelling of the Polish word *ksiądz,* "priest, Father."

Translation — This document was read to the declarant and illiterate witnesses and was signed by us alone. Administrator of the parish of Szczutowo and keeper of vital records. — Rev. W. Kiński.

Document #3: Short-Form Certificate

This versatile standardized certificate was used for birth, marriage, and death records. Its contents are extracted from the longer, paragraph-type documents of which Document #2 was a sample.

On the opposite page is reproduced a short-form registry certificate, and beneath it is a rendering of its contents in standardized print and cursive fonts that presumably will make the original a bit easier to decipher and thus give readers practice that will help them decipher their own records.

№ —9 акта съ 1897 года Ломжинской губерніи, Кольненскаго уѣзда, прихода Пжитулы, гмины Кубра

Here the place of issue is detailed, specified by administrative divisions of the Russian Empire in descending order. There are no exact equivalents for these divisions, of course, in the United States, but one can use English terms as approximations of the originals.

№ —9 акта съ 1897 года — "No. —9 record from 1897." The phrase *с ... года* means "from/of such-and-such year." The full record number was cut off when the copy was made.

Ломжинской губерніи — "of Łomża Province." "*Ломжа*" is the Cyrillic rendering of the Polish city of Łomża. A "*губернія*" was a high-level division of the Empire, more or less the equivalent of a *województwo* (province) in Poland. This phrase, like the following ones, is in the genitive case because this is "Record #—9 of the year 1897 of Łomża province, etc."

Кольненскаго уѣзда — "of Kolno County." *Кольненскаго* is the adjectival form of the city of Kolno, and has the (archaic) masculine genitive singular ending *-аго* to agree with its noun, *уѣзда.* An *уѣздъ* (modern spelling *уезд*) can be translated as "county" or "district."

прихода Пржитулы — "of the Parish of Przytuły." Here *прихода,* "parish," is in the genitive (the nominative is *приход*), but *Пржитулы* is in its standard nominative form, as it would be in the equivalent Polish phrase, *parafii Przytuły.*

гмины Кубра — "of the district of Kubra." The word *гмина* (nominative form of *гмины*) is a borrowing from Polish *gmina,* "community, district." As in the equivalent Polish expression, *gminy Kubra,* the name of the *gmina* itself is left in the nominative, *Кубра.*

Translation — Record No. 9 for the year 1897 of the Province of Łomża, County of Kolno, Parish of Przytuły, District of Kubra.

Метрическое Свидѣтельство, Къ книгамъ народонаселенія или воинской повинности

метрическое свидѣтельство — "A Registry Certificate." A *свидѣтельство* (modern spelling *свидетельство*) is a certificate or license; *метрическое* comes from the same root as *metryka* in Polish and *metrices* in Latin and means "of the registry, of vital statistics."

къ книгамъ народонаселенія — "for the books of the [permanent] population." *Къ* (modern spelling *к*) is a preposition followed by the dative case, and *книгамъ* is the dative plural of *книга,* "book." *Народонаселеніе* (modern spelling *народонаселение*) means "population," especially as applied to permanent populace rather than transients.

или воинской повинности — "or [for] military obligation." This phrase, too, is the object of preposition *къ* and therefore is in the dative case. *Воинская повинность* is a term meaning "military obligation."

Translation — A Registry Certificate for Population Records or Military Obligation.

№ акта
съ 189? года.

гу. Ломжинской губерніи.
.... уѣзда
прихода ....
гмины Кудра

МЕТРИЧЕСКОЕ СВИДѢТЕЛЬСТВО.
Къ книгамъ народонаселенія или воинской повинности.

ИМЯ И ФАМИЛІЯ.	Родился умеръ бракосочетались. Въ д. Хржанова			Имена и фамиліи родителей.
	Дня.	Мѣсяца.	Года.	Антони и Антонина
Янъ Крыщинскій	6 18	Декабря	1897	урожден.. ля Ковалевская

Прописью: Тысяча восемьсотъ девяносто седьмаго года

Съ подлиннымъ актомъ вѣрно:

Въ Пржитулахъ 5/18 дня Марта 1913 года.

Содержащій акты гражданскаго состоянія

[signature illegible]

Собственноручную подпись чиновника
гражданскаго состоянія свидѣтельствуетъ

.... мѣсяца .... дня 19 ... г.

ломж. губ. тип.—Ф. № 117.

№ — 9 акта
съ 1897 года

Ломжинской губерніи
Кольненскаго уѣзда
прихода Пржитулы
гмины Кудра

МЕТРИЧЕСКОЕ СВИДѢТЕЛЬСТВО
Къ книгамъ народонаселенія или воинской пвинности

ИМЯ И ФАМИЛІЯ	Родился [умеръ] [бракосочетались] Въ д. Хржаново			Имена и фамилія родителей
	Дня	Мѣсяца	Года	Антони и Антонина
Янъ Крыщинскій	6 18	Декабря	1897	урожденная Ковалевская

Прописью: Тысяча восемьсотъ девяносто седьмого года
Съ подлиннымъ актомъ вѣрно:
Въ Пржитулахъ 5/18 дня Марта 1913 года
Содержащій акты гражданскаго состояня
[signature illegible]
Собственноручную подпись чиновника
гражданскаго состоянія свидѣтельствуетъ

– 203 –

Имя и фамилія: *Янъ Крыщинский*

    имя и фамилія — "First name and surname." Фамилия is the modern spelling of the noun meaning "surname."

    Translation — First Name and Surname: Jan Kryszczyński.

Родился Умеръ Бракосочетались въ д. Хржаново

    Родился — "[He] was born," past tense masculine of *родиться,* "to be born." Note that only *родил* is printed so that the clerk can write in either *ся* to make *родился,* the masculine form, or *ась* to make *родилась,* the feminine form. Also printed is *умеръ,* "[he] died" — if a female died the suffix *ла* would be filled in to make it feminine, *умерла* — and *бракосочетались,* "they got married," to be filled in or crossed out as appropriate. So this certificate could serve for births, marriages, or deaths, with a few slight changes. Here *умеръ* and *бракосочетались* are crossed out, so it's a birth certificate.

    въ д. Хржаново — "in the village of Chrzanowo." Here *въ д.* is an abbreviation for *въ деревнъ* (modern spelling *в деревне*), from *деревня,* "village."

    Translation — Was born in the village of Chrzanowo.

Дня *6/18* Мѣсяца *Декабря* Года *1897*

    Translation — 6/18 December 1897. [See explanation of double dates under the analysis of *шетого / девятнадцатого марта,* Document #2, page 199].

Имена и фамилія родителей *Антони и Антонина урожденная Ковалевская*

    Имена и фамилія родителей — "First names and surname of parents." *Имена* is the plural nominative of *имя. Родителей* is the genitive plural of *родитель,* "parent."

    урожденная Ковалевская — "née Kowalewska."

    Translation — First names and surnames of parents: Antoni [Kryszczyński] and Antonina, née Kowalewska.

Прописью: Тысяча *восемьсотъ девяносто седьмого года.* Съ подлиннымъ актомъ вѣрно: Въ *Пржитулах 5/18* дня *Марта* 1913 года. *Содержащій акты гражданскаго состоянія* — Собственноручную подписью чиновника гражданскаго состоянія свидѣтельствуетъ

    Прописью — "Written out:" (an adverb signifying that the year follows, written out in words).

    Тысяча восемьсотъ девяносто седьмого года — Literally, "of the thousand eight hundred ninety-seventh year," i. e., 1897.

    Съ подлиннымъ актомъ вѣрно — Literally, "in conformance with the original record," but generally translated as "a certified true copy."

    Въ Пржитулахъ 5/18 дня Марта 1913 года — "In Przytuły, the 5th/18th of March, 1913." Note that in Polish *Przytuły* is a plural form and the phrase "in Przytuły" is *w Przytułach,* with the locative plural ending -*ach.* Russian does likewise and adds the same ending, -*ахъ.*

    Содержащій акты гражданскаго свидѣтельствуетъ состоянія — *Собственноручную подпись чиновника гражданскаго состоянія* — "The keeper of the civil records *[signature illegible]* witnesses the signature, in his own hand, of the official of the civil records." *Подпись* is "signature" (literally "under-writing"), a *чиновник* is an "official," and the verb *свидѣтельствуетъ* is no mystery once one has seen the words *свидѣтельство* (certificate) and *свидѣтель* (witness).

Translation — In words: the year one thousand eight hundred ninety-seven. A true copy of the original. In Przytuły, the 5th/18th of March, 1913. The keeper of civil records witnesses the signature, in his own hand, of the official of civil records.

Document #4: A Jewish Birth Certificate

Свидѣтельство.

Видано Одесскимъ Городовымъ Раввиномъ за надлежащею подписью и печатью въ томъ, что въ метрической тетради о родившихся евреяхъ, г. Одессы за 1902 г. значится подъ № 1478 женской — графы актъ слѣдующаго содержанія: Тысяча девятьсотъ второго года, Августа четвертаго дня, у Запаснаго рядового Янкеля Санева Клюр-фельда и жены его Этли родилась дочь, нареченная именемъ Тауба Ривка

Одесса, Февраля 15 дня 1911 года.

И. д. Одесскаго Городового Раввина

Свидѣтельство. Выдано Одесскимъ Городовымъ Раввиномъ за надлежащею подписью и печатью въ томъ, что ...

- *Выдано Одесскимъ Городвымъ Раввиномъ* — Issued *(выдано)* by the Odessa City Rabbi." *Одесскимъ* is the instrumental singular masculine of the adjective formed from the name of the city Odessa; *городовымъ*, same case form, is an adjective derived from the word for "city" (modern spelling *город*); and *Раввиномъ* is the instrumental singular of the noun *раввинъ* (modern spelling *раввин*) meaning "rabbi."
- *за надлежащею подписью и печатью* — "with the appropriate signature and seal." In this usage the preposition *за* is followed by the instrumental case, and *надлежащею подписью и печатью* show the appropriate feminine instrumental endings.

въ томъ что — "to the effect that..." (literally, "in this, that...")

Translation — A Certificate. Issued by the Odessa City Rabbi with the appropriate signature and seal to the effect that...

въ метрической тетради о родившихся евреяхъ, г. Одессы за 1902 г. значится подъ №. 1478 женской графы актъ слѣдующаго содержанія:

въ метрической тетради — "in the registry book. *Метрическая книга* is the more common way of saying "record book"; a *тетрадь* is literally a "notebook."

о родившихся евреяхъ — "for Jews being born." *О*, a preposition most often taking the prepositional (as here), generally means "of, about, regarding," but can sometimes mean "for." The word *еврей*, which sounds like "Yev-ray," comes from the same root as the English word "Hebrew." *Родившихся* (nominative *родившиеся*) is from *родиться*, "to be born," and here sounds best in English if translated as "births," i. e., "the births of Jews."

г. Одессы за 1902 г. — "city of Odessa, for the year 1902." The first *г.* is an abbreviation of *город*, "city," and the second is short for *год*, "year."

значится подъ №. 1478 — "is found under #1478." The verb *значить* is usually translated "to mean," but with the reflexive suffix *-ся* it can be used to mean "is found, appears." *Подъ* (modern spelling *под*) is a preposition meaning "under" or occasionally "near."

женской графы — "of the female column." This means that the entry in question is to be found under #1478 of the column for females. Compare Document #1.

актъ слѣдующаго содержанія — "a record of the following contents."

Translation — ...in the record book of Jewish births in the city of Odessa for the year 1902 is found under Number 1478 in the female column a document of the following contents...

Тысяча девятьсотъ второго года, Августа четвертаго дня

второго — "second."

Августа четвертаго дня — "on the fourth day of August."

Translation — On August 4, 1902...

у Запасного рядового Янкеля Санева Клюрфельда и жены его Этли

у Запасного рядового Янкеля Санева Клюрфельда — "to reserve private Yankel Sanev Klyurfeld." The preposition *у* takes the genitive case and means "of, at, to."

и жены его Этли — "and his wife Etlya." The nominative form of *жены* is *жена*, and changing the genitive form of the wife's name to the nominative yields "Etyla."

Translation — ...to private in the reserves Yankel Sanev Klyurfeld and his wife Etlya...

родилась дочь, нареченная именемъ Тауба Ривка. Одесса, Февраля 15 дня 1911 года.

родилась дочь — "a daughter was born." Note the feminine form of the verb, *родилась*, as opposed to the masculine form *родился* seen in earlier documents.

нареченная именемъ Тауба Ривка — "given the name Tauba Rivka." *Нареченная* is the feminine singular nominative (modifying *дочь*) of the past passive participle of the verb *наречь*. *Нареченный* or feminine *нареченная* can also mean "betrothed," but the explicit use here of *именемъ*, the instrumental singular of *имя*, specifies that it means "named." Note that although the name *Таубка Ривка* is basically an appositive of *именемъ* the name itself is in the nominative while *именемъ* is instrumental; presumably this construction is used to show the name in the nominative case, free from declensional variation and easy to get right.

Одесса, Февраля 15 дня 1911 года — "Odessa, February 15, 1911."

Translation — ...a daughter was born, named Tauba Rivka. Odessa, February 15, 1911.

Document #5: An Islamic Birth Record

Reproduced on the next page is an Islamic birth record which features a number of useful expressions and terms. The reproduction has been electronically reduced and cleaned up to make it easier to read, and a rendering in standardized cursive is given alongside it.

Выпись изъ метрической книги о родившихся при Новогрудской мечети Минской губ. состоявшихся въ 1911 году.

Тысяча девятьсотъ одиннадцатаго года сентября 16го дня въ городѣ Новогрудкѣ отъ законныхъ супруговъ дворянъ отца Самуила Давидова и матери Фелиціи Хасляновны изъ Асеановичей Корицкихъ родилась дочь коей дано имя по обряду магометанской вѣры Аминя. Обрядъ нареченія совершилъ мулла Новогрудской мечети Бекиръ Шалидевичъ. Что настоящая метрическая выпись значится записанной по метрической книгѣ за № 10.

И выдается Фелиціи Хасляновнѣ Корицкой на предметъ полученія паспортной книжки.

Въ томъ подписомъ и приложеніемъ мечетной печати удостовѣряю. Августа 17 дня 1915 года. Г. Новогрудокъ.

Мулла Новогрудской мечети Бекиръ Шалидевичъ

Выпись изъ метрической книги о родившихся при Новогрудской мечети Минской губ. состоявшихся въ 1911 году.

выпись изъ — "an excerpt from"

при Новогрудской мечети — "at the Novogrudok mosque." *При* is a preposition meaning "at, with, by" and takes the prepositional case; *мечети* is the prepositional singular of the feminine noun *мечеть*, "mosque," and *Новогрудской* is the adjectival form of the name of the town Novogrudok.

Минской губ. — "of the Province of Minsk." *Губ.* is an abbreviation of *губернія.*

состоявшихся въ 1911 году — "occurring in 1911." *Состоявшихся* is the prepositional plural of the participle *состоявшийся*, from *состояться*, "to happen, take place."

Translation — An excerpt from the birth register at the Novogrudok Mosque, Province of Minsk, for the year 1911.

Тысяча девятьсотъ одиннадцатаго года сентября 16го въ городѣ Новогрудкѣ отъ законныхъ супруговъ дворянъ отца Самуила Давидова и матери Фелиціи Хасляновны изъ Асеановичей Корицкихъ родилась дочь

> *одиннадцатаго* — "eleventh"
>
> *сентября* — "of September" (nominative *сентябрь*)
>
> *въ городѣ Новогрудкѣ* — "in the city of Novogrudok." In modern spelling this phrase would read *в городе Новогрудке.*
>
> *отъ законныхъ супруговъ дворянъ* — "of the legally-married noble couple." *Законный* is an adjective meaning "lawful"; a *супруг* (genitive plural *супругов* in modern spelling) is a "husband," while a *супруга* is a "wife," so the plural denotes a married couple. *Дворянъ* is the genitive plural of *дворянинъ*, "noble, aristocrat."
>
> *отца Самуила Давидова* — "the father Samuil Davidov." The whole phrase is in the genitive case because it is the object of the preposition *отъ*, which takes the genitive. So the masculine singular genitive noun ending *-а* is detached from the names to get their standard, nominative forms: Samuil Davidov.
>
> *и матери Фелиціи Хасляновны изъ Асеановичей Корицкихъ* — "and the mother Felitsiya Haslyanovna, née Aseanovich Koritski." This phrase, too, is in the genitive for the same reason that the father's name was. *Матери* is the genitive singular of the noun *мать*, "mother." Feminine nouns generally take the ending *-ы* (hard) or *-и* (soft), so to obtain the nominative form one must remove that ending and replace it with the standard feminine nominative ending, *-а* (hard) or *-я* (soft). Thus the genitive *Фелиціи Хасляновны* gives nominative *Фелиція Хасляновна*, "Felitsiya Haslyanovna." The expression *изъ* + the genitive plural, when following a married woman's name, signifies her maiden name; the standard form of her surname (the nominative feminine singular) is *Асеанович Корицкая*.

Translation — In the year 1911, on the sixteenth day of September, in the city of Novogrudok, to a legally married noble couple, the father being Samuil Davidov and the mother Felitsiya Haslyanovna, maiden name Aseanovich Koritskaya, a daughter was born...

коей дано имя по обряду магометанской вѣры Амины.

> *коей дано имя* — "to whom was given the name." *Дано* is the past passsive participle of *дать*, "to give."
>
> *по обряду магометанской вѣры* — "in accordance with the rite of the Islamic faith." The preposition *по* can mean many things, but one of the most common usage is with the dative to mean "by, according to, in accordance with." *Вѣры* is the genitive of *вѣра* (modern spelling *вера*) and means "faith, creed." The adjective *магометанский (magometanskiy)* is formed from the name "Mohammed"; sometimes Russian uses *-г-*, the hard *g*-sound, where other languages use an *h*, other times it uses the letter *-х-* to approximate the *h* sound.

Translation — ...who was given the name "Aminya" in accordance with the rite of the Islamic faith.

Обрядъ нареченія совершилъ мулла Новогрудской мечети Бекиръ Шалидевичъ

> *обрядъ нареченія* — "the ceremony of naming."
>
> *совершилъ* — "performed, completed" (from *совершить*).
>
> *мулла Новогрудской мечети Бекиръ Шалидевичъ* — "Bekir Shalidevich, the mullah of the Novogrudok mosque."

Translation — "Mullah Bekir Shalidevich of the Novogrudok mosque performed the naming ceremony."

Что настоящая метрическая выпись значится записанной по метрической книгѣ за № 10

> *что* — "[and] that." *Что* is a busy word in Russian; it can serve as the conjunction "that," as it does here, and it can be a pronoun meaning "what" or "that" or even sometimes "which." With the particle *-то* it means "something" (something definite) and with *-нибудь* it means "anything." In its various declined forms (*чего, чем, чом, чему*, etc.) it can mean about a thousand other things over and above its basic meaning of "that."
>
> *настоящая* — "this, the actual" in the sense of "the one we're currently talking about." In form *настоящий* is a present active participle from the verb *настоять*.
>
> *записанной* — "recorded, entered," from the verb *записать*.
>
> *по метрической книгѣ за № 10* — "in the registry book under #10."

Translation — And that the actual registry entry appears recorded in the register under #10.

И выдается Фелиціи Хасляновнѣ Корицкой на предметъ полученія паспортной книжки.

> *выдается* — "[it] is issued," from *выдаваться*.

Фелицíи Хасляновнѣ Корицкой — "to Felitsiya Haslyanovna Korickaya" (dative case).

на предметъ — "for the purpose of." *Предмет* (modern spelling) is a masculine noun meaning "subject, object, topic," but in this particular expression is translated as shown.

полученія паспортной книжки — "of receiving a passport." *Получение* (modern spelling, nominative case) is a neuter verbal noun from *получить*, "to get, receive." A *книжка* is a small book (diminutive of *книга*), and a *паспортная книжка* is a passport booklet. Literally the phrase means "[for the purpose of] the getting of a passport booklet," and thus the genitive case is used.

Translation — And [this certificate] is issued to Felitsiya Haslyanovna Koritskaya for the purpose of obtaining a passport.

Въ томъ подписомъ и приложеніемъ мечетной печати удостовѣряю. Августа 17 дня 1915 года. Г. Новогрудокъ. Мулла Новогрудской мечети Бекиръ Шалидевичь

въ томъ — "in this, to this."

подписомъ и приложеніемъ мечетной печати — "by the signature and the affixing of the mosque's seal." *Подписомъ* and *приложеніемъ* are in the instrumental, "by means of the signature and affixing." (In standard Russian *подпись* is a feminine noun and this should read *подписью*.)

удостовѣряю — "I certify," from *удостовѣрять.*

Translation — I certify the above with [my] signature and the attachment of the mosque's seal. The city of Novogrudok. Mullah of the Novogrudok mosque, Bekir Shalidevich.

Document #6: Russian Booklet-Type Passports

Russian passports can range from the familiar booklet-type documents to single-sheet documents of various sizes. The booklet-sized passports were often trilingual, in Russian, French, and German, but some were only in Russian. Here is a sample of a booklet format, and the next document exemplifies the other style.

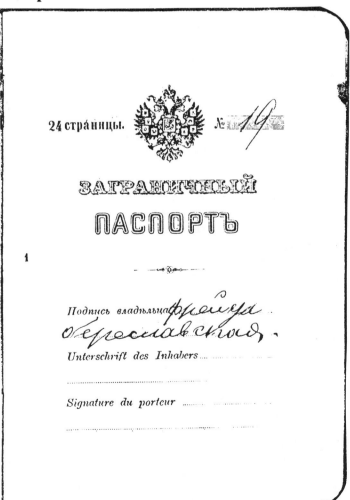

24 страницы   № 19

ЗАГРАНИЧНЫЙ

ПАСПОРТЪ

Подпись владѣльца Фрейда Ъереславская

страницы — "pages" (nominative singular *страница*)

заграничный — "foreign"

паспортъ — passport

подпись — "signature"

владѣльца — "of the bearer" (nominative *владѣлецъ*, modern spelling *владелец*)

Фрейда Ъереславская — the bearer's name, Freida Bereslavskaya. Note that on the next page her name is clearly written *Ъраславская*, "Braslavskaya."

Unterschrift des Inhabers, Signature du porteur — "Signature of the bearer" (in German and French)

Analysis of pages 2-3

предъявитель сего — "The bearer of this [document]."

Бобринецкая — "of Bobrinetz," an adjective formed from a place name.

мѣщанка — "a middle-class woman." This is the feminine form of the noun *мѣщанинъ* (modern spelling *мещанин*), which Russian dictionaries printed in the U.S.S.R. defined as "petty bourgeois" and in Soviet circles was virtually synonymous with "soulless middle-class philistine." In fact it historically meant only that the person was neither peasant nor aristocrat, but middle-class (usually dwelling in a town or city); all that, of course, changed when Communists took over Russia.

Фрейда Лейбова Браславская — "Freida Leibova Braslavskaya." *Леибова* is another form of patronymic, formed from the common Jewish name "Lejb" or "Lejba."

вдова, 48 л. — "a widow, age 48." A *вдова* is a widow, and a *вдовец* is a widower. The abbreviation *л.* after a number almost always stands for *лет*, "years."

съ дочерьми — "with daughters." The preposition *съ* when used with the instrumental usually means "with, along with"; all the names of the daughters, which follow, will also be in the instrumental case because they are the objects of the preposition *съ* (modern spelling *с*). As for *дочерьми*, the form is confusing because the nominative singular is *дочь*, but other forms add endings to the stem *дочер-*. Several other common words act similiarly, e. g., *мать*, "mother," adds endings to the stem *матер-* (*матери, матерью*, etc.)

Сурой, 18 л. — "Sura, age 18." *Сурой* is the instrumental case; to find the standard, nominative form one must remove the instrumental ending, *-ой*, and add the nominative ending *-a*.

Брухой, 7 л. — "Brukha, age 7"

Брухой-Ривкой, 5 л. — "Brukha-Rivka, age 5."

отправляется за границу — "is departing abroad." *Отправляется* is the present active 3rd person of *отправляться*, "to set out, leave." *Граница* means "border, boundary," and the expression *за границу* or *за границей* means "abroad."

за паспортъ уплачено 15 руб. - коп. — "15 rubles, no kopecks [were] paid for the passport." *Уплачено* is a participle of the verb *уплатить*, "to pay for, pay off."

во свидѣтельство чего — "In witness whereof, in certification of that"

и для свободнаго проѣзда — "and for free passage"
данъ сей паспортъ — "this passport is given"
съ приложеніемъ печати — "with the affixing of the seal"
Въ гор. Херсонъ Января 15 дня 1908 года. — "in the city of Kherson [on the Black Sea, east of Odessa], January 15, 1908." The abbreviation гор. is, of course, short for городъ, and since both this word and the name of the city follow въ both have the locative ending -ѣ.
И. д. Губернатора, Вице-Губернаторъ, Управлящий Канцеляріею — "Acting for the Governor [illegible], the Vice-Governor [illegible], Office Manager [illegible].

Translation — The bearer of this document, the middle-class resident of Bobrinets Freida Leibova Braslavskaya, a widow, age 48, with her daughters Sura, age 18, Brukha, age 7, and Brukha-Rivka, age 5, is departing abroad. 15 rubles, no kopecks were paid for this passport. In witness whereof and for free passage this passport was issued with the affixing of the seal. In the city of Kherson, January 15, 1908. For the governor, Vice-Governor —, Office Manager —.

Document #7: A Single-Sheet Russian Passport

ПАСПОРТЪ

Left Column

1. Вѣроисповѣданіе: *Іудейское*
2. Время рожденія или возрастъ: *род.*
   1 сентября 1896 года
3. Родъ занятій: *приказчик* [?]
4. Состоитъ ли или состоялъ ли въ бракѣ:
   Холостъ

1. Religion: Jewish
2. Time of birth or age: born
   1 September 1896
3. Type of work: shop assistant, salesperson [?]
4. Will enter or has entered into marriage:
   Single

– 211 –

5.Находятся при немъ: —

5.Accompanied by [literally, "are found with him] --

6.Отношеніе къ отбыванію воинской повинности:
   *Подлежитъ при-
   зыву съ 1917 г.*

6.Relationship as to service of military
   obligation: Subject to the draft of 1917

7.Подпись (владѣльца паспорта):
   Х. Г. Б. Финкельглузъ

7.Signature (of passport's bearer):
   H. I. B. Finkelgluz

При неграмотности предъявителя
   обозначаются его примѣты:
Ростъ: *средній*
Цвѣтъ волосъ: *черные*
Особыя примѣты: *нѣтъ*

In the event of the bearer's illiteracy his
   distinguishing marks are noted:
Height: medium
Color of hair: black
Distinguishing marks: none

Right Column

ПАСПОРТЪ
Выданъ *Ровенской Мѣщан. Управой*
   Issued by the Rovno Burghers' Council
БЕЗПЛАТНО на срокъ не болѣе одного года
   Free of charge for a period not more than one year.
Предъявитель _____ сего *Волынской гуд.,*
   The bearer of this [document], of Volyn' province,
Ровенскаго уѣзда, *мѣщанинъ* г. *Ровно*
   County of Rovno, a burgher of the city of Rovno
Хаимъ Госифъ Берковъ Финкельглузъ
   Haim Yosif Berkov Finkelgluz
уволенъ въ разные города и селенія Россійской Имперіи отъ нижеписаннаго числа
   is free [to travel] into the various cities and villages of the Russian Empire as of the date written below
по *двѣнадцатого Октября 1913* года.
   until October 12, 1913.
Данъ, съ приложеніемъ печати, *тысяча девятьсотъ*
двѣнадцат. года *Октября 12* дня.
   Issued, with seal affixed, October 12, 1912.

Предсѣдатель Управы [signature illegible]
   President of the Council —
Членъ Управы [signature illegible]
   Member of the Council —

ОТСРОЧКА — "Postponement, deferment." If for some reason a postponement was needed, the taking effect of this passport (*дѣйствіе сего паспорта*) would be postponed (*отсрочена*) to a given date.

A few points of interest in this document bear further explanation:

Ростъ — "Height," after which possible entries include: *малый* "small," *низкий* "short," *средний* "medium," and *высокий* "tall."

Цвѣтъ волосъ — This means literally "color of hairs," and there are a number of possible answers, including *бѣлый* "white," *свѣтлый* "light," *темный* "dark," *серый* "grey," *русый* "light brown," *рыжий* "red," and *с проседью* "greying."

Предъявитель _____ — The reason this word, meaning "the bearer," is followed by a line is so that the clerk filling out the passport can write in the suffix -ница if the bearer is female; almost any Russian noun ending in -ель can be made feminine by adding -ница. Here, of course, the bearer is a man and the feminine suffix is not added.

Document #8: A Ship Ticket

On the right is a reproduction of a third-class ticket for passage by ship from Liepaja, Latvia to New York. On the left are given a few notes to help in decipher and translating it.

Русско-Американская Линія — Russian-American Line

ПАССАЖИРСКИЙ БИЛЕТЪ — passenger ticket

междупалубній — between decks

на проѣздъ — for passage

въ III кл. — 3rd-class (literally "in 3rd class")

на пар. — "on the steamship" (*пар.* = *пароход*, "steamship")

русскаго — "of the Russian" (*русский* = "Russian")

Восточно-Азіатскаго — "Eastern Asiatic"

Пароходства — "steamship line"

отходящій — "departing" (from the verb *отходить*)

новаго стиля — "New Style" (i. e., as reckoned by the Gregorian calendar accepted in the West)

изъ Либавы — "from Libava" (the Russian name for Liepaja, Latvia).

въ Нью-Іоркъ — "to New York"

для дальнѣйшаго слѣдованія — "for further passage"

въ Bridgeport, Con. — "to Bridgeport, Connecticut"

для слѣдующихъ лицъ — "for the following persons"

имя и фамилія пассажира — "Passenger's Name and Surname"

Возрастъ — "age"

Плата — "Payment"

руб. — "rubles" (*рубль*)

коп. — "kopecks" (*копейка*)

согласно указаннымъ на оборотѣ сего условіямъ — "in accordance with (*согласно*) the terms (*условіямъ*) stated (*указаннымъ*) on the other side (*на оборотѣ*) of this (*сего*)

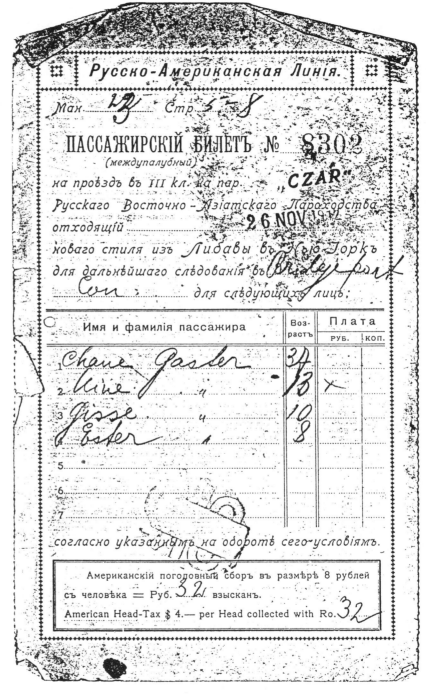

Translation — Russian-American line. Passenger Ticket No. 8302 (between decks), for 3rd-class passage on the steamship "Czar" of the Russian Eastern-Asiatic Steamship Line departing 26 Nov 1912, New Style, from Liepaja to New York for further passage to Bridgeport, Conn., for the following persons — Chane Gasler, 34; Mine Gasler, 13; Gisse Gasler, 10; Ester Gasler, 8 — in accordance with the terms stated on the other side of this ticket. [Note that the names are not written in Cyrillic!]

Selected Vocabulary Terms

As with any highly-inflected language, it is difficult to know how much information to give in a vocabulary list of Russian words. A truly comprehensive list would give all the words one can expect to find in documents; it would show them in standard printed Cyrillic, in Cyrillic "italics," and in cursive; it would give them in both archaic and modern spellings; it would indicate all declensional or conjugational forms one might encounter; and it would at least include examples of the words in context, since a simple word like стан can have any of a dozen meanings. Such a list would probably be of enormous value for those who want to master Russian, but it would surely confuse and frustrate readers wishing to invest only the effort needed to make out a few facts in a given document. Besides, there are books that attempt to give that information — they're called "dictionaries" — and even the thickest don't have enough room to provide all that data.

So this list includes only terms likely to appear in documents important to family historians, and it shows those words in standard Cyrillic printed form and in cursive (the italics are a cross between printed and cursive forms anyway, and thus should fool no one familiar with the printed and written forms). The words are alphabetized according to Russian order (to facilitate use of and comparison with dictionaries). The part of speech is shown, and the meaning of the word **in genealogical context** is given. All words are given in modern spelling, because the difference between modern and pre-Revolution spelling is usually quite minor — substitute "e" for "ѣ" and "и" for "i," and ignore final "ъ" — but in a few instances where the archaic spelling might prove tricky that form is also given in parentheses. Nouns and pronouns are usually listed under their standard (nominative) forms, but frequently-seen declensional variations are also listed with cross-reference to the nominative forms, where such usages and common phrases are mentioned. Most verbs are given in the form commonly encountered in documents, with indication of the infinitive form, but where different forms of the same verb appear frequently all those forms are brought together in a listing under the infinitive. Adjectives and participles are usually given in the standard nominative masculine singular, but one should remember that, for instance, выданный can appear in short form (masculine выдан, feminine выдана, neuter выдано) or with a number of different declensional endings.

а *а*— (conj.) and, but

август *август* — (masc. noun, gen. *августа*) August

администатор *администатор* — (masc. noun) administrator

азиатский *азиатский*— (adj.) Asiatic

акт *акт* — (masc. noun) record, document; акты гражданского состояния — vital statistics

акушерка *акушерка*— (fem. noun) midwife

апрель *апрель*— (masc. noun, gen. апреля) April

башмачник *башмачник* — (masc. noun) shoemaker

безплатный *безплатный*— (adj.) free of charge

белый *белый*— (adj.) white

билет *билет*— (masc. noun) ticket

борода *борода*— (fem. noun) beard

брак *брак*— (masc. noun) marriage

бракосочетались *бракосочетались* — (v., past plur. of бракосочетаться) they got married

бракосочетание *бракосочетание* — (neut. noun) marriage, getting married

брат *брат*— (masc. noun) brother

брачный *брачный*— (adj.) matrimonial, wedding

булочник *булочник*— (masc. noun) baker

бургомистр *бургомистр* — (masc. noun) mayor (from German *Bürgermeister*)

был, были *был, были* — (v., from быть) was, were

быть *быть*— (v.) to be

в *в*— (prep.) in, to

вдова *вдова*— (fem. noun) widow

вдовец *вдовец*— (masc. noun) widower

венчание *венчание* (вѣнчаніе) — (neut. noun) wedding ceremony

верный *верный*(вѣрный) — (adj.) true, faithful

вероисповедание *вероисповедани* (вѣроиспо-вѣданіе) — (neut. noun) faith, creed

вечер *вечер*— (masc. noun) evening; вечером — in the evening

виленский *виленский*— (adj.) of Vilno

владелец *владелец*(владѣлецъ) — bearer, owner

вне *вне*— (prep.) outside of; (as a prefix) extra-

внебрачное дитя *внебрачное дитя* — (neut. noun) illegitimate child

внук *внук*— (masc. noun) grandson

внучка *внучка*— (fem. noun) granddaughter

воинский *воинский*— (adj.) military

войт *войт*— (masc. noun) wójt (Polish community official)

волос *волос* — (masc. noun) hair (usually used in plural)

волость *волость*— (fem. noun) rural district

волынский *волынский* — (adj.) of Volyn' (Volhynia, Wołyń)

восемнадцатый *восемнадцатый* — (adj.) eighteenth

восемнадцать *восемнадцать* — (num., gen. восемнадцати) eighteen

восемь *восемь*— (num., gen. восьми) eight

восемьдесят *восемьдесят* — (num., gen. восьмидесяти) eighty

восемьсот *восемьсот* — (num., gen. восьмисот) eight hundred

восприемник *восприемник* — (masc. noun) godparent

восприемница *восприемница* — (fem. noun) godmother

восток *восток*— (masc. noun) east

восточный *восточный* — (adj.) eastern

восьмидесятый *восьмидесятый* — (adj.) eightieth

восьмисотый *восьмисотый* — (adj.) eight hundredth

восьмой *восьмой*— (adj.) eighth

возраст *возраст*— (masc. noun) age

время *время*— (neut. noun, gen. времени) time

второй *второй*— (adj.) second

вчера *вчера*— (adv.) yesterday

выдается *выдается* — (v., from выдаться) is issued

выданный *выданный* — (part. from выдать) issued (short form выдан/а/о)

выдано *выдано*→ выданный

выдать *выдать*— (v.) to issue

выпись *выпись*— (fem. noun) extract

высокий *высокий*— (adj.) high, tall

выше *выше* — (adv.) above, previously; вышеописанный — described above

где *где*— (adv.) where

глаза *глаза*— (masc. noun, plur.) eyes

гмина *гмина*— (fem. noun) community, district

год *год*— (masc. noun) year

гора *гора*— (fem. noun) mountain

город *город*— (masc. noun) city

гражданский *гражданский*— (adj.) civil

графа *графа*— (fem. noun) column

граница *граница* — (fem. noun) border, boundaries; за границу, за границей abroad

губерния *губерния* (губернія) — (fem. noun) province

д. *д.* — (abbreviation) день or дня, day; деревня — village

дальнейший *дальнейший* — (adj.) farther, further

дан *дан* (neut. form дано) — (v., part. from дать); [was] given

два *два*— (num., gen. двух) two

двадцатый *двадцатый*— (adj.) twentieth

двадцать *двадцать* — (num., gen. двадцати) twenty

две *две* → два (feminine form)

двенадцатый *двенадцатый*— (adj.) twelfth

двенадцать *двенадцать* — (num., gen. двенадцати) twelve

двести *двести* — (num., gen. двухсот) two hundred

дворянин *дворянин* — (masc. noun) noble, nobleman

двоюродная сестра *двоюродная сестра*— (fem. noun) cousin

двоюродный брат *двоюродный брат* — (masc. noun) cousin

двухсотый *двухсотый*— (adj.) two hundredth

деверь *деверь* — (masc. noun) brother-in-law (husband's brother)

девица *девица*— (fem. noun) girl, maiden, virgin

девяносотый *девяносотый* — (adj.) nine hundredth

девяносто *девяносто* — (num., gen. девяноста) ninety

девяностый *девяностый* — (adj.) ninetieth

девятнадцатый *девятнадцатый* — (adj.) nineteenth

девятнадцать *девятнадцать* — (num., gen. девятнадцати) nineteen

девятый *девятый*— (adj.) ninth

девять *девять*— (num., gen. девяти) nine

девятьсот *девятьсот* — (num., gen. девятисот) nine hundred

действие *действие* (дѣйствіе) — (neut. noun) validity, functioning, operation

декабрь *декабрь* — (masc. noun, gen. декабря) December

день *день* — (masc. noun, дня) day; днем — during the day, in the afternoon. p.m.

деревня *деревня*— (fem. noun) village

десятый *десятый*— (adj.) tenth

десять *десять*— (num., gen. десяти) ten

дети *дети*— (plural noun) children

дитя *дитя*— (neut. noun) child

для *для* — (prep. with genitive) for

днем *днем* → день

дня *дня*→ день

договор *договор*— (masc. noun) agreement

документ *документ*— (masc. noun) document

дочь *дочь* — (fem. noun, gen. дочери, instr. plur. дочерьми) — daughter

дядя *дядя* — (masc. noun) uncle

еврей *еврей*— (masc. noun) Jew

еврейский *еврейский*— (adj.) Jewish

ее *ее*— (pron.) her

его *его* → он, оно

ей *ей* → она

ему *ему*— (dative of он or оно) [to, for] him, it

жена *жена*— (fem. noun) wife

женский *женский*— (adj.) female, feminine

живый *живый* — (adj.) alive, living; находящийся при живых — still alive, among the living

жительство *жительство* — (neut. noun) residence; место постоянного жительства — place of permanent residence

жительствующий *жительствующий* — (part. from жительствовать) residing, living

жизнь *жизнь* — (fem. noun) life

за *за* — (prep.) for; behind, beyond

заграничный *заграничный* — (adj.) foreign

заключить *заключить* — (v.) to perform, conclude, contract; заключено — (part.) [it was] performed; заключил — (past tense) [he] concluded, contracted

законный *законный* — (adj.) legal

занятие *занятие* — (neut. noun) occupation

запад *запад* — (masc. noun) west

западный *западный* — (adj.) western

запасный *запасный* — (adj.) reserve (i. e., in the military)

записанный *записанный* — (part. from записать) entered, recorded

заявлено *заявлено* — (part. from заявить) [it was] announced, declared

звание *звание* — (neut. noun) calling, profession

здешний *здешний* (здѣшний) — (adj.) local, of this place

земледелец *земледелец* — (masc. noun) farmer

земледелие *земледелие* — (neut. noun) agriculture

значит *значит* — (v., from значить) it means

значится *значится* — (v., from значиться) it is found, it appears

золовка *золовка* — (fem. noun) sister-in-law (husband's sister)

зять *зять* — (masc. noun) brother-in-law (sister's husband)

и *и* — (conj.) and

или *или* — (conj.) or, either

им *им* — (dative of они) them

имена *имена* → имя

ими *ими* — (instrumental of они) them

империя *империя* (имперія) — (fem. noun) empire

имя *имя* — (neut. noun, plur. имена) (first) name

их *их* — (gen./acc. of они) them, their

из *из* — (prep. with genitive) from, of

июль *июль* — (masc. noun, gen. июля) July

июнь *июнь* — (masc. noun, gen. июня) June

к *к* — (prep. with dative) to, towards

кабатчик *кабатчик* — (masc. noun) barkeeper, innkeeper

какой *какой* — (pron., adj.) what, which

книжка *книжка* — (fem. noun) booklet; паспортная книжка — passport

книга *книга* — (fem. noun; dat. plur. книгам) book

кольненский *кольненский* — (adj.) of, from Kolno

кончина *кончина* — (fem. noun) demise, death

коп. *коп.* — (abbreviation) kopeck (копейка)

копия *копия* — (fem. noun) copy

костел *костел* — (masc. noun) [Roman Catholic] church

которому *которому* → который (dative, "to which/whom")

который *который* — (rel. pron.) who, which, that

которых *которых* → который (genitive, "of which/whom")

крестник *крестник* — (masc. noun) godson

крестница *крестница* — (fem. noun) goddaughter

крестьянин *крестьянин* — (masc. noun) farmer, peasant

крестьянка *крестьянка* — (fem. noun) peasant (female)

крещение *крещение* — (neut. noun) baptism

ксендз *ксендз* — (masc. noun) priest (esp. Polish Catholic)

кто *кто* — (pron.) who, who?

кузнец *кузнец* — (masc. noun) blacksmith

купец *купец* — (masc. noun) merchant

л. *л.* — (abbreviation of лет) age, of — years

легитимационный *легитимационный* — (adj.) identity; легитимационная книжка — kind of identification papers

Ленинград *Ленинград* — (masc. noun) Leningrad

лет *лет* — (n., gen. plur. of рок) years

ли *ли* — (particle) whether (also signifies a question)

Либава *Либава* — (fem. noun) Libava, Liepaja (Latvia)

линия *линия* — (fem. noun) line

Литва *Литва* — (fem. noun) Lithuania; на Литве — in Lithuania

литевский *литевский* — (adj.) Lithuania

лицо *лицо* — (neut. noun) face; person, individual

лично *лично* — (adv.) in person, personally

ломжинский *ломжинский* — (adj.) of, from Łomża (Poland)

май *май* — (masc. noun, gen., мая) May

малый *малый* — (adj.) small

март *март* — (masc. noun, gen. марта) March

мать *мать* — (fem. noun, gen. матери) mother

мачеха *мачеха* — (fem. noun) stepmother

между *между* — (prep. with instrumental) between, among

мечеть *мечеть* — (fem. noun) mosque

меня *меня* → я

мещанин *мещанин* (мѣщанинъ) — (masc. noun) middle-class male, burgher

мещанка *мещанка* (мѣщанка) — (fem. noun) middle-class female, burgher

мертвый *мертвый* — (adj.) dead

место *место* (мѣсто) — (neut. noun) place

месяц *месяц*— (masc. noun) month

метрический *метрический*— (adj.) registry

меховщик *меховщик*— (masc. noun) furrier

младенец *младенец* — (masc. noun, gen./acc. младенца) baby, child

мне *мне*— (dative of я) [to] me

мной *мной*→ я

Москва *Москва*— (fem. noun) Moscow

муж *муж* — (masc. noun) husband

мужской *мужской*— (adj.) male, masculine

мулла *мулла*— (masc. noun) mullah

мясник *мясник*— (masc. noun) butcher

на *на*— (prep.) on, at, in, to

надлежащий *надлежащий*— (adj.) appropriate

нам *нам*— (pron., dative, from мы) [to, for] us

нами *нами*— (pers. pron, instrumental case of мы) [by] us

наочный *наочный* — (adj.) with one's own eyes, eyewitness

наречение *наречение*— (neut. noun) naming

нареченный *нареченный* — (part. from наречь) betrothed; нареченная именем — given the name

народонаселение *народонаселение* — (neut. noun) population

нас *нас*— (pers. pron., from мы) us

настоятель *настоятель* — (masc. noun) dean (of church, cathedral)

настоящийся *настоящийся*— (adj.) present, real

находиться *находиться* — (v.) to be found, be located; to be; находящийся — (part.) located, finding oneself; находятся — (pres. plural) are found

не *не*— (adv.) not

невеста *невеста*(невѣста) — (fem. noun) bride

невестка *невестка* — (fem. noun) sister-in-law (brother's wife)

неграмотность *неграмотность* — (fem. noun) illiteracy

неграмотный *неграмотний*— (adj.) illiterate

незаконный *незаконный*— (adj.) illegitimate

нем *нем*→ он, оно

нему *нему*— (dative of он or оно) him, it

нет *нет*— (adv.) no; there is/are no —

ниже *ниже*— (adv.) below

нижеписанный *нижеписанный* — (part. from ниже + писать) written below

низкий *низкий*— (adj.) short, low

ним *ним*— (dative of они) them

ними *ними*— (instrumental of они) them

них *них*— (prep. of они) them

новобрачные *новобрачные* — (plur. adj. used as noun) the newlyweds

новогрудский *новогрудский* — (adj.) of Novogrudok

новый *новый*— (adj.) new; новаго стиля — New Style (dating by Gregorian calendar)

номер *номер*— (masc. noun) number

нос *нос*— (masc. noun) nose

ночь *ночь*— (fem. noun) night; ночью, ночи — at night

ноябрь *ноябрь* — (masc. noun, gen. ноября) November

о *о*— (prep.) about, for

оба *оба*— (num., gen. обоих) both

обозначаются *обозначаются* — (v., from обозначаться) are noted

оборот *оборот* — (masc. noun) revolution, turnover; на обороте — on the reverse, the other side

обряд *обряд*— (masc. noun) rite, ceremony

объявлять *объявлять* — (v.) to declare, state; объявляемся — we declare; объявляющий — (adj.) declaring; (noun) declarant; объявляя — (gerund) declaring, stating; объявляют — (plural present) they declare

оглашение *оглашение* — (neut. noun) announcement

одесский *одесский*— (adj.) of, from Odessa

один *один*— (num., gen. одного/одной) one

одиннадцатый *одиннадцатый*— (adj.) eleventh

одиннадцать *одиннадцать* — (num., gen. одиннадцати) eleven

одна *одна*→ один (feminine form)

одно *одно*→ один (neuter form)

октябрь *октябрь* — (masc. noun, gen. октября) October

он *он*— (pers. pron.) he; его — his, its

она *она*— (pers. pron.) she; ей — [to] her; ее — her

они *они*— (pers. pron.) they; их — their, them

оно *оно*— (pers. pron.) it; его — its

описанный *описанный* — (part. from описать) described

основание *основание* — (neut. noun) basis; на основании — on the basis [of]

особа *особа*— (fem. noun) person

особый *особый*— (adj.) special, distinguishing

от *от*— (prep. with genitive) from, of

отбывание *отбывание*— (neut. noun) service

отец *отец*— (masc. noun, gen. отца) father

отношение *отношение* — (neut. noun) relationship (to, with: к)

отправляется *отправляется* — (v., from отправляться) is departing

отсрочка *отсрочка* — (fem. noun) postponement, deferment

отходящий *отходящий* — (part. from отходить) departing

отчество *отчество*— (neut. noun) patronymic

отчим *отчим*— (masc. noun) stepfather

падчерица *падчерица*— (fem. noun) stepdaughter

пароход *пароход*— (masc. noun) steamship

пароходство *пароходство* — (neut. noun) steamship line

паспорт *паспорт*— (masc. noun) passport

паспортный *паспортный*— (adj.) passport

пассажир *пассажир*— (masc. noun) passenger

пассажирский *пассажирский*— (adj.) passenger

пасынок *пасынок*— (masc. noun) stepson

пекарь *пекарь*— (masc. noun) baker

первый *первый*— (adj.) first

печать *печать*— (fem. noun) seal

пивовар *пивовар*— (masc. noun) brewer

писать *писать*— (v.) to write

плата *плата*— (fem. noun) payment

племянник *племянник*— (masc. noun) nephew

племянница *племянница*— (fem. noun) niece

плотник *плотник*— (masc. noun) carpenter

по *по* — (prep.) by, according to, in, after; по полудни — in the afternoon; по полуночи — after midnight

повар *повар*— (masc. noun) cook

повинность *повинность* — (fem. noun) duty, obligation

погребение *погребение*— (neut. noun) burial

под *под*— (prep.) under, near

подбородок *подбородок*— (masc. noun) chin

подлежит *подлежит* — (v., from подлежать) is subject to (dative)

подлинный *подлинный* — (adj.) authentic, original

подписан *подписан* — (part. from подписать) [was] signed

подписом *подписом*— with [my] signature

подпись *подпись*— (fem. noun) signature

позволение *позволение*— (neut. noun) permission

поконый *поконый*— (adj.) deceased

пол *пол*— (masc. noun) sex; мужского пола — of the male sex

пол *пол*— (num.) half

полдень *полдень*— (masc. noun) noon, midday

полночь *полночь*— (fem. noun) midnight

полтора *полтора*— one and a half

получение *получение* — (neut. noun) receiving, obtaining

портниха *портниха*— (fem. noun) dressmaker

портной *портной* — (adj. used as masc. noun) tailor

постоянный *постоянный* — (adj.) constant, steady, permanent

потому, что *потому, что*— (conj.) because

почему *почему*— (conj.) why

прабабка *прабабка* — (fem. noun) great-grandmother

православный *православный* — (adj. used as noun) Orthodox

прадед *прадед*— (masc. noun) great-grandfather

прапрабабка *прапрабабка* — (fem. noun) great-great-grandmother

прапрадед *прапрадед*— (masc. noun) great-great-grandfather

предмет *предмет* — (masc. noun) object, subject, topic; на предмет — for the purpose of

предшествовали *предшествовали* — (v., past plural of предшествовать) preceded

предъявил *предъявил* — (v., from предъявить) [he] presented, showed

предъявитель *предъявитель* — (masc. noun) the bearer

при *при* — (prep.) at, by, on the occasion of, near, with

приложение *приложение* — (neut. noun) attachment, affixing

приметы *приметы* — (masc. noun, plural) [distinguishing] marks

присутствие *присутствие* — (neut. noun) presence; в присутствии — in the presence of

присутствующий *присутствующий* — (part. from присутствовать) present, in attendance

приход *приход*— (masc. noun) parish

приходский *приходский*— (adj.) parochial, of the parish

призыв *призыв*— (masc. noun) call, appeal, levy, draft

проезд *проезд* (проѣзд) — (masc. noun) passage; билет на проезд — ticket for passage

прописью *прописью*— (adv.) written out

проседь *проседь* — (fem. noun) streaks of grey; с проседью — greying

прочитан *прочитан* — (part. from прочитать) [was] read

прочтение *прочтение*— (neut. noun) reading

псаломщик *псаломщик* — (masc. noun) psalm-reader

публикованный *публикованный* — (part. from публиковать) published

пятидесятый *пятидесятый*— (adj.) fiftieth

пятисотый *пятисотый*— (adj.) five hundredth

пятнадцатый *пятнадцатый*— (adj.) fifteenth

пятнадцать *пятнадцать* — (num., gen. пятнадцати) fifteen

пятый *пятый*— (adj.) fifth

пять *пять*— (num., gen. пяти) five

пятьдесят *пятьдесят*— (num., gen. пятидесяти) fifty

пятьсот *пятьсот* — (num., gen. пятисот) five hundred

работа *работа*— (fem. noun) work, labor

работник *работник* — (masc. noun) worker, laborer

работница *работница* — (fem. noun) female worker

рабочий *рабочий* — (adj. used as masc. noun) worker

раввин *раввин* — (masc. noun) rabbi

разный *разный* — (adj.) various, sundry, different

река *река* — (fem. noun) river

рекрутский *рекрутский* — (adj.) of recruiting

религиозный *религиозный* — (adj.) religious

римско-католический *римско-католический* — (adj.) Roman Catholic

ровенский *ровенский* — (adj.) of, from Rovno

род *род* — (masc. noun) kind, sort; birth; от роду — from birth, age

родитель *родитель* — (masc. noun) parent

родиться *родиться* — (v.) to be born; родился — (past, masculine) he was born; родилась — (past, feminine) she was born; родившиеся — (part., plural, gen. родившихся) born, births;

рождение *рождение* — (neut. noun) birth

российский *российский* — (adj.) Russian

рост *рост* — (masc. noun) height

рот *рот* — (masc. noun) mouth

руб. *руб.* — (abbreviation) ruble (рубль)

русский *русский* — (adj.) Russian

русый *русый* — (adj.) light brown

рыжий *рыжий* — (adj.) red (hair)

рядовой *рядовой* — (adj. used as noun) private, regular soldier

с *с* — (prep.) with (with instrumental); from (with gen.)

садовник *садовник* — (masc. noun) gardener

сапожник *сапожник* — (masc. noun) shoemaker

свекор *свекор* — (masc. noun) father-in-law (husband's father)

свекровь *свекровь* — (fem. noun) mother-in-law (husband's mother)

светлый *светлый* — (adj.) light

свидетель *свидетель* (свидѣтель) — (masc. noun) witness

свидетельство *свидетельство* (свидѣтельство) — (neut. noun) certificate

свидетельствует *свидетельствует* — (v., from свидетельствовать) witnesses

свояченица *свояченица* — (fem. noun) sister-in-law (wife's sister)

святой *святой* — (adj.) holy, sacred; (n.) saint

священник *священник* — (masc. noun) priest

север *север* — (masc. noun) north

северный *северный* — (adj.) northern

сего *сего* → сей

сегодня *сегодня* — (adv.) today

седьмой *седьмой* — (adj.) seventh

сей *сей* — (pron.) this; сего — [of] this

селение *селение* — (neut. noun) settlement, village

семидесятый *семидесятый* — (adj.) seventieth

семисотый *семисотый* — (adj.) seven hundredth

семнадцатый *семнадцатый* — (adj.) seventeenth

семнадцать *семнадцать* — (num., gen. семнадцати) seventeen

семь *семь* — (num., gen. семи) seven

семьдесят *семьдесят* — (num., gen. семидесяти) seventy

семьсот *семьсот* — (num., gen. семисот) seven hundred

сентябрь *сентябрь* — (masc. noun, gen. сентября) September

серый *серый* — (adj.) grey

сестра *сестра* — (fem. noun) sister

сия *сия* (сія) — this (fem. nominative) → сей

скорняк *скорняк* — (masc. noun) furrier

следование *следование* — (neut. noun) movement, passage

следующий *следующий* — (adj.) [the] following

словесно *словесно* — (adv.) orally, verbally

слово *слово* — (neut. noun) word

слуга *слуга* — (masc. noun) servant

служанка *служанка* — (fem. noun) female servant

смерть *смерть* — (fem. noun) death

сноха *сноха* — (fem. noun) daughter-in-law

собственноручный *собственноручный* — (adj.) with one's own hand

совершить *совершить* — (v.) to perform, complete; совершил — (masc., past) [he] performed, completed; совершенный — (part.) performed

согласно *согласно* — (adv.) in agreement with (dative, or с with instrumental)

содержащий *содержащий* — (part. of содержать used as noun) keeper

содержащийся *содержащийся* — (part. from содержаться) making a living

сорок *сорок* — (num., gen. сорока) forty

сороковой *сороковой* — (adj.) fortieth

состоит *состоит* — (v., from состоить) enters

состояние *состояние* — (neut. noun) state, condition, status; акты гражданского состояния — vital statistics

состояться *состояться* — (v.) to happen; состоялось — (neuter, past) it happened; состоявшийся — (part.) occurring

сотный *сотный* — (adj.) hundredth

союз *союз* — (masc. noun) union; религиозный брачный союз — a religious marriage, union

способ *способ* — (masc. noun) means, way; способ жизни — way of making a living

средний *средний* — (adj.) medium

срок *срок* — (masc. noun) term, period

сто *сто* — (num., gen. ста) one hundred

столарь *столарь* — (masc. noun) carpenter

страница *страница* — (fem. noun) page

супруг *супруг* — (masc. noun) husband

супруга *супруга* — (fem. noun) wife

счет *счет* — (masc. noun) number

сын *сын*— (masc. noun, nom. plural сыновья) son

таинство *таинство*— (neut. noun) sacrament

текущий *текущий* — (adj.) current, present; текущего года — this year

темный *темный*— (adj.) dark

тесть *тесть* — (masc. noun) father-in-law (wife's father)

тетрадь *тетрадь*— (fem. noun) notebook

тетя *тетя*— (fem. noun) aunt

тех *тех*→ тот

теща *теща* — (fem. noun) mother-in-law (wife's mother)

ткач *ткач*— (masc. noun) weaver

того *того*→ тот

только *только*— (adv.) only

том *том*→ тот

тому *тому*→ тот

тот *тот*— (pron.) that; в том — in this, to this

третьий *третьий* — (adj.) third; третья часть — 3rd part, (records of) deaths

трех *трех*→ три

трехсотый *трехсотый*— (adj.) three hundredth

три *три*— (num., gen. трех) three

тридцатый *тридцатый*— (adj.) thirtieth

тридцать *тридцать* — (num., gen. тридцати) thirty

тринадцатый *тринадцатый*— (adj.) thirteenth

тринадцать *тринадцать* — (num., gen. тринадцати) thirteen

триста *триста* — (num., gen. трехсот) three hundred

тысяча *тысяча*— (num., gen. тысячи) thousand

тысячный *тысячный*— (adj.) thousandth

уволен *уволен* — (part. from уволить) is free, is discharged, is given leave

удостоверение *удостоверение* — (neut. noun) certification; по наочнем удостоверании — after visual confirmation

удостоверять *удостоверять*— (v.) attest, certify; удостоверяю — (present tense) I certify

уезд *уезд*(уѣздъ) — (masc. noun) county

указанный *указанный* — (part. from указать) listed

Украина *Украина*— (fem. noun) Ukraine

умер *умер*— (v., from умереть) [he] died; умерла — she died

умерший *умерший* — (part. from умереть) deceased, late

умеющий *умеющий* — (part. from уметь) knowing how to, able to

уплачено *уплачено*— (part. from уплатить) [was] paid for

управа *управа*— (fem. noun) council, board

управление *управление* — (neut. noun) administration

урожденный *урожденный*— (adj.) born, née)

условие *условие*— (neut. noun) condition, term

утро *утро*— (neut. noun) morning; утра — (gen.) in the morning; утром — (instrum.) in the morning

фабрикант *фабрикант* — (masc. noun) manufacturer

фамилия *фамилия*— (fem. noun) surname

февраль *февраль* — (masc. noun, gen. февраля) February

холост *холост*— (masc. noun) bachelor, groom

холостой *холостой*— (adj.) single, bachelor

хозяин *хозяин* — (masc. noun, gen./acc. plur. хозяев) landowner

церковный *церковный*— (adj.) church

церковь *церковь* — (fem. noun) church (esp. an Orthodox church)

цвет *цвет*— (masc. noun) color

час *час* — (masc. noun) hour; o'clock; в десять часов — at ten o'clock

часть *часть*— part

чего *чего*→ что (genitive singular, "of that")

черный *черный*— (adj.) black, dark

четвертый *четвертый*— (adj.) fourth

четыре *четыре*— (num., gen. четырех) four

четыреста *четыреста*— (num., gen. четырехсот) four hundred

четырехсотый *четырехсотый* — (adj.) four hundredth

четырнадцатый *четырнадцатый* — (adj.) fourteenth

четырнадцать *четырнадцать* — (num., gen. четырнадцати) fourteen

чиновник *чиновник*— (masc. noun) clerk, official

число *число* — (neut. noun) date, numeral; сего числа — on this date

член *член*— (masc. noun) member

что *что*— (conj.) that; (pron.) that

швея *швея*— (fem. noun) seamstress

шестидесятый *шестидесятый*— (adj.) sixtieth

шестисотый *шестисотый*— (adj.) six hundredth

шестнадцатый *шестнадцатый*— (adj.) sixteenth

шестнадцать *шестнадцать* — (num., gen. шестнадцати) sixteen

шестой *шестой*— (adj.) sixth

шесть *шесть*— (num., gen. шести) six

шестьдесят *шестьдесят* — (num., gen. шестидесяти) sixty

шестьсот *шестьсот*— (num., gen. шестисот) six hundred

шинкарь *шинкарь*— (masc. noun) innkeeper

шурин *шурин* — (masc. noun) brother-in-law (wife's brother)

юг *юг*— (masc. noun) south

южный *южный*— (adj.) southern

этому *этому*→ этот

этот *этот*— (pron.) this

я *я* — (pers. pron.) I; меня — me; мной — [by] me
явился *явился* — (v., from явиться) he appeared

январь *январь* — (masc. noun, gen. января) January

Selected Personal Names

Russian personal names are something of a problem. Russia has long controlled or included so many different regions and ethnic groups that one finds Russified versions of names from languages as varied as Estonian, Georgian, and Mongolian; such names have no equivalents in English. European Russia harkens back to the same basic cultural sources as western countries, but more from the Greek and Byzantine traditions than Latin; so again, many of the names simply have no English equivalents. Trying to read Russian novels will demonstrate the pointlessness of equating most Russian names with anything familiar to Americans.

Some first names are roughly equivalent to ones used in Europe, and the most common of them are listed below with those equivalents. In general, however, the best bet with Russian names is to sound them out — in this regard the Cyrillic alphabet is a pretty reliable phonetic guide to pronunciation — and accept them as they are. The main instance where seeking equivalents is appropriate would be with natives of regions such as Poland or Lithuania, when someone named *Stanisław* might appear in Russian-language documents as Станислав. Otherwise, let Аркадий be Arkady, let Глеб be Gleb, and let Фёдор be Fyodor, not "Theodore."

Аврам *Аврам* — Avram (Abraham)
Александр *Александр* — Aleksander (Alexander)
Анатолий *Анатолий* — Anatoly
Андрей *Андрей* — Andrej (Andrew)
Артур *Артур* — Arthur
Борис *Борис* — Boris
Василий *Василий* — Vasiliy (Basil)
Вероника *Вероника* — Veronika (Veronica)
Виктор *Виктор* — Viktor (Victor)
Виталий *Виталий* — Vitaly
Вильгельм *Вильгельм* — Vilgelm (William)
Владимир *Владимир* — Vladimir
Дмитрий *Дмитрий* — Dmitri
Генрих *Генрих* — Genrikh (Henry)
Георг *Георг* — Georg (George)
Герман *Герман* — German (Herman)
Даниил *Даниил* — Daniil (Daniel)
Давид *Давид* — David
Екатерина *Екатерина* — Yekaterina (Catherine)
Елена *Елена* — Yelena (Helen)
Елизавета *Елизавета* — Yelizaveta (Elizabeth)
Евгений *Евгений* — Yevgeniy (Eugene)
Иван *Иван* — Ivan (John)

Иисус *Иисус* — Iisus (Joshua)
Иосиф *Иосиф* — Iosif (Joseph)
Ицаак *Ицаак* — Itsaak (Isaac)
Карл *Карл* — Karl (Charles)
Кирилл *Кирилл* — Kirill (Cyril)
Лаврентий *Лаврентий* — Lavrenty (Lawrence)
Лев *Лев* — Lev (Leo)
Марк *Марк* — Mark
Матфей *Матфей* — Matfey (Matthew)
Михаил *Михаил* — Mikhail (Michael)
Моисей *Моисей* — Moisey (Moses)
Николай *Николай* — Nikolay (Nicholas)
Павел *Павел* — Pavel (Paul)
Пётр *Пётр* — Pyotr (Peter)
Самуил *Самуил* — Samuil (Samuel)
Сергей *Сергей* — Sergey (Serge)
Фёдор *Фёдор* — Fyodor (Theodore)
Фелиция *Фелиция* — Felitsiya (Felicia)
Фридрих *Фридрих* — Fridrikh (Frederick)
Христофор *Христофор* — Khristofor (Christopher)
Эдуард *Эдуард* — Eduard (Edward)
Юрий *Юрий* — Yuri

Other Languages:

Hungarian and Lithuanian

The three language families seen so far — the Germanic, Romance, and Slavic — include the best-known European languages, the ones spoken by the greatest number of people; but they by no means exhaust the linguistic diversity of Europe. There are a number of other languages, perhaps not so well known to Americans but still spoken by millions, including immigrants to the United States. Prominent among these are Hungarian (called "Magyar" by native speakers) and Lithuanian.

Both Hungarian and Lithuanian are members of language families in their own right, as is discussed in their respective sections. Readers interested in linguistics should know that Lithuanian belongs to the Balto-Slavic branch of the Indo-European family, whereas Hungarian is a member of the Finno-Ugrian family, which is not even related to the Indo-European.

The map below, like the other maps in this book, is meant only to provide a general notion of the "homelands" where these languages originated. Lithuanian has, of course, long been the primary language in the country of Lithuania, but one should note that many ethnic Poles and Russians live in Lithuania and so Polish and Russian are widely spoken there, as well.

As regards Hungarian, the map of Europe has been shifted here and there so much over the centuries that it is something of an oversimplification to point to the country known as Hungary and say "Here is where Magyar is spoken." Other languages are heard in Hungary, and Hungarian is often heard in parts of neighboring countries. But the country of Hungary does comprise the core region where Magyar predominates.

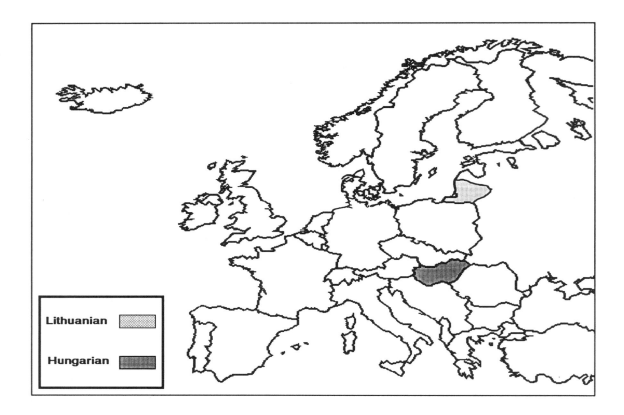

Lithuanian

Hungarian

Magyar

The Hungarian Alphabet

Printed	Cursive	Printed	Cursive	Printed	Cursive
A, a	$\mathcal{A}$, a				
Á, á	$\mathcal{A}$, á				
B, b	$\mathcal{B}$, b	R, r	$\mathcal{R}$, r	Ú, ú	$\mathcal{U}$, ú
C, c	$\mathcal{C}$, c	S, s	$\mathcal{S}$, s	Ü, ü	$\mathcal{U}$, ü
Cs, cs	$\mathcal{C}$s, cs	Sz, sz	$\mathcal{S}$z, sz	Ű, ű	$\mathcal{U}$, ű
D, d	$\mathcal{D}$, d	T, t	$\mathcal{T}$, t	V, v	$\mathcal{V}$, v
E, e	$\mathcal{E}$, e	Ty, ty	$\mathcal{T}$y, ty	Z, z	$\mathcal{Z}$, z
É, é	$\mathcal{E}$, é	U, u	$\mathcal{U}$, u	Zs, zs	$\mathcal{Z}$s, zs
F, f	$\mathcal{F}$, f				
G, g	$\mathcal{G}$, g				
Gy, gy	$\mathcal{G}$y, gy				
H, h	$\mathcal{H}$, h				
I, i	$\mathcal{I}$, i				
Í, í	$\mathcal{I}$, í				
J, j	$\mathcal{J}$, j				
K, k	$\mathcal{K}$, k				
L, l	$\mathcal{L}$, l				
Ly, ly	$\mathcal{L}$y, ly				
M, m	$\mathcal{M}$, m				
N, n	$\mathcal{N}$, n				
O, o	$\mathcal{O}$, o				
Ó, ó	$\mathcal{O}$, ó				
Ö, ö	$\mathcal{O}$, ö				
Ő, ő	$\mathcal{O}$, ő				
P, p	$\mathcal{P}$, p				

The Hungarian language uses the Roman alphabet, but with a number of modifications. Specifically, it features the consonant combinations *cs, gy, ly, ny, sz, ty,* and *zs* (*cz* is seen only in names and has become otherwise obsolete) and the short/long vowel pairs *a/á, e/é, i/í, o/ó, ö/ő u/ú,* and *ü/ű.* It also lacks the letters *q, w,* and *x,* except in foreign words. The consonant and vowel combinations may look intimidating, but in fact most of the sounds represented by these letters have approximate equivalents in English. Alphabetical order in Hungarian dictionaries and lists of names can present a few difficulties; each short/long pair is treated as the same vowel for listing purposes, but *ö/ő* follows *o/ó* and *ü/ű* follows *u/ú,* so that *több* follows *továbadd* and *tüdő* follows *túró.* The sensible rule of thumb is always to check above and below the place in a list where one would expect to see a word according to English alphabetical order.

Hungarian comes from an entirely different family from the Indo-European languages (Italian, German, Russian, and so on), but its vowel sounds are like those of most European languages. The *á* sounds like the *a* in "car," the *é* like the *a* in "gate," the *í* like the *i* in "machine," the *ó* like that in "tore," and the *ú* like the *oo* in "moon." The short sounds *a, e, i, o, u* are just that, shorter versions of the long vowels; the *a* and *o* are most unlike their English counterparts, more like the sounds in "hut" and "horn" respectively. The *ö/ő* pair is a short/long version of the sound in German "Goethe," almost like saying "fir" but not quite pronouncing the *-r*. The *ü/ű* pair is a short/long version of the German *ü* or French *u,* somewhat like saying "ee" with rounded lips. As in German, the *ö/ő* and *ü/ű* have sometimes been spelled *oe* and *ue,* a fact that may be significant in searching old records for specific words or names.

The pronunciation of most Hungarian consonants is comparable to that of their English counterparts, but a few require attention. The *c* is pronounced like *ts* as in "gets," the *g* is always hard as in "go," and a *j* sounds like English *y* as in "yes." The consonant pairs are initially tricky; *cs* is pronounced like English *ch* in "cheek," *ly* is pronounced like *y* in "yes," *sz* is pronounced like *s* in English "sing" (but Hungarian *s* is pronounced like English *sh* in "short": "Budapest" is pronounced "Budapesht"), and *zs* is pronounced like the *s* in "pleasure." The *gy, ny,* and *ty* pairs are palatized sounds, like a combination of *d + y, n + y,* and *t + y* respectively; something similar is heard in "would you," "can you," and "let you" in British or very precise American pronounciation.

Hungarian words are always stressed on the first syllable, and the stress has no effect on the quality or length of vowels.

The Hungarian Language

Hungarian, also known as "Magyar," is unlike the language spoken in Hungary's immediate geographical neighbors, in that it does not belong to the Indo-European family of languages. Hungarian is classified as a member of the Finno-Ugrian language family, other members of which are Turkish, Finnish, and Estonian. Hungarian is spoken not only in Hungary but in several pockets of settlements in neighboring nations — Romania, Czechoslovakia, Yugoslavia — as well as in emigré communities in North and South America and Australia.

Hungarian has no declensional system and is remarkably phonetic; its complex set of grammatical relationships are expressed by means of numerous agglutinative suffixes, e. g., for *ablak* (window):

ablaktől — "from the window"   *ablakok* — "windows"
ablakon — "on the window"   *ablakomba* — "into my window"

Thus the challenge to the researcher is to determine the root and the meanings of the suffixes.

Since it is not practical to try to give a grammatical analysis of passages in Hungarian — especially in this limited space — the two sample documents reproduced here are not closely analyzed. Instead, key words and phrases are identified and the gist of the documents given. This should provide researchers with examples that will help them analyze their own records, and it is realistic to expect that many of expressions shown here will be the key words and phrases researchers need to decipher the documents they have.

Document #1: A Hungarian Birth Certificate

Abaúj-Torna Varmegye/(város) — "county/(town) of Abaúj-Torna"
Születési anyakönyvi kivonat — "Certificate of Birth"
Somodiban 1897 (ezer *nyolczszáz kilenczven hetedik évi Julius* hó *20 huszadik*) napján — "In Somodi, the
   year 1897 (one thousand eight hundred ninety-seven), month of July, the 20th day." In modern spelling
   kilenczven has dropped the -z- *(kilencven)* and *nyolcz* is *nyolc*.

Megjelent az alulirott anyakönyvvezető — előtt *Bablonka Ferdinánd,* akinek állása (foglalkozása): *gépész
kovács,* lakóhelye: *Somodi,* s aki*t* személy*esen ismerete,* és bejelentette a következő születést:
   megjelent — "appeared"
   anyakönyvvezető előtt — "before *(előtt)* the Director of the Register of Births"
   foglalkozás — "profession"
   lakóhelye — place of residence
   személyesen ismerete — "personally acquainted, known"
   bejelentette a következő születést — "announced the following birth" (*születés* — "birth")
   Summary — This section tells us that Ferdinánd Bablonka, a blacksmith residing in Somodi, appeared before
the undersigned Director of the Registrar of Births, with whom he is personally acquainted, and announced the
following birth...

A törvényes atya családi és utóneve: *Bablonka Ferdinánd,* vallása: *római katholikus,* állása (foglalkozása):
gépész kovács, lakóhelye: *Somodi,* születéshelye: *Somodi,* életkora: *32 (harminczkét)* éves, ...
   a törvényes atya — "the legal father"
   családi és utóneve — "surname and first name"
   vallása: római katholikus — "religion: Roman Catholic." Other possibilities: *görög katholikus,* Greek
      Catholic; *görög keleti,* Greek Orthodox; *református,* Reformed; *izraelita,* Jewish; *evangélikus,*
      Evangelical Lutheran.
   lakóhelye: Somodi — "place of residence: Somodi"
   születéshelye: Somodi — "place of birth: Somodi"
   életkora: 32 (harminczkét) éves — "age: 32 (thirty-two) years"
   Summary — This section gives the father's name, occupation, place of birth and residence, and age:
Ferdinánd Bablonka, Roman Catholic, a blacksmith, born and residing in Somodi, age 32.

Abauj Torna ~~város~~ varmegye

Születési anyakönyvi kivonat.

57 szám.

Kelt: *Jomodiban*

1897 (*ezer nyolczszáz kilenczvenhetedik*) évi

Julius hó *20* (*huszadik*) napján.

Megjelent az alulírott anyakönyvvezető _____ előtt

Bablonka Ferdinánd,

akinek állása (foglalkozása): *gépész kovács*,

lakóhelye: *Jomodi*

s aki *A*

személy *esen ismerte*,

és bejelentette a következő születést:

A törvényes atya

családi és utóneve: *Bablonka Ferdinánd*

vallása: *római katholikus*

állása (foglalkozása): *gépész kovács*

lakóhelye: *Jomodi*

születéshelye: *Jomodi*

életkora: *32* (*Harminczkét*) éves,

Az anya

családi és utóneve: *Lébray Katalin*

vallása: *római katholikus*

állása (foglalkozása): *háztartás*

lakóhelye: *Jomodi*

születéshelye: *Jomodi*

életkora: *30* (*harmincz*) éves,

- 225 -

N. r.-sz. Várnav L., Szegea. 12. számu minta az A. U. 115. §-ához.

helye: *Somodi*

A születés

ideje: 1 *897* (ezer *nyolczszáz kilenczven hetedik*

évi *Julius* hó *14* (*tizennegyedik*)

napjának dél *előtt* 3 (*harmadik*) órája.

A gyermek

neme: *fiu* ; vallása: *római katholikus*

utóneve: *János*

Mégjegyzés:

Felolvastatván

helybenhagyatott és *aláíratott*

Schuster Kálmán s.k.
anyakönyvvezető.

Bablonka Ferdinánd s. k.
bejelentő.

Az anya családi és utóneve: *Létray Katalin,* vallása: *római katholikus,* állása (foglalkozása): *háztartás,* lakóhelye: *Somodi* , születéshelye: *Somodi,* életkora: *30 (harmincz)* éves, ...

az anya — "the mother"

ház — "house" (*házastárs* is "spouse")

harmincz — "thirty" (modern standard spelling *harminc*)

Summary — This section gives the same data for the mother: Katalin Létray, Roman Catholic, a housewife, born and residing in Somodi, age 30.

A születés helye: *Somodi,* ideje *1897* (ezer *nyolczszáz kilenczven hetedik* évi *Julius* hó *14 tizennegyedik* napjának dél *előtt* 3 *(harmadik)* órája. **A gyermek** neme: *fiu;* vallása: *római kathólikus,* utóneve: *János.* Mégjegyzés: —. Felolvastatván — helybenhagyatott és *aláíralott.*

ideje — "date (*születési ideje* — "date of birth")

nap — "day"

délelőtt 3 (harmadik) órája — "at 3 a.m." (*óra,* "hour"; *délelőtt,* "in the morning, before noon")

gyermek — "child"

neme: fiu — "sex: boy" (*lány* — "girl")

mégjegyzés — "observations, remarks"

Summary — János Bablonka was born in Somodi on July 14, 1897, at 3 a.m. Sex: male, religion: Roman Catholic. [The remainder is legalese attesting this copy's conformity to the original.]

Document #2: A Hungarian Passport

(12 oldalt tartalmaz. — Contlent 12 pages.)

A kláilltó hatóság szdma: *11084*
Numero de l'autorité :

Ő FELSÉGE
· ELSŐ FERENCZ JÓZSEF
AUSZTRIAI CSÁSZÁR, CSEHORSZÁG KIRÁLYA STB. STB.
· ÉS
· MAGYARORSZÁG APOSTOLI KIRÁLYA NEVÉBEN.

AU NOM DE SA MAJESTÉ
· FRANÇOIS JOSEPH I-ER
EMPEREUR D'AUTRICHE, ROI DE BOHÈME ETC. ETC.
· ET
· ROI APOSTOLIQUE DE HONGRIE.

ÚTLEVÉL. — PASSEPORT.

Szám:
Nr. : *A. 978.378*

Körtvélyfai Istvánné
szül. Kender Margit

magyar állampolgár részére.

Pour le sujet hongrois :

Mme Etienne Körtvélyfai
née Marguerite Kender

Érvényes: *egy*
Valable pour: *Jun*   évre.
                        an.

Az utazó állása vagy foglalkozdsa *nap —*

Számosnő

Profession   *journalière*

Lakhelye   *Hidasnémeti*

Abaujtorna vármegye

Domicile   *Hidasnémeti*

comitate Abaujtorna

Kora ⎱
Áge ⎰   *30 éves*
           ans

Saját aldirdsa :
Signature du titulaire :

Körtvélyfaju Istvánné

---

oldal — "page"
szám — "number"
Első Ferencz József — Francis Joseph I (*első* — "first")
ausztriai császár — "Emperor of Austria"
csehország királya — "King (*király*) of Bohemia" ("Czechoslovakia" is *Csehszlovákia*, but this document dates from when Bohemia was part of the Austro-Hungarian Empire and there was no Czechoslovakia)
stb. — "and so on, etc."
magyarország — "Hungary"
nevében — "in the name of"
útlevél — "passport"
szül — "née"
állampolgár — "citizen"

érvényes — "valid"
állása vagy foglalkozása — "job or profession"
napszámosnő — "day-laborer"
Lakhelye: *Hidasnémeti, Abaujtorna vármegye*— "Residence: Hidasnémeti, Abaúj-Torna county"
Kora: 30 éves— "Age: 30 years."
Saját aláirása — "Signature of the bearer"

Page one of this passport reveals interesting data on the recording of Hungarian surnames. A married woman was most frequently known by using her husband's first name with the particle *-ne*, meaning "wife of," attached to it. Here note *Istvánne* (Mrs. István [Stephen]). The maiden name is indicated by *szül*, "née," followed by the woman's given and maiden surname — in this case, Margit Kender.

Page 3 (passport, handwritten)

Az állam vagy világrész, hova az utazás terveztetik

Északamerikai Egyesült Államok

Voyageant en (allant à) *Etats-Unis de l'Amérique du Nord*

Mely kikötőn át történik az utazás

Lieu d'embarquement

Az utazás czélja *kivándorlás*

But du voyage *émigration*

Page 4 (passport, handwritten)

Az utazó személy leírása. — Signalement.

Termete — Taille *alacsony - petite*

Arcza — Visage *kerek - rond*

Haja — Cheveux *szőke - blonds*

Szakálla — Barbe

Bajusza — Moustache

Szeme — Yeux *kék - bleus*

Szája — Bouche *rendes - régulière*

Orra — Nez

Különös ismertető jelei *Passport dated Aug 4-1915 Kathes Margit Körtvélyfai age 30 + children Elizabeth Körtvélyfai 14 y Stephen 9 y Margit 6 y Anna 3 y born Hidasnémeti Hungary*

Signes particuliers

Page 3

Az állam vagy világrész — "the country or part of the world"

hova — "where"

utazás — "journey, trip"

Északamerikai Egyesült Államok — "North America, United States"

mely kikötön — "which port"

az utazás czélja: kivándorlás — "purpose of journey: emigration"

Page 4

leirás — "description"; az utazó személy leirása — "description of the person traveling"

termete: alacsony — "stature: short"

arcza: kerek — "face: round" (in modern spelling the root word for "face" is arc)

haja: szőke — "hair: blond"

szakálla: -- — "beard: --"

bajusza: -- — "moustache: --"

szeme: kék — "eyes: blue"

szája: rendes — "mouth: regular"

orra: rendes — "nose: regular"

különös ismertető jelei — "distinguishing marks"

Summary — The passport is issued to Mrs. István Kortvélyfai, née Margit Kender, a Hungarian citizen, for the period of one year. She is a laborer, age 30, a resident of Hidasnémeti, county of Abaúj-Torna. She is journeying to the U.S.A. for the purpose of emigration. She is short in stature with a round face, blond hair, and blue eyes, with no distinguishing marks.

Selected Vocabulary Terms

Compiling a brief but useful list of Hungarian terms is a difficult task. Hungarian is a complex language; furthermore, its grammatical complexities work in a way totally alien to the linguistic understanding of those who speak English or any other Indo-European language. The only alternative to lengthy discussions of the different forms and suffixes words can take is to give the basic forms of a number of words most likely to appear in documents; you may not find in this list the exact form you are looking for, but with the help of this list you should be able to get the gist of a given document. If this list and study of the sample documents analyzed above cannot enable you to make sense of a record or certificate, the record's level of linguistic complexity probably demands the expertise of a competent translator or a well-educated native-speaker.

Words are identified by part of speech — noun, verb, etc. — or synonym when necessary to avoid ambiguity; thus *helyes* is identified as "(adj.) correct, right" to make clear that it is not the verb "to correct," and *jobb* is specified as "right (opposite of left)" so that it is clear *jobb* does not mean "right" in the sense of "correct." Not specified, but important to remember, is Hungarian's preference for postposition, i. e., *előtt* meaning "before" usually comes after, not before, a noun; "before noon" is *délelőtt*, literally "noon-before." As a rule, when you see a word translated as a preposition in English, expect the preposition's object to precede it, not follow it, in Hungarian.

a, az — the
aki, akit — who, whom
alacsony — short
aláirás — signature
alatt — during, under
áll — chin
állam — country, state; *Egyesült Államok* — United States
állampolgár — citizen
állandó lakhely (lakcím) — permanent residence
állás — job
állomás — station
alulirott — undersigned
amely — which
ami — that
angol — English, Englishman
anya — mother
anyakönyv — register
anyakönyvvezető — civil registrar
anyós — mother-in-law
apa — father
após — father-in-law
április — April
ár — price
arc — face
asszony — woman
asztalos — carpenter
atya — father
augusztus — August
-ba, -be — into
bajusz — moustache
baleset — accident
balra — left (opposite of right)
-ban, -ben — in

barna — brown
Bécs — Vienna
belül — inside, within
belváros — downtown
beszélni — to speak
beteg — ill
betegség — disease
-ből, -ből — out of
borbély — barber
bűn — crime
bűnöző — criminal
cél — purpose
cím — address
címer — coat of arms
cipő — shoe
család — family; *családnev* — family name
családi — marital, family; *családnév* — surname
családi állapota — marital status
császár — emperor
csecsemő — infant
Csehország — Bohemia
Csehszlovákia — Czechoslovakia
csónak — boat
csütörtök — Tuesday
czél → *cél*
de. — (abbreviation) a.m.
december — December
dél — noon; *délben* — at noon
dél — south; *déli* — southern
délelőtt — in the morning, before noon
délután — afternoon
diák — student

Duna — Danube
egészséges — healthy
egy — one
egyedül — alone
egyén(i) — individual
Egyesült Államok — United States
egyetem — university
egyház — church (organization)
együtt — together
éjfél — midnight; *éjfélkor* — at midnight
éjszaka — (at) night
élet — life
életkor — age
előtt — before, in front of
első — first
elvált — divorced
ember — man, person; *emberek* — people
én — I
engedély — permission
Erdély — Transylvania
érkezés — arrival
érvényes — valid
és — and
esküvő — wedding
este — evening
észak — north; *Észak-Amerika* — North America
év — year; *évszázad* — century
evangélikus — Evangelical Lutheran
ez a — this
ezelőtt — ago
ezer — thousand
falu — village

február — February
fehér — white
fej — head
fekete — black
felelet — answer
feleség — wife
felett — over, above
fénykép — photo
férfi — male
férj — husband
férjes, férjezett — married
festő — painter
fia — son
fiatal — young
fiú — boy
fivér — brother
fog — tooth
foglalkozás — profession
folyó — river
fontos — important
fordítás — translation
Földközi-tenger — Mediterranean Sea
főváros — capital (city)
Franciaország — France
fül — ear
gépészkovács — blacksmith
gesztenye — chestnut
görög — Greek; Görögország — Greece
görög katholikus — Greek Catholic
görög keleti — Greek Orthodox
gyár — factory
gyermek — child
ha — if
háború — war
hadsereg — army
haj — hair
hajadon — single (unmarried)
hajó — ship
halál — death
halott — dead
harmadik — third
harminc[z] — thirty
harminc[z]két — thirty-two
három — three
hat — six
határ — border
hatodik — sixth
hatvan — sixty
ház — house
haza — native country
házasság — marriage
házastárs — spouse
háztartás — housewife

hegy — mountain
hely — place
helyes — (adj.) correct, right
helyett — instead of
hentes — butcher
hét — seven; week
hetedik — seventh
hétfő — Monday
hetven — seventy
hiba — mistake
hivatal — office
hol — where?
holmi — belongings
holnap — tomorrow
homlok — forehead
hova, hová — where
hölgy — lady
hónap — month
húsz — twenty
húszadik — twentieth
ide — here
ideje — date; születési ideje — date of birth
idő — time
-ig — till, e. g., 8 óraig — till 8 o'clock
igaz — true; igazság — truth
igazolás — certificate
igen — yes
ikrek — twins
indulás — departure
irat — document
író — writer
is — too, also
iskola — school
Isten — God
itt — here
izraelita — Jewish
január — January
jegy — ticket
jelenlét — presence; jelenlétemben — in my presence
jó — good
jobb — better; right (opposite of left)
jog — law
jövő — next; a jövő héten — next week; jövőre — next year
július — July
június — June
katona — soldier
kedd — Tuesday
kék — blue
kelet — east; keleti — eastern
kérdés — question

kerek — round
kérés — request
kereskedő — merchant
keresztelő — baptism
keresztény — Christian
keresztnév — Christian name
kerület — town district
kétszer — twice
két[tő] — two
kéz — hand
kezdet — beginning
ki — who?
kicsi — little
kié — whose?
kikötö — port
kilenc — nine
kilencedik — ninth
kilenc[z]ven — ninety
kinek — to whom?
király — king; királyi — royal
kisbaba — baby
kit — whom?
kopasz — bald
-kor — at (at a particular time)
kor — age
kórház — hospital
kormány — government
könyv — book
következő — following, next
közel(i) — near
közep — middle, center
középiskola — secondary school
között — a...között — between
köztársaság — republic
külföldön, külföldre — abroad
különös — strange, special
lakóhelye — place of residence
lakosság — population
lány — girl
lánya — daughter
lánykori név — maiden name
leány — daughter
legjobb — best
leirás — description
lelkipásztor — pastor
Lengyel — Pole; Lengyelország — Poland
lenn, lent — below
levél — letter
levéltár — archive
ma — today; ma este — tonight
magas — high
magyar — Hungarian
Magyarország — Hungary
május — May
március — March

más — other
második — second
másolat — (n.) copy
matróz — sailor
megjelent — appeared
mégjegyzés — observations, remarks
megye — county
mely — which
melyik — which?
menyasszony — bride, fiancée
menye — daughter-in-law
méret — size
mérnök — engineer
mert — because
mészáros — butcher
mi — we; mi(csoda)? — what?
miatt — because of
miért — why?
mikor — when?
minden — all
mindig — always
minket — us
mivel — (conj.) since
most — now
munka — work; munkás — worker
nagy — big
nagybácsi — uncle
nagynéni — aunt
nagyon — very
nagyszülők — grandparents
nap — day
napszámosnő — day-laborer
néger — black
négy — four
negyedik — fourth
negyven — forty
nélkül — without
nem — no, not; (noun) sex
német — German; Nemetország — Germany
nemzet — nation; nemzeti — national
név — name
november — November
nő(stény) — female, woman
nős — married
nőtlen — single (unmarried)
nővér — sister
nulla — zero
nyelv — language
nyilatkozat — statement
nyilvános — (adj.) public
nyolc[z] — eight
nyolcadik — eighth

nyolc[z]száz — eight hundred
nyolc[z]van — eighty
nyugat — west; nyugati — western
oda — there
okmány — document
oktatás — education
október — October
olasz — Italian; Olaszország — Italy
oldal — page
-on — on, e. g. szombaton, on Saturday
óra — hour, o'clock; njolc órakor — at eight o'clock
orosz — Russian
orr — nose
ország — country
osztrák — Austrian
ott — there
otthon — home
ovális — oval
ő — he, she
ők — they
öreg — old
ősz — grey (e. g., hair)
összeg — amount
öt — five
ötödik — fifth
ötven — fifty
övé — hers
pap — priest
pár — pair, couple
paraszt — peasant
pecsét — stamp, seal
pék — baker
péntek — Friday
pénz — money
piros — red
poggyász — baggage
polgár — citizen
református — Reformed (religion)
reggel — morning
rendes — regular
rendör — policeman
rész — part
rokonok — relatives
római katolikus — Roman Catholic
rossz — wrong, bad
saját — [one's] own
semmi — nothing
sógor — brother-in-law
sógornő — sister-in-law
soha — never

sok — many
sötét — dark
stb. — and so on, etc.
súly — weight
süket — deaf
Svájc — Switzerland
szabó — tailor
száj — mouth
szakács — (n.) cook
szakáll — beard
szám — number
száz — hundred
század — century
szem — eye
személy — person; személyes — personal
személyazonossági — identity card
személyesen ismerete — personally acquainted, known
szeptember — September
szerda — Wednesday
sziget — island
szín — color
szív — heart; szívroham — heart attack
szó — word
szóbeli — verbal
szobrász — sculptor
szombat — Saturday
szomszéd — neighbor
szótár — dictionary
szőke — blond
szül — nee, born
születés — birth
születéshelye — birthplace
szülők — parents
szürke — grey
tag — member
tanár — teacher
távolság — distance
te, ti — you
téged — you
tegnap — yesterday
temetés — burial
temető — cemetery
templom — church (building)
tenger — sea
termete — stature, height
terület — territory
test — body
testvér — brother
téves — wrong
tilos — forbidden
titeket — you
tíz — ten

tizedik — tenth
tizenegy — eleven
tizenhárom — thirteen
tizenhat — sixteen
tizenhét — seventeen
tizenkettő — twelve
tizenkilenc — nineteen
tizennégy — fourteen
tizennegyedik — fourteenth
tizennyolc — eighteen
tizenöt — fifteen
tó — lake
tolmács — interpreter
-től — from
török — Turkish
törvényes — legal
tulajdonos — owner
túra — trip
új — new
újra — again
újság — newspaper

unoka — grandchild
unokafivér — cousin
unokanővér — niece
út — road
után — after
utas — passenger
utazás — journey, trip
utca — street
úticél — destination
útlevél — passport
utóneve — first name
ügyvéd — lawyer
vadasz — hunter
vagy — or
vagyok — I am
vagyunk — we are
vak — blind
-val, -vel — with
valahol — somewhere
valaki — somebody
valami — something

válasz — answer
vallás — religion
vám — duty, customs
vámvizsgálat — customs-control
varmegye — county
város — town, city
városháza — town hall
vasárnap — Sunday
végösszeg — sum, total
vezetéknév — surname
vonat — (noun) train
vőlegény — bridegroom
völgy — valley
zenész — musician
zöld — green
zsidő — Jewish
zsinagóga — synagogue

Personal Names

Popular Hungarian personal names differ in origin. A number of names come from other languages (especially Latin, Hebrew, and Greek), largely through the influence of the Christian church and the names of saints; as is evident from the list, these names have generally been modified to sound a bit more "Hungarian" — Steven → István, Elizabeth → Erzsébet — but they are usually not too hard to recognize. Many other names are of Hungarian origin, however, and have no equivalent in English. They are often of ancient significance, e. g., Árpád is the 9th-century Magyar chieftain, conqueror, and national hero regarded as the founder of Hungary. A number of those names are also listed below, and those with no real equivalent in English are marked with asterisks.

Ágota — Agatha
Ákos — Ákos*
Álmos — Álmos*
Amalia — Amalia
Anikó — Anikó*
András — Andrew
Aranka — Aranka*
Árpád — Árpad*
Bálint — Valentine
Béla — Bela*
Botond — Botond*
Bulcsú — Bulczú*
Csaba — Csaba*
Csilla — Csilla*
Domokos/Domonkos — Dominic
Elemér — Elemér*
Elöd — Elöd*
Emese — Emese*

Emma — Emma, Irma
Erzsébet — Elizabeth
Eva — Eve
Farkas — Farkas*
Ferenc[z] — Francis
Fülöp — Philip
Gábor — Gabriel
Géza — Geza*
György — George
Gyula — Julius
Ilona — Helen
Imre — Emery
István — Stephen
Janka — Janka*
János — John
Jénő — Jénő*
Jolán — Yolanda
József — Joseph
Kamilla — Camilla

Károly — Charles, Carl
Kinga — Kinga*
László — Ladislaus
Lajos — Louis
Lehel — Lehel*
Lukács — Luke
Magda — Magda
Mária — Mary
Mihály — Michael
Miklós — Nicholas
Pál — Paul
Réka — Réka*
Rózália — Rozalia
Rózsa — Rose
Sándor — Alexander
Vencel — Wenceslaus
Zoltán — Zoltan*
Zsolt — Zsolt*
Zsuzsanna — Susan

Lietuviškas

The Lithuanian Alphabet

Printed	Cursive
A, a	A, a
Ą, ą	A, ą
B, b	B, b
C, c	C, c
Č, č	Č, č
D, d	D, d
E, e	E, e
Ę, ę	Ę, ę
Ė, ė	Ė, ė
F, f	F, f
G, g	G, g
H, h	H, h
CH, ch	CH, ch
I, i	I, i
Į, į	Į, į
Y, y	Y, y
J, j	J, j
K, k	K, k
L, l	L, l
M, m	M, m
N, n	N, n
O, o	O, o
P, p	P, p
R, r	R, r
S, s	S, s
Š, š	Š, š

Printed	Cursive	Printed	Cursive
T, t	T, t	V, v	V, v
U, u	U, u	Z, z	Z, z
Ų, ų	Ų, ų	Ž, ž	Ž, ž
Ū, ū	Ū, ū		

Lithuanian uses the Roman alphabet, with the omission of the letters *q, x,* and *w,* which appear only in words of foreign origin, and with several additional letters formed by adding diacritical marks to standard Roman letters. There are three of these modified consonants, *č, š,* and *ž,* and six special vowels, *ą, ę, ė, į, ų,* and *ū.*

Lithuanian vowels and diphthongs are especially complicated and are distinguished by length, i. e., there are short and long versions. It is impossible to portray the complexity of these sounds adequately in this space, as there are some eleven basic vowel sounds and it is hard enough for a person unused to hearing spoken Lithuanian to distinguish them even when hearing them, let alone reading about them. As a point of departure one should realize that the basic vowels are closer to the vowels of most European languages than to those of American English; in other words, *a* is more like the sound in "father" than the *a* in "hate" or "cat"; *e* is more like the *a* sound in "fable" than the *e* in "keep,"; *i* is more like the *i* in "machine" than in "high"; and *u* is more like the *oo* in "coop" than the *u* in "cut." Lithuanian vowels are pure, that is, they do not slide off into diphthongs; compare the way the long *e* in English "tee" glides into a *y* at the end — Lithuanian holds single vowel sounds unless one is specifically dealing with a diphthong (among which are *ai, au, ei, ie,* and *uo*).

Consonants are somewhat less intimidating, but they, too, are characterized by a rather high degree of complexity. It is essential to realize that all consonants, other than the *j* (sounded like the *y* in English "yacht") have both palatalized and non-palatalized versions, that is, versions in which the palate is used in articulating the sound (compare the *n* sounds in "not" and "onion" — the latter is palatalized). Consonants are palatalized before front vowels *(i, į, y, e, ę, ė),* and before vowels spelling conventions call for indicating the palatalization by inserting an *-i-.*

Some of the consonants that require special attention from English-speakers are:

š, pronounced like *sh* in English "shirt"
ž, pronounced like *s* in English "measure"
c, pronounced like *ts* in English "cats"
č, pronounced like *ch* in English "church"
j, pronounced like *y* in English "yellow"
ch and *h,* found mainly in words of foreign origin, are pronounced in a manner resembling either English *h* or the *ch* sound in German "Bach."

Researchers studying Lithuanian sources should pay special attention to the aforementioned sounds as they are most prone to Anglicization, particularly in surnames or place names, e. g., *Arbačauskas* vs. *Arbachauskas* or *Česnavičius* vs. *Chesnavichius.* The spelling of *š* as *sh,* of *č* as *ch,* and of *ž* as *zh* can occur frequently and perplex the unwary.

The Lithuanian Language

The Lithuanian language, spoken in Lithuania and by emigrés in Canada, the United States, and other nations where Lithuanians have settled, is a member of the Baltic branch of the Indo-European family of languages. Said to be one of the oldest modern Indo-European languages, it is the frequent object of study of scholars engaged in comparative Indo-European linguistics; like Sanskrit, it provides a view of the Indo-European family at a very early stage of its development, but Lithuanian is a living, modern language spoken every day. Other members of the Baltic language sub-group include Latvian and the now extinct Old Prussian.

Lithuanian inflection of nouns, adjectives, and pronouns is complicated, with a wide range of grammatical endings. The same cautions apply when translating Lithuanian documents as do with other highly inflected languages: to arrive at a correct name or geographical designation, the case endings may need to be deleted. It is also well to note that Lithuanian surnames, like their Polish and Russian counterparts, have different endings to distinguish sex and marital status:

male	*married female*	*unmarried female*
Miškinis	Miškienė	Miškinytė
Ruzgys	Ruzgienė	Ruzgytė
Bukauskas	Bukauskienė	Buskauskaitė

Document #1: Lithuanian Baptismal Certificate I

A Lithuanian baptismal certificate is reproduced on the opposite page. Here are the key phrases.

Ištrauka iš — "excerpt from"

gimimo — "birth" (from *gimimas*)

metrikų akto — "registry document"

Garliavos Rym. kat. parapijos — "the Roman Catholic parish (*parapija*) of Garliava"

vardas ir pavardė: Elzbieta Povilaitytė — "name and surname: Elzbieta Povilaitytė." Note that this document gives the expected ending on the surname for an unmarried female, *Povilaitytė*. Compare this to the rendition of the father's surname in the last column, *Povilaitis* — this is the name that would be considered the standard form for purposes of research.

kada gimė (žodžiais): Liepos 4 dieną tūkstantis devyni šimtas septintais metais— "when born (in words [i. e., written out in full]): July 4 day, thousand nine hundred seventh year," i. e., 4 July 1907

kur gimė: Marvodvare— "where born: Marvodvare [?]"

tėvų vardai ir pavardės: Baltrus Povilaitis ir Katarina Adamavičiūtė — "Parents' names and surnames: Baltrus Povilaitis and Katarina Adamavičiūtė."

23 dieną Rugpiučis mėn. 1922 m. — "23rd day of the month of August of the year 1922"

Document #2: Lithuanian Baptismal Certificate II

The second document on the opposite page is also a baptismal certificate. The original was very faded and the reproduction has been enhanced electronically to make it as legible as possible.

Lietuvos Respublika — "The Republic of Lithuania" (the independent country that existed after World War I until the Soviet Union annexed it in 1940).

Alytaus R. K. Bažnyčia — "Alytus Roman Catholic Church"

Metrikos ištrauka iš Alytaus bažnyčios 1884 metų gimusiųjų ir pakrikštytųjų metriku knygų — "Registry excerpt from the Alytus church, year 1884, register of births and baptisms"

Valerija Golokvosčiute gime tūkstantis aštuoni šimtas astuonias dešimtys ketvirtais metais birželio mėn. devintą dieną— "Valerija Golokvosčiute born [the] 1884th year (i. e., 1884), month of June, 9th day."

kaime — "village" (from *kaimas*)

Kūdikio tėvu vardai ir pavardės: Aleksandro Golokvosčiaus ir Alena Monginaitės — "Parents' names and surnames: Aleksander Golokvosčiaus and Alena Monginas."

duktė — "daughter"

Bažnyčios Klebonas — "Pastor (*klebonas*) of the church"

1933 m. Sausio-mėn. 30 dieną —- "year 1933, month January, day 30," i. e., issued 30 January 1933.

Ištrauka iš GIMIMO metrikų akto. N 231. 1907. m.

G-a-r-l-i-a-v-o-s Rym. kat. parapijos. Kauno apsk.

Vardas ir pavardė	Kada gimė (Žodžiais)	Kur gimė	Tėvų vardai ir pavardės
Elzbieta Povilaitytė	liepos 4 dieną tūkstantis devyni šimtai septintais metais	Marvo dvare	Baltrus Povilaitis ir Katarina Adamavičiūtė

Paduotos žinios atatinka originalui.

23 dieną Rugpiūčio mėn. 1927 m.

Garliavos R-K. parapijos Klebonas Kun. P. Raciunas

LIETUVOS RESPUBLIKA

LITUANIA

Kaišedorių Vyskupija

Alytaus R. K. Bažnyčia

Metrikos ištrauka

Iš Alytaus Bažnyčios 1884 metų gimusiųjų ir pakrikštytųjų metriku knygu [illegible] reikalu

Eilės Nr.	Kokiuo vardu kūdikis pakrikštytas? Kada ir kame gimęs?	Kūdikio tėvu vardai ir pavardės ir kur prisirašė?	Pastabos
56.	Valerija Golovočiutė gim. tūkstantis aštuoni šimtai aštuoniasdešimtys ketvirtais metais birželio mėn devintą dieną Bazorų kaime	Aleksandro Golovočiaus ir Alenos Morgun[illegible] drutė	

Šios ištraukos žinių tikrumą liudiju.

Alytus I 1933 m. Sausio mėn. 30 dieną 35 Nr.

Alytaus Kun. K. [illegible] Bažnyčios Klebonas

Document #3: A Lithuanian Passport

On the opposite page is a reproduction of a Lithuanian passport issued in 1921. Here are the most important words and phrases.

Kaunas, 1920 m. Rugpiūčio 12 d. — "Kaunas, August 12, 1920"
skyrius — "department, division"
užsienio passas No. — "foreign passport #"
Pavardė: Vainerienė — "Surname: Vainer[ienė]" Note the children's names and ages entered after the surname ("sons *[sun]* Mošе, age 14; Hiršu, age 11; Calel, age 6; daughter *[dukt.]* Feigle, age 8"). Note also the female suffix *-ienė* on the surname (but she signs her name, under her photograph, in Russian script as *М. Вашнеръ, M. Vainer*).
Vardas: Mina — "First name: Mina."
Pilietybė: Lietuvos — "Citizenship: Lithuanian"
Užsiemimas (profesija, amatas) krautuwininkė — "Profession: shopkeeper"
Gyvenamoji vieta: Kuršenai, Šiaulių ap. — "Residence: Kuršenai, Šiauliai district"
Gimimo diena 1883 amžiaus 37 metų — "Date of birth: 1883; age 37"
Gimimo vieta: Kuršenai — "Place of birth: Kuršenai"
galioja iki 1921 m. Vasario 12 d. — "Valid until February 12, 1921"
parašas — "signature"

Summary — This passport was issued to Mina Vainer, traveling with her children (Mošе, age 14; Hiršu, age 11; Calel, age 6; and Feigle, age 8), a Lithuanian citizen, occupation shopkeeper, residing in Kuršenai, Šiauliai district, born 1883, at Kuršenai, age 37. The passport is valid till February 12, 1921.

Additonal Useful Terms

Months
balandis, balandžio — April
birželis, birželio — June
geguže, gegužės — May
gruodis, grudžio — December
kovas, kovo — March
lapkritis, lapkričio — November
liepa, liepos — July
rugpiūtis, rugpiūčio — August
rugsėjis — September
sausis, sausio — January
spalis, spalio — October
vasaris, vasario — February

Cardinal Numbers
aštuoni — eight
aštuoniasdešimt — eighty
aštuoniolika — eighteen
dešimt — ten
devyni — nine
devyniasdešimt — ninety
devyniolika — nineteen
du — two
dvidešimt — twenty
dvylika — twelve
keturi — four
keturiasdešimt — forty
keturiolika — fourteen
penki — five
penkiasdešimt — fifty

penkiolika — fifteen
septyni — seven
septyniasdešimt — seventy
septyniolika — seventeen
šeši — six
šešiasdešimt — sixty
šešiolika — sixteen
šimtas — one hundred
trylika — thirteen
trys — three
trisdešimt — thirty
tūkstantis — one thousand
vienas — one
vienuolika — eleven

Ordinal Numbers
antras — second
aštuntas — eighth
aštuoniasdešimtas — eightieth
aštuonioliktas — eighteenth
dešimtas — tenth
devintas — ninth
devyniasdešimtas — ninetieth
devynioliktas — nineteenth
dvidešimtas — twentieth
dvyliktas — twelfth
keturiasdešimtas — fortieth
keturioliktas — fourteenth
ketvirtas — fourth
penkiasdešimtas — fiftieth

penkioliktas — fifteenth
penktas — fifth
pirmas — first
septyniasdešimtas — seventieth
septynioliktas — seventeenth
septintas — seventh
šešiasdešimtas — sixtieth
šešioliktas — sixteenth
šeštas — sixth
šimtasis — one hundredth
trečias — third
tryliktas — thirteenth
trisdešimtas — thirtieth
tūkstantas — one thousandth
vienuoliktas — eleventh

General
apylinkė — district
bažnyčia — church
brolis — brother
diena — day
duktė — daughter
gimęs — born
kaimas — village
klebonas — priest, pastor
krautuvininkas — shopkeeper
latvis — Lett, Latvian
lenkas — Pole; *Lenkija* — Poland
lietuvis — Lithuanian
mėnuo — month

Kaunas, 192 0 m. *Rugpjūčio 12* d.

VIDAUS REIKALŲ
MINISTERIJA
PASŲ SKYRIUS

Užsienio pasas No 8326.

Pavardė *Vaineriene* ou *sun: Mozė -14m. Hirša-11, Calet-6m.*

Mina *dukt. Feige -9m.*

Vardas *Mina*

Pilietybė *Lietuvos*

Užsiėmimas (profesija, amatas) *krautuvininkė*

Gyvenamoji vieta *Kuršėnai Šiaulių ap.*

Gimimo diena *1883* amžiaus *37* metų

Gimimo vieta *Kuršėnų*

Šiuo liudijama, kad šio paso savininkas yra fotografijos pažymėtasis asmuo ir kad po fotografija jo paties pasirašyta.

Galioja iki 192 1 m. *Vasario 12* d.

Vidaus Reikalų Ministerija
Pasų Skyrius

Šio paso galiojimo laikas pratęsiamas
1 mėn. laikui, būtent iki 1927 m.
Kovo mėn. *13* d.
Kaunas, 1927 m. *Vasario* mėn. *3* d.

Pasų Skyriaus
Viršininkas

Paso savininko parašas
Unterschrift des Inhabers
La Signature

metai — year
miestas — city
motina — mother
rusas — Russian (man)
rusiškas — Russian
senelė — grandmother
seneliai — grandparents
senelis — grandfather
sesuo — sister
šeima — family
tėvai — parents
tėvas — father
valanda — hour, o'clock
Vokietia — Germany
vokietis — German man
vokiškas — German

Personal Names
Adomas — Adam
Albinas — Albin
Aldona — Aldona
Algirdas — *
Antanas — Anthony
Dominikas — Dominic
Elzbieta — Elizabeth
Emilija — Emilia
Gediminas — *
Jonas — John
Julija — Julia
Juozas — Joseph
Jurgis — George
Katarina — Catherine
Kazimeras — Casimir
Marija — Mary

Ona — Anna
Petras — Peter
Povilas — Paul
Pranas — Francis
Stanislovas — Stanislaus
Vincas — Vincent
*Vytautas** — Vitold, Witold

* Many Lithuanian first names are those of saints, as in other Catholic nations. Names of Lithuanian origin, some of the pre-Christian era, continue to be popular as well; those with no close English equivalent are marked with an asterisk (*).

Appendix A: Bibliography

The following list is meant to provide the names of several works which will help readers conduct genealogical research involving various European languages and countries. The list names a number of works readily available, but clearly is not comprehensive or exhaustive. Also worthy of mention are the introductory guides to a variety of European languages which have been compiled by the staff of the Family History Library (FHL) in Salt Lake City, Utah, and are available through local Family History Centers. To obtain more detailed advice on sources from people who specialize in research in specific countries or areas, we recommend studying Appendix B, A List of Genealogical Organizations. Members of those Societies and Groups are best equipped to refer you to publications that meet your individual needs. But for general introduction, the works listed below, and the FHL guides, should be helpful.

General

In Search of Your European Roots: A Complete Guide to Tracing Your Ancestors in Every Country in Europe. Angus Baxter. Genealogical Publishing Co., Inc., Baltimore, 1988.

Where Once We Walked: A Guide to the Jewish Communities Destroyed in the Holocaust. Gary Mokotoff and Sallyann Amdur Sack. Avotaynu, Inc., Teaneck, NJ 07666. This is an excellent gazetteer of central and eastern European countries. It lists some 22,000 towns in Austria, Belarus, Bulgaria, Czech Republic, Estonia, Germany, Hungary, Latvia, Lithuania, Moldavia, Poland, Romania, Russia, Slovakia and Ukraine.

Czech / Slovak

Genealogical Research for Czech and Slovak Americans. Olga K. Miller. Gale Research Co., Detroit, 1978.

German

If I Can, You Can Decipher Germanic Records. Edna M. Bentz. Genealogy Unlimited, Inc., P.O. Box 537, Orem, UT 84059-0537.

Tracing Your German Roots, Maralyn A. Wellauer. Milwaukee, published by author.

Hungarian

Handy Guide to Hungarian Genealogical Records. Jared H. Suess. Everton Pub., Logan, UT.

Italian

Handy Guide to Italian Genealogical Records. Everton Pub., Logan, UT, 1978.

Jewish

A Dictionary of Jewish Surnames from the Russian Empire. Alexander Beider. Avotaynu, Inc., Teaneck, NJ 07666, 1993.

Finding Our Fathers: A Guide to Jewish Genealogy. Random House, New York, 1977.

From Generation to Generation: How to Trace Your Jewish Genealogical and Personal History. Arthur Kurzweil. Schocken Books, New York, 1981. To be republished and updated in 1994 by Harper-Collins, New York.

Polish

A Translation Guide to 19th Century Polish-Language Civil Registration Documents, compiled and edited by Judith R. Frazin. The Jewish Genealogical Society of Illinois, 1989, c/o 1025 Antique Lane, Northbrook, IL 60062.

Polish Parish Records of the Roman Catholic Church, Their Use and Understanding in Genealogical Research. Gerald A. Ortell. Genealogy Unlimited, Inc., P.O. Box 537, Orem, UT 84059-0537.

Russian

Russian Language Documents from Russian Poland: A Translation Manual for Genealogists, Jonathan D. Shea. Genealogy Unlimited, Inc., P.O. Box 537, Orem, UT 84059-0537

Appendix B: A List of Genealogical Organizations

Listed below are a number of societies and organizations willing and able to answer specific questions about ethnic family history research. Undoubtedly there are many organizations not on this list, and addresses of individual groups may have changed since we found them, but on the whole this list should help you get off to a good start by contacting others pursuing the same goals you are. Readers who possess personal computers with modems should also be aware that there are many bulletin boards with valuable genealogical information, and several of the better known services — CompuServe, Prodigy, and Genie among them — have excellent bulletin boards and features devoted to genealogical research.

Croatian-Serbian
— Croatian-Serbian Genealogical Society, 2527 San Carlos Ave., San Carlos, CA 94070

Czech
— Czechoslovak Genealogical Society, P.O. Box 16225, St. Paul, MN 55116
— Czechoslovak Genealogical Society, 72 Appleberry Dr., San Rafael, CA 94903

Dutch
— Dutch Family Heritage Society, 2463 Ledgewood Dr., W. Jordan, UT 84084

French
— American-Canadian Genealogical Society, P.O. Box 668, Manchester, NH 03105
— American-French Genealogical Society, P.O. Box 2113, Pawtucket, RI 02861

German
— German Genealogical Society of America, P.O. Box 291818, Los Angeles, CA 90029
— Immigrant Genealogical Society, P.O. Box 7369, Burbank, CA 91510-7369
— Germans from Russia Heritage Society, 1008 E. Central Ave., Bismarck, ND 58501

Hungarian
— National Archives: Leveltarak Orszagos Kozpontja, Uri Utca 54-56, Budapest 1, Hungary

Irish
— TIARA, Box 619, Sudbury, MA 01776
— Irish Genealogical Society, P.O. Box 16585, St. Paul, MN 55116

Italian
— POINT, c/o Dr. Thomas Militello, P.O. Box 2977, Palos Verdes, CA 90501

Jewish
There are some 55 Jewish genealogical societies in the United States and Canada and 10 other countries. For a list of societies, write Association of Jewish Genealogical Societies, P. O. Box 900, Teaneck, NJ 07666.

Lithuanian
— Balzekas Museum of Lithuanian Culture, 6500 S. Pulaski, Chicago, IL 60629

Norwegian
— Norwegian Genealogical Group, 1046 19th Ave. SE, Minneapolis, MN 55414

Polish
— Polish Genealogical Society of America, 984 N. Milwaukee Ave., Chicago, IL 60622
— Polish Genealogical Society of California, P.O. Box 713, Midway City, CA 92655-0713
— Polish Genealogical Society of Connecticut, 8 Lyle Rd., New Britain, CT 06053
— Polish Genealogical Society of Michigan, Detroit Public Library, 5201 Woodward Ave., Detroit, MI 48202
— Polish Genealogical Society of Texas, 15917 Juneau Lane, Houston, TX 77040-2155

— Polish Genealogical Society of Western New York, 299 Barnard, Buffalo, NY
— Polish Genealogical Society of Wisconsin, P.O. Box 37476, Milwaukee, WI 53237

Portuguese
— American-Portuguese Genealogical Society, P.O. Box 644, Taunton, MA 02780

Slovenian
— Slovenian Genealogical Society, 2018 Springdale Dr., Martinsburg, WV 25401.

Spanish
— Hispanic Genealogical Society, P.O. Box 810561, Houston, TX 77281-0561

Swedish
— Swedish Pioneer Historical Society, 5125 N. Spaulding Ave., Chicago, IL 60625
— Swedish American Genealogist, c/o Nils Walson, P.O. Box 2186, Winter Park, FL 32790.